CW00797525

The Royal School of Church Music:

The Addington Years

by

John Henderson and Trevor Jarvis

The Royal School of Church Music

19 The Close, Salisbury, Wilts, SP1 2EB. England
Email: press@rscm.com Website: www.rscm.com
Registered charity 312828

Copyright © 2015 John Henderson & Trevor Jarvis

John Henderson and Trevor Jarvis have asserted their moral rights to be identified as
the authors of this work under the Copyright, Designs and Patents Act, 1988

First published 2015

All rights reserved. No part of this work may be reproduced or transmitted in any form or
by any means, electronic or mechanical, including photocopy, recording or any information
storage or retrieval system, without the authors' written permission.

ISBN-13:

978-0-85402-250-2 (Paperback)

978-0-85402-251-9 (Hardback)

Cover Design by Heather Bamber
Type face: Trebuchet MS
Printed in Great Britain on acid-free paper by
Charlesworth Press, Wakefield.

This book is dedicated to the thousands of RSCM affiliates, members and friends without whom the organisation would not have flourished.

Contents

Appendices

Foreword

By The Rt Revd and Rt Hon Lord Carey of Clifton, RSCM Vice-President.

Choral music is one of the glories of the Anglican tradition and one greatly envied by other Christian denominations. As a former Archbishop of Canterbury, I have heard some of the very best choirs in the world — and most of these have been Anglican — and regard the choral tradition as one of our most noble treasures and central to our mission. This is not to denigrate other ways of leading worship, which all have their place in the repertoire of music, but there is nothing to compare to a choir, well trained and in full voice.

In this third book in the series of Royal School of Church Music historical books, the focus falls on the Addington Years. Addington Palace was for many years the home of Archbishops of Canterbury, but, for a variety of reasons, left the control of the Church and became a private home. Unexpectedly, it became available again in 1952 and, at the suggestion of Dr Fisher, the then Archbishop of Canterbury, Addington Palace became the new home of the RSCM.

And what a beloved home it became! This volume by John Henderson and Trevor Jarvis tells the story of the Addington years through the eyes of those who attended the many courses. It is a fascinating and human story of brilliant musicians, gifted organists, devoted choir masters and mistresses, ordinary boys and, later, girls, struggling to raise the level of their singing and music to the glory of God. Although very hard work is described, the human aspects of fun and relaxation are brought out too which, in my experience of choirs, is usually an essential part of the fellowship that choirs share.

The authors also bring out delightfully the varied personalities of the men and women who filled the Palace with their music and their desires to raise the standard of Church music in the country and abroad. Gerald Knight, deservedly for the length of time he was Director, stands out as one of the giants in the narrative of Addington but he is far from being alone. Great people jostle in this story because of their passion and vision of music for the greater glory of God.

It was one of my great pleasures when Archbishop to sponsor the Millennium Youth Choir of the RSCM which continues to thrive.

It is my sincere hope that this third volume will help to increase interest in the RSCM and its mission today. The RSCM now welcomes other denominations into membership, thus strengthening worship in other traditions and being enriched in the process. If we really want to see our churches flower and the Anglican Communion to prosper, support for the valuable work of the RSCM must continue and grow.

George Carey served as Archbishop of Canterbury and President of the RSCM from 1991 until 2002 during the final years at Addington Palace.

On retirement, he became a Vice-President.

Prologue

'You are standing in the majestic sweep of the drive at Addington. You let your eyes roam over the Palace, with its solid Georgian lines, its spacious windows promising large airy rooms inside. You drink in the calm of the green acres all around you: up in the great trees the rooks are cawing in their hundreds: birds are singing: your spirit responds to all the beauty you can see and hear.' This splendidly vivid — albeit somewhat extravagant — piece of prose, penned by the then Warden of Addington, the Revd Cyril Taylor, introduced the RSCM membership to their new home.

In the same article, Taylor goes on to invite the reader to visualise what the future will hold. 'Students from this country and overseas, sharing a common life there for a year or more, training to be organists and choirmasters: and many others you see who have come for a week or less.' Here he lists clergy, lay readers, students of church music, who have come to consult books in the library, Commissioners and Representatives keeping in touch with Headquarters, choirmasters and affiliated choirs who have come either for a day, or on a course, to sing services in the chapel. This may all seem a rather fanciful picture that Cyril Taylor painted in the January 1954 issue of *English Church Music*, and yet, for the most part, this vision became a reality.

'Vision' is a recurring theme in the course of the RSCM's history. We encounter it first in Sydney Nicholson's vision for the future of church music back in 1927, when he decided to devote all his time towards putting the recommendations of the Archbishops' *Music in Worship* report of the previous year into practice[1].

The outbreak of the Second World War caused the first disruption into what had hitherto seemed to be a well-established, and latterly flourishing, set-up. Closure of the Chislehurst property, involving both the College and the SECM's offices, meant that new premises were needed. Tenbury Wells and then Leamington Spa served as temporary locations, but there was a need to find a permanent home as the war drew to an end. The Chislehurst property, although still owned by the SECM, was occupied by the Bromley Technical School for girls, and because of post-war building restrictions, no date for returning there could be envisioned. A move to a location in the city of Canterbury had already been considered as a possible option, when a lease offer from the Dean and Chapter of a house (No 17) within the precincts of the cathedral, to be followed by a similar lease offer on Roper House, a large building just outside the precincts, was made. This became the home of the RSCM from November 1945 until the end of 1953[2]. The Canterbury years seemed to be ideal in terms of location and profile. Gerald Knight later wrote[3]: 'People came to see the cathedral and, partly because we happened to be there, they came to see us too... It was a

---

[1] Full details of this vision and how it was realised may be found in our companion volume *Sydney Nicholson and the College of St Nicolas: The Chislehurst Years* 2011: ISBN 9780952805045.

[2] Built in the late 18C, Roper House in St Dunstan's Street was at one time St Dunstan's Brewery, but had also been occupied as a private house and as a private school.

[3] in *RSCM: The First Forty Years* 1967.

great privilege to live and work under the shadow of so great a cathedral as that of Canterbury.'

However, at the end of 1951 the cathedral gave notice that the lease on No 17 The Precincts would not be renewed, and consequently would expire at Christmas 1952, whereas the lease on Roper House, used as a student hostel, still had some time to run. It became imperative that a new home be found within the year. The RSCM Executive Committee's view was that the geographical position of the College should be either 1) London or 2) Canterbury, and that other possibilities should not be considered. By London they meant 'anywhere with a radius of 20 miles from Charing Cross, say, Hatfield to the North to Redhill in the South.' Gerald Knight, then Warden of the RSCM, discussed the question of the College's future home with Dr Geoffrey Fisher, Archbishop of Canterbury. Dr Fisher mentioned that Addington Palace, formerly the Archbishop of Canterbury's Summer Residence and which had recently been acquired by Croydon Corporation, was looking for a tenant. He suggested that the building may well suit the RSCM's needs. Gerald Knight reported this to RSCM Council on 22nd January 1952 and Council appointed a Committee to investigate the possibility[4]. On 5th February two members of the Finance Committee visited Addington Palace for the first time and in April RSCM Council made the decision to negotiate for a lease. With the help of the Archbishop, negotiations were started which led to a lease between the RSCM and Croydon Corporation being ratified in June 1952[5]. Apart from the 1953 Coronation choristers being accommodated and rehearsed at Addington Palace during May and June of 1953, the actual move from Canterbury to Croydon was to be made in January 1954. The plans for that first year at Addington were that the new term would begin on 22nd January with 11 full-time students, and that the administration offices would follow at the end of the month. Courses would start soon thereafter, the first being for theological students in March, followed by a choirboys' course in April, starting on Easter Monday[6].

For an organisation that has worldwide membership and influence, that is much loved by so many people whose lives have been enriched or transformed by its activities, and which has now passed its 87th birthday, it seems extraordinary that there is no full chronicle of the RSCM and its work available. In 1948, on the death of the founder, Sir Sydney Nicholson, the RSCM published *The Nicholson Memorial* in Canterbury. Although the memorial was intended as a £60,000 fund-raising exercise, it also outlined the achievements and activities of the SECM and RSCM to that time. In 1967 Gerald Knight, by then Director of the RSCM, gave a lecture at Church House in Westminster which was subsequently published (together with a diary of major RSCM milestones) as *RSCM: The*

---

[4] There was also an offer to take up a Manor House in Somerset. Hilary Chadwick-Healey was sent to investigate, but nothing came of this.

[5] The five-month period from the first idea of a move to Addington to ratification of the lease seems remarkably short but then planning the renovations and modifications to the building took just over a year so that building work did not begin until July 1953.

[6] 41 boys attended this first course with Edred Wright as Director; Frederic Waine was Housemaster, John Hooper, a College student, was assistant housemaster and Cyril Taylor was Chaplain.

First Forty Years. Ten years later, for the Golden Jubilee celebrations, a brochure was issued[7] which included a profile of the organisation and a substantial historical article by Stanley Webb[8] under the general editorship of RSCM Director Lionel Dakers. Finally, in 1997, Dr Watkins Shaw's monograph *Vocation and Endeavour: Sir Sydney Nicholson and the early years of the Royal School of Church Music* was published posthumously by the RSCM and Church Music Society.

These then are the official publications, but one more valuable document exists, a thesis submitted for the MA degree at the University of Sheffield by Barry Neil Sampson[9] in October 1971 entitled *The Royal School of Church Music: A study of its history, its organisation and its influence*. At almost 700 pages in two volumes, this fine work has been of great value to the present authors and is the most complete factual history we possess[10]. A severe handicap for the present authors has been the lack of archival records at the RSCM. The preparation of our two previous books, *Sydney Nicholson and The College of St Nicolas: The Chislehurst Years*[11] and *Sydney Nicholson and his Musings of a Musician*[12], was made considerably easier by the fact that Sydney Nicholson was a hoarder of documents, letters and photographs as well as a keen diarist. His legacy provided a wealth of material for these first two books. The RSCM as an organisation however does not appear, at any time, to have had much thought about keeping records for historians. It was too concerned with surviving financially from year to year and too focussed on the work that it was doing day by day to ever really consider that one day someone might be interested in how the organisation developed.[13] Most of the information used by Sampson in his thesis and by the present authors has been gleaned from the pages of the RSCM magazines but, as RSCM activities multiplied, more and more was necessarily left out of *Promoting Church Music* and *Church Music Quarterly* because of limited space. As a simple example, the Special Commissioners'[14] reports of choirs visited and reports of Area Festivals were initially very thorough, but, as the years went by, both of these activities became too numerous to report and so only edited highlights were included in the magazines.

Barry Sampson did have the advantage of being able to interview the staff and students in 1970, just as we have greatly benefited from information, photographs and recollections of

---

[7] This was subsidised by the Guinness brewing family!

[8] Stanley Webb was a journalist and writer on musical matters. He was best known for his contributions to the New Grove dictionaries, for many years of writing programme notes for David Willcocks and the Bach Choir and, for 13 years, of reviews to the Gramophone magazine. In 1980 he was made an Honorary Member of the Royal College of Organists.

[9] At the time of writing, Barry's interest and work for the RSCM continues as Secretary for the RSCM Sheffield Area Committee.

[10] One cannot but help thinking that, in the 21C world of education, Barry Sampson's thesis would probably merit a Doctorate.

[11] 2011: ISBN 9780952805045

[12] 2013: ISBN 9780854022267

[13] In the subsequent moves from Addington to Dorking, and then from Dorking to Salisbury, a certain amount of down-sizing inevitably took place. Some archive paperwork was disposed of which, if storage space had not been such an issue, would surely have been kept.

[14] The RSCM Commissioners were designated 'Special' in the same way as 'Special Constables', i.e. they were part-time and not full-time employees.

many past Addington students and RSCM staff and volunteers today. He also had access to some registers and office files which no longer exist, so we owe a considerable debt to his work.

Barry Sampson observed in 1971 that 'The history of the School is not complete, for it is being made at the moment. The RSCM is not a static institution; it is a living thing; a vast collection of people with one aim and enthusiasm — to foster and improve the music and worship offered up in churches day-by-day throughout the length and breadth of the Anglican Communion and in the churches of the many other denominations who are now members of the School. Without a clear purpose and the loyal support of its members everywhere it would stumble and fall. This purpose must be maintained in the face of many obstacles.'

If anything, the obstacles today seem even greater than when the above was written 45 years ago, but the Founder's vision remains alive and well. And so, Chislehurst, Tenbury Wells, Leamington Spa, Canterbury and Croydon (to which list must now be added Dorking and Salisbury) may sound to the uninitiated like a random selection of railway destinations, but they are in fact the locations occupied by the RSCM over the last 87 years. The longest spell at any one place (so far) is Addington Palace, with a total of 43 years. This is the story of the work of the RSCM during the Addington years.

John Henderson, Trevor Jarvis

Acknowledgments

We most gratefully thank the many former Addington students, choristers and RSCM staff members who have contributed their reminiscences to this book, and especially Mr Martin How and Dr Harry Bramma, who have made valuable suggestions in addition to providing individual chapters. Indeed, we have received so much help from so many people that perhaps we should call ourselves editors or compilers rather than authors.

Our special thanks also extend to former Archbishop of Canterbury, Lord Carey of Clifton, Vice-President of the RSCM, for consenting to write the Foreword; to Lord Gill, current RSCM Council Chairman, for an Afterword; to Geoff Weaver for his contribution about Harry Bramma, to Roy Massey for his reflections as former Warden and to Jenny Setchell of Christchurch, New Zealand for photographs and for permission to reprint her recollections of the 1981 Addington Summer Course.

Disclaimer

The views expressed by the authors in this book on RSCM matters are personal and do not necessarily represent the official view of the RSCM today.

Abbreviations

Direct quotations from the personal contributions sent by former members of staff and students are acknowledged in the text by name or by these abbreviations:

AA	Adrian Adams (1967-1970)	JM	John Morehen (1960/61)
AB	Anita Banbury (1963-66)	LS	Lionel Sawkins (1958/59)
AC	Anthony Cridland (1969-71)	MB	Michael Bailey (1960-63)
AH	Antonia Harman (1970-74)	MD	Michael Deasey (1969/70)
AS	Alan Snow (1972/73)	MJRH	Martin How (staff)
DRH	David Harrison (1955/56 & 1958/59)	MS	Michael Smith (1955/56)
DH	Derek Holman (staff)	PP	Peter Philips (1972)
ES	Elizabeth Salmon (1962/63)	PS	Paul Spicer (1970/71)
GRW	Guyon Wells (1957-59)	RA	Roger Allen (1970/71)
GCW	Gillian Weir (1962-64)	RB	Robert Bell (1958/59)
HB	Harry Bramma (staff)	RG	Robert Gower (1971)
HM	Hume McGrath (1966/67)	RM	Roy Massey (staff)
IB	Ian Barber (1960-65)	RS	Robert Smith (1961-63)
IH	Ian Henderson (staff)	TA	Terence Allbright (1965-68)
IM	Ian McKinley (1958/59)	TS	Tim Schofield (1972/73)
JB	James Burchell (1961/62)	VEW	Vincent Waterhouse (staff)
JE	John Eagles (1971/72)	WF	William French (1963-65)

General Abbreviations

A&M	*Hymns Ancient & Modern*
ADCM	The Archbishop of Canterbury's Diploma in Church Music [formerly ACDCM]
AIRMT	Associate of The Institute of Registered Music Teachers [of New Zealand]
AOC	Archbishop of Canterbury
AP	Addington Palace
BNS	*The Royal School of Church Music: A study of its history, its organisation and its influence*, Barry Neil Sampson, 1971, Sheffield University MA Thesis
CBE	Commander of the British Empire
CMQ	*Church Music Quarterly*
CS	Cathedral Singers
CMS	Church Music Society
CTS	Chorister Training Scheme
CVT	Cyril Vincent Taylor
DMA	Doctor of Musical Arts
DSCM	Diploma of the State Conservatorium of Music [Sydney, NSW]
ECM	*English Church Music*
FSB	Festival Service Book
GHK	Gerald Hocken Knight
GPC	General Purposes Committee

GSM	Guildhall School of Music (GGSM – Graduate, LGSM – Licentiate, HonFGSM – Honorary Fellow)
IAO	Incorporated Association of Organists
IOW	Isle-of-Wight
LCM	London College of Music
MAB	Musical Advisory Board
MSM	Master of Sacred Music
n/a	Information not available
OAM	Order of Australia Medal
ODS	One-Day School
PCM	Promoting Church Music
RAH	Royal Albert Hall
RAM	Royal Academy of Music (ARAM – Associate, LRAM – Licentiate, FRAM – Fellow)
RCM	Royal College of Music (ARCM – Associate, FRCM – Fellow)
RCCO	Royal Canadian College of Organists (FRCCO – Fellow)
RCO	Royal College of Organists (ARCO – Associate, FRCO – Fellow), the suffix (CHM) indicates Choirmaster Diploma
RMCM	Royal Manchester College of Music (later RNCM Royal Northern College of Music)
RSCM	Royal School of Church Music
SECM	School of English Church Music
SHN	Sir Sydney Hugo Nicholson
SNCSN	Sydney Nicholson and The College of St Nicolas: The Chislehurst Years (publ 2011)
SNMOM	Sydney Nicholson and his Musings of a Musician (publ 2013)
SPCK	Society for Promoting Christian Knowledge
TCL	Trinity College of Music, London (GTCL – Graduate, ATCL – Associate, LTCL – Licentiate, FTCL – Fellow)
TDC	Three-Day Course

US, Australian and Canadian States are identified by their usual 2-letter codes.

All degrees, diplomas and awards are abbreviated without punctuation.

Photographs

Most of the photographs used in the book are from the RSCM archives and from former students and staff; these are not individually acknowledged. Some photographs may well be copyright to professional photographers, especially the late Howard Marmaduke King of Croydon, who was employed frequently by the RSCM and died around 1960. Most of our archival photographs were trimmed for use in the RSCM magazines and so may have had the photographer's name removed. We apologise if any copyrights have been infringed.

Some readers may notice an imbalance of photographs, with a relative paucity of photographs from the period 1985-1996. This is due to there being no CMQ archive for those later years, but a wealth of photographs from the earlier period.

Chapter I. The move from Canterbury.

A) Finding and securing a new home:

The offices of the RSCM had opened their doors in Canterbury in November 1945, with the College of St Nicolas following in January 1946 at what many people thought would be a permanent home. Alas this was not to be. No 17 The Close was leased from the Dean and Chapter, and the first intimation that the sojourn at Canterbury was going to be of limited duration came in July 1951, when the Cathedral authorities announced that the lease on some of the buildings being used by the RSCM would henceforth be renewed on a yearly basis only. This was inevitably unsettling, even more so when on 13th December of the same year the Council of the RSCM 'received notice to deliver up the premises [No 17] at Christmas 1952; no suitable alternative accommodation was offered.'[15] The lease on Roper House, used both as offices and as a student hostel, still had some time to run, but the building was not large enough to accommodate the contents and activities of No 17 as well. This would, at first sight, appear to be a somewhat high-handed attitude on the part of the Dean and Chapter. However, a recently-discovered letter written by the Dean shows that it was with extreme reluctance on the Cathedral's part that this decision was reached. 'Many of us feel deeply grieved ... that the exigencies of the Chapter and its finances, including in these their responsibility to the King's School, have compelled them to break a direct connection which many of us valued so highly.'[16] He goes on to offer both his large library and a staff flat in the Deanery for the RSCM's use, and expresses a wish that one day they may return. Generous as this gesture was, the accommodation offered would not meet the needs of the organisation, even should they continue to lease Roper House. Thus, there was an immediate need to find alternative accommodation. The RSCM's Executive Committee's view was that the geographical location of the College should be either London (by which was meant anywhere within a twenty-mile radius from Charing Cross) or an alternative site in Canterbury.

As mentioned in the Prologue, it was the Archbishop of Canterbury, the RSCM's President, who first suggested Addington Palace. These negotiations moved very rapidly and led to the lease between the RSCM and Croydon Corporation being ratified in June 1952. The Archbishop, who had shown himself to be an enthusiastic and active supporter of the organisation, wrote in *ECM* July 1952: 'On many grounds I shall greatly regret the departure of the RSCM from Canterbury, but the contiguity to London will bring many advantages, and I console myself that the School will still be in my own diocese, while nothing could be more splendid than that it should be in a former home of the Archbishops of Canterbury.' In the same issue of *ECM*, the Council confirmed the appointment of Gerald Knight as Director on 20th June. Hitherto, he — together with John Dykes Bower (St Paul's Cathedral) and William McKie (Westminster Abbey) — had held the fort as Honorary Associate Directors following the death of the Founder Sir Sydney Nicholson in 1947. The appointment was

---

[15] *ECM* July 1952.
[16] Personal letter written by Dean Hewlett Johnson to the RSCM Secretary Leslie Green, dated Dec 1951.

made very rapidly for it was only at Council Meeting on 29th April that it was decided to approach three people as potential Directors — Mr Gerald Knight of Canterbury, Dr Henry Havergal of Winchester and Dr Gordon Slater of Lincoln.

The Hon Associate Directors of the RSCM 1946-1952
Left: Dr John Dykes Bower, Right: Mr Gerald Knight, Bottom: Dr William McKie

Some mention must be made of Sir John Dykes Bower, an important supporter of the RSCM and its work, but who does not really fit into any one category within this book. As already mentioned, he was one of the three Honorary Associate Directors of the RSCM appointed following the death of Sir Sydney Nicholson in 1947 and he had been a Council member since 1944. In addition to his role as Associate Director and Council Member, Dykes Bower's RSCM work included acting as Deputy Director during GHK's absence on foreign tours, acting as organist on the 1963 Toronto trip, serving on the RSCM Music Advisory Board, allowing his house to be used for many Council and other meetings and acting as Director of RSCM Publications from 1952. He retired from Council in 1975.

Sir John Dykes Bower CVO DMus b.13th August 1905, Gloucester; d.29th May 1981, Orpington, Kent. A pupil of Herbert Brewer at Gloucester Cathedral, he was organ scholar of Corpus Christi College in Cambridge from 1922. He rapidly progressed to be organist of Truro Cathedral (1926-1929), New College, Oxford (1929-1933), Durham Cathedral (1933-1936) and St Paul's Cathedral (1936-1968). He lost all of his possessions in the fire-bombing of London in 1940, and during the war he served at the War Ministry with the rank of Squadron Leader in the Royal Air Force Volunteer Reserve. Oxford University made him an honorary DMus in 1944. He was a professor at the RCM from 1936 until 1969, and his retirement from this and from St Paul's Cathedral was precipitated by the sudden onset of blindness. He was master of the Worshipful Company of Musicians in 1967/68 and knighted in 1968. Corpus Christi, Cambridge, made him an honorary fellow in 1980. He was Chairman of the Council of Hymns A&M and the hymn writer J B Dykes (1823-1876) was his forebear. A perfectionist in everything, it is alleged that he was never heard to play a wrong note. The *Oxford Dictionary of National Biography* records that 'Dykes Bower's fastidiousness and relentless quest for flawless performance made him hard to please, and could combine with his quiet reticence to make him silent where a word of encouragement could have been beneficial. A very private man with a horror of the limelight, he asked only to be allowed to offer perfection through music in the worship of the Church of England. He inspired awe but also deep affection in everyone who worked alongside him.'

Events for the move from Canterbury now moved fairly swiftly. In July 1952 the work of transforming Addington Palace to fit its new purpose began, although it wasn't until a year later that any major building work started. A date for the move had yet to be set, depending on when the various licenses would be granted, and the transfer of the Golf Club, which had been using the Palace, to new premises. By October, planning consent for the building work required had been received from the Town Clerk of Croydon. In the same month all the furniture and equipment from No 17 The Precincts was moved out, and put in store at both Roper House and the Deanery. With Roper House now full, space was at a premium — and three further rooms were urgently required as office space and as overflow accommodation for the hostel. An agreement was reached with Edred Wright,

3

Headquarters Choirmaster, to rent three rooms in his own house in Canterbury. On moving out of No 17, the RSCM was responsible for 'redecorating and dilapidations', the cost of which amounted to £602, but the Dean and Chapter settled for just £400. With the generous offer of both this reduction of the bill and of storage space in the Deanery, it would seem that the Dean and Chapter were making an attempt to 'sweeten the pill'.

Now appointed full-time Director of the RSCM since June, Knight stepped down as Organist and Master of the Choristers at Canterbury Cathedral on 31st December 1952, in order to devote all his time to the impending move. By the end of April 1953, the lease for Addington Palace was signed and sealed by the Executive Committee at 5 Amen Court, London, this being the home of Dr John Dykes Bower, Organist of St Paul's Cathedral and also Chairman of the Committee since 1951. The lease would run for fifty years at a rate of £1000 per annum — a modest sum, even at 1953 prices. There was however some dissatisfaction in the local Croydon area over the low rent being charged (to a 'church organisation'), which made its way into the local press. The first residents at Addington were to be the Coronation choristers (see Chapter II), who were little more than camping out in a building largely devoid of furniture. By July of the same year, building work began and the exterior of the Palace painted. The major work involved a complete re-wiring, the installation of 'new heating apparatus', the building of a new kitchen and the conversion of a conservatory and men's changing room into the Chapel of St Nicolas. Redecoration 'on a modest scale, of about 100 rooms, as well as the painting of three hundred windows, was also undertaken.' Work continued until lunch time on 10th July 1954, the day of the official opening by HM the Queen Mother (see Chapter III), but enough work was complete to allow term to start as planned in January 1954.

The time to move from Canterbury finally arrived. Gerald Knight wrote affectionately of the home he was about to leave. 'The seven years in Canterbury have been happy ones, and many of our students ....will recall with pleasure the time that they spent beneath the shadow of the great Cathedral. Members of the staff will leave Canterbury with unconcealed regret, but full of hope for the future which Addington holds in store.'[17] One of the last services held by the College was in the crypt at Canterbury on the occasion of the RSCM annual carol service on 17th December 1953, after which the College choristers adjourned to Roper House for the traditional 'Boy Bishop's Feast', a tradition started by Nicholson at Chislehurst.

January 1954 saw the first van-load of furniture arriving at Addington, and on the 22nd of that month the first students arrived for the start of the Spring Term. Over a four week period, twenty van-loads of furniture were moved to the Palace, the move being subsidised by The Pilgrim Trust and Hymns A&M. The last severing of any connection with Canterbury came in the first week of February, when the RSCM office finally moved out of Roper House. The Bishop of Croydon blessed the Palace on the 2nd February, and so a new chapter in the RSCM's history had begun.

---

[17] *ECM* Jan 1954.

Interestingly, back in the January 1947 issue of the RSCM magazine *English Church Music*, Sydney Nicholson wrote an article entitled 'A Nightmare and a Dream'.

'The nightmare was queues of choirboys for courses, and of a demand not being met through lack of money, buildings and staff. The dream was both a vision and a plea for a large mansion in the country with a chapel that would hold up to a hundred boys.'

Unfortunately, he did not live to see his vision realised.

Canterbury Summer School 1949 outside Roper House
Gerald Knight (in surplice with medal) seated in the centre
To his right are Hubert Crook, Edred Wright and Leslie Green

Harry Bramma:

'The move to Addington in 1953 brought much new life to the RSCM. Addington Palace was an important factor along with the development of membership networks at home and abroad. Leslie Green was very keen to make Addington work. He was the chief advocate of the move because he thought it would be seen as a new Spring with all the added facilities which would be available. He was right in all this. It was a bold move to relocate from Canterbury to Croydon. It aroused great interest and demonstrated that the RSCM was a force to be reckoned with. Of course there were some detractors who imagined how the Director and staff were moving into a life of grandeur in a Palace — paid for by the membership, but most members were excited by this manifestation of new life and forward thinking.'

B) The History and Layout of Addington Palace:

The original building which occupied the site, which was later possibly a fortified Manor House, predates the Norman Conquest, for it is mentioned in the Domesday Book of 1084. The exact details are lost somewhat in the mists of time. In an article for *Treble Clef*, Peter White mentions 'It seems that 600 years ago there was a castle here, and that this was probably the original building. A little later on (about 30 years) this was replaced by a building called Addington Palace'[18] [Place]. Whatever the building was approximately 600 years ago, it was replaced by a building called Addington Place. The building and its estate then passed on to the Leigh family, who remained the owners for over 300 years, until the estate was bought in 1768 for £38,500 by one Barlow Trecothick, an Alderman of London (and subsequently Lord Mayor in 1770). He lived in the old mediæval building whilst the new Addington Palace was being built. Both these names, Leigh and Trecothick, were subsequently used for rooms on the second floor, and would have been familiar to choristers attending residential courses.

Addington Place, *in* Surry, *the Seat of* James Ivers Trecothick *Efq.*
Published as the Act directs, May 1st, 1780, by W. Watts, Kemp's Row, Chelsea.

The current building was started in the latter part of the 18th century, between 1773 and 1779, and the architect was Robert Mylne. Barlow Trecothick did not live to see the building work completed as he died in 1778, and so it was left to his nephew, James Trecothick, to complete the work. James also had the grounds laid out by Capability Brown, which is when many of the trees were planted. The completed house was of

---

[18] *RSCM News* No 7 July 1964.

Portland stone in the Palladian style, modelled on the building style of ancient Rome, with the overriding emphasis on strict proportions and a perfect symmetry of aspect: a style popular at this time for many great houses of the period. At the time of completion, the Old Palace nearby, which had belonged to the Archbishops of Canterbury for over 500 years[19], was sold, and Addington Palace was bought for him, by Act of Parliament, some 25 years later in 1807/8.

ADDINGTON PLACE,
Surrey.
The Seat of the Archbishop of Canterbury.

London Published by John Harris St Pauls Church Yard Aug 1 1823

It then became the country residence of six successive Archbishops: Manners-Sutton, Howley (who had extensive and major alterations carried out between 1830 and 1833), Sumner, Longley, Tait and Benson. (All these names were also used to name different rooms within the Palace.) Archbishop Frederick Temple decided to take up residence at Canterbury, rather than Croydon, and the Palace (known as Addington Park during the Archbishops' residency) was sold in 1898. The entire estate (3500 acres) was bought by a South African millionaire, Frederick English, who had the interior reconstructed for the sum of £70,000[20]. English employed the eminent architect Richard Norman Shore to carry out the work, the result being the aspect we see today from the front drive. Following his death in 1909, the building was put up for auction, but the reserve price was not reached, and the sale was withdrawn in 1911. Two years later, part of the parkland was sold to the Addington Golf Club.

---

[19] Some buildings of the Old Croydon Palace are still in use by Whitgift School.
[20] *Addington Palace Golf Club 1930-2005* gives the figure £100,000.

Addington Palace War Hospital.

Then, during the First World War, the unsold house was used from 1914 to 1919 by the Red Cross as a War hospital specialising in enteric [intestinal] disease, mainly infectious diarrhoea of which typhoid and dysentery were two of the most common conditions. The Trustees of Addington Park offered the property to the Ministry of Defence and it opened on 13th December 1914 with 130 beds. The cost of running the hospital (£20,000 a year) was underwritten by the War Office, and the cost of the equipment for the hospital and the laboratory (£5,000) was provided by the Joint War Committee of the British Red Cross Society and the Order of St John of Jerusalem. Local isolation hospitals dealt with acute cases and Addington Palace was a clearing-house for convalescents. Most patients were held at AP from six to eight weeks until bacteriological tests showed they were free of disease. Patients who remained persistent carriers of bacteria were eventually invalided out of the army and returned to their homes[21].

After the war, the Palace remained empty until 1928 when Addiscombe Garden Estates bought it and had the park laid out as a golf course, using the Palace as the clubhouse, and the adjacent bungalow to the side of the Palace became the 'Pro Shop'. Peter White concluded his article in *Treble Clef* with the following tantalising piece of information: 'I've left one piece of information till last. There exists, between the Palace and the village church an underground passage. It's not still in use of course; in fact it's now sealed up! I've no doubt it's been the scene of some interesting bits of history.'[22]

It would now be appropriate to take a virtual tour around the Palace during the RSCM's tenure.

---

[21] Information from the 'Lost Hospitals of London' website.
[22] *RSCM News* No 7 July 1964.

The Entrance Hall:

> 'Constructed in 1900, this is a square, cold harsh room having little artistic or architectural value. Against the east wall is a flight of narrow steps leading down to the Basement. Immediately to the right of the door through to the Salon [Great Hall] is a narrow access through a short awkward slanting passage into the adjacent room in the South wing. As planned by Shaw (the architect) this was a Ladies Cloakroom and is now the RSCM Warden's office.'[23]

This somewhat uncompromising description marks the Entrance Hall as one of the least attractive rooms in the Palace, and probably one of the coldest. The rest of the ground floor makes up for this!

AP Front door with crib scene

The Great Hall:

This, the grandest of the Palace rooms, was originally the Salon and is dominated by both a large, ornate fireplace of polished Istrian marble and alabaster, and a magnificent candelabrum containing 120 lights hanging from the centre of the ceiling. Shaw had the candelabrum brought over from a chateau in France. The RSCM later had it restored to its original condition[24]. The other striking feature of the Great Hall, which stands two storeys high, is the Gallery, with its supporting pillars, made of Italian walnut.

The Hall was used for larger concerts, and contained two grand pianos, where GHK would often improvise to the gathering before going into dinner. There was also a small chamber organ (for details see Chapter IX). In the northwest corner leading to the Music Room was the RSCM bookstall.

---

[23] *Addington Palace* by Frederick Shorrocks, RSCM, 1985.
[24] See Appendix 7, Summer 1976.

Great Hall
Above: as seen from the Music Room
Below: as seen from the Entrance

The First Common Room / Music Room:

When the College closed in 1974, there followed a re-organisation and renaming of many of the rooms and this room was one such.

Situated off the Great Hall, it had formerly been Archbishop Howley's Chapel before Shaw remodelled it as a dining room, adding a moulded ceiling, carved oak dado and fireplace. The RSCM used it first as a Common Room and then latterly as a general Music Room. Later visitors to the Palace will remember that the Peter Collins organ, originally placed in the Great Hall, was kept in here during the 1990's.

The Common Room ca 1955; this photograph taken for a postcard and brochure

The Dining Rooms:

The Large Dining Room, also accessed from the Great Hall and adjacent to the Common Room/Music Room, has seen a number of different uses. It had been the Archbishop's study, was then converted by Shaw into a library for the new owner Frederick English, before being used by the resident RSCM community and visiting courses as the Large Dining Room. Passing through this one comes to part of the original structure built for Trecothick as a music room. It was later used as a Small Dining Room and was the scene of those famous 'candle-lit' dinners.

Above: Addington Summer Course 1981 in the Large Dining Room, a view towards the Small Dining Room

Below: a view of the Large Dining Room looking towards the Great Hall

The Kitchen:

This part of the building was remodelled and expanded by the RSCM, to make it fit for purpose. Beyond the kitchens on the ground floor were the female student's quarters, guarded by the kitchen staff.

The First Library / Lecture Room:

To the left of the fireplace in the Great Hall is the very fine doorway to the Lecture Room[25]. This room had been in use as the Ladies drawing room by the Golf Club up until 1953[26], and is referred to as the 'Adam Drawing Room' on contemporary plans. Frederick Shorrocks gives a good description of this room, starting with the marble fireplace with its jasper columns and frieze: 'The carved classic tableau in the centre matches the Wedgewood-style plaques at each end of the ceiling and over the doors. The moulding surrounding the plaques over the doors is finely carved from wood and the tiny musical instruments are hollow. The doors are of solid mahogany. Regency symmetry dictated the provision of four doors, whereas there are only two entrances. Two of the doors are false, one concealing a cupboard and the other having only a wall behind it.' This has confused many a new student in the past!

---

[25] Before 1976 the legend over the door read 'COLLES LIBRARY'.
[26] See Photograph in Appendix 1.

Above: Student Rodney Ford at work in the Library 1956

The Library became the Lecture Room in 1976. This view taken 1981

The Colles Library in its first location, with Head Student Malcolm Cousins seated.
Hon Librarian C E S Littlejohn standing at the back, with student Peter White bending ca 1955

The Norman Shaw Room:

Accessed from the Lecture Room was the first home of the Colles Library. This room was originally designed as a dining room before being used by Trecothick as a Morning Room. In a catalogue of 1911 it was described as having Chinese hand-painted wallpaper, and the room was known as the Chinese Drawing Room. This wallpaper was removed sometime between 1911 and 1953. The £2000 raised by the 1975 Christmas Fayre was used to convert this into a fully-equipped lecture room. It later became the Resources Room and in 1982 the small Hill, Norman & Beard extension organ was placed in here.

The main staircase:

Above: viewed from above in 1992
Below: viewed from below in 1981

The Main Staircase:

The staircase was constructed by Shaw in the 1900 conversion, and only gives access from this point to the first floor rooms. In the corner were located the pigeon holes for in-coming post, the pay phone and the large gong.

The Second Common Room:

This room has had a number of different uses: as a parlour designed by Mylne, then as the Breakfast Room, and from 1930 as the 'nineteenth hole' of the Golf Club. When the Golf Club vacated the premises, the bar was replaced by the Cleverley Organ from Canterbury and the RSCM named the room 'The Nicholson Practice Room'[27]. It subsequently became the Common Room and the bar was reinstated under Lionel Dakers' Directorate for the benefit of members of the various short courses using the facilities.

Above: The Common Room in 1992, Below: in 1981 with the reinstated bar visible

---

[27] The Cleverley Organ can be seen clearly in the photograph of GHK teaching in here on p. 159.

The Main Corridor:

This corridor, leading to the Chapel at the end, has on the left-hand side an electric lift installed by Shaw, but no longer operational, access to the Common Room bar, stairs up and down and access to the rear lawns, and the Director's office. On the right-hand side is the Robing Room.

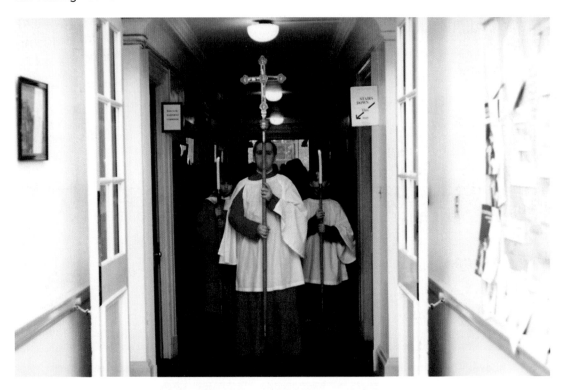

The Nicholson Singers in procession down the Main Corridor from the Chapel before the final service in the Great Hall in 1996. Access to the basement was down the stairs to the left.

The Robing Room:

This large room, dominated by another Shaw fireplace, and with a moulded ceiling, was originally the billiard room from 1900. The RSCM used it as a rehearsal room and installed an organ which was later replaced by a larger instrument. (For details of the Robing Room organs, see Chapter IX). The choir robes were stored here, hence the name.

Formerly, a Billiard Room, other sports have since been played there!

The Robing Room, 1956

Above:
An ordinand receives singing tuition with Robert Poole

Left:
Marjorie Spence adjusting a ruff on Martin Bennett

19

The Chapel:

Shorrocks' account reads:

'In 1953 when the building was occupied by the RSCM, the Pavilion interior was rebuilt as a delightful chapel. The west wall was demolished at this time and an organ inserted in the arch created. The organ projects into a narrow lobby added by Shaw for no other purpose apparently but to match the stairs vestibule built on the front of the North Pavilion.'

Full details of the Chapel and its organ may be found in Chapter IV (Section A) and Chapter IX.

Above and below Left: Chapel photographs taken for publicity use
Top Right: the 1976 Altar Frontal designed by Elizabeth Elvin
Bottom Right: Photographs of the St Nicolas Window used for an 'open out' calendar

The Chapel pews came from St Sepulchre, Holborn, via Chislehurst
and Canterbury, but were exchanged in 1986 for soft chairs

The Basement:

As the house is built on a site which slopes down from the front to the rear, the basement area — not visible from the front aspect — enjoys a full-height aspect at the rear. The whole basement area is surprisingly large, and it contained various RSCM offices and living quarters for staff. The Publications Department, together with the courses music library was also located there, enjoying more space when the new Practice Block came into use.

Above: The General Office, 1960's, Leslie Green standing
Below: The General Office ca 1979

The Practice Room Block:

In 1967 a new Practice Room block was built at the north end of the building, incorporating the old Summer House (or possibly dairy) known, because of its shape, as the Octagon. Built on the site of the kitchen yard back in the Archbishops' residency, it later contained garages and various outbuildings, which were then cleared away to make room for the new block containing twelve practice rooms and a music room. Details of the organs in both the music room and the Octagon may be found in Chapter IX.

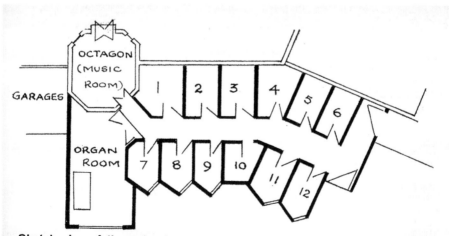

Sketch plan of the extension to Addington Palace, newly built with the exception of the Octagon. The 12 Practice Rooms, numbered on this plan, are to be named as are other rooms in the Palace.

The First and Second Floors:

These mainly contained the accommodation for the students and staff including:

The Empire Room:

This was located on the first floor, and enjoyed a view over the forecourt. This was GHK's sitting room and, as well as comfortable chairs and elegant furniture, it contained a grand piano[28]. In pride of place on the mantelpiece was a photograph of the Queen's visit in 1963. It was in this room that students took tea with the Director and played Scrabble.

The Empire Room in 1992

The Second Library:

In 1976 the Colles Library moved upstairs. During the later Addington years there were effectively two libraries for in addition to the Colles collection a 'Resource Room' was provided downstairs containing an extensive collection of specimen copies of choral and organ music from most of the important publishers, together with bound sets of journals such as *The Organ* (back to issue one of 1923), *The Musical Times* (back to 1906) and the bound collections of choral music inherited from SHN and GHK.

---

[28] At one time there must have been two grand pianos present as some students recall playing duets with GHK who left a substantial collection of two-piano music.

The final home of the Colles Library photographed in 1981

Golf Cottage:

Built in about 1930, this had been the laundry for the original Palace, with living quarters for laundry maids. It had a walled garden which can just be seen through the Chapel windows on p. 21. When the Dakers arrived they renamed it Nicholson House and lived there throughout Lionel's directorate.

The Bungalow:

The bungalow, set at right angles to the main Palace, is the first building to be seen as you come up the front drive. With its prominent clock on the front, this bungalow was formerly the second pro's shop of the Golf Club from the mid 1930's, the golf clubs and APGC (Addington Palace Golf Club) carved on the door posts revealing its former use. It was used by the RSCM as staff accommodation, and housed at various times: Sidney Campbell, Derek Holman, Roy Massey and Martin How. In Martin's time the bungalow was divided into two sections, with Martin occupying the front portion, and Colin Yorke the rear, smaller portion. When Martin How moved out to his own accommodation in Croydon, Colin Boniface (appointed Steward in 1989) and his wife Daphne (who was appointed housekeeper in 1990) moved in. The bungalow forms the backdrop for many of the course photographs taken at Addington over the years — see p.131. [MD] recalls:

> 'Martin How had his own little cottage next to the palace with a clock above the front door. At his first lecture he observed how it was all very well for us to be able to look out the window at his clock, but he had to come all the way outside in 'the foulest weather' in order to check the time.'

Above: Addington Golf Club Ladies Drawing Room ca 1949
used by the RSCM as Library and then as a Lecture Room

Below: In addition to the vast fireplaces in the Great Hall and Music Room, many rooms at Addington had Norman Shaw marble fireplaces. This example was in the Common Room

Chapter II. The Coronation Choristers at Addington — the first residents.

During April and May 1953 the country's local press was full of articles and photographs of young boys in choir robes. These were the lucky few: the 20 boys selected from the 3000 RSCM affiliated choirs who would sing at the Queen's Coronation in June.

Dr William McKie, organist of Westminster Abbey and Honorary Associate Director of the RSCM from 1947 to 1953, was in overall charge of the music. Sir Sydney Nicholson's plans for the 1937 Coronation Choir were so successful that they had been committed to paper and were used again as the basis for planning the 1953 Choir. Gerald Knight was appointed Hon Sec of the Coronation Choir in October 1952.

The choir was to be 400 strong[29], the core of which would be from the Royal Foundations — singers from the choirs of Westminster Abbey, St George's, Windsor, the four Chapels Royal and representatives from seven colleges (including Eton). Added to this Royal nucleus were selected singers from eight historic cathedral choirs — St Paul's, Southwark, Canterbury, York, St Mary's, Edinburgh, Llandaff, Belfast and Dublin. The last is perhaps a surprise being outside the Kingdom, but they were also present at the 1937 Coronation. Parishes within London were represented, including St Margaret's, Westminster, whose connection with the Abbey is obvious, but also by All Saints', Margaret Street. When asked why they were included Dr McKie replied 'They come because they have always come. I don't quite know why.' Such is the power of tradition in the church and state! Australia, Canada, New Zealand and South Africa contributed nine professional[30] and 27 other singers nominated by the Commonwealth High Commissioners. The *Birmingham Post* commented:

'Twenty of these 36 Commonwealth singers will be women, who form a tiny soprano-contralto oasis[31] in a force which otherwise is exclusively male (202 men and 178 boys) in accordance with tradition.'

The *Post* went on to mention the inclusion of 'sixty or so eminent British tenors and basses who happen to be versed in church music.' By virtue of this 'happenchance', several RSCM staff, course tutors and council members[32] managed to get into the choir or act as stewards[33].

Last, but not least, there was the RSCM contingent of 20 choristers representing parish churches and parish church cathedrals outside London. These boys were chosen by GHK, Edred Wright and Hubert Crook consulting with key choir-trainers around the country. Hubert, from his travels around the country and from RSCM residential courses, knew many of the best boys.

---

[29] The Ministry of Works actually provided 390 numbered seats. GHK's final list showed 394 singers, so hopefully nobody had to stand for all those hours.

[30] Chosen from singers already resident in the UK.

[31] It is rumoured that this group were deliberately seated behind a pillar so as to be out of sight! A sad, but typical, reflection on that era.

[32] These included Hilary Chadwick-Healey, Lionel Dakers and Revd George Sage.

[33] Edred Wright, Hubert Crook, Leslie Green and Sir Kenneth Swan.

GHK wrote in February 1953 to Thomas Duerden, organist of Blackburn Cathedral, hard-working Special Commissioner and enthusiastic RSCM supporter:

My dear Tommy,

Hubert, Edred and I have been thinking out and drawing up a list of choirs from which we may select the 20 boys... Here are our ideas.

1. Blackburn Cathedral
2. Chelmsford '
3. Wakefield '
4. Derby '
5. Truro '
6. Barkingside, Holy Trinity
7. Leeds Parish Church
8. Chesterfield Parish Church
9. Dartford, Christ Church
10. College of St Nicolas
11. ditto
12. Tenbury, St Michael's College
13. Norwich, King Edward VI School
14. Wolverhampton, St Peter
15. Bristol, St Mary Redcliffe
16. Belfast, St Bartholomew
17. Hawick, St Cuthbert
18. Barry, St Paul
19. Bury Parish Church
20. [here is pencilled 'All Saint's, Eastleigh']

As you see, we have not decided number 20 and wonder whether you have any suggestions to make. The accompanying draft letter will show you the principles which have guided our choice – geographical and long service to the RSCM. The Old Cathedrals are represented in the official list drawn up by Dr McKie and schools are well represented in it too.

Gerald

It is likely that this list was drawn up with knowledge of specific boys. Why, for instance, would St Bartholomew's Church in Belfast appear in this list unless one knew that their chorister Harry Gordon had won prizes in the Dublin 'Feis' and the 'coveted Broadhead Cup at the Blackpool Music Festival'[34] during the previous year? Certainly there was insider knowledge leading these suggestions.

---

[34] *The Irish Times* 12th May 1953.

Initially the invitations went to the incumbents of the selected churches[35] saying:

'The task of deciding which of our many hundred affiliated choirs should be chosen for this signal honour has been formidable. In order to ensure that our selection gave as wide representation as possible to the various categories of choirs affiliated to the RSCM — Parish Church Cathedrals, Parish Churches and Schools — we have aimed at spreading our invitations over as many regions of the country as possible, remembering especially those choirs which have rendered outstanding services to the cause of Church music through their membership of the RSCM. With these considerations in mind, we invite your Church to name one boy (treble) who, in the opinion of yourself and your Choirmaster, would be suitable for this very important task.'

'It is realised that so long an absence from school is serious and cannot be permitted without the consent of the Headmaster of the boy's school. It may help to know that arrangements will be made within the time available for boys to do under supervision such 'homework' as may be set them by their schools. If you are able to nominate a boy, we should be grateful if you would complete the enclosed form with the necessary signatures, and we will then communicate with the boy's headmaster to find out whether he is willing to agree to his going.'

'It need hardly be said that the opportunity to sing on such an occasion as this is one which falls to few people during a lifetime. The RSCM is immensely proud of being asked to be responsible for selecting some singers for the Coronation Choir, and we feel sure that you will share this feeling. We look forward to receiving your nomination on the enclosed form not later than March 7th, 1953.'

'The boys will arrive at Croydon not later than the evening of Friday, May 8th, and will reside there continuously until Wednesday, June 3rd. Where the journey is not too long or difficult, it will be permissible for boys to go home for the Whitsun week-end after the rehearsal on Friday, May 22nd, provided that they return in time for the Full Rehearsal in the Abbey at 5 p.m. on Whit Tuesday.'

There was also a financial commitment — 'The cost of board and lodging and all travelling expenses between Addington and London will have to be guaranteed by the parish or by the boy concerned, and it is hoped that £16 will cover this. In addition the cost of travel between the boy's home and Addington will have to be found.'

After the nomination of choristers by the churches, personal invitations were sent to the boys in March and, following their acceptance, the choristers' names and churches were released to the press on 10th April[36].

---

[35] In brackets at the bottom it suggested that 'a copy be sent for information to the organist & choirmaster' but the invitation to nominate a boy was sent to the priest.
[36] 18 choristers were named that day; the final two were appointed a few days later.

The final contingent of RSCM choristers was:

Anthony Holt, Holy Trinity, Barkingside	David Bainbridge, Christ Church, Dartford
Anthony Morse, St Paul, Barry	Graham Neal, All Saints', Eastleigh
Harry Gordon, St Bartholomew's, Belfast	Dennis Whitehead, St Cuthbert's, Hawick
Stanley Roocroft, Blackburn Cathedral	Michael Roberts, Leeds Parish Church
Malcolm Tanner, St Mary Redcliffe, Bristol	David Reeve, King Edward VI School, Norwich
Peter Hampson, Bury Parish Church	Michael Hartley, St Michael's, Tenbury
Nicholas Swain, College of St Nicolas	Richard Radcliffe, Truro Cathedral
John Fryer, College of St Nicolas	Philip Hutchings, St Peter's, Wolverhampton
Clive Plumb, Chelmsford Cathedral	John Sinnett, Holy Trinity, Leamington
Kenneth Yates, Chesterfield Parish Church	Barry Smith, St Peter's, Stockton-on-Tees

The boys, who had been sent the music in advance and had already learned the notes before they arrived in Croydon, trained for a month at Addington before the Coronation together with 12 boys from six provincial cathedrals (two each from the cathedrals in Edinburgh (St Mary's), Llandaff, Armagh, Belfast, York Minster and Dublin).

Edinburgh:	Alan Hazel & Douglas Jackson
Llandaff:	David Bevan & Peter Graper
Armagh:	Roger Dormer & Samuel Greenaway
Belfast:	Dermot McDonnell & Walter Officer
York Minster:	Beverley Jones & K Hopper
Dublin:	Kenneth Turner & Norman Williams

GHK was nominally in charge, but Edred Wright trained the boys. There were also three Masters[37] and a Matron (Mrs M F Carnes[38]). The boys' parents were sent a substantial list of instructions, what and how many items of clothing to take, information about Railway vouchers for cheap fares, pocket money instructions, details of how laundry and health matters would be managed, that they must, of course, take their Ration Books[39] and so on. He also wrote at length about the accommodation saying 'the address — Addington Palace — may conjure up in the minds of boys a spectacle of splendour and four weeks of luxury. It would be unfair to them if we did not dispel this misapprehension.'

---

[37] One of these was Mr Robert Kidd, assistant organist at St Mary's Cathedral in Edinburgh, who came down with the Scottish boys and himself sang bass in the coronation. He had previously sung at the 1937 coronation as a boy treble representative from St Mary's Cathedral. In 2006 he was awarded the Cross of St Augustine by the Archbishop of Canterbury for 72 years' service to church music in Edinburgh. There is no record of the other staff members.

[38] Mrs Carnes was a former Matron of Canterbury Cathedral Choir School.

[39] Confectionary rationing had ceased two months previously, so the choristers were not restricted for chocolate. Sugar, meat and all other food rationing ceased within the next 12 months.

SINGERS

THE SONG SCHOOL,
THE CLOISTERS,
WESTMINSTER ABBEY, S.W.1

March, 1953

CORONATION OF HER MAJESTY QUEEN ELIZABETH II
JUNE 2ND, 1953

DEAR SIR,

I have the pleasure to invite you to sing   TREBLE   in the Choir at the Coronation Service.

You will, I am sure, take this invitation as an honour, carrying with it the obligation to do everything in your power to make the Choir worthy of so great an occasion. This will necessarily involve much hard work for all concerned.

It must therefore be understood that if you accept this invitation, it is essential that you attend and remain throughout all the rehearsals specified below. Anyone not fulfilling these obligations will automatically forfeit his place in the Choir. No deputies are allowed.

You will be allowed to claim up to   Ten shillings   for expenses.

The rehearsals are as follows:—

IN ST. MARGARET'S, WESTMINSTER

Tuesday,	May	12 at 5.30 p.m.	Boys only		
Wednesday,	,,	13 ,, 5.30 ,,	,,	,,	
Friday,	,,	15 ,, 5.30 ,,	,,	,,	
Monday,	,,	18 ,, 5.30 ,,	,,	,,	
Tuesday,	,,	19 ,, 5.30 ,,	Full Choir, 2 hrs., approx.		
Wednesday,	,,	20 ,, 5.30 ,,	,,	,,	,,	,,
Friday,	,,	22 ,, 5.30 ,,	,,	,,	,,	,,

IN THE ABBEY

Tuesday, May 26 at 5 p.m.   Full Choir and Orchestra, 3 hrs. approx.

The Final Rehearsals are summoned by the Earl Marshal and will be:—

Possibly Wednesday, May 27, in the morning, in the Abbey, and Friday, May 29, in the morning, in the Abbey.

Every singer must provide himself with a cassock and surplice, without which he cannot be admitted on June 2nd.

Kindly fill in and return to me the attached form before March 18th April

Mr. Gerald H. Knight has kindly consented to help me in the organisation of the Choir.

The service is to be broadcast, televised, recorded and filmed. Your acceptance of my invitation by signing the attached form involves also your acceptance of this fact, and empowers me to conduct any negotiations that may be necessary with the B.B.C., the Gramophone Company, etc. I have convened a temporary committee to consider any problems that may arise, which will make its recommendations in due course.

Yours very truly,

Gerald H. Knight, Director, R.S.C.M.

for the   *Director of Music for the Coronation Service.*

To Dennis William Whitehead   [P.T.O.

The attached form to be returned to The Director,
R.S.C.M., Roper House, St Dunstan's St., Canterbury.

Indeed, the Palace was in a desolate state and far from palatial, but hopefully not too cold in May/June time. Scottish chorister 13-year-old Dennis Whitehead from St Cuthbert's in Hawick was one of the lucky boys and we are very fortunate that he kept a diary of the experience. He wrote to his parents to say 'They were wrong when they said it was more like camping out because the palace is just like a palace.' Oh for the hardiness of youth! One thing he did not mention, however, was that on Monday 18th May part of a ceiling in the music room fell down and the boys were moved to another part of the building to rehearse. The *Croydon Advertiser* correspondent[40] wrote 'Hopefully, I enquired whether this was an occasion when it could accurately be recorded that their singing 'literally raised the roof.' It was not. The boys, fortunately, were not there when the ceiling came down.' In fact there had been a concert in there the night before and chorister David Reeve apparently sang something containing a top B-flat and wondered whether he had done the damage!

Dennis Whitehead wrote:

> Rehearsals began the day after I arrived and for the first week our daily routine was as follows:—
> Breakfast – 9 a.m.
> Choir Practice – 10 – 1 p.m.
> Dinner and Break – 1 – 3.30 p. m.
> Rehearsal at St. Margarets with other boys 3.30 – 8.3
> Supper – 8.30 p.m.
> Dormitories 9.15.
> Lights out 9.45.

The choristers and staff were provided with meals by the Golf Club at 8/- a day per head.

During their stay the boys had billiards, table-tennis, or ping-pong as they called it then, for their entertainment and there was cricket outside when the weather was good. They also went swimming at the Croydon Baths and each Sunday they attended a local church in the morning and held a concert in the evening — mostly performed by the boys themselves (they were nearly all instrumentalists as well as singers) and the staff.

There were several photographs in the press of Edred Wright processing round the grounds of the Palace 'practising a ceremonial procession' whilst singing. These were probably staged publicity moments for, during the Coronation service itself, there was no singing in

---

[40] 22nd May 1953.

procession. A choir of 400 singing in procession would have been a logistical nightmare, as anyone reading this who has attended a large Diocesan Choral Festival will know only too well!

There were four boys' and three full choir rehearsals held in St Margaret's, Westminster, followed by one full rehearsal with orchestra and Kneller Hall trumpeters in the Abbey one week before the event. During that final week there were full musical rehearsals with organ and orchestra and two Earl Marshal's rehearsals. These latter were a complete run through of the service, at the second of which 'the Peers, Peeresses and everyone took part except the Queen whose place was taken by the Duchess of Norfolk.'[41]

When Coronation Day dawned Dennis wrote:

> 'On the morning of the Coronation we were wakened at 4 a.m. and at six o'clock we arrived at the Chapter House in the Abbey where we robed. At 6.30 we lined up in the cloisters and stood there in the cold for an hour.'

Each boy had been provided with a picnic to fit into their cassock pockets.

> 'By 8 o'clock we were in our places armed with Ovaltine tablets, glucose tablets, barley sugar, bread and butter, an apple, ¼lb slab of chocolate, all of which was consumed before the service began. Between 9.30 and 11.00am the orchestra played various selections and during this time it was interesting to look around at the various nobilities. I was very fortunate in being in a position to see most of the ceremony.
>
> There were twenty ladies in the choir representing various countries and one of them caused a mild sensation by starting to read the morning paper. When this was noticed a body of stewards descended on her and she was ordered to put it away. I also noticed Mr Atlee [former Prime Minister] immediately opposite me fortifying himself and his friends with Ovaltine Tablets.'

> 'At last the great moment arrived. The organ and orchestra began to play the introduction to the first anthem *I was glad* by Parry and we knew the Queen had arrived at the West Door.
>
> I must confess I could not sing the first few notes because of a lump in my throat. I shall never forget as long as I live the thrill of that moment when the Queen and her ladies in waiting in all their splendour slowly entered the Coronation Theatre. This was the moment I had looked forward to for so many weeks and the picture will remain forever in my memory. It might interest you to know that we sang in all 19 anthems and choruses. Most of us by this time knew the music outside in and could sing it easily from memory.

---

[41] From Dennis Whitehead's diary. The Earl Marshal in charge of 'stage management' was the Duke of Norfolk and so perhaps it is no surprise that his wife was the Queen's understudy!

Sir William McKie was the conductor and he had three sub-conductors[42]. The service ended at 2.00pm but it was 3 o'clock before we were allowed to leave the theatre and proceed to the buffet and eat to our heart's content.'

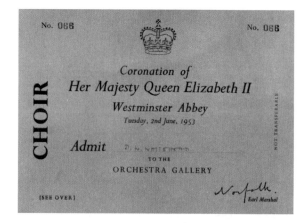

Many of the singers at the Coronation were perched on stools, specially made for the occasion[43]. Later that year the boys were offered the chance to buy one of these and some did so, though at £4 each (equivalent to £100 today) they were not cheap. Coronation chorister David Bainbridge recalls that he was visiting a wealthy lady in the USA many years later who proudly showed him such a stool that she had acquired. He did not like to tell her that it was a fake; the originals had an identification marking which was not present on this specimen. It seems that there has been a niche market in fake

Coronation stools and today originals of these small chairs change hands for around £400.

The choristers also each received a medal to commemorate the occasion.

At the end of Dennis's account he wrote:

'We then hurried back to Addington and enjoyed watching the procession on TV and we also saw the great fireworks display on the Thames embankment. By this time I was feeling very tired as it had been a most strenuous and exciting day. The next morning we were all dispatched to our homes as quickly as possible and I arrived back in Hawick feeling a bit dazed and bewildered after all that had happened.'

---

[42] Most other accounts give two conductors: William Harris and John Dykes Bower, but Dennis was perfectly correct because at the last moment Edred Wright was brought in as an additional sub-conductor.
[43] 15' wide for boys and 18' for men.

Dennis Whitehead: Coronation Chorister

Upper Left:

Press photo of Dennis Whitehead in 1953

Above:

Dennis was one of the singing group 'The Sarum Clerks' in 1972

Lower Left:

Pictured in October 2013 in Sarum College following the Coronation Anniversary Service held in Salisbury Cathedral where he served as a Lay Clerk for 27 years

Chapter III. The Dedication and Official Opening of Addington Palace

A) The Dedication: February 1954

The first term at Addington began on 22nd January 1954 and the first students began to arrive. The Dedication and Blessing of Addington by Bishop Cuthbert Bardsley, Bishop of Croydon, took place ten days later on a wintery day, Tuesday 2nd February. It is curious that this event received no mention in the RSCM Magazine, which was focussed entirely on the forthcoming Royal Opening in July. Nonetheless photographs show an adult choir, some members of which were students from the College in Canterbury, processing with GHK and the Bishop. Workmen and scaffolding are also present in some photographs.

The Bishop of Croydon with Crucifer Eriya Kaizi (a Ugandan student at both Canterbury and Addington) alongside Cyril Taylor, Gerald Knight and Horace Spence

The Blessing and Dedication of Addington Palace with scaffolding (top), snow (bottom left) and workman on the stairs (bottom right)

B) The Official Opening: July 1954

> 'Her Majesty Queen Elizabeth the Queen Mother has graciously consented to open Addington Palace as the Headquarters of the Royal School of Church Music on Saturday, 10th July, 1954.'

Thus read the announcement of the official opening in the April 1954 issue of *English Church Music*. It was entirely appropriate that it should be the Queen Mother, as she had had a long association with both Sir Sydney Nicholson and later with the RSCM. Nicholson, whilst Organist and Master of the Choristers at Westminster Abbey, had not only helped plan the music and play for her marriage to the then Duke of York in April 1923 and, whilst Director of the SECM, organise the Coronation Choir in May 1937, he had also obtained both her support and attendance at the Choirboys' Festival Service held at Westminster Abbey in October 1945. The Queen Mother's association with the RSCM was further strengthened when she accompanied the King (George VI) on an official visit to the College of St Nicolas in Canterbury on 11th July 1947.

With the announcement in *ECM* came a request for men to help on the day by acting as stewards, and for affiliated choirs to 'send their Head Choristers to line the lawns in cassocks during the procession. We shall need about 60 boys.'[44] Application for tickets was open to all members, albeit with the proviso that no more than two tickets per choir would be available. In order to help offset the costs of the day, the article goes on to suggest that: '...members attending should pay 7/6d and receive a copy of the souvenir programme and a ticket for tea.'[45] This souvenir programme contained not only the full order of service, illustrated articles on the history of the RSCM, photographs of current officials, but also an inserted copy of William Harris's newly-composed anthem *Behold the Tabernacle of God*. After the event, the programme was offered for sale at the reduced price of 1/-.

Given the amount of preparation required for such an auspicious day and considering that workmen were still very much an ongoing presence at Addington, there must have been some anxious moments as to whether all the building work would be completed in time. However, all was ready for the day which, although a sunless one, was at least dry.

From 2.30pm onwards guests were received by the Director and Council on the South Lawn, before making their way to their allotted seats in the chapel. At 3.00pm Dr Sidney Campbell, Director of Studies, began a short and (commented some afterwards) 'restrained' recital on the Chapel organ. At 3.15pm the Queen Mother arrived and was greeted by the Lord Lieutenant of Surrey, the Archbishop of Canterbury and the Mayor of Croydon. The procession then formed up as follows: a Crucifer carrying the cross of the College, the Warden, the Choir, the Honorary Chaplains, the Director, Members of Council, the Vicar of Addington, the Archdeacon of Croydon and, escorting Her Majesty the Queen Mother, the Archbishop of Canterbury, preceded by his Primatial Cross. The Choir for the occasion consisted of two boys each from the choirs of Westminster Abbey, St Paul's,

---

[44] *ECM* Apr 1954.
[45] *ibid.*

Canterbury, Southwark, Rochester and Blackburn Cathedrals, and the Chapel Royal, St James. The men included not only students, but also some who had sung at the opening service at Chislehurst in 1927. The choir was rehearsed and conducted by Edred Wright, the College Choirmaster. The hymn *Christ is our Corner-stone*, a favourite of Sir Sydney Nicholson, was sung in procession (unaccompanied) — as it had been sung both at the opening of the College at Chislehurst, and also at Canterbury — followed by Psalm 121 to plainsong, with Nicholson's fauxbourdons. The service in the chapel was brief, during which the Queen Mother unveiled a tablet, which the Archbishop then dedicated. The inscription read:

> This Chapel of St Nicolas was dedicated by Geoffrey Francis Fisher,
> Archbishop of Canterbury, in the presence of Her Majesty Queen Elizabeth
> the Queen Mother, July 10th 1954.

The lesson was read by the Bishop of Croydon, then followed Harris's new anthem *Behold the Tabernacle of God*; the final prayers were given by the Warden (Revd Cyril Taylor) and just before the Blessing by the Archbishop, the congregation sang the hymn *Jesus where'er thy people meet*, to the tune 'Wareham', with Nicholson's descant.

After the service, the Queen Mother, accompanied by the Archbishop and Director, made their way to the marquee on the South Lawn for the speeches. The Archbishop, who spoke first, made the comment that it had taken him some time to reconcile himself to the fact that the move from Canterbury was a good thing. 'It [the RSCM] had to leave Canterbury, and it nearly broke my heart.'[46] However, he lightened the mood by following this with, 'I have never been to Addington Palace until this afternoon, and when I first saw it I asked myself 'Why on earth aren't I living here?' Then I remembered that the Palace contained over a hundred rooms.' It was now the turn of the Queen Mother who, having made reference to the achievement of the Founder, and to the inaugural meeting in the Jerusalem Chamber in 1927, went on to say:

> 'From time immemorial in this country, music has formed an integral and vital part of our worship. We possess a tradition of church music unequalled either in volume or in splendour, and we owe it to the generations of gifted and devoted men to ensure that what they have handed down to us shall continue to rise in beauty and integrity to the glory of God.'[47]

In reply, Gerald Knight thanked the Queen Mother, not only for her part in the day, but also for all the interest she had shown in the work of the RSCM. As the Queen Mother left the marquee, she stopped to speak to a number of College choristers, students and boys drawn from affiliated churches who had formed a double line along the route, before re-entering the Palace where Members of Council, RSCM staff and others were presented to her. Tea was then served to all the guests in the dining rooms and in a marquee on the West Lawn.

---

[46] *ECM* Oct 1954.
[47] *ibid.*

Above: HM The Queen Mother with Gerald Knight and Archbishop Geoffrey Fisher

Below: The Speeches

Presentations to HM in the Great Hall   HM The Queen Mother meets the choristers

After tea, the Queen Mother was shown round the Palace and 'so great was her interest that the official time for the end of her visit was long overrun, and it was nearly half past five before her car drove off.'[48] This statement alone bears ample testimony to both her enjoyment of the day, and her continued interest in the organisation.

From the outset of the SECM, and later the RSCM, meticulous planning and organisation have marked all the great occasions, and this day was no exception. There must have been considerable work done behind the scenes, by the Secretary, the Bursar and others, to get both the building and the grounds ready in time for what must rank as one of the 'great occasions' in the history of the RSCM.

---

[48] *ibid.*

Chapter IV. The Palace in Action:

A) The Chapel[49]

As with both Chislehurst and Canterbury, the hub around which all activities of the college would centre in the new home of Addington Palace would be the chapel. This precept was so firmly held, and adhered to, that its restatement by the Warden (Revd George Sage) in the first issue of *RSCM News* was entirely apt:

> 'The heart of any course of training must be the practical work in which theory and precepts find their embodiment. The Chapel of St Nicolas is the heart and centre of Addington Palace and there, in Eucharist and Daily Office, in the context of our common prayer and praise, the purpose for which we exist and all the work done to further it become one.'[50]

The location selected was originally known as the South Pavilion, and had been variously a smoking room for the gentlemen of the house, a winter garden (or conservatory), for unspecified use whilst occupied by the Red Cross as a war hospital, and, from 1930, a locker room for members of the golf club. This room, located on the ground floor at the southern end of a wide corridor, was ideally suited to become the new Chapel of St Nicolas, a room benefitting from plenty of natural light and capable of seating a maximum of 100 persons. It was reported in *ECM*[51] that Mr S E Dykes Bower, Surveyor of the Fabric to Westminster Abbey, had 'kindly given his services, and is now working on the plans.' By the word 'given' one may conclude that his services were offered for free. The Proprietors of *Hymns Ancient & Modern* had made a generous donation of £850[52] towards the cost of establishing a chapel worthy of the headquarters of church music. The Harrison & Harrison organ, moved from Canterbury, was duly installed in 1954[53]. The re-leading of the St Nicolas stained glass windows, the work of Sir Sydney Nicholson's brother Archibald which had been placed in the chapel at Chislehurst, were reinstated in the Addington chapel in time for the official opening in July 1954[54]. This work was undertaken — and paid for — by the designers Mr G E R Smith and Mr H L Pawle, who carried on the work of the late Archie Nicholson[55]. The window depicts St Nicolas blessing three boys: a Westminster Abbey chorister (in a red cassock), a Chislehurst chorister (in a blue cassock) and a boy scout. The choir stalls were designed by Sir Christopher Wren for the Church of the Holy Sepulchre, Holborn, and subsequently obtained by Nicholson for use at Chislehurst. Many of the fittings and fixtures from both Chislehurst and Canterbury were also relocated in the new chapel, along with the many gifts of communion plate etc. Of especial note were the

---

[49] Photographs of the Chapel can be found in Chapter I.
[50] *RSCM News* No 1 Jan 1963.
[51] Apr 1953.
[52] About £20,000 in 2015.
[53] See Chapter IX.
[54] See Chapter III.
[55] Archibald Keightley Nicholson (1871-1937) was one of Sir Sydney Nicholson's older brothers (see *SNCSN*). A stained glass artist with a studio in Gower Street, London, his apprentice Gerald Smith carried on the business after his death.

processional cross (a gift from the Society of Faith) and the College banner depicting St Nicolas (a gift of Mrs Wright).

There is little doubt that the chapel was in almost constant use. 'In a year there are no less than 250 choral services, sung by at least seven different kinds of choirs.' In addition to this, choir rehearsals and an almost constant demand for organ practice meant that the chapel became the hub that had been envisioned.

A service in Chapel, Summer School September 1961

B) Of Choirs and Choristers

In order to trace the history and development of the chapel choirs at Addington, it is necessary to first look back to what was in place before the move to Croydon. At the outset of the then SECM, Sydney Nicholson, in setting up the College of St Nicolas at Chislehurst, had stressed the importance of having a choir of boys and students to maintain a daily round of sung services. To this end, he had put in place a residential choir (a choir school in all but name) of ten boys who, together with the students, established a pattern of daily worship in a broad spectrum of choral styles and traditions. The ten choristers also provided an in-house choir, on which the students could practise their choir-training skills. When the move to Canterbury was made at the end of the Second World War, it was decided to dispense with what had proved to be the somewhat expensive arrangement of a resident boys' choir, and concentrate on recruiting local day-boys from the Canterbury area. These boys were to sing services during the week at the relocated St Nicolas College, and to provide a choral resource for student choir trainers. At weekends, these boys were encouraged (and no doubt expected) to sing in their own home church choirs. This would seem to have been a far better use of the rather war-depleted funds of the RSCM, than to revert to a residential choir school set-up. Furthermore, there had been some criticism in the past that the Chislehurst choristers, brought to a high standard under the expert tuition of both Nicholson and their choirmaster Harry Barnes, had become a somewhat elite group of singers, which hardly represented the typical parish choir set-up the aspiring choir-trainer would encounter.

Edred Wright, a former chorister under Nicholson at Westminster Abbey, and latterly a student at the College in Canterbury, was appointed Choirmaster in 1946. He quickly proved to be a gifted and successful choir-trainer. 'Singers who have had the privilege of working under Mr Wright know that he is a master of his craft'[56]. Not long after the opening of Addington for business in January 1954, the recruiting of boys from the surrounding area to form a Palace choir began, and Wright was able to start a choir. This initial batch of boys came mostly from John Ruskin, John Newnham and Gilbert Scott schools. Edred Wright had already submitted a scheme to Council for recruitment. This scheme was based on payment according to grade, the grades being Probationer, Singing Boy and Chorister, and a bonus payment to be made when each boy left. Wright envisioned that the total number of boys required to set up a choir would not exceed 66, and that the cost could not be more than £100 per annum.[57] The Council meeting, at which, it was noted in the minutes, the Director was absent, approved the scheme. The payment of choristers was phased out in later years. Even before the move to Addington, RSCM Council had decreed that the RSCM needs 'to maintain at Headquarters a constant standard of well-ordered worship, to serve as an object-lesson and inspiration to those anxious to learn'[58], and this proposal fitted well with their intentions. And so it was, in less than five months, a newly-formed choir of boys, named the Tallis choir, sang their first service on 6th May 1954, albeit with a modest repertoire.

However, all was not well, as was revealed in a Council minute dated 28th July of the same year. The Warden, Cyril Taylor, had reported at that meeting that 'although he had great admiration for the Headquarters Choirmaster's abilities as a choir-trainer, he felt that Mr Wright did not fit easily into the communal life of Addington Palace, and that a change of occupation was desirable in the interests of both Mr Wright himself and of the College. It was resolved to offer him the appointment as a full-time Commissioner in the field from 1st September 1954, and that from January 1955 his work would be concentrated in the Northern Province and based on York.' Whether the problem was one of personality clash or whether the fact that Edred Wright was still living in Canterbury and commuting to Addington which possibly made him more of an outsider and less of a community member is not clear. At some point Wright had been offered the post of Choirmaster at King's School, Canterbury presumably starting in September 1954, so it may have been thought that he would be able to give less time to his post of Headquarters Choirmaster than was originally envisioned; but the fact that he was offered a full-time post, albeit somewhat removed from Canterbury (perhaps deliberately), leads one to the assumption that he was still regarded as a valuable addition to the RSCM staff.

On his own initiative, Gerald Knight went to see Wright, possibly to put the proposal of being Northern Commissioner to him. As a result of this meeting and without consulting any of the RSCM Management Committees, GHK terminated Edred Wright's contract as

---

[56] William McKie in his foreword to Edred Wright's book *Basic Choirtraining* - RSCM 1955.
[57] Finance Committee Minute No 327.
[58] Council Minutes Jan 1953.

Headquarters Choirmaster. Council was not entirely happy with this unilateral action, but agreed however to back up the Director's action. Fred Martin-Smith (Hon Treasurer of the Finance Committee) subsequently went to see Mr Wright and offered him six months' salary and allowances. In return Edred tendered his written resignation on 13th September 1954. Nevertheless, he received an appreciative write-up in the members' quarterly magazine: 'During his association with very many activities of the RSCM, Mr Wright's outstanding gifts were probably best exemplified in his training of the choir at Cathedral courses over the last five years, and he has shared the secret of his skill with the readers of this magazine in a series of articles.'[59] What may be noteworthy here is the lack of any mention of his work with the Addington choir, although there is the danger of reading too much into this omission. Edred Wright continued to work for the RSCM directing several courses over the next 20 years and he was assistant conductor of the major 1970 *Jubilate Deo* Festival in the Royal Albert Hall.

Addington Postcard No 409 was issued early in 1955 and so this photograph of Hubert Crook directing the Chapel Choir probably dates from 1954

Sidney Campbell[60], Organist of Southwark Cathedral, and also appointed Director of Musical Studies at Addington in January 1954, briefly stepped into the breach in the Christmas Term of 1954, with Hubert Crook assisting. However, towards the end of term Crook, the Chief Commissioner, took over completely: 'things were so unsettled that it was necessary to ask four of the boys to leave: After this it was possible to build up.'[61] One wonders if this

---

[59] *ECM* Oct 1954.
[60] For biography see Sub Wardens.
[61] From a 'Headquarters Choir Log' kept by Martin How.

may have been a result of Sidney Campbell's well-known volatility! Crook, who normally spent a considerable portion of his time 'on the road' visiting affiliated choirs and conducting events up and down the country, was required to spend much of his time during the remainder of the Autumn Term, and the following two terms, at Addington. During this period, Crook reorganised and expanded the College choir (the Tallis Choir), and, by contacting local schools, was able to recruit many more boys. Such was his success in this work, that the Director, on 17th November 1954, was prompted to recommend to the Executive Committee that Hubert Crook be appointed Headquarters Choirmaster, provided that a suitable person could be found to take over his role as Chief Commissioner. Melville Cook, Organist of Leeds Parish Church, was approached, but declined the offer and so Crook continued his work with the Palace choir combined with his field trips as Chief Commissioner — a heavy work-load indeed! In the Lent Term of 1955, Crook's recruiting skills had led to his being able to start a second choir called the Nicholson Choir, which became the foundation stone of what was to follow. The original Tallis Choir had at this time 'reached their potential.'[62] By July 1955 the Nicholson Choir were able to sing their first service — with the Tallis Choir. By the end of term they had reportedly performed two anthems, *Lead me, Lord* by S S Wesley and *Bow down Thine ear* by A Arensky.

However, help was on the horizon. It was announced in *ECM* April 1955 that a new Headquarters Choirmaster had been appointed, and would commence his duties at the start of the Autumn Term in 1955. His name was Martin How, late Organ Scholar of Clare College, Cambridge and himself a former student of the RSCM at Canterbury. Martin had arrived at Addington in January 1955, as a student intending to resume his studies which had been interrupted by National Service. There can be little doubt that Martin's expertise in choir-training, together with his organisational skills[63], was quickly realised, and that he would be the ideal person to take over the running of the choirs at Headquarters at the start of the new academic year.

Stepping down from his role as interim Headquarters Choirmaster, Crook summed up his own contribution in the July 1955 issue of *ECM*: 'I have continued at Addington my task of organising the two choirs of boys. By the end of July [1955] that will be completed, and I want here to pay tribute to the splendid co-operation of the boys themselves in helping me to carry out this important piece of work. Briefly, the task has been to re-organise the Tallis choir (started by Edred Wright in May 1954) on a proper age-group basis, to recruit a second choir of boys (which started work in January 1955 and is known as the Nicholson choir); to establish the proper administrative machinery, and to concentrate on the basic training. Although all this has brought much of my normal work to a standstill, it has been a richly rewarding experience for which I am grateful.' Martin How's appointment now released Hubert Crook to resume his full-time post in the field as Chief Commissioner.

---

[62] *ibid.*
[63] Martin How maintains to this day that any organising skills were entirely due to his National Service training.

Martin How commenced work as Headquarters Choirmaster in September 1955, with the Tallis Choir, now about a year old, and the Nicholson Choir about two terms old. He saw an immediate need to recruit and train some leaders in both choirs. By the end of the Christmas Term, he records 'Carol party to Mrs Scott's[64], and simple carols in the Great Hall afterwards: First time that the choir really 'performed' they just made it!'[65]

Nevertheless, Martin quickly made his mark. In the Lent Term, following further recruitment and reorganisation of both choirs and timetables, and also concentrating on a group of Probationers, standards started to improve. In the May 1956 issue of *ECM* we read:

'The work of the College choirboys, under Mr Martin How, goes from strength to strength. We have two large choirs (Nicholson and Byrd), each of which sings one evensong a week, and two groups of probationers to fill vacancies as they occur. This means that something like seventy to eighty boys come regularly to the Palace every week.'

The writer of this article concludes, with what may be regarded as a truism by those acquainted with the set-up: 'Being Headquarters Choirmaster is no rest cure. This large number of choristers speaks volumes for the time and dedication put in by their Choirmaster.'

The timetable of choirs, practices and services varied over the years and by 1958 there were four choirs, as follows:

Purcell Choir	(14 boys)	Monday practice and service (fortnightly)
Nicholson Choir	(18 boys)	Monday practice, Wednesday service
Byrd Choir	(14 boys)	Monday practice, Thursday service
Tallis Choir	(16 boys)	Thursday practice, Friday service (fortnightly)

Martin commented 'At last we have a real working plan for the organisation of choirs, thanks to George Sage's sane ideas about things, and his permission for fortnightly schemes (Purcell and Tallis choirs). Each choir can support a secure treble line.'[66]

On weekdays, boys would arrive straight from school between 4pm and 5pm, by which time they should have eaten their tea. They then departed after evensong, normally by 7pm, or if staying on for a run round the golf course, 7.30pm. These runs inaugurated by MJRH seemed to have been popular, as were other sporting activities ranging from table tennis to football and cricket matches against other teams.

The Saturday morning choir was held in connection with the inauguration of an Addington Palace scout troop, with Martin as Scoutmaster and Lindsay Colquhoun as Assistant Scoutmaster, with the following timetable: Choir Practice 10am–11am, Scouts 11am–12 noon. Initially, volunteers were asked for, and the idea became well established. The

---

[64] Martin continued to take a choir to sing carols at Mrs (later Lady) Scott's for some time after the College Choir was disbanded using hand-picked singers. The tradition went on for over 30 years. Lady Scott was the wife of RSCM Council Member Sir Hilary Scott (1906-1991), President of the Law Society, and a staunch RSCM supporter who lived locally.

[65] From a 'Headquarters Choir Log' kept by Martin How.

[66] *ibid.*

Summer Term also saw the introduction of student choirmasters on a permanent basis; four students were in charge of four groups respectively, and they each organised their own services — valuable training indeed.

Above: The scouts welcome GHK home 1960

Below: Addington Troop Camp 1959

Above: Scout Camp 1959, at rear Martin How cooking, Lindsay Colquhoun eating

Below: Scouts lookout tower 1959

Miscellaneous Chorister Photographs

ADDINGTON BOYS AT TEA
July 1988

AND THE DOG DOESN'T EVEN LOOK!

Above Right: John Cooper up-ended in 1955

Above Left: Tea time for boys

Middle Right: Elevenses

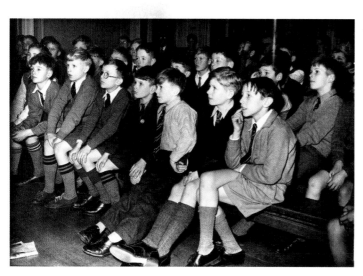

Bottom: Possibly the conjurer has more eyes on him than does the average choirmaster! This taken at the 1956 St Nicolas party

Left: Choristers (L) Richard Barnes, (R) David Ursell

Below: The RSCM Chorister Football Team 1956

Examination of the roll of choristers for the start of the Autumn Term 1958 shows that there were 73 boys on the books. Fourteen of these boys, who were more advanced, were termed as College Choristers. There were six Leader choristers and a Head Chorister. Ten of the boys were also listed as belonging to the Scout Troop based at the Palace. All of these boys were recruited from schools in the area, mainly Winton House School, Gilbert Scott School and Elmhurst School.

Martin then briefly sought pastures new: firstly, to return to Cambridge for a year in 1960, to finish his studies at his old College, and then taking the post of Organist and Choirmaster at Grimsby Parish Church, which had a choir school attached, from 1961. In his absence, Michael Brimer had been appointed acting Choirmaster, on the condition that if a university teaching post in Australia should come up, he would be free to apply for it.

In order to give a clearer picture of the set-up of the Headquarters Chapel Choir at Addington, Brimer wrote an account primarily intended for younger readers, which gives a good insight into the routine of a Chapel choirboy. 'The top line [of the choir] is provided by boys who live in the Croydon area. They apply to join and, if accepted, come up to Addington straight after school on a certain afternoon. They have their tea, amuse themselves (mess about) in the games room or on the wide lawns until practice begins at 5.00 pm. They practise until 6.10 pm, and Evensong is at 6.15 pm. The boys are away by 7.00 pm. There are about 70 boys in the choir ….divided into three choirs, which come on Tuesdays, Thursdays and Fridays. The best boys from those three choirs come on Mondays [and] a small group of boys come for practice on Saturday mornings as well.'[67]

However, a lectureship in Australia did come up, rather sooner than expected, and Brimer resigned in December 1961 to take up the post in the Music Department of the University of Western Australia. Martin How writes: 'In his one year he [Brimer] made a superb contribution to the College choir by extending the repertoire and using to the full the now fully-experienced set of boys.'[68] The extent to which the repertoire had been extended may be judged by the following: 'We sing so much music [in order that] the students at Addington shall have the experience of hearing and singing a representative selection from the whole range of church music. To keep up a different anthem for every day of three terms and a different setting for every day of a term, requires quite a lot of work.' [69] Rather an understatement!

Peter White, a former Addington student and organ scholar at St John's College, Cambridge, then took over the reins, beginning as Headquarters Choirmaster in March 1962. He continued Brimer's excellent work in recruiting boys from local schools, and maintained a large choir divided into various groups. 'He was much influenced by George Guest's technique in making his boys sing with a continental tone, and the Addington boys had a similar bright sound which I didn't care for very much.' [RM]

Upon White subsequently taking the post of Director of Music at Merchant Taylor's School in 1966, Alan Fen-Taylor, a former organ scholar and an accomplished harpsichordist, was appointed from September 1966. He was regarded by the Warden Roy Massey as a brave appointment, as the advertisement had brought in very few applications. However, things did not work out well. 'All the students almost without exception felt that he was such a mixed-up soul. Even though he had all the right qualifications and background, he was unable to pass on the information in a proper and cohesive form.' The boys' choirs, previously with about eighty on the books, rapidly dwindled to [virtually] nothing and the choristers' parents were understandably concerned. Eventually matters came to a head, and Fen-Taylor agreed to leave in November 1967, after being told that his position could not be confirmed after his year's probationary period.

---

[67] *Choristers' Leaflet No 73* February 1961.
[68] *Unpublished Memoirs* Martin How.
[69] *Choristers' Leaflet No 73* February 1961.

Meanwhile, by August 1964, Martin How was back at the Palace having been offered the post of Headquarters Commissioner. This post involved working 'in the field' with much travelling around the country, visiting and helping affiliated choirs, fulfilling the role previously undertaken by Hubert Crook. However, following the departure of Alan Fen-Taylor, Martin How was recalled from 'the field' in autumn 1967, to take up the post of Headquarters Choirmaster (once again) starting in January 1968. Gerald Knight had said to him:

> ' 'Now, dear, we want you back at Addington — to put things right you see!' …
> Immediately I had to look to the boys' situation. There were only six left…
> fortunately three of the boys were extremely good… [they were] Peter Floyd,
> Andrew Cole and Stewart Norris. Upon them we were able to rebuild the choir.' [70]

So, Martin restarted his work as Headquarters Choirmaster at the beginning of the Spring Term 1968, and was immediately faced with the task of recruiting and rebuilding. 'I was required to re-establish the choral side of things… in particular to restore morale amongst the boys and students alike.'[71] Innovations brought in by MJRH included the institution of May Concerts, and a demonstration choir. Sampson sums up the reason for this success in his thesis of 1971:

> 'Mr How is well-known for the skilful, yet informal way in which he quickly
> establishes a successful relationship with [his] choristers. The easy chat by him in the
> columns of 'Treble Clef'[72] show some evidence of this ability; but the skill, efficiency
> and size of the Headquarters' choirs testify to his ability.'

In September 1970 Martin was able to resume his duties as Headquarters Commissioner when Colin Yorke was appointed Resident Choirmaster. By this time there were over a hundred boys belonging to the four choirs, although only about thirty came at any one time. There were many highlights, one of which was when some boys from the Chapel Choir sang in 'Parsifal' at Covent Garden in 1971.

However, all was to change. In *PCM* October 1973, the Bishop of Ely, Chairman of Council, announced to the RSCM membership that the College of St Nicolas would close at the end of the academic year 1974, and instead of taking residential students, the RSCM would henceforth concentrate on a programme of short courses on a wide variety of subjects. This spelled the end of 'College Choristers' as such. Colin Yorke, in consequence, stepped down as Headquarters Choirmaster in the summer of 1974. John Ottley, who had been appointed as a general assistant in the secretarial office from December 1974, was listed as Headquarters Choirmaster in 1976, but by this time the choir was living on 'borrowed time'.

In June 1977, Lionel Dakers reported to Council 'that it was no longer possible to find a place for the boys of the choir in the new scheme at Addington. The original purpose of the

---

[70] *Unpublished Memoirs* Martin How.
[71] Choirmaster's Report Summer 1970, MJRH.
[72] The central page insert in the RSCM magazine.

boys' attendance at Addington had disappeared with the ending of the course for full-time students and, after discussion with the staff, had decided that the choir would be disbanded in July 1977. The Director then informed Council members that boys from choirs in the Croydon Archdeaconry would be used when a choir was needed for the short courses.'[73]

So ended a tradition of boys singing regularly at chapel services which extended back not only to the early Addington days, but further back to both the Canterbury and Chislehurst days as well. Ah, well, *Tempora mutantur, nos et mutamur in illis*. However, a Phoenix was to rise…

The Monday Choir — recalled by Martin How.

'The College Choristers did to some extent out-live the College itself and the students. John Ottley, a member of the office staff and Organist and Choirmaster at St John's Church, Selsdon, took them on, giving them a weekly practice. I think John would be the first to admit that it was hard to find a true purpose for the boys now that the College and its services were no more. After a while the choir was discontinued, not without some heated objections from certain parents.

Although now back 'in the field' as Commissioner for the South I could be back at Addington on some Mondays. I therefore put forward a scheme to Lionel Dakers for an 'occasional' choir, mostly on a fortnightly basis to begin with, whereby promising boys from local choirs can be given some coaching towards Cathedral Singers events and Cathedral courses. LD was understandably cautious if not slightly 'anti' to begin with, having just overseen the closing of the College Choir. However he agreed on the condition that the boys were not known as the College Choristers.

The group began with the invaluable support of Bob Prizeman at St Philip's Church, Norbury, Bob Stewart at Beddington, Bob Soper at Caterham, David Squibb at Trinity School, Croydon and others. The boys in the group were quite reasonably competent, and they made all the difference to the various RSCM events that they helped to lead. Starting the enterprise in the late 70's, by the early 80's the group had become well-established and met on a weekly basis, unless my travels absolutely forbade my returning to Addington. So it became The Monday Choir and now we added many more boys from local choirs, making it not just a choir of 'experts' but a training choir. Martin Dales, in charge of the choir at St Paul's, Crofton, and Bob Soper of Caterham, St Mary's were key supporters. Also there were our friends at St Mary's, Hayes, who included the ever-supportive Matthew Burrows and of course, as always, St Mildred's, Addiscombe with Derek Dorey as Choirmaster. John Ottley was a true ally.

In time the tradition was established of finishing the Monday practice with an epilogue of ten minutes' duration (6.pm-6.10pm) round the grand piano in the Great Hall. This was in front of the parents who had come to collect their offspring and take them home. The

---

[73] From *Council Minutes* June 1977.

event became quite popular, and provided a short time of reflection and relaxation for the parents, and sometimes members of any course which happened to come into residence on the Monday. Some members of the office staff would stay on and sing ATB parts, and we would have the choirmasters of some of the choirs represented, and various adult singers who liked to join us for this venture. One of the features of these epilogues was the regular making of a recording on an old-fashioned portable tape recorder. The results form a rather novel and valuable archive of the Monday group. We were able on these occasions to reflect the various church seasons or saints' days as they occurred. We were also able to work in a full opportunity for various solos, giving experience to boys at all stages of their development. These solos made full use of the various Sentences found in the experimental ASB services (one of the better features of the ASB surely?).

I do sometimes wonder if more use could be made of the epilogue/round the piano idea at the end of church weekday choir practices, involving parents who have come to collect their kids. Of course everyone always says 'we would never have time!' but what an opportunity to bring parents into the church if they don't usually come — or even if they do.'

May Concerts

In January 1968, now Headquarters Choirmaster once again, Martin How set about recruiting for the boys' choirs, which had dwindled somewhat under the previous Choirmaster. With the help of David Squibb (Director of Music at Trinity School, Croydon), he was able to recruit boys of the calibre of Robert Jones (now DOM at St Bride's, Fleet Street) and Tony Britten (now well-known in the Music Show business).

'These two lads, as leaders of opposite sides in the choir, rivalled each other in their musical prowess and leading ability. With their ability, we were able to start 'May Concerts' along with the students, doing such works as Tony Hewitt-Jones' *Sea Songs* and Mozart's *Requiem*. The orchestra we employed was the Croydon-based Erato Orchestra.'[74]

The choir used the title the 'Addington Palace Singers' for the concerts. There was an influx of some highly able students following the Warden (Freddie Waine) setting up the 'London Students' scheme, whereby students at London colleges with an interest in choral and vocal studies could reside at Addington Palace, and join in chapel services and concerts. Among these students were Stephen Roberts (baritone), Michael George (bass), Paul Spicer (choral conductor), Vaughan Meakins (bass) and Susan Campbell (soprano). 'We can claim, I think, that Michael George and Stephen Roberts were singing some of their first solo roles in our May Concerts.'

Major works were performed such as Handel's *Messiah* and Mozart's *Requiem*, and Martin recalls that the standard was very high and that 'these [concerts] became a central part of the students'/choristers' year.' Colin Yorke, Martin How's successor, showed a particular

---

[74] *Unpublished Memoirs* Martin How.

flair with the orchestra and developed the May Concert tradition in the few years left of the College's life before closure. There is no doubt that the full resources of the College were brought together for these concerts, which included choristers, students, visiting singers (from Monday night evensongs) and instrumentalists.

'Vincent Waterhouse (Secretary) undertook to look after the finances [of the Addington Palace Singers] and got us affiliated to the National Federation of Music Societies. In all instances we were so lucky to have Addington Palace as a near-by base for all participants.'[75]

C) Chapel Services

Over the years some of the Chapel service times were changed, but a general pattern was as follows:

Morning Prayers (Mondays):

'On a Monday morning there were prayers for all the students and there was at least one hymn. A different student played it each week and [afterwards] Dr Knight always had a comment to make.' [IB] These prayers, which included prayers for specific places both nationally and internationally on a rota basis, were held at 9am, and latterly included two hymns. The chapel service sheet for 17th March 1969 included prayers for RSCM members in the diocese of Chelmsford and York, and also in the Province of the Pacific in the USA.

Evensong (Weekdays):

Evensong was sung on most weekdays, by one or other of the various boys' choirs, with students supplying the lower parts, as required. On Wednesdays there was a plainsong evensong sung at the earlier time of 3.00pm, later changed to 3.15pm, by a student choir under Ernest Warrell, and latterly Michael Fleming — with Fr Capenor of St George's, Shirley, as Cantor. There was a late Students' Evensong every fortnight on Monday evenings at 9.00pm, to which a few extra singers from local churches would come and join the residents for a rehearsal after dinner '...followed by evensong at which some ambitious music was sung. These late evensongs were often very enjoyable and this is where our London sopranos and other first study singers really came into their own.' [RM] For one student at least [RG], the Wednesday plainsong evensong was a highlight of the week.

Also on Wednesdays there was an early service of plainsong Matins alternating with Litany at 8.00am — before breakfast. 'The women sang these services because they were at times when the choirboys were not available.'[AB]

John Eagles says of the Wednesday morning Plainsong services:

'For students, it was customary to treat Wednesdays as a plainsong day. This meant that there was a (very) early service in the chapel at some God-forsaken hour, which was often one of the monastic offices such as Prime or Matins. As I was the only student who, being a local chap, was not residential (and to this day I have never

---

[75] *ibid.*

spent a night at Addington Palace), this entailed an onerous start by getting up an hour earlier than everyone else, tackling the ascent of Ballards Way and the descent of Gravel Hill, and arriving in a bleary-eyed and semi-conscious state to sing a service that did not appeal. Naturally, there were a number of these early starts when I decided to absent myself. This clearly did not receive the approval of the then Warden, Frederic Waine, who saw the experience as indispensable for a student in church music. On a rare occasion when I did manage to show up, later in the day he would say to me, 'Nice to see you at Prime, John, this morning!', as if to rub the point in.'

Early Eucharist (Fridays):

The 7.30am Eucharist on Friday mornings was probably the least popular service of the week, mainly because of the early hour[76] and also because it was often less than satisfactory in performance terms. The service was before breakfast; however, exceptions to a strict fast seem to have been made on occasions. 'We could have a biscuit before Schubert in G owing to its length.' [AB][77]. It had become a student tradition to provide a cold bath afterwards for those who failed to rouse themselves to sing. 'I fear the choral efforts at that time of day lacked certain finesse.' [RG]. 'Early morning Eucharist was a particular challenge!' commented [IB] though [AH] recalls '7am Sung Eucharist on a Friday morning was a challenge for most of us students, but we sopranos soared up to those notes even at that time in the morning!'

With the appointment of Lionel Dakers as Director in 1973, a review of the overall structure of the College was undertaken. Martin How makes the comment about this early service: '...try not only singing a Sung Eucharist before breakfast, with a hesitant student conductor and an uncertain organist, and then going into corporate breakfast where everyone is in a bad mood!'[78] Dakers obviously had little love for this service.

> 'They [the London students] owed little allegiance to Addington, which was in many respects understandable. One of the most futile features of this scheme was the Mass sung with a full complement of music at 7.30 each Friday morning. Because it was so early, absenteeism, legitimate or otherwise, was rife, while the service, because it was resented, was seldom what it ideally should have been.'[79]

John Eagles again:

> 'Before breakfast on Fridays, there was a fully choral Eucharist in the chapel at which the Chaplain, Revd Leslie Katin (the brother of Peter Katin, the concert pianist) would usually celebrate. The housekeeper (whose name escapes me) would bring her spaniel into the service and for most of the time the dog would lie asleep

---

[76] Wendy Faulkner (née Pearce) recalls that on Friday mornings at 7.00am the students were woken 'by old Harry [Blacktin] leaning on the rising bell for several minutes.'

[77] Anita Banbury also mentions that Addington observed the tradition of being 'meatless' on Fridays.

[78] *Unpublished Memoirs*, Martin How.

[79] *Places where they Sing*, Lionel Dakers, Canterbury Press, 1995.

oblivious to what was going on. On occasions, however, it produced canine snoring which was clearly audible in the chapel. I remember one occasion when the organist – a fellow student – was giving the intonation for the *Sursum Corda* but had not quite drawn the stops sufficiently to allow enough wind to reach the pipes. The result was a bizarre combination of pitches that bore little resemblance to what was intended. Together with the sound of the snoring animal, it is a wonder that Revd Katin managed to find any approximate note whatsoever! This in turn created much amusement among us students, and I remember Revd Katin giving us a stern glare in admonition for taking this moment in the service so light heartedly.'

Evensong (Saturdays):

The plan from the very outset was that Saturday Evensong would be sung by an affiliated choir[80], which would be invited to spend either the day, or just the afternoon if not travelling a great distance, at Addington, rehearsing for evensong in the chapel, either under the Headquarters Choirmaster or another member of staff, tea – which was to be provided – and then Evensong. After the service there would be an opportunity of listening to the playback of the service, recorded on a reel-to-reel tape recorder. Roy Massey wrote: 'This was in the early days of tape recorders, when such machines were quite a novelty, and hearing themselves sing was a new experience for many of them.'

St Mary Cray was the first affiliated choir to begin the tradition on Saturday 3rd April 1954. They were followed by Enfield Parish Church on 15th May, St James, Elmers End on 29th May, High Wycombe Parish Church on 12th June, St Margaret, Putney on 19th June and St Mary's, Thakenham on 26th June. Later in the year, choirs from further afield visited – from Leeds, Southampton, Reading and Cambridge. This was a popular outing for parish choirs and, until 1957, there was a waiting list of choirs hoping to visit.

Ten years later *RSCM News* No 1 January 1963 reported that: 'All this means that apart from the resident students and the regular Addington boys, some four hundred different members sing at least one service in the year at Addington.'

In addition to choirs visiting to sing Evensong on Saturdays, other choirs came from time to time to hold a residential training course, usually at weekends. On the first weekend of April 1977, The choir of St John & St Philip from The Hague in The Netherlands were resident for four days, the first of at least four biennial weekends they held in Croydon. Occasionally choirs would use AP as a hostel such as in January 1974 when the choristers of Salisbury Cathedral stayed for two days whilst making a recording in London for Decca.

Eucharist (Sundays):

On Sundays there was a simple said Communion service at 8.00am, but after that Roy Massey writes:

---

[80] Friday Evenings and the weekends were kept free for the students so that they might be involved with other local choirs or attend concerts in London.

'Sunday was free of services to enable the students to go into London to sample the wide variety of music on offer in the City and one or two of them already had their own local church. All Saints', Margaret Street, was a much favoured destination as Michael Fleming's choir of men and boys was spectacularly good in their exotic repertoire of Viennese masses at High Mass, and occasionally some students came down to see what I was doing at the parish church in Croydon.'

D) Carols at Addington

Many people in the Croydon area will remember Carols at Addington. The first format was the concert of carols given by the College Choir with Martin How which started at Christmas 1955.

These concerts became so popular that, from 1958, two carol evenings were held. After the demise of the College choir, Martin selected a balanced choir for these occasions, latterly using singers from the Southern Cathedral Singers. In 1983 the hall was so full that Lionel Dakers, on the grounds of safety, had to turn away 20 people, including chorister mothers and someone who had come all the way from Southampton. It was decided to make this a ticketed event in the following years but chorister families and Addington staff had priority in applying for the tickets and so the public were hard-pressed to gain admittance.

Carols 1956:

Martin How practising carols in the Nicholson Practice Room

**Singing Carols in the Great Hall
It appears the RSCM could only afford minimalist tree decorations!**

Carols 1957:
Left: in the Great Hall; Above: on the Stairs

In 1982 Dakers began a second format of carols at Addington, namely a half-day course for visiting singers. We don't have attendance figures for the early years but this was popular enough to become an annual event and in 1988, 151 singers attended with Lionel, and then in the following year 166 sang with the new Director Harry Bramma. Martin How was usually the accompanist, though in 1988 the Dakers family assisted with a family 'orchestra'.

Over the years there were a great many additional services sung by the Chapel choirs, both at Addington and elsewhere, too numerous to list here in full. In addition to the Carols mentioned above, some of these events quickly established themselves into ongoing traditions. Here is but a selection of events in 1956:

- The first performance of the new publication *Cross of Christ*, given in the Great Hall in March.
- First performance of 'The life of a choirboy through the ages' to the Mothers' Union (a show that was later used in connection with the launch of the CTS).
- Recording for ITV in St Mildred's Church.
- Singing at the consecration of the Bishop of Madagascar in Lambeth Palace Chapel, by invitation of the Archbishop in June.
- Singing hymns for the Hymn Society of Great Britain with Vaughan-Williams.
- Singing evensong at the Summer Garden Party. This became an on-going tradition.

In 1957, there were several additions to the list of events, including:

- Singing at the Presentation of ADCM Diplomas at Lambeth Palace.

- Recording a selection of psalms, for use as official RSCM records.
- A Choristers' Weekend in July based at Addington but including a visit to Brighton where the boys sang Evensong in the Church of the Good Shepherd. These weekends continued for some years and Martin How comments now that all these additional events did as much as anything to give a much needed 'morale-raiser'.

Broadcasts

Broadcasts (some live, some recorded) of Choral Evensong from the Cathedral Courses were almost routine, especially up until the mid-1970's. Recordings and broadcasts made by the Addington choir(s) or at Addington itself include the following:

1955

Oct 11th   First of two recitals given by the BBC Singers and the BBC Chorus, directed by Leslie Woodgate, recorded for broadcast on the BBC Home Service at 9.45pm. Programme: *Mass in G-minor* – Vaughan Williams.

Nov 29th   Second of two recitals given by the BBC Singers and the BBC Chorus, directed by Leslie Woodgate, and recorded for broadcast on the BBC Home Service at 9.45pm. Programme: *Songs of Farewell* by Parry.

Dec 7th   The choir record a selection of carols for broadcast on the BBC overseas service.

1956

Spring   Recital by the Renaissance Singers directed by Michael Howard recorded for broadcast on the BBC Home Service, and transmitted on 6th March at 9.45pm. Programme: *Mass for Four Voices* and *Justorum animae* by William Byrd.

1957

Easter   In St Mildred's, Addiscombe, Associated Rediffusion record music sung by the College choristers for use in their Friday night Epilogue programmes. MJRH directs with student Ian Bridge (organist of St Mildred's) at the organ.

July 6th   Compline from Chapel broadcast by BBC, directed by E H Warrell; students David Gatward and Michael Holman were cantors.

Nov 24th   Morning Service (the Sunday nearest St Cecilia's day) broadcast from chapel at AP. Entry from the *Radio Times* reads:

'Morning Service on the Sunday after the Feast of St Cecilia, Patron Saint of Music: From the Chapel of Addington Palace, Croydon (the Royal School of Church Music), conducted by the Warden, the Revd Cyril Taylor, and the Revd Horace Spence, Clerical Commissioner of the RSCM. Versicles and Responses, Venite, Psalm 148, First Lesson: from 2 Chronicles 6, Te Deum Laudamus, Second Lesson: Revelation 4, Benedictus, Creed, Versicles, Collects, Anthem: *Praise to God* by Sidney Campbell, Prayers, *Christ is our corner-stone* (*A&M Revised* 243), Address: by Gerald Knight, Director of the

RSCM[81]. *Let all the world in every corner sing* (*A&M Revised* 376), Blessing, Choirmaster, Martin How, Organist, Derek Holman. The choir consists of students from England, South Africa, Australia, New Zealand, Canada, and the USA, now training at Addington to be organists and choirmasters, two of whom are reading the lessons. The boys are drawn from the neighbourhood.'

1958

Easter   During the Easter Holidays the College Choristers make a recording of hymns and anthems for ITV in St Mildred's Church, Addiscombe.

July 16th   BBC 3rd Programme at 18.45: 'Christian Outlook' included [from *Radio Times*]: 'Triennial Festival of the Royal School of Church Music: Gerald Knight, Director of the RSCM at Addington Palace, describes some aspects of the work of the School and introduces recordings of some of the choral music performed during last Thursday's festival at the Royal Albert Hall.'

Dec   A recording of carols made for the BBC Overseas Service.

Dec 14th   BBC TV broadcast Martin How taking a choir practice in the *Sunday Special* series at 18.10, repeated on 22nd Feb 1959.

Above and next page: December 1958 Live BBC Studio broadcast of
'Sunday Special: Choir Practice' with Martin How

---

[81] This can be heard on the CD that accompanies this book.

1959

May 24th/28th Martin How's diary mentions TV recordings on these dates.

Summer   The College choristers record a programme for ITV's 'Abide with me'.

1965

July 7th   *Choral Festival Service* at Royal Albert Hall, attended by HM Queen Elizabeth the Queen Mother and The Archbishop of Canterbury with 800 singers. The BBC recorded the whole service, and broadcast an edited 45 minutes on the Home Service on 4th August in the Choral Evensong slot.

1966

Dec 3rd   College students sing a Eucharist at St Sepulchre, Holborn, for St Nicolastide in the morning. In the afternoon at St Martin-in-the-Fields, John Churchill gives a demonstration 'Congregational Practice', with hymn singing. At 5.30pm Evensong is sung in Holy Trinity, South Kensington.

1968

Aug 25th   The closing service of the Lambeth Conference from St Paul's Cathedral, London, broadcast on BBC1 TV at 10.15am. From *Radio Times*:

'Nearly five hundred bishops of the Anglican Communion, delegates to the Tenth Lambeth Conference, attend a service of Holy Communion to mark the completion of their consultation. Celebrant, The Archbishop of Canterbury surrounded by the Metropolitans as concelebrants. Preacher,

The Metropolitan of India, Pakistan, Burma, and Ceylon. Epistle read by The Archbishop of New Zealand 1 Peter 3, vv. 8-15. Gospel read by The Archbishop of Uganda St Luke 5, vv. 1-11. Hymns: *To the name of our salvation, Glorious things of thee are spoken, Let all the world in every corner sing, Holy, holy, holy, Alleluia, sing to Jesus, Deck thyself, my soul, with gladness.* The Choir of The Royal School of Church Music under the direction of Dr Gerald Knight, Organist, Roy Massey, Commentator, Richard Baker, TV presentation by John Vern.'

1969

Aug 14th   A one hour programme about the RSCM broadcast on BBC Radio 4 produced by a free-lance journalist — Mr Leigh Crutchely.

Aug 24th   Professor Sir Bernard Lovell broadcasts on behalf of the RSCM in 'The Week's Good Cause' on BBC Radio 4.

1974

Mar 26th   The BBC record one of their 'Seeing and Believing' series of programmes at AP. Entitled 'Which way now' and broadcast on 12th May, it was a survey of trends in church music featuring Lionel Dakers, Erik Routley, Ian Hall, and Cyril Taylor, interviewed by Judith Jackson. Producer R T Brooks.

Seeing and Believing recording

At the same time the BBC also recorded 'They would have been a hundred' a programme about Gustav Holst and G K Chesterton, broadcast on BBC1 23rd June at 11.00am. Both programmes featured music sung by the AP Choir and Students directed by Colin Yorke with Michael Fleming at the organ.

Summer   A recording of 'Sunday Half Hour' made for broadcast by BBC Radio 2 on 4th Aug. Choirs from in and around Croydon were conducted by Martin How and Colin Yorke with David Bruce Payne at the organ and Michael Fleming at the piano. Hymns introduced by Lionel Dakers. From the *Radio Times*:

'Recorded in the Royal School of Church Music, Addington Palace, Croydon. *Let all the world* (Augustine); *There's a spirit in the air* (Lauds); *Hail, true body* (Standish); *Lift high the Cross* (Crucifer); *Behold, the tabernacle of God* by Sir William Harris; *Father, Lord of all creation* (Abbot's Leigh); *For the fruits* (East Acklam); *All my hope on God is founded* (Michael); *The splendours of thy glory* (Crediton).'

1975

Sept 7th   A broadcast on BBC1 at 11.00am in the *'Seeing and Believing'* series. It was repeated on 20th June 1976 on BBC 1 at 11.00am. From the *Radio Times*:

'New Songs to Sing — Leonard Pearcey talks to John Wilson, Brian Morris and Cindy Kent about three new hymn-book supplements. Choir of Students of the Royal School of Church Music, conductor Michael Fleming and organist Lionel Dakers. The Countrymaids, Accompanist Sue Farrow. From the Royal School of Church Music, Addington Palace.'

Dec 31st   BBC2 televise a Watchnight Service (at 23.30) from the Great Hall conducted by the Archbishop of Canterbury. *PCM* April 1976 reports that 'Within seconds of coming off the air, the Archbishop, choir, congregation and BBC cameramen spontaneously linked arms and burst into *Auld Lang Syne*, spurred on Martin How on the piano — a delightfully informal ending to a memorable occasion.'

1976

Mar 9th   Recital on the Peter Collins organ by Peter Hurford. Recorded by the BBC and broadcast on BBC Radio 3 on Sept 13th 1976 at 16.30. From the *Radio Times*:

'Bach, *Prelude and Fugue in G major* (BWV 541); Pescetti, *Sonata in C-minor*; Buxtehude *Chorale Fantasia on 'Wie schön leuchtet'*; Bach, *Seven Fughette* and *Chorale Preludes on Christmas Chorales*.'

1977

July 24th   *In Every Corner Sing* broadcast on BBC Radio 3. A 50-minute feature on the RSCM's first 50 years, narrated by Robert Prizeman with LD, GHK, MJRH, John Cooke and Allan Wicks taking part.

Sept 25th   BBC1 broadcast a *Songs of Praise* programme at 18.40 which looks at the people and preparations for the June RSCM Festival. From *Radio Times*:

'This programme recalls the June night when 700 choristers from all over Great Britain, members of church choirs affiliated to the Royal School of

Church Music came to the Royal Albert Hall, London, for a 50th anniversary celebration. The service was attended by HM Queen Elizabeth The Queen Mother, Geoffrey Wheeler was there and also talked to some of the people involved during their preparations. *All people that on earth do dwell* (Old 100th); *Christ is made the sure foundation* (Westminster Abbey); *O praise ye the Lord* (Laudate Dominum); *The true glory* by Peter Aston; *Far shining names* (St Nicolas); *Ye watchers and ye holy ones* (Lasst Uns Erfreuen); *Let all the world* (Luckington); *The day thou gavest* (St Clement). Conductor Lionel Dakers, Organist Martin How, Film director Andrew Barr, Series producer Raymond Short.'

1985

June 28th The Diamond Jubilee Service *Let all the World* in Albert Hall is recorded and broadcast on BBC1 TV on 28th June at 10.30am.

July 8th The Overseas Summer Course record a service at AP for the BBC.

1987

Aug 2nd BBC World Service broadcast a Service from Addington Summer School.

1988

July 29th BBC World Service broadcast a Service from Addington Summer School.

1993

July 11th BBC Radio 2 *Sunday Half Hour* broadcast at 20.30. From *Radio Times*:

'Roger Royle presents favourite hymns from Addington Palace, Headquarters of the Royal School of Church Music. *All Praise To Thee*; *God Has Spoken*; *We Rest on Thee*; *O Holy City, Seen of John*; *Jesus Stands Among Us*; *There's a Spirit in the Air*; *Jerusalem the Golden*; *Now Thank We All Our God*. Musical Director James Whitbourn.'

The 50th Anniversary of *The English Hymnal*.

In June 1956 the 50th anniversary of *The English Hymnal* was marked by a conference of The Hymn Society at AP. The many lecturers included RVW, Prof Arthur Hutchings and Joseph Poole. Students and college choristers sang hymns, directed by MJRH, with Derek Holman, organ, in West Croydon Methodist Church on 13th June. Martin How recalls that he was asked to be present at RVW's lecture to play any hymn requested by RVW.

Hymn Society Conference June 1956 with Vaughan Williams

Michael Smith (1955/56) recalls:

'I spent many happy hours in the Colles Library researching all sorts of things that I had not had the resources to explore before, and that THE HIGHLIGHT of the year was the English Hymnal 50th anniversary lecture by Ralph Vaughan Williams — complete with ear trumpet in which he received questions. Someone asked him why the editors had included some very dull tunes like 'Rhuddlan' with all those repeated notes to '*Judge Eternal*', to which he responded by asking the questioner whether then he considered that the *Overture to the Magic Flute* — with all those repeated notes — very dull.'

E) Student life and routine, including anecdotes

Routine matters

An article in *RSCM News*[82] entitled 'What it's like being a student at the RSCM' by Fred Graham, a Canadian student, gives a general picture of some of the student routine, by explaining what an imaginary visitor would encounter when visiting the Palace.

'At 7.30 in the morning our visitor would hear a bell, soon after which several young people would stroll towards a door marked 'Dining Room' for breakfast. (That is excepting Wednesdays and Fridays when there was an early service.) At nine o'clock another bell would sound, signifying the beginning of the choir-training class. Were our visitor to walk the short distance to the Practice Room, he would find a student explaining to the class his interpretation of an anthem which he will be responsible for conducting later in the week. The student's idea as to how the music should be played and sung is examined by the other students and commented upon by them, as well as by the choirmaster[83], who is present to lead the discussion and correct errors in interpretation. This anthem will be presented later to the chapel choir, consisting of men (the other students) and either trebles (boys) or women. At any time during the day, our visitor would find people ascending a wide and beautiful staircase and disappearing to the second floor. Here are the rooms of the men students [the girls' accommodation was beyond the kitchen on the ground floor], where they live, work and sleep.'

[MD] mentioned breakfast:

'There was Gerald Knight, magisterial and every inch the director, who always sat in the same place for breakfast at the end of a table. I overcame my initial awe and often sat next to him to absorb first-hand anecdotes of notable organists and clergy. Also he liked to be challenged on Psalms. He would get me to read a verse and he would identify the psalm faultlessly, even the obscure ones. I suppose most current and former English cathedral organists could have done the same.

At the far end of another table would be Michael Fleming surrounded by students as he read out excerpts from the morning paper usually with typical dry witty comments on the world situation. There was always much laughter at his end.'

[AH] remembers:

'Michael Fleming often took us for choir practice and it was an honour to sit next to him at the dining room table for breakfast or dinner. He had a great sense of humour and was always flapping his tie about something! I remember two female students who were in love with him and they would compete to sit next to him at breakfast! He did eventually marry someone local and we were all delighted at the news.'

---

[82] *RSCM News* No 16 Oct 1966.
[83] At the time of writing this was Peter White.

Afternoon tea

That quintessentially English tradition of taking afternoon tea was faithfully observed at Addington. Upstairs, in the Empire Room, at 4pm, Gerald presided over what became quite an institution. 'He loved inviting folk up to afternoon tea in his rooms and one quickly learned that 'tea, milk, water my dear' was the correct order when pouring him a cuppa.'[RM] On Wednesdays, the ritual included listening to the BBC live broadcast of Evensong on the radio. 'I remember we were listening to a Choral Evensong with him one Wednesday and the setting was by Leighton. His comment was 'I can't imagine the Virgin Mary singing that.' '

Downstairs, in the Common Room, the students had a more informal gathering, also at 4pm, and on Wednesdays this too would also include listening to Choral Evensong broadcast on the radio [BBC Third Programme] which followed straight after a plainsong evensong sung in the chapel at 3.15pm. 'At around 5.15pm, GHK (if he was in residence) would walk through to catch the 5.30 post, from the private collection [box] provided for the RSCM offices, with a hand-written card for the cathedral organist concerned. I often wondered what was said if the music was not well received.'[RG]

Dinner

Dinner was a formal affair[84], except for Sundays, which was informal normally consisting of sandwiches with fruit in the Common Room, having had the main (roast) meal in the middle of the day. Roy Massey recalls that 'During the week [Gerald] used to sit and improvise in a most elegant manner at the Blüthner piano in the Great Hall as we all assembled for dinner in the evening. Those entitled to them, wore their [academic] gowns, and with candles on the two long tables in the elegant dining room, the meal had a touch of formality which impressed me from the start.' Ian Barber remembers hearing Derek Holman and Gerald Knight improvising on the two grand pianos in the Great Hall before dinner. 'They played a bit each and then the other took over. Whatever key one ended up in, the other took over seamlessly.' There seems to be no doubt about the effect all this formality had on the student body. One student, newly arrived, recalls 'I well remember my first evening at Addington, sitting down in the elegance of the candlelit dining room and wondering if all student life could be like this. The College of St Nicolas was surreal indeed.'[RG]

Fr Anthony Cridland also recalled that 'the candle light dinners every evening created an atmosphere that did everyone good.'

However, with the arrival of a new Director, a more critical voice was soon heard: 'I was faced with a college which aped Oxbridge in its wearing of academic gowns, and the holding of candlelit dinners on any pretext.'[85] The old order was soon set to change, with the closing of the College of St Nicolas, and the end of taking residential students. Dining after this almost certainly became more economic (previously, many students and staff commented on how well they were fed) but also, I suspect, more prosaic.

---

[84] [AH] recalls: 'everyone dressed for dinner and it was always something special.'
[85] In *Places where they Sing* by Lionel Dakers, Canterbury Press, 1995.

Leisure moments

'There were many amusing incidents which caused us many a laugh during those years, but I remember us all sitting in the Common Room after lunch on Saturdays to listen to the famous radio programme *Round the Horne* and being in stitches of laughter at the jokes which were rather *risqué* in those days.'[HM]

The local pub was 'The Cricketers', which seems to have been frequented by the students — and some of the staff too, no doubt. Given the confines of the Palace, coupled with the fact that it was both a place of study as well as a place of leisure, inevitably there was friction among the resident students. [AS] in the penultimate year of the College recalls '...but it was the arbiter Michael Fleming who often came to the rescue, and quietly and steadfastly sorted out problems which had arisen.'

Addington Students June 1970

Front Row: Anthony Caesar; Frederic Waine; GHK; Michael Fleming; Martin How, Colin Yorke.

Second Row: Catherine McClurg; Shirley Tomlins; Maggie Rawlings; Wendy Pearce; Adrian Adams. Christine Asher is behind Wendy and Adrian.

Third Row: Carol Felton; Stephen Dickinson; ??; Sheila Olsen; Michael Walsh; Carl Nittinger.

Fourth Row: Michael George; Eric Freeman; Jonathan Gregory.

Fifth Row and up the steps: Andrew Small; Chris Berriman; Neil Houlton; Jonathan Hellyer Jones; David Thorne; Geoffrey Gilfillan; Revd Anthony Cridland; David Wyatt; Emmanuel Oni; Michael Deasey; John Matthews; ??; Michael Hedley; Nigel Allcoat; Guðjón Guðjónsson; John Leek; Nicholas Smith; Brian Wilmot.

Student pranks

What follows serves as a fairly typical illustration of what college and university students of the fifties and sixties used to get up to in their moments of relaxation. Obviously, the Addington students were no different from other institutions!

Anita Banbury (1963-66) recalls the time when 'One day some incense was put in the blower room and this was foreign to her [Secretary Dorothy Yorke's] religious inclination. The smell pervaded mid-morning when we practised on the robing room organ. Her reaction was puzzlement for a time.' Roy Massey, Warden at the time, also recalls what surely must be the same incident 'On the whole the students were well behaved except on one occasion when someone lit incense before a service in the organ blower room under the chapel, with the result that the organ blew out incense when the first chord was played. The stale smell was horrendous for days afterwards. I thought I knew who was responsible, and quietly suggested to him that a repeat performance would not be appreciated.'

Martin Roberts (1960-62) recounts the night when he, together with two fellow students, placed an Austin 7 in the [Old] Common Room. 'It required merely the use of a screwdriver, a medium-sized floor mat, and a few moments of thought and muscle.' There are several versions of this story, but photographs exist which show both the result and the perpetrators.

The Austin 7 which did not quite make it to the Great Hall in 1961

The proud perpetrators of the Austin prank

Another student prank involved re-siting exactly the contents of one of the rooms overlooking the golf course, onto the flat roof over the front porch. 'From that same roof, we also disgorged the contents of the fire hose onto the unfortunate Colin Yorke.'[RG] One wonders why Colin Yorke deserved such treatment!

Elizabeth Salmon, a student from New Zealand, recalls that some of the boys [by which she means the male students and not the choristers, we hope] used to collect elderberry flowers from the grounds to make elderberry wine, which '...turned into more of a liqueur — strong in alcoholic content. It made a late night party outside on the golf course a very merry affair, with a bit of dancing. Sadly, we were not so merry the next morning when we were castigated as a result of a complaint from the golf course management: we women had been wearing high heels which had left their imprint on the treasured golf green. Oh dear! The silliness of youth, but it was a great party!'

Derek Ferris (1954-57) remembers 'how we unofficially converted one old piano into a 'harpsichord' with the insertion of thumb-tacks ('drawing pins' to a Brit) into the hammers.'

Student impressions of Addington

Many former students have written with reminiscences of their time at Addington and quotations have been liberally used throughout the book. Further impressions are quoted here.

Ian McKinley arriving from Australia to study at Addington writes a colourful account of his first experience: 'I found Addington as beautifully English as I had hoped, set among woods whose leaves were coloured and starting to fall, and on the edge of a golf course.' Lionel Sawkins arriving from Australia in less attractive weather writes: 'It was a depressingly foggy overcast day... when I travelled through Clapham Junction to East Croydon and then took the 130 bus to Addington Palace. I had a warm welcome from Miss Yorke but Gerald Knight who had encouraged me to take 3 years' leave from my job as Director of Music at a large school in Australia, ignored me for the first two weeks; I eventually worked out that, as I had shaved off my moustache on the way over, he just simply failed to recognise me.' At the end of the memorably hot summer of 1957, Guyon Wells, in glowing terms, fondly recalls his arrival at the Palace. 'After the warmest of welcomes, I was taken on a tour of the facilities by Audrey [the wife of Warden Cyril Taylor] and shown the full scope of this beautiful Georgian building. From the grandeur of the Great Hall overlooked by the upper balcony of the Empire Room on the first floor, to the superb library with its Adam Ceiling, and on to the beautifully-proportioned Chapel with its Dykes Bower designed St Nicolas window and the fine Harrison organ, this initial experience was truly memorable.' The setting of the Palace in its spacious grounds impressed many of the students. 'The surroundings were gracious ... how many students sat doing harmony with a view of the golf course and fountain out of the window?'[AB] 'I am so grateful to have been at Addington. It provided a stable life, and was a warm and happy atmosphere for a student.'[IB]

James Burchell, hailing from Halifax, Nova Scotia, summed up what many other former students have commented on:

> 'For me, my time at Addington was exactly right: small classes and individual tuition, the constant exposure to the English tradition of church music, the challenge of the practical experience of playing and directing in front of tutors and fellow students who couldn't always be fooled.'

Warden Roy Massey remembers:

> 'The student body numbered about three dozen and were a very mixed bunch. Addington students consisted of youngsters from this country and others recruited from abroad, and they followed what was basically a one year course on all aspects of church music. The second category were the Londoners, students who lived with us but were taking a full time course at one of the Colleges of Music. They were expected to take part in any choral activity which fitted in with their timetable and were allowed to practise on the College organs and use our facilities. They added a significant dimension to the musical life of the place and were much appreciated. Among their number were six young ladies who added colour to an otherwise rather

monastic establishment and a useful soprano line when required. Therefore, at any one time there might be a youngster from a remote tropical region learning to put together hands and feet in a hymn tune side-by-side with someone already well *en-route* for an ARCO. As Warden and *ipso facto* Director of Studies, one had to try and accommodate this wide diversity of accomplishment. In my time — as best as I can remember — the teaching staff consisted of the Warden taking organ, ear training and history lectures; John Foster taught paperwork; John Bigg — a splendid performer — taught piano; Norman Platt taught singing and voice production: Mrs Martindale Sidwell taught piano under her maiden name [Barbara Hill]; Canon Dr Ronald Jasper lectured on liturgy; GHK lectured on the history of church music; Timothy Farrell from the Chapel Royal taught organ; Michael Fleming from All Saints', Margaret Street, taught plainsong and Peter White taught organ and choir training. Canon Jasper was chairman of the Liturgical Commission at the time and I had to meet him from the station every Saturday morning and take him back afterwards. He later became Dean of York where his enthusiasm for revised liturgy was not entirely welcomed by his Chapter.'

Anita Banbury (1963-66):

'The students put on a concert at Christmas. I remember singing about 'Madam Noel' (the local laundry service) to the First Nowell; and at one of these was my introduction to Swingled Bach.'

Ian McKinley (1958/59):

'Most of the time was solid work, involving choral singing, chapel services and associated rehearsals, sight-reading both vocal and keyboard, musicianship, and individual lessons in singing, organ, theory of music and improvisation. At the latter, I was hopeless, causing the lively Derek Holman to pronounce me as 'musically egg-bound.''

Dr Roger Allen (1970/71):

'I arrived at Addington Palace on 20th September 1970 as a callow eighteen year-old youth. I remember the date distinctly as it was the day before the Patronal Festival of St Matthew's Northampton, my home church and where I had first become involved with the work of the RSCM. I spent a year as an Addington student before heading north as a not so callow youth to read music at the University of Liverpool. My lifelong friends and former fellow students Robert Gower and Paul Spicer have written eloquently of the Tutors and students who formed the musical community in what turned out to be the last years of the College of St Nicolas. I have nothing to add, except to say that I fully endorse their warm remembrances of and gratitude for the collective musical wisdom of Gerald Knight, Freddie Waine, Michael Fleming and Martin How, and all they so freely gave to those of us aspiring to be the next generation of church musicians and musical educators. But what of the rich cast of characters who staffed and ran the Palace? Addington at that time, with its grand interiors, richly furnished state rooms (Empire and Wellington) set amidst a golf course often frequented by the diminutive comedian Ronnie Corbett, not to mention the dungeon-like basements occupied by the administrative offices of the RSCM presided over by the urbane and cultivated Vincent Waterhouse, had more than a dash of *Brideshead Revisited*. Such an establishment required a domestic hierarchy to maintain the inhabitants in a style to which we as students, though not exactly entitled, quickly came to relish.

The Palace (and the Director Dr Knight!) was ruled over by the then Housekeeper, Mrs Gordon, occasionally assisted by her daughter Anthea. Mrs Gordon (I don't think we ever knew her Christian name) was an indomitable *grande dame* of the old school who, it was said, was descended from the family of General Gordon of Khartoum. This was anecdotal but entirely plausible as she would have been perfectly at home in any of the grand houses of the late Victorian aristocracy. Mrs Gordon was a formidable presence with a shock of snowy white hair who more than made up for in force of personality what she lacked in physical stature. The door to her elegantly-furnished rooms was half way up the main staircase adjoining the Wellington Room. From here she presided over the running of the Palace like a Queen Dowager, but a very benevolent Dowager. Not much escaped Mrs Gordon's eagle eye. She was generous to a fault and unwaveringly supportive of those in her care. If it reached her ear (and it usually did) that a student was out of sorts for any reason, they would be summoned (not invited — summoned!) for 6.15pm prompt and plied with copious quantities of sherry before supper. There was no false sentiment or unwarranted sympathy on offer; but after a conversation with Mrs Gordon and a dose of her brisk good sense (together with the effect of the sherry) the world somehow seemed a better place. She would imbibe freely from the decanter herself and continue to hold forth in her inimitable way once we had gone down to dinner, much to the delight of the students within earshot (which was most of the room) and to the consternation of the Warden's wife, Beryl, who took a rather different view of what constituted appropriate conversation at table!

Daily life at Addington generally followed the rituals and rites of a theological college. The kitchen was presided over by Therese, a voluble German who in turn was ably supported by the kitchen factotum, the imperturbable Harry Blacktin. Harry was another Palace institution much loved by the students. One morning someone dropped a full plate of kedgeree (a Therese speciality) which spread itself over what seemed like most of the dining room floor. Entirely unfazed, Harry slowly emerged from the kitchen, approached the resulting mess with a dustpan and brush, planted himself in the way whilst solemnly intoning in a cadaverous voice, 'mind out chaps, danger'! Simple and economical of expression, when uttered by Harry these words had all the force of the knell of doom. The Palace was always immaculate and kept in pristine condition throughout by the 'Pledge Ladies'. This army of domestics would proceed around the rooms large and small, carefully ensuring that no speck of dust was allowed to settle on the exquisite antique furniture that adorned the Great Hall and the State Rooms. They took their collective title from a certain well-known brand of spray polish which they wielded to great effect.

Another Palace worthy was Captain Billy Rivers. Where Billy Rivers fitted into the scheme of things was not entirely clear — at least to the students — but he was a much-loved Palace character with a heart of gold. He held, as far as I was aware, no official position[86], but was devoted to the RSCM and all its works. Billy would appear at around 9.00am each morning and could always be relied upon to cash a cheque from the bundle of used banknotes he carried in his back pocket. This was a great help if cash ran short as the nearest bank was in East Croydon! Not that we needed much cash as, with the exception of occasional visits to the Cricketers' Arms, there was no call for it and little to spend it on. Billy was there to support in whatever way he could: no call for help ever went unanswered, although when it came to transport there was always a marked reluctance ever to accept a lift in his battered old Rover! Billy Rivers drove a motor vehicle as if he were driving an armoured car across the military training grounds of Salisbury Plain. Even in those days, when the flow of traffic on Gravel Hill was far less than it is now, this could be an unnerving experience.

There were, to me at least, welcome breaks in the weekly routine of classes, chapel services and the twice-weekly ritual of broadcast Choral Evensong on the radio which was listened to in a solemn silence broken only by Dr Knight's incantation of 'tea, milk, water m'dear' when he wanted his tea cup refreshing. Two events in particular stand out in the memory. Firstly, the annual Addington Palace Fayre (sic), held in mid-November, always concluded with a game of 'murders'. This arcane exercise was much beloved of Dr Knight, and involved, as far as I remember, trying to navigate the many recesses of the Palace in the pitch dark whilst someone played victim and someone else detective. Time has mercifully drawn a discreet veil over how this all ended. Another highlight was the piano recital given by Dorothy Grinstead. Dorothy, a lovely lady of indeterminate age who bore more than a passing resemblance to Dr Evadne Hinge of Hinge and Bracket fame, had generously donated the fine Blüthner grand piano which stood in the Great Hall. A condition of the donation was that Dorothy should be invited to give an annual recital for the benefit of the students. I don't recall the contents of the programme except that it was drawn from the mainstream classical repertoire; but I do vividly remember that Dorothy's free approach to the notes demonstrated beyond doubt the theory that, in order to realise the spirit of the composer's intentions, every musical performance should contain an element of improvisation.

On a rather higher musical plane the proximity of London was a siren call to those of us who sometimes found the atmosphere at Addington precious and rather

---

[86] See p. 321.

claustrophobic — and I have to say that I did. The early 1970s were heady days indeed in London's musical life. Rudolf Kempe and Otto Klemperer (just!) were still active on the South Bank; Georg Solti was in the last year of his decade as Music Director at Covent Garden and amongst the high points of the 1970/71 season was Peter Hall's visually beautiful production of *Tristan und Isolde* with the incomparable Birgit Nilsson, then at the very height of her powers, as Isolde. That is the only time in my life I have ever slept out overnight on the pavement in order to be well at the head of the queue for a day ticket; I didn't have the financial resources of some of the rich American students at the Palace and I couldn't afford to pre-book. Reginald Goodall was just beginning the odyssey which would in 1973 culminate in the now legendary English *Ring* cycle at the London Coliseum. I think I attended four performances of *The Valkyrie* in the early months of 1971, arriving back at the Palace in the early hours of the following morning. On more than one occasion I was quite rightly reprimanded by Freddie Waine with the Addington equivalent of a black spider memo for missing Evensong without permission. I was, and am, entirely unrepentant; but then I have to confess to being a bit of a rebel and was not a very pliant Addington student. Goodall actually visited the Palace in the spring of 1971 when he was preparing *Parsifal* for Covent Garden in order to rehearse the Addington boy choristers in the voices from on high in Act 1. The performance given on 8 May 1971 can be heard on the recording issued in the Royal Opera House heritage series. Goodall was at home in the Addington environment: he had after all begun his musical career as a chorister at Lincoln Cathedral and as organist of St Alban's Holborn, a post subsequently occupied by Michael Fleming. It was only later that he found fame as conductor of the premiere of *Peter Grimes* and as an esteemed Wagnerian. Amongst the Tutors Freddie Waine, Michael Fleming and Martin How also demonstrated catholic musical tastes extending well beyond the sphere of church music: Freddie Waine demonstrated an eclectic musical knowledge through weekly classes in music history that considered such figures as Richard Strauss and Schönberg; Michael was a committed Elgarian and would frequently insert quotations from *Gerontius* or the two Symphonies into his organ improvisations; Martin was (and I'm sure still is) a fine pianist and could frequently be heard playing Chopin late into the night in the small bungalow he occupied to the left of the Palace frontage. I remember with great pleasure how in September 1971, after I had left Addington but before going up to university, he and I sat together in the slips at Covent Garden for a performance of the complete *Ring* cycle.

These remembrances and reflections come from nearly half a century ago; an age almost unimaginably different in pace to that of the technology-driven world of today. It has been a pleasure to dig back in the memory and recall with gratitude the rich gallery of characters who gave such glow and savour to our lives as members of the College of St Nicolas. It is easy with hindsight and at the other end of a musical career to put a gloss on all this, but the truth is that even by the *mores* of the early

1970s the residential college at Addington Palace was an institution that had somehow strayed into a world to which it did not belong. The 'gentleman' cathedral organist, so wonderfully realised in the stately personage of Gerald Knight, was already an historic figure. The days when cathedral organists took articled pupils had long since given way to the Oxbridge organ scholar system of professional training; liturgical reform was gathering momentum and with the appointment of Area Commissioners the RSCM was expanding its activities in the field and beyond. The profession was changing and the model on which the College was originally founded by Sydney Nicholson was becoming unsustainable. A little over a decade later in 1985 Frederick Ouseley's much older foundation at St Michael's Tenbury was to fall victim to a similar shift in historical circumstance. It must in all honesty be said that there were Addington students in my year who were there more for their ability to pay the fees rather than their suitability for professional training. It was therefore not entirely surprising that with the accession of Lionel Dakers as Director and the subsequent root and branch review of the RSCM and all its associated activities that the announcement was made that the College was to be wound up. Its day was done and it had fulfilled its purpose; but for what it gave me and I know others in musical instruction and experience, quality of life, and most important of all the lifelong friendships forged during that year, I shall always be deeply grateful.'

Dame Gillian Weir (1962-1964):

'During the 1950s and 60s the Director of the RSCM, Dr Gerald Knight, was an indefatigable traveller, carrying its message around the world. I had listened to the recordings of the wonderful British choirs throughout my childhood in New Zealand, and was lucky enough to meet him on one of his visits there. I had just won a scholarship to study at the Royal College of Music in London, and he said, in his magisterial way, 'You must come and live at Addington Palace, my dear!' Learning that four female students were permitted at Addington Palace on the grounds of their usefulness in singing the daily services I demurred, saying that I couldn't sing (literally, as an unfortunate tonsils operation had brought an end to my constant childhood warbling), but he was undeterred. My voyage to England was traumatic, as I was one of several hundred passengers who contracted food poisoning — several died — and I left the ship in Italy, making my way to London by train. It is hard these days to convey what a huge step it was at that time, for a shy, nervous young New Zealander who knew nothing of the world to take, and I was not encouraged when coming at last through Customs at Southampton to be told dismissively by the Customs Officer 'Well, you can come in; you don't look as though you've got too many bugs on you.' Incurable Romantic as ever, and in love with the British poets, I survived being told my luggage from the ship was lost (temporarily, it fortunately proved) and I set off at once for Grantchester, in Cambridgeshire, to see for myself whether a thousand Vicars danced down the lawn and whether the church clock did indeed still stand at ten to three. I then arrived at Addington Palace.

My arrival caused consternation as it was the vacation. A concert was in progress and no room was available for me. Still without luggage I was told where I could purchase a raincoat (a strange new name: 'Marks & Spencer's') and a new friend took pity on me, spiriting me off to spend a few weeks waiting at his family's home till I could come back to Addington. In retrospect I realise how lucky I was that I did not end up chained to a post in someone's basement or floating in the Thames. The next shock was almost as bad, which was finding that in fact my inability to sing did of course matter. Fortunately there was Miranda, a fellow student with amazing top As, and Elizabeth, a singer who had been trained by the legendary Peter Godfrey and with superb pitch and technique. My skill (necessarily) was mouthing the words, and away from these histrionic displays I spent happy days practising on the subterranean organ in the basement and in the chapel. Later, into our little world swept Violet Chang, from the Far East. An aspiring opera singer, Violet had a wonderfully charismatic personality, radiating presence on stage, and it is not surprising to see that in her busy life in Philadelphia, USA, she continues to energise the musical world and is known for her philanthropy. Timothy Farrell, languidly brilliant, was a superb pianist as well as organist, playing concertos or canticles with equal ease; I'm sure a great many former Addington students were tuned in when he later provided his expert skills in playing for the wedding of Princess Anne at Westminster Abbey, when he was assistant there.

Several of the students were also enrolled at the Royal College of Music, and one of them, Nicholas Zelle, possessed a small car. We packed into it gratefully, and zoomed along the A23 from Croydon to London, an exhilarating achievement long gone; one would need a helicopter to accomplish the journey so quickly now. Once we were held up by a lorry, with a large, menacing driver; Nicholas saw him off by jumping out of his Mini and rushing up to the cab. 'Please, Sir' he said breathlessly, 'could you let us past? My wife is having a baby!' Consternation, crashing of gears with swift reversing and turning, and we were on our way. I was extremely sad when I learned of Nicholas's death a year or so ago just as we had made arrangements to meet. He was the kindest of men. Even sadder, because of the manner of his death, was the horrifying murder in his native Uganda of Michael Kalule, a few years after he had returned. Michael was a calming influence at the Palace and a shining example of goodness, slightly bemused by the English way of pretending an airy dismissiveness of anything serious but insistent on striving to resolve any disputes and keep us all happy.

My first winter in England was proclaimed the worst ever, and despite coming from the land of Everest's conqueror (with a few mountains of its own) I had never seen snow. The temperature was so low that the girls were given permission to bring blankets and sleep in front of the roaring fire in the Hall. This was quite a concession as the girls' rooms were in a separate wing; we were corralled behind the kitchens, where the formidable but very popular German cook reigned supreme. Hungry foxes were often seen at the windows, desperate for food, and we battled not only snow but fog, endemic then before the clean-up laws of future years. I eventually acquired my own Mini, and lost in the fog one night and struggling to find my way back to a main road I found myself on a station platform at Waterloo. Kind students took me into their homes at holiday times, and I fell in love with the Roman remains and the famous Rows in Chester, staying with Campbell Hughes, and in Gloucester when Christopher Phelps invited me there. Campbell became my chief page-turner when I began playing recitals, progressing to making an invaluable contribution throughout my career as an incomparable engineer for my recordings for the BBC. He has won prizes in his field, being a major contributor to recording, from the Proms to many independent projects. His page-turning appearance however was nearly his last. Before walking on stage at Westminster Central Hall for my first recital there, I warned him against dropping any of the pile of scores he was carrying, arranged carefully in order. I drifted on stage, Campbell following anxiously. Reaching the console I turned to face the audience and bowed low — only to hear a resounding crack and see stars, as Campbell's head, lowered in concentration, met mine. The audience loved it; perhaps my career should have taken another route, as a comedienne. During one vacation we both intrepidly went off to Fernando Germani's course in Siena, Campbell spending several weary weeks painting drainpipes for a plumber to raise the money. I nearly didn't make it, as setting off to the prize-giving of the RCM just before the flight I was hit by a speeding hit and run driver while crossing the road from the Palace to the bus. I was picked up sans glasses, earrings, and worst of all without the priceless LPs of Vierne improvising at Notre Dame which I was due to return to Nicholas Danby at the RCM and which were now in bits. I also missed picking up a prize at the hands of the Archbishop, but was mollified when he sent a kind message. I seem to have been quite lucky to have survived life at the Palace: just after the release of the film Cleopatra the students thought one night it would be fun to hoist me onto an improvised bier, a candelabra in each hand, and parade me around the carpark. This was going fine until other students were spied on the roof, carrying hoses; my increasingly frantic cries were ignored, the slaves at the front ran one way and those at the back the other, and I fell on my head with a thump on the concrete. The formidable Matron, Mrs Gordon (a relative of General Gordon of Khartoum it was rumoured), was scathing in her criticisms of all of us as I was picked up and delivered into medical care. (On another occasion she withered the Warden, a gentle cleric, in a dispute over the lights, with a stentorian 'Warden! You are a foolish virgin!' See Matthew 25: 1-13.)

Evenings were often spent happily playing Pick Up Sticks with Dr Knight, or playing piano duets with him — mostly Grieg's arrangements of Mozart concertos. It was generally thought to be diplomatic to turn a blind eye when his Sticks quivered, which I was more than happy to do as he helped considerably for a while with my homework for my RCM tutor in paperwork, although it became clear after a while that their views did not always accord. Gerald was a remarkable man; wholly committed to the work of the RSCM, a perfectionist in every respect ('we shall start at 3.57') and completely ruling church music throughout the land at that time. His aspect concealed what I think was a fundamental shyness, and those of us who love choirs and places where they sing owe him a tremendous debt. The Tutor was Derek Holman, a splendid musician and one whose show of cynicism lightly covered a cunning sense of humour. He claimed that he had sent one of his compositions to a noted publisher who had returned it saying they would publish it if he moved either the right hand part or the left up or down one semitone. (The compositional style of the sixties cast a long shadow...) Peter White, later director of music at Leicester Cathedral, was another fine teacher there and also with a sly sense of humour; when one evening I had demonstrated a shade too enthusiastically my agreement with the RSCM policy of clear enunciation of consonants he quietly indicated that he was available to run me to the station with my suitcases. I was sad to learn that he too is now with the choirs above. Michael Fleming, the superb musician in charge at All Saints', Margaret Street, was another hugely admired member of staff, chiefly responsible for teaching the students about plainsong; we trooped up to All Saints and sat (men on one side and women on the other, as was compulsory then) to listen in awe to his choir there. Always kind and friendly, he was regarded with great affection. The Addington students were so fortunate to have also the brilliant Martin How as choir trainer; he not only instilled the highest of standards in the students but went on to create the Chorister Training Scheme to further the RSCM's work globally.'

Robert Smith (1961-63):

'Richard Hui was a [Malaysian] London student with a deep, powerful, resonant voice. On one of about three occasions I remember singing in the Addington choir at Lambeth Palace, for the wedding of the Archbishop's son I think, Richard distinguished himself by taking on too much of the glorious white wine that flowed in archiepiscopal abundance at the following reception, then having to leave early, steering as steady a course as he could manage to the middle of the palatial hall, drawing himself up to survey a route to the nearest door which he then negotiated with equal unsteadiness. Surprisingly he had managed to return to Addington before our coach and on entering the front door we were regaled with his stentorian tones that shook the whole palace as he thundered a solo performance of *The Holy City* flat on his bed two floors above.'

Also from Robert Smith regarding Richard Hui:

'...on Wednesday early afternoons at plainsong evensongs, in the absence of trebles we were all two pews closer than usual and the slightest incongruity in our august proceedings inevitably tested self-control, when two rows of heads were customarily bowed very low with surplices stuffed in mouths to contain any unseemly outburst of half-stifled hilarity. On one such day after the Psalm(s), behold no reader appeared for the Old Testament lesson. Like a bolt of lightning Richard suddenly remembering it was his turn, shot up from his seat like a rocket, tripped on the step on his way to the lectern and in very broken English stumbled through his first reading as he could best manage. After the Magnificat when surplices were already well drenched Richard delivered his coup de grace announcing 'Ze second lesson is from Chapter (?), Werces 19 to 17' when our surplices received their all-time greatest challenge.'

Regarding accommodation, [AH] remembers:

'When I first went to Addington I was in a four shared room called Stanford (all the rooms were named after church music composers or Archbishops of Canterbury e.g. Benson, Longley). I liked this to start with (and especially the huge bath with a big metal plug, that weighed a ton to manoeuvre into place) but the longer I stayed the more privileged we were, ending up in private rooms down near the kitchen. The men mostly had to share, 2 or 4 to a room. This was normal in those days!'

Catherine McClurg (1969/70):

'I remember Carol Felton worked on an egg farm at week-ends for pocket money. She demonstrated from the roof window that an unfertilised egg falling from a great height, in this case onto the lawn below, would not break. We dashed down and found this to be true.'

F) Housekeeping, Catering, Summer Fete and other Social Activities

Warden Roy Massey on College domestic life recalls:

'I very rapidly discovered that the mainspring of life at the College was undoubtedly the Housekeeper, Mrs Gordon. She was a quite remarkable woman in her capacity to organise the workings of a great house; and, though I never discovered her antecedents, I'm quite sure she had been brought up in a large country house somewhere. She had high standards in everything she did as she organised the various routines necessary to make the place run smoothly. Her domestic staff were very faithful to her and did a remarkable job in cleaning and maintaining the premises. Harry, the handyman was a familiar sight with his floor polisher and George, who lived at the Lodge at the bottom of the drive, was another useful fellow around the place. Her catering staff were also highly efficient, Teresa the German cook was a wonderful character with a slightly mercurial temperament, but the meals she produced were of a high standard and in my three years at Addington I put on weight. Teresa also had the endearing habit of putting out some food by the kitchen door for the foxes in the park. Mrs Gordon also made herself responsible for the flower gardens behind the palace and her green fingers regularly produced a splendid array of colour in the summer and there was little that went on in the college that she didn't know about. She was quite demanding in her relationship with the students and her admonition to an individual that such and such behaviour was 'not palace manners' pulled up many a student who might have erred and strayed. On the other hand, she had a heart of gold and any youngster with a problem would often seek her out for a bit of comfort and motherly advice. At first she had very mixed feelings about a Warden who was a thirty year old organist from Birmingham, as she had been appointed when the position was held by a clergyman of mature years who died in 1964, and for my first few months I realised that she didn't really approve of me. Eventually I challenged her on the subject, I cannot remember the exact circumstances, and she asked to see me in the presence of GHK. She then accused me of something in front of him and GHK quietly took my part and then, to the surprise of both of us, she suddenly burst into tears and ran from the room. Nothing was ever said again, but that cleared the air and ever afterwards I could not have had a greater ally or, as time went on, a greater friend who couldn't do enough for me. One day, about half way through my time as Warden, she suddenly said quietly to me that I was very effective in the job because I was so kind. She was undoubtedly a unique and wonderful character, excellent with visitors and welcoming folk to the palace, superb with the students and marvellous at organising the day to day workings of a large and complex establishment.'

Roy Massey continued:

'How was I finding the job when I eventually discovered how to cope with it? It was indeed varied and fascinating in many ways, but I often found myself pulled in several directions at once. As Warden I often had to receive visitors, take telephone calls, attend meetings, some of them in London, write letters, discuss domestic matters with Mrs Gordon, take college prayers on Monday morning, attend services as much as possible and find time to talk to individual students as required. I also had to interview any prospective candidates. All this as well as a fairly full organ teaching commitment. I was also expected to take part in periodic courses such as those for ordinands, which I found very stimulating, courses for organists and choirmasters and Summer Schools. I ran my first Summer School at the end of my first term. I shared a secretary with the Director, and Miss Dorothy Yorke was a great support and help to me. She was a good church lady from Sanderstead and she adored GHK who, of course, wrote letters in meticulous style which delighted her heart. At first I was less assured in this area as I'd never dictated a letter in my life, but she politely corrected my infelicities of language and kept a wary eye on my timetable. She was an absolute treasure. There were other delightful folk on the staff. Little Mrs Hunt looked after my bungalow as if it were her own and made a lovely job of treating with non-slip my wooden block floor. She also made my bed every day. Mrs Clegg, the widow of one of GHK's Canterbury tenors was in the publications department and was marvellous at finding music for me and also giving me brown paper with which to cover my organ music. She also had a wicked sense of humour. Old Miss Foat was another stalwart of the publications dept. She sang at St John's, Upper Norwood, with a voice described by her choirmaster as like a fruitcake with a wobble, but she was a delightful person.'

G) Resident staff including Chaplains and Main Administrative Personnel

Wardens

This post was held by Sydney Nicholson from the opening of the School until 1939. When the School was reopened in Canterbury after the war, Gerald Knight held the post on a part-time basis, as he was also organist at the Cathedral. Revd Cyril Taylor was the first full-time Warden, who was appointed just before the organisation moved to Addington Palace in 1954. From this time the Warden was responsible for the internal work of the RSCM at Headquarters[87]. This included the following: responsibility for the resident academic staff, the administration and training of both full and part-time students, and the organisation of residential and short courses held at Addington.

Revd Cyril Taylor	1953-1958	also Chaplain
Revd George Sage	1958-1964	also Chaplain
Derek Holman	1964-1965	previously Tutor and Sub-Warden
Roy Massey	1965-1968	
Frederic Waine	1968-1972	
Michael Fleming	1973-1979	
Allen Ferns	1979-1982	
Janette Cooper	1982-1990	
Llywela Harris	1990-1993	the last Warden at Addington

Taylor, The Revd Cyril Vincent MA, FRSCM: b. 11th Dec 1907, Wigan, Lancashire; d. 20th June 1991, Petersfield, Hampshire. Cyril Taylor was educated at Magdalen College School in Oxford, and at Christ Church College in Oxford before entering Westcott House in Cambridge for ordination in 1931. He was curate at Hinckley in Leicestershire and at St Andrew's in Kingswood, Surrey, before appointment as Precentor and Sacristan of Bristol Cathedral in 1936. He was assistant to the Head of Religious Broadcasting at the BBC from 1939 until 1953 when he was appointed Warden and assistant Chaplain at Addington Palace (announced in *ECM* Jan 1953). He was one of the compilers of the *BBC Hymn Book*. He was not without a sense of humour, but often, when told a

joke, would respond with the single, long drawn out word 'extra-ordinary'.[88] He was well thought of by the staff and students alike, and effectively established the new College of St Nicolas at Addington. On leaving Addington in 1958, he became vicar of Cerne Abbas in

---

[87] RSCM Annual Report 1953.
[88] From MJRH.

86

Dorset and was appointed Precentor and Residentiary Canon of Salisbury Cathedral in 1969. He was made FRSCM in 1974. A memorial service was held at Salisbury Cathedral on 4th Oct 1991, after which his ashes were interred in the cloisters there (see right).

Taylor, Mrs Audrey: The wife of Cyril Taylor, Audrey looked after the domestic affairs at AP as Housekeeper. She was initially offered a salary of £150 p.a. but wrote accepting the post at a reduced salary of £100 for which the RSCM was very grateful!

Guyon Wells (1957-59):

'Then there was the time when the Warden's wife who always sat at the lower end of the dining room, overheard a group of students who had been isolated for a few days following an outbreak of some sort of sickness, discussing how they had rubbed rear ends with the Queen Mother when using the toilet specially provided for her in the Empire Room at the opening of Addington in 1954.'Oh!' she exclaimed, 'but it was so much more beautiful then. I had filled it with sweet peas and roses.' Polite giggles all round as can be imagined as it dawned on her that we were talking of different facilities.'

(L to R) Lionel Dakers, Audrey Taylor, Elisabeth Dakers, Cyril Taylor and Roy Massey after the Jubilee Service in July 1979

Sage, The Revd George Ernest MA: d.14th June 1964. Formerly vicar of South Mymms Parish Church, appointed Warden and Chaplain of AP in autumn 1958. He was a chorister at St John's College, Cambridge, an organ scholar of St Catherine's College, Cambridge, and was ordained in 1938. During the war he took musical charge of the Canterbury Cathedral choristers who had been evacuated to Cornwall, and was then appointed Minor Canon and Sacrist and later Succentor of St Paul's Cathedral. Latterly he accepted livings at St John's Church, Hyde Park and St Michael's Church, Star Street, Paddington. He died in 1964 after a short illness. The funeral service was held in AP Chapel.

Lionel Sawkins (1958/59):

'[I remember] the very informative lectures on liturgy and its origins by the Revd George Sage, the Warden. On the down side, George thought all students should be in bed by a respectable hour, and late arrivals by students from an evening out could mean climbing in a window, plus a little lecture the next morning to the sinner.'

Ian Barber (1960-65):

'He was one of the kindest people you could meet. He always had time to talk to the students and gave very genuine advice.'

Revd George Sage teaching, 1962[89]

[89] Another photograph of George Sage is on p. 101.

Holman, Derek DMus (London), FRCO(CHM), FRAM: b. 16th May 1931, Redruth, Cornwall. He was educated at Truro School and the RAM and by 1955 was organist & choirmaster at St Stephen's in Westminster and taught at Westminster Abbey Choir School. He started as Resident Tutor at AP in organ and paperwork in January 1956, taking over the work of Sidney Campbell and Gordon Phillips. Appointed Assistant Sub-organist at St Paul's Cathedral at the same time as his AP appointment, he was married to his fiancée Margaret just two weeks before arriving at AP. In September 1957 he was appointed Sub-Warden and in 1958 he was appointed Organist and Choirmaster at Croydon PC. On the death of George Sage in 1964, he (reluctantly) became Warden but resigned on 31st March 1965, to take up the post of Organist at Grace-church-on-the-Hill, Toronto, Canada. MJRH comments that Derek Holman was popular with the students. Soon after leaving Addington he was awarded the FRAM and a London DMus. About his post, Derek Holman says[90]:

> 'My work as Resident Tutor consisted mainly in preparing students for the RCO exams, in particular for the much-dreaded paper-work and dictation tests. To add some 'gravitas' to the harmony and counterpoint department, Sir William Harris of St George's, Windsor, was recruited as 'Director of Musical Studies'[91], and paid a visit to Addington every two or three weeks to see the students and their work. His visits often ended with a sight-read performance of a choral work, for example Bach's Cantata *Ich hatte viel Bekümmernis* (but 'auf English') or Handel's *L'Allegro* — an agreeable change from Anglican Chant.'

Derek Holman teaching in 1956

---

[90] In a letter March 2015.

[91] Several people have implied that the appointment of Sir William was more a cosmetic one, to add credibility to the RSCM's educational credentials. Nonetheless many of the better students benefited from his occasional one-to-one lessons.

Robert Bell (1958/59):

'As Canadians, we[92] had our own concept of central heating, of which the Palace boasted but of which we could feel little evidence. A history lecture in the Colles Library found us seated on opposite sides of a library table. Derek Holman, the lecturer, on entering the room pronounced it 'stuffy' and threw open one of those huge library windows letting in a blast of cold, foggy air. Norman and I looked at one another, each crumpled up a sheet of notepaper, and lit a small bonfire in an ashtray and sat warming our cold hands. Derek responded with good humour and lowered the window, but did not close it.'

Ian Barber (1960-65):

'Dr Derek Holman was a wonderful inspiration, very generous with his time and criticism.'

John Morehen (1960/61):

'I took the full course at Addington. We were very lucky so far as the academic staff were concerned. Our Academic Tutor was Derek Holman, who later forged a highly successful career in Toronto. He was far and away the most naturally amusing person I have ever met. His humour often came when one least expected it, and was usually delivered with a dead-pan face and expression. If one was not 'on the ball' one could very easily miss his humorous touches. But behind it all lay tremendous musicianship, reinforced by a sound knowledge of music history and a fine academic judgement. He knew all the major London musicians, and arranged for Addington students to meet the Organists of Westminster Abbey, St Paul's Cathedral, etc.'

Martin Robert (1960-62):

'[DH] had a very quick and dry wit and could instantly see through any instance of flummery.'

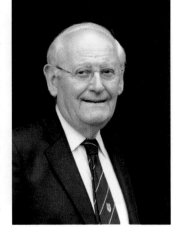

Massey, Roy Cyril, DMus (Lambeth), ARCM, FRCO(CHM), FRCCO, ADCM, FRSCM: b. 9th May 1934, Birmingham. A pupil of David Willcocks, he studied at the University of Birmingham. He was Music Master of King Edward's Five Ways Grammar School in Birmingham from 1959 to 1965, and organist of St Augustine's, Edgbaston. Appointed Warden on April 1st 1965 in succession to Derek Holman, like his predecessor, he was also organist of Croydon Parish Church. In 1968 he was appointed Organist of Birmingham Cathedral and Director of Music at King Edward's School, Birmingham and in 1974 he moved onto Hereford Cathedral. In 1972 he was made FRSCM and in 1991 he was awarded a DMus (Lambeth) — see photograph on p. 396.

---

[92] 'We' meaning himself and Norman Hurrle (1958/59).

Waine, Frederic, MA, BMus, FRCO, ARCM, Hon RSCM: b. 1911, Croydon; d.16th May 1974. He was appointed Warden in 1968, succeeding Roy Massey. He and his wife lived in Golf Cottage. He was formerly Director of Music at St Peter's School, York, where he had gained a good reputation and had been Master-in-Charge of a number of RSCM boys' residential courses. He had also been a Special Commissioner since 1954[93]. He made useful links with London music colleges, and also got concerts going at the Palace. It was noted in council minutes that he had evidently played a major part in getting official approval of the RSCM as an 'efficient establishment of further

education.' He retired on 31st December 1971, on doctor's orders, and moved to Yorkshire, where he died after a long illness.

Peter Phillips (1972):

'Freddie was a pale presence, very quiet and undemonstrative.'

Robert Gower (1971):

'Adjacent to the Palace was the Warden's lodging, occupied by the gentle scholar Frederic Waine, who had forsaken the storms of teaching and came south from St Peter's School, York to the calmer waters of Surrey. Freddie was an encourager, rather than a disciplinarian, so never really addressed the inevitable pushing of the boundaries from a lively co-educational group. Blessed with serenity and patience, he was remorselessly teased by the student body, who latched eagerly onto his phrases such as 'the underestimated prune' (as he consumed a spoonful at breakfast). His pastoral concern was clear, though — and I owed much to his advice.'

Martin How:

'Although getting on in years (he had reached retirement age) and maybe 'past his best' in some ways, he nevertheless quietly and effectively introduced new measures into the scheme of things... I don't think he was ever fully appreciated by his colleagues, or by the students for that matter.'

Antonia Harman (1970-74):

'Freddie Waine (and his wife Beryl) were lovely people who were very homely and if there was ever a personal problem they would be there to lend an ear. I kept in touch with them after they left and even went to stay with them once in Yorkshire.'

---

[93] Martin How's unpublished *Memoirs*.

Fleming, Michael Paschal Marcon. BA, BMus, FRCO(CHM), ADCM, FRSCM, MA(Lambeth):

b. 8th[94] Apr 1928, Oxford; d.10th Jan 2006, Croydon, Surrey. Michael sang under SHN in the first Cathedral Course at Gloucester Cathedral in 1942[95]. He was educated at St Edmund's School, Canterbury and was Lady Mary Trefusis Scholar at St Nicolas College in Canterbury in 1946 and again, following National Service, in 1948. After graduating from University College, Durham, he was organist of St Giles in Cambridge, of Chingford Parish Church and then of All Saints', Margaret Street from 1958 where he had developed the choir to a very high standard and had become an authority on plainsong. He was subsequently plainsong editor to the *New English Hymnal* published in 1986 and continued on the governing body of this throughout his life[96]. He joined the staff at AP in spring 1960 as tutor in plainsong, visiting on Wednesdays and directing the Plainsong Evensongs. On closure of the Choir School at All Saints', Margaret Street at Easter 1968, he became Resident Tutor of Addington (the post had been vacant for 3 years since Derek Holman had left), and Organist and Choirmaster of Croydon PC in succession to Roy Massey. On the sudden retirement of Frederic Waine, he became Acting Warden and from 1st April 1973 he was appointed full Warden. In January 1979 he was appointed Resident Staff Tutor, relinquishing the post as Warden, to lecture and teach at AP, undertake more outside work through festivals and

one-day schools for affiliated churches, and take charge of the Colles Library. Allen Ferns replaced him as Warden in 1979. In 1980 he became organist of St Alban's, Holborn. MF moved out of AP in 1982, married in 1985 and retired as Staff Tutor on his 65th birthday, 8th April 1993. He continued to direct the Nicholson Singers which he had founded in 1981 until 2000 when they were disbanded. He also continued as a music reviewer for *CMQ* until 2000. In 1999 he received a Lambeth MA from Archbishop George Carey (photo on p. 397).

In 1998, whilst he was DOM at St Alban's, Holborn, Michael was approached by the PCC of St Michael and All Angels in Croydon and asked if he would revive the musical life of the church and on All Saints' Day in 1998 his newly-formed choir sang its first service.

Father Anthony Cridland (1969-71):

> 'I remember Michael Fleming, my organ tutor with affection because I realised he accepted where each one of us was musically and built on our skills.'

---

[94] Born on Easter Day in 1928, hence his middle name.
[95] MF said that all he could remember of this event was the bickering between SHN, the conductor, and GHK, the organist!
[96] He was also on the council of the Church Music Society.

Robert Gower (1971):

'Michael's musicianship oozed consistently. With his genial smile, his flapping of his tie and murmuring (followed by laughter). Michael was adored for his modesty, talent and for his empathy with the young. I learned so much about accompaniment and organ management from him, as well as fundamental instrumental technique and repertoire in our lessons. His plainsong lectures and accompaniments were wonderfully crafted, plainsong evensong on a Wednesday afternoon at 3.15pm being a highlight of his [our?] week.'

Peter Phillips (1972):

'He was a difficult man to talk to, but he had an air of authority which I appreciated.'

Alan Snow (1972/73):

'I was grateful to the staff for the help and guidance they gave. I must make mention of the man who made the greatest impression on me and that was Michael Fleming. He became Warden upon the retirement of Freddie Waine, having been promoted from Resident Tutor, a role he fulfilled admirably enough. I believe that Michael has had a profound influence on my life both musically and socially. He was a gentle gentleman. He was an undemonstrative man and practising Christian with a sense of humour that was second to none. Coupled with that infectious little laugh which I found so comforting he was such good company to be with. His anecdotes were charmingly delivered and he could never have caused offence to whoever he might have highlighted. His social and professional generosity was overwhelming. Many was the time that he took some of us out for a meal and a jovial time it was.

I sang for him at Croydon Parish Church and as ever he was an inspiring and encouraging director. I remember his conducting on two memorable occasions. First, at St Michael's in West Croydon, where he conducted Vaughan Williams's *Mass in G-minor* and then, in the following Lent, at Croydon Parish Church the *St Matthew Passion*. My admiration for his musicianship was unbounding. Both performances will stay with me all my days.'

John Eagles (1971/72):

'Lecture sessions that day [Wednesdays] were often led by Michael Fleming, a noted authority in plainsong, who had come from the hallowed sanctuary of All Saints', Margaret Street. We had lectures on the development of plainsong, the various modes and intonations, and in the art of plainsong accompaniment. The latter was augmented by Michael's study book on the topic published by the RSCM, and at evensong we used the *Manual of Plainsong* by Briggs and Frere. These Wednesday evensongs did become an experience that grew on me as time progressed. The chapel faced across the broad sweep of Addington Park which was clearly in view as we sang the liturgically-appropriate antiphons throughout the year. As these changed in their musical nature revolving around the ordinary, penitential and festal seasons of the Church's year, so too did the landscape outside. The whole experience was a visual mirage of the music as the two elements blended to form an inseparable entity. I began my time as a student with little or no practical knowledge of plainsong, craving more for the rich harmonic sonorities of the music found in Howells and the like; I came away converted by the power of such simple, platonic and subtly-crafted melodic lines.'

Michael Fleming with Croydon Parish Church Choir in 1969

Ferns, (Martin) Allen ARSCM: b. 1921; d. March 1998. Organ tutor at AP from October 1976. He was Director of Music at Lord Weymouth's Grammar School in Warminster, Scarborough College and at Reigate Grammar School, resigning from the latter to take up the appointment as Warden in January 1979. He was also a Special Commissioner. He took over from Michael Fleming, who became Resident Tutor. He and his wife Margaret (Molly) moved into AP, with Molly acting as assistant housekeeper under Elisabeth Dakers. In addition to his Warden's duties, he was either housemaster or master-in-charge of sixty RSCM residential courses over the years. HB wrote that '... the work was frequently hectic, and entailed one course departing after breakfast with the next one coming in a few hours later. Although there were inevitable pressures, Allen was quite unflappable.'[97] Made ARSCM in 1977, he retired in 1982. The service book *O Come let us sing* was devised by him.

Allen Ferns ca 1979

Cooper, Miss Janette: b. 1937. Formerly Director of Music at Roedean School, she was appointed Warden to succeed Allen Ferns in September 1982. She pioneered the very successful 'Reluctant Organist' courses in 1974 and, in conjunction with this, produced a 3-part hymn book. She was very popular with her many followers. She resigned as Warden in April 1990, but continued to run courses at AP. By February 1996 she had clocked up 120 of these which were usually attended by between 12 and 20 participants. Harry Bramma writes:

> 'Janette Cooper continued to run these courses even after she retired from the RSCM in 1990. They were a mixture of residential weekday courses with the occasional one-day sessions. Those frog-marched to the organ console because they played the piano were in desperate need of basic organ tuition. Over the course of time, such was the skill of Janette Cooper, these courses developed into a kind of club where people bent on improving their skills looked forward to meeting up again with friends who they had met on previous courses. When it was no longer possible to have residential days, Janette successfully maintained one-day 'follow-up' courses for those who had been motivated and taught at the residential sessions.'

Harris, Llywela: b. 11th April 1931, St David's College, Lampeter. Llywela took over from Janette Cooper as Warden in September 1990 and retired in September 1993. She then served as organist for the Welsh language Communion Service at St David's Cathedral[98] from 1994 until 2011, in which year she received the Archbishop of Wales's Award for Church Music.

Harry Bramma:

> 'I appointed Llywela Harris who was at the time Director of Music at SS Mary & Anne, Abbots Bromley, a Woodard School for Girls, where she had a long and distinguished career. She brought great elegance to the job and remarkable efficiency. During her three years she made a notable contribution.'

---

[98] Her father was a canon of St David's Cathedral and Precentor of the Chapel at St David's College in Lampeter.

Sub-Warden

The post of Sub-Warden was created to relieve the Director from some of his administrative duties. This post, together with that of Director of Musical Studies (held in turn by Ernest Bullock, Sidney Campbell and William Harris), was later made redundant when it was decided to appoint a professional musician as Warden.

Dr Sidney Campbell	1947-1949
Derek Holman	1957-1964 (see under Warden)

Campbell, Sidney Scholfield, MVO, DMus, ARCM, LRAM, FRCO(CHM), FRSCM: b. 7th June 1909, West Ham, London; d. 4th June 1974, Windsor. After working as a bank clerk, he turned to music and studied with Sir Ernest Bullock and Harold Darke, achieving the FRCO 1931 and a BMus 1940 followed by DMus 1946 at Durham University. After serving at St Peter's in Croydon from 1937 to 1943 and at St Peter's Collegiate Church in Wolverhampton from 1943 to 1947, he was appointed Sub-Warden of the College of St Nicolas at Canterbury 1947-49. Whilst working for the RSCM he directed the two-week summer RSCM Cathedral Course in Ely Cathedral during August 1948. He got on so well with

Sidney Campbell in 1972

the Dean and Chapter at Ely that they appointed him as successor to Marmaduke Conway in 1949 without seeking further applicants[99]. From there he became Organist of Southwark Cathedral from 1953 to 1956, then Organist and Master of Choristers at Canterbury Cathedral from 1956 until his move to St George's Chapel, Windsor in 1961. He was Director of Musical Studies at Addington from January 1st 1954 assisted by Gordon Phillips and Robert Poole until he resigned on doctor's advice in 1956. A man with a fiery temper, he was regarded as somewhat eccentric. He was appointed MVO in 1972.

David Harrison (1955/56 & 1958/59):

> 'Sidney Campbell lived in the building to the left of the Palace as one viewed it from the front. He seemed to regard me as someone to be taken under his wing and I was pressed into service as an alto in the Southwark Cathedral choir. His penchant for modern trends in organ building and playing led the students to christen his dwelling 'The Baroquery'. He himself told me of the occasion, just before I arrived, when the Palace was formally 'opened' as the headquarters of the RSCM; naturally a service was planned and included an outside procession which was choreographed to pass by his window. For some reason he was not involved in the celebration but was at home at the time. As the procession drew nearer his front window, approaching it from the rear of the palace, the Director, Gerald Knight, seemed unaware that there was to

---

[99] Mentioned in *A Country Choirmaster Looks Back,* 2005, the autobiography of Brecon Cathedral organist David Gedge, who recounts various anecdotes underlining Campbell's eccentric personality but also describes him as brilliant and lovable.

be a halt at this point. Campbell looked out of his window to see Mr Knight solemnly processing entirely on his own towards the front of the house. I gather that a stentorian laugh from the Baroquery accompanied him on his way.'

One anecdote about Sidney Campbell recalls his appearance one day for lessons with a dressing on his head. It seems that a Lay Clerk had thrown a copy of *Hymns Ancient & Modern* at him, though it is not recorded why this happened.

Revd Michael Smith (1955/56):

'Sidney was always a little 'different' and would irritate CVT easily by 'misbehaviour' at the Dinner table. Later, when I was teaching in Canterbury, he invited me on a number of occasions to play for parts of the service when he needed to get away — the fee was always 50 Players No 3 left on the stool. He was an inveterate smoker of cigarettes — usually Piccadilly No 1 — as Gerald was an inveterate pipe smoker. Between them they were responsible for my own downfall in that direction.'

The cigarette dangling from his mouth was a common feature and many of his contemporaries, including singers, smoked regularly. – the photograph here shows a cigarette/pipe break in 1962 with (L to R) George Sage, Mervyn Callaghan, Sidney Campbell and Malcolm Cousins.

Director of Musical Studies

Sidney Campbell	1954-1956	See above under 'Sub-Wardens.'
William Harris	1956-1961	
Geoff Weaver	1994-1996	Title changed to 'Director of Studies'

Harris, Sir William (Henry) KCVO, MA, DMus, FRCM, FRCO: b. 1883, London; d. 6th September 1973. He was educated at New College, Oxford and the RCM. Tutor and Director of Musical Studies at AP visiting once a fortnight (recorded in *ECM* May 1956). 'Every fortnight we enjoyed a visit from Sir William, who gave a chosen few an organ lesson and provided an evening's entertainment with a short talk followed by a sing-along, which he directed from the piano in the Great Hall – all very memorable, if not of the highest musical standard!' (From Guyon Wells, student 1957-1958) 'Addington in those days was an unduly inward-looking community, so his [Sir William's] visits had particular importance; and not only for that reason, but because his complete musicianship fitted him so perfectly for this task. However, he had a strange propensity for dissembling this.' (LD in *CMQ* July 1983) He was the long-serving Organist and Master of Choristers at St George's, Windsor from 1933 to 1961. On his retirement from St George's in 1961 he also retired from AP. He was known to the students at AP as 'Sir Bill.'

Ten years after Harris's death, in *CMQ* July 1983 Canon Cyril Taylor recalled:

> 'In the evenings he sometimes presided at the piano over the 'singing through' of some major work in the Great Hall, and on other occasions he came to our large sitting-room, which provided superb acoustic for the then new hi-fi recordings, and introduced students to some work on disc. They were much amused, I recall, when his final introductory comment on the Elgar *Enigma Variations* was, 'I knew Dorabella.'

> It was in the same room that he accepted the suggestion that he should write an anthem on *This Joyful Eastertide*, which Novello in due course published and where – in 1958, I think – he handed me the manuscript of *Bring us, O Lord* with the characteristic words, 'Do you think this will do?'

> A few weeks before my wife and I left Addington in 1958 for Cerne Abbas in Dorset, we received a postcard in his hand, written in the village, enthusing over its beauty, asking to be considered for the next vacancy on the organ-stool, and signed Henry G Ley, William H Harris: organ-blowers (unpaid).'

Ian McKinley (1958/59)

> 'We had, presumably as a special privilege, the odd lesson from an irascible Sir William Harris. He was not impressed with the overseas students, branding us scornfully as 'colonials.' This was felt to be an intolerable insult, so lessons ended suddenly on a bad note.'

Ian Barber (1960-65)

'Sir William Harris taught us paperwork. This was a great experience. I remember he used to smoke cigarettes as he taught. He would forget to knock the ash off and I remember sitting waiting for it to fall on his suit.'

Guyon Wells (1957-59):

'Every fortnight we enjoyed a visit from Sir William Harris DOM at St George's Chapel, Windsor, who gave a chosen few an organ lesson and provided an evening's entertainment with a short talk followed by a sing-along with he himself directing from the piano in the Great Hall. All very memorable if not of the highest musical standard! After all, it was all very much of an improvised nature.'

Weaver, Geoff MA, ARCO, ALCM, FRSCM: b. 1943. Geoff was educated at the City of Bath Boys' School, before going on to Caius College, Cambridge to read music. He was then appointed DOM at Bristol Grammar School, before moving abroad to undertake work for the Church Missionary Society in Hong Kong. On returning to the UK, he served as organist at Bradford Cathedral from 1982 until 1986. He then worked as Warden and Tutor for the Church Missionary Society at Crowther Hall (the CMS training centre in Selly Oak), Birmingham for the next eight years. Here he was involved in a wide range of educational work, and published a collection of melodies from around the world entitled *World Praise*. In April 1994 he was appointed Director of Studies at Addington, replacing the post of Warden[100], with a brief to co-ordinate the RSCM's educational work. He initiated the Foundation Certificate course in Church Music Studies. After the move to Cleveland Lodge, his post was changed to Director of Outreach.

Geoff in action at the 2010 Residential Course at Kingswood School in Bath

---

[100] But including many of the duties of the Warden.

Chaplains

The first Chaplain of the SECM had been Revd George Salter until his appointment as Vicar of St Sepulchre's, Holborn[101]. Succeeded by the Revd Dr Charles Stanley Phillips, when the College opened again after the war, the post became part-time. The main task of the Chaplain was to take services in the chapel, undertake the pastoral care of the students and lecture on a part-time basis.

Revd Cyril Taylor	1953-1958 (See under Wardens)
Revd George Sage	1958-1964 (See under Wardens)
Revd Anthony Caesar	1965-1970
Revd Leslie Katin	1970-1972
Revd John Henry Diehl (Acting Chaplain)	1973

When Diehl returned to the USA, the post fell vacant and, following reorganisation of the courses in 1974, a resident Chaplain was no longer required.

Caesar, Revd Anthony LVO, MA, MusB, FRCO: b. 1924, Educated at Magdalene College, Cambridge. He was Assistant Music master at Eton College, before going on to ordination. A former Precentor of Radley College, he was appointed Chaplain at Addington serving from 1st April 1965 until 31st August 1970 and combining his Palace role with duties as a selection secretary for CACTM (Central Advisory Council for the Ministry). The Chaplaincy post carried no salary but emoluments in kind consisted of an attractive flat with free board and lodging at AP. In 1968 he was appointed Priest-in-Ordinary to HM the Queen. In 1970 he was elected an Honorary Chaplain of the RSCM. He became Precentor of Winchester Cathedral, then Sub-Dean of HM Chapels Royal[102].

Roy Massey:

> 'The Chaplain to the College was the Revd Anthony Caesar who arrived at the same time as I did in 1965. He worked in Church House Westminster in the department selecting ordinands and arrived home each day in time to sing Evensong. Occasionally he would be held up so I had to sing the service. This taught me that singing the versicles is not an entirely straight-forward pastime and, consequently, I've always been very sympathetic to anyone having to do it. I found it advisable not to eat nuts or chocolate before being a Cantor! Anthony was a gifted composer in his own right and an utterly delightful person who was a great asset to the community. He went on to a Canonry of Winchester and then to the position of Sub-Dean at the Chapels Royal at St James's Palace. In retirement he lives in Cheltenham.'

Katin, Revd (Herbert) Leslie: b. 22nd Aug 1923; d. 20th Oct 1972. He trained at St David's College, Lampeter, and was ordained priest in 1951. Vicar of St Bartholomew in Camberwell (demolished 1994) from 1955, he then taught in private and state secondary

---

[101] He served at St Sepulchre from 1929 to 1962 having previously been Precentor at Winchester Cathedral (see *SNCSN*).

[102] He can be seen, front left, on the 1970 student photo on p. 72.

schools. He was appointed Chaplain in September 1970 on the retirement of Revd Anthony Caesar but died unexpectedly in office. He was the elder brother of concert pianist Peter Katin.

Diehl, Revd John Henry: b 1933 or 1934, Lancaster, PA; d. 7th May 2004. He was a student at Addington from 1972 to 1974 and was offered the post of Chaplain at Addington on the death of Revd Leslie Katin, but he declined it. He subsequently served as Rector of St Mark's in Lehigh Valley KY until January 1976, then as Canon Rector of St Stephen's Cathedral in Harrisburg and as Rector of St John's Episcopal Church in Hagerstown from 1979 until retirement in 1991.

Sage, The Revd George MA: See under 'Wardens'.

Leslie Green and Revd George Sage, 1963

In addition to these clergy, the Revd Alan Norton, Vicar of Addington, helped out in 1964 when a resident Chaplain could not be found.

General Secretaries

Green, (Herbert) Leslie (Arnold) FRSCM: b. 11th Aug 1903; d. 1995, Canterbury. Leslie Green's musical education began with his father Mr H J Green, organist of St Mellitus in Hanwell and from his service as a chorister at Durham Cathedral with Revd Arnold Culley (organist of Durham Cathedral). Leslie was the first Secretary of the SECM from 1928 at Chislehurst, then at Canterbury and finally at Addington. His job title

was changed to General Secretary in 1954 to reflect the increased responsibilities given to him. He held this post until his retirement in 1964 and was in charge of the general organisation of the RSCM, which included large-scale festivals and overseas tours but did not include the running of Headquarters, which was done by the Bursar, Alec Jackson. LG lived at AP from Monday to Friday, returning to his wife and home at the weekends. Apart from war service in the RNVR, he had continuously handled the School's organisation since 1928, making him a knowledgeable and resourceful member of staff. He relinquished his post at the end of July 1964. A Memorial service was held in Canterbury Cathedral on 6th February 1995. 'LG was held in high esteem. From his naval days he continued to show a certain correctness and efficiency found in ex-service officers — with a good eye for detail' [MJRH]. In Harry Bramma's address at Green's memorial service he said: 'It is no exaggeration to say that, without the dedication of Leslie Green, the RSCM would not exist

in its present form today.' Here, HB is reinstating LG's unique position, for LG had fallen out of favour with GHK at a personal level following LG's privately expressed disapproval of GHK's appointment as Director in 1952. MJRH recounts that LG, together with Hubert Crook, went up to the Empire Room one evening shortly after Gerald's appointment, and told him so. However, much to his credit, GHK had recognised and accepted LG's part in the organisation. It was not until 1986 that he was awarded an FRSCM. Robert McDowall recalls (in a private letter) that HLAG was well-known for his little tips and *bon mots*, one of the most important of which was:

'we [the RSCM] live on goodwill.'

West Byng, Commander Anthony Hastings RN: d. 15th April 1986, Brighton. He was appointed Secretary in succession to Leslie Green from January 1st 1965. He had served in the Royal Navy for 25 years, mostly involved with secretarial and administrative work. West Byng planned and organised the Royal Albert Hall Festival in 1965, which must have been quite a 'baptism of fire'. He retired in 1968 after only three years in the post and was succeeded by Vincent Waterhouse. He was known as 'The Commander'. For some unknown reason he changed his name by Deed Poll in Nov 1965 from West-Byng to the un-hyphenated West Byng.

Roy Massey:

> 'Another character was Anthony West Byng who had been appointed General Secretary on the retirement of H L A Green. He was a pleasant but slightly enigmatic chap with a naval background who I suspected was not really on top of the job. I also came to the conclusion that he lifted his elbow fairly regularly. One night my assistant at the Parish Church and I arrived back at the Palace quite late and spotted in the car headlights what seemed to be a pile of old rags in the drive. It turned out to be West Byng absolutely legless and quite unable to stand. John and I took an arm each and started to get him as he burbled incoherently through the front door of the palace and up to his bedroom at the top of the house. Unfortunately, to do this, we had to get past Mrs Gordon's door whose light was still on. Fortunately, she didn't hear us — she was probably listening to her wireless — and we got him on to his bed and tip-toed away. He was most apologetic the next morning.'

Waterhouse, Vincent Edward: b. 1927; d. 2006. He was appointed Bursar in September 1966. He was organist of St Nicholas Parish Church, Sutton, until taking up his Addington responsibilities. In April 1968 he became Secretary on West Byng's retirement, and also appointed Chief Administrative Officer at the same time. Two of his first major initiatives were to rationalise the RSCM journals into one (*CMQ*) and to negotiate with the London Colleges that the RSCM become a provider of Church Music education enabling the RSCM to become recognised by HMI Education as an establishment of further education. It was intended that he should share Mactrevor House with Mr Meekison but planning permission to turn the house into two flats was rejected. He therefore bought a house: 22 Abbots Green (adjacent to the Addington estate). As it was always RSCM policy to provide accommodation for senior staff, Council agreed to buy the house from him for £8000 and charge him rent as for all other resident staff. In July 1975 the house was sold and VEW moved into a flat at AP. He retired from Addington in July 1990, after 24 years with the RSCM.

In tribute to him Monty Durston (Vice-Chair of RSCM Council) wrote 'I have had the pleasure of knowing him over the entire span of his years at the RSCM and have admired his intellectual gifts: he is a man of firm opinions who expresses himself unequivocally. His mind is a veritable filter which he has used brilliantly when converting accurately long discussions, either in the General Purposes Committee or in meetings of the Council, into near-perfect minutes within an hour or two.' Lionel Dakers also recalled: '[VEW] often said 'When you are a secretary to a committee, always write up the minutes without delay while everything is fresh in your mind.' How true this is, so I dutifully left him in peace the day following an important meeting.' Dakers went on to say in the tribute to VEW's 24 years of service

Lionel Dakers (L) and Vincent Waterhouse (R) In the Director's Office

published in *CMQ* in July 1990 that 'Immaculately dressed during office hours, he [was] a stickler for etiquette – rightly so in the slap-happy informal world we inhabit.' VEW was an enthusiastic opera lover and Harry Bramma also noted in this same tribute that, as he moved from the RSCM to the RCO, 'We wish him well in his new sphere of work – and in his new home in London, not surprisingly within walking distance of his beloved opera houses.'

Harry Bramma recalls Vincent Waterhouse:

'Vincent Waterhouse was another key member of staff who made a considerable contribution. He had originally worked for a Livery Company in the City of London, coming to work for the RSCM in 1965. When the post of Secretary fell vacant in 1968, the Council, at the suggestion of Dame Betty Ridley, decided to promote him. From then until 1990, he very efficiently oversaw the finances and buildings. He had quite a good grasp of the stock market and as an organist himself, knew about the musical administration of the RSCM. During his time the number of affiliated churches rose to 8,000 and remained at that level until 1990. He was good at getting to know those who ran committees at the local level, both at home and abroad.

A Yorkshireman, he had moved south to work in London on leaving school at Cottingham near Hull. One suspects he was one of those of very real ability who, like many others, did not receive the educational opportunities after the war which they ought to have had. This I think engendered a certain bitterness in his personality. He had style, ability and could be very charming, but he was not always easy in personal relationships. It was well-known amongst staff at Addington that he was best avoided

104

on Monday mornings! But, for 25 years, he was a key player at the RSCM, giving his time and interest in church music without stint. Despite his idiosyncrasies, he should be remembered generously as someone who gave so much to the RSCM. He liked to appear rather grand, and somehow managed to expunge any trace of Yorkshire from his speech (except when speaking to me!). His telephone manner was noticed frequently with amusement. On answering, he managed to lengthen the word 'Secretary' in the most remarkable way — it went something like 'say — c — re — terrae.' It was an affected mannerism which could be relied on to appear as he lifted the receiver!

My personal relations with him were mixed. At bottom, I think he thought me an iconoclast and dangerous radical. I was a different kind of Yorkshireman who was perhaps, to him, unfathomable. We had to move from the RSCM 'comfort-zone' which I think he very much regretted. Curiously, when he moved to be Clerk of the RCO, of which I was Hon Treasurer in 1990, our relationship was much more cordial and constructive. Perhaps I was less of a threat in that role, but any history of Addington Palace would be incomplete without substantial reference to him.'

(Henry) Richard George Lawrence: He was appointed Secretary and Chief Executive in July 1990, in succession to Vincent Waterhouse. He had previously worked for 15 years with the Arts Council of Great Britain. He was a boy chorister at Westminster Abbey, under Sir William McKie, educated at Haileybury and Worcester College, Oxford. He left in 1994, and was replaced by Charles King re-titled as 'Chief Executive'.

King, Charles: Appointed Acting Chief Executive (a new title for the General Secretary) in 1994, the title 'Acting' being dropped after 6 months in office. Harry Bramma writes:

'It was he who did much of the work of closing down the Palace and moving into Cleveland Lodge. After he left in the spring of 1997, the administrative work was undertaken by two members of Council — Roger Butler, the Vice-Chairman, and Ian Fraser. They worked with great commitment and with considerable financial success. Alas this involved making cuts in the publications department but was helped by the considerable profit made by the 'Come and Sing' events that I organised in the great churches[103]. In fact, my last year (1997/98) was the only year since the mid-eighties that the RSCM broke even financially.'

---

[103] There were nineteen of these (10 Stainer and 9 Fauré), raising £29,000. [HB] writes: 'I was overwhelmed by the support and generosity I encountered. All the conductors and organists gave their services and in only two places did we have to pay a facilities fee. At several cathedrals, the Dean and Chapter paid the fees of soloists. This series is worth putting on record as witness to the esteem and affection the RSCM was held in cathedral circles in 1998.'

H) Headquarters Choirmasters

Edred Wright	1954	(two terms only before he resigned)
Hubert Crook	1954-1955	
Martin How	1955-1960	
Michael Brimer	1960/1961	
Peter White	1962-1966	
Alan Fen-Taylor	1966/1967	
Martin How	1968-1970	
Colin Yorke	1970-1974 (the College Choir ceased after this)	

Wright, Edred John, BMus (Lambeth), FRSCM: b. 14th Feb 1911, Wimbledon; d. 3rd Jan 2004, Canterbury. He was a chorister at Westminster Abbey under Sydney Nicholson, then Dulwich College. After the war, he became a student at the College of St Nicolas at Canterbury, and was then appointed its choirmaster (1946-1953). Whilst choirmaster he directed, or assisted GHK and Hubert Crook with, 35 chorister and cathedral residential courses. He announced his resignation in 1954, when appointed Choirmaster at King's School, Canterbury, though see Chapter IVb regarding his departure. Between 1965 and 1970 he again directed residential Easter and Summer courses at Addington. He was very successful at King's School[104] mentoring many musicians who would become well-known such as Mark Deller, Simon Carrington, Stephen Varcoe and Harry Christophers. Edred conducted the Canterbury Operatic Society and, for 20 years, the outdoor City Carols on Christmas Eve for the Mayor's Fund. He was a founder member, and ultimately conductor, of the Westminster Abbey Purcell Club. He was awarded an ARSCM in 1967, upgraded to FRSCM in 1996[105] and Archbishop of Canterbury, Michael Ramsey, awarded him a Lambeth BMus in 1970.

---

[104] King's Canterbury pupil Michael Morpurgo wrote: 'He was short, stocky and balding. He dressed untidily and smoked like a chimney, but Edred Wright, the music director at King's School in Canterbury, was a ball of energy who inspired me to love music and to sing well above everyone's expectations. I had an ordinary voice and musical ability, but Edred, as we called him, was an extraordinary choirmaster. He taught me between the ages of 13 and 18, and when he was teaching me, I felt as if I was on fire. By the time I finished singing, I was breathless with the sheer joy of it. As with all great teachers, he lifted mediocre pupils like me to new heights.'

[105] See Harry Bramma's appreciation on p. 295.

Above: Edred received a Lambeth BMus from Archbishop of Canterbury Michael Ramsey in 1977

Below: Edred's ARSCM was upgraded to an FRSCM at the Addington Farewell Service in 1996

Crook, Hubert: see Chief Commissioner

How, Martin: see Headquarters Commissioner

Brimer, Michael MA, DMus, FRCO(CHM), LRAM, ARCM, ADCM: b. 8th Aug 1933, South Africa. After study at the University in Cape Town, he was a student at Addington 1954/55, at the RCM and concurrently organist of St Peter's in Cranleigh Gardens, London. He went on to be organ scholar at Clare College, Cambridge.

John Morehen (1960/61):

> 'The Choirmaster during my time was Michael Brimer. In a sense he was the proverbial 'square-peg-in-a-round-hole', as I didn't feel that his heart really lay in church music. His real strength was as a formidable pianist. There was a fine grand piano in the Great Hall at Addington, but it was strictly 'off limits' to students. Occasionally after dinner Michael would treat us to a Beethoven sonata, always played from memory.'

Indeed, despite his expertise in church and organ music, Brimer went on to a successful career as a concert pianist and conductor. In the year after leaving Addington he premiered Malcolm Williamson's 2nd Piano Concerto and has performed complete cycles of the Beethoven piano sonatas at least five times. As an academic he has taught at the University of Western Australia, Monash University, the University of Natal, the University of Cape Town and the University of Melbourne, becoming Professor Emeritus in 2010.

White, Peter Gilbert, MA, MusB, FRCO(CHM), ARSCM: b. 21st Jan 1937, Plymouth; d.2007, an Addington student, studying at the RAM, he went on to St John's, Cambridge as organ scholar, was appointed Assistant Organist at Chester Cathedral in September 1960. He was appointed Choirmaster at AP in succession to Michael Brimer and began work on 1st March 1962. He was the editor of the 'Treble Clef' section of *RSCM News* and was made ARSCM in 1965. He went on to be Assistant organist of Chester Cathedral, DOM at Merchant Taylors' School in Northwood 1966, and then in 1969 was appointed Master of the Music at Leicester Cathedral serving there until 1994.

Fen-Taylor, Alan BA, FRCO, ARCM: Oxford graduate, harpsichordist and specialist in early music. Became HQ Choirmaster in September 1966 but the appointment was not a success and he was asked to resign in November 1967. One student (Hume McGrath) comments: 'we all felt that the choirmaster (Alan Fen-Taylor) was such a mixed-up soul even though he had all the right qualifications and background, he was unable to pass on the information in a proper and cohesive form.' By 1973 he was a professor at the International School of the Sacred Heart in Tokyo.

Roy Massey comments:

> 'a former Oxford organ scholar and a gifted musician — but, sadly, he didn't fit the position at all well. In spite of his considerable gifts, in the end we could not confirm him in the job after his probationary period. Consequently GHK and I had a very uncomfortable interview with his father as a result, but he was not for us.'

108

Yorke, Colin: MMus, LRAM, b. 1941, Cape Town, South Africa. He was a student at Addington in 1967/68 before appointment as resident choirmaster in September 1970, after Martin How had returned to working in the field as Commissioner. He was also assistant organist at Croydon PC. Colin was very successful in arranging and directing the 'May Concerts' started by Martin How, but left at the end of the Summer Term in 1974 when the College Choir was disbanded. He returned to South Africa as senior music programme producer with the SABC and Radio Allegro. Apart from 1993-96 when he returned to London, he was an inspirational director of the Johannesburg Bach Choir from 1990 until 2006.

Colin Yorke ca 1990[106]

I) Events from the Diary including Royal Visits

The Queen's Visit

It was in the April 1963 issue of *RSCM News* that the membership read the following announcement: 'We are greatly honoured to be able to tell all our members that Her Majesty the Queen, who is our patron, will visit Addington Palace on Monday 20th May, 1963.' The Queen had consented to become a Patron of the RSCM in July 1952, but had yet to visit the Palace and meet the staff who worked there. Queen Elizabeth The Queen Mother, the first Patron, had paid an official visit in July 1954 for the opening of the Palace (see Chapter III). Understandably, there followed a period of intense preparation in order to prepare the Palace for such an auspicious occasion.

On the day, the Queen, arriving at 12.35 pm, was greeted at the front door of Addington Palace by the Mayor of Croydon

The Chairman greets HM The Queen

(Councillor J L Aston), and the Bishop of Kensington (Rt Revd Edward Roberts) who, in his role of Chairman of the RSCM Council, became host to Her Majesty for the duration of her visit. After presenting Mrs Roberts, Gerald Knight (Director), the Revd George Sage (Warden and Chaplain) and Mrs Gordon (Housekeeper) to the Queen, the welcoming party moved through to the Great Hall for a sherry party, at which members of RSCM Council and

---

[106] Photograph by courtesy of the Johannesburg Bach Choir.

their wives, together with senior members of staff and tutors were presented to Her Majesty. It is worth noting here that the inclusion of the Housekeeper Mrs Chloe Gordon among the welcoming party at the front door shows the high regard in which she was held.

Following the sherry reception, the Queen lunched in a private room, whilst Council, staff and other residents lunched in the College dining rooms. At the private lunch party for the Queen, the following were present: the Chairman of Council, the Director, the Warden, the General Secretary (Leslie Green), the Bursar (Alec Jackson) and the Appeals Secretary (Capt Rivers), together with the Lord Lieutenant of Surrey (the Earl of Munster), the Mayor and Mayoress of Croydon, the High Sheriff (Sir George Erskine), the Queen's Lady-in-Waiting (Lady Susan Hussey), Lord Plunket and Sir Edward Ford. A choir of students sang Grace before and after the meal. However, such were the number of guests requiring lunch, which took it beyond the capacity and resources of the Palace, that Sir William and Lady McKie entertained those doctors of music, musicians and workers for the RSCM who were due to receive diplomas that afternoon to a lunch in Croydon. After lunch coffee was served in the Great Hall, and further presentations were made, as follows: Sir William McKie, Dr Leo Sowerby, George Maybee and Mervyn Byers, followed by members of the office and domestic staff.

Above: Senior Chorister Peter Hood meets HM The Queen

Left: Her Majesty with GHK and RSCM Chairman walking in the grounds

The Queen was then taken on a conducted tour of the ground floor of the Palace including the Colles Library, the Walford Davies Lecture Room and the Nicholson Practice Room. Further presentations were made including students from overseas. In the Practice Room the Choirmaster (Peter White) was rehearsing the choristers who were later going to sing to

Her Majesty. Peter Hood[107], as senior chorister, was presented — and told the Queen that he had been in the choir for seven years.

There followed a short recital in the chapel, where the choir of boys and students sang Stainer's *How beautiful upon the mountains*, followed by Britten's *Jubilate in C*, sung by a mixed student choir. Robert Smith, as senior student, played Stanley's *Bell Allegro* on the Chapel organ.

It was now time for the Queen to leave, after the signing of the Visitors' Book and presenting a signed photograph of herself. It was a day when the Palace was *en fete*, with all turned out in their finery — the bishop suitably gaitered, the Mayor in morning dress, ladies suitably clad in hats and gloves and the teaching staff in academic regalia. Judging by the pertinent questions she asked, there seems to have been little doubt concerning the genuine interest shown by the Queen, knowing of her knowledge of church worship and the music which goes with it.

> 'Never has such an important occasion been spent in an atmosphere of greater ease and relaxation. We were all enchanted…and we hope that we are not deceiving ourselves in thinking that Her Majesty enjoyed the time she spent with us as much as we did in having her in Addington Palace.' [108]

At some point in the afternoon, whilst GHK was showing the Queen around the palace, he was heard to use his characteristic phrase 'mind the step m'dear.'

George Sage introduces College Students to HM
L-R: Michael Bailey, Adrian Perkins, Michael
Taylor, Michael Kalule and unknown

[107] b.1948, a pupil at Selhurst Grammar School.
[108] *RSCM News* No 3 July 1963.

Royal Visit 1963 — waiting in the Great Hall

In 1982 HM Queen Elizabeth the Queen Mother made a private visit on 15th July to meet members of the Summer Course for Overseas Students. This visit had been planned for 1981, but illness prevented Her Majesty attending and the visit was deferred. Following a tour and presentation of both students and staff, HM heard a short programme of music in the Chapel and the students sang for her in the Great Hall after tea and again prior to her departure. When the chapel recital ended she was heard to say 'Oh dear, is that all?'

LD commented that:

> 'The fact that we live in a very different world from when the last royal visit took place was emphasised by the number of policemen and women patrolling the grounds and sniffer dogs going through the house prior to the Queen Mother's arrival. Nor could the royal car and its police escort avoid the traffic delays of South London caused by the rail strike. The fact that the Queen Mother arrived twenty minutes late, with mannerly regal apologies, is perhaps a further reflection on the changing face of life today which even affects royalty.'[109]

---

[109] *CMQ* Oct 1982.

Chapter V. Education at the Palace

Introduction

From its very first beginnings, the RSCM promoted certain 'Principles and Recommendations'[110] and on the application form for Affiliation choirs declared that:

> 'The above-name choir desires to be affiliated to the Royal School of Church Music. Its members undertake to do their best to promote the cause of good church music. In this they will be guided by the Principles and Recommendations set forth by the RSCM.'

Each choir was given these Principles and Recommendations in the form of a leaflet together with a vestry notice 'so that the fundamentals of their membership are constantly before them.' During his Wartime sojourn at St Michael's, Tenbury, Sydney Nicholson elaborated upon the three pages of Principles by adding 'notes and comments' and the whole was published as a 60-page book *The Principles and Recommendations* (first of the SECM and then of the RSCM). This was reprinted several times and GHK noted in the 1950 edition 'That this book has proved helpful to many choirmasters is evident from the continued demand for copies,' and indeed it was a simple textbook for amateur choir trainers.

In his preface to the 1957 edition, GHK observes that: 'Every clergyman and every organist and choir-master ought to make a point of reading it again at least once a year, asking himself how far his church is putting into practice its concentrated wisdom.'

In the beginning the teaching programme at Addington was little changed from that at Canterbury. The 1947 prospectus indicates three types of student. The 'Full Course Student', with three 12-week academic terms @ £50 a term, was prepared for any or all of the RCO exams in organ and choir-training or for the ADCM. They received private tuition in theory and organ-playing as well as group lectures, classes and choir-practice training if they wished. A few students were non-resident @ 20 guineas a term for all subjects or 4 guineas a term for each single subject.

Secondly, there were 'Special Course Students' attending courses specially arranged for diploma exams and lasting for two weeks. Thirdly, there were 'Short Course Students' coming to the College for refresher courses, lectures, choir-practices and services.

The 1946 to 1953 Canterbury years of the RSCM do not merit a whole book, and perhaps have been unfairly side-lined in our trilogy of RSCM historical books, but it is worth noting that this was a very special time for all those concerned. The proximity of Canterbury Cathedral, the close involvement with worship there, the interaction with the cathedral clergy (especially Canon Joseph Poole, the Precentor) and with GHK who was still cathedral organist as well as Warden of the College, made for an inspirational period for many students.

---

[110] See Appendix 2d.

Michael Foad (1952-1954) recalled[111] that he did not enjoy the first and his only term at Addington as his heart was in Canterbury. He admired the way CVT had set things up and managed to get AP going, but both he, and some others, who had moved from Canterbury felt that AP under CVT was 'more church and less music' — a reversal of what they had experienced at Canterbury. He mentions that Edred Wright was a genius at choir training and taught him a lot and that GHK was an amazing psalm accompanist, but not a great recitalist. Part of the Crypt at Canterbury Cathedral was an 'RSCM area' for services and he recalls that often he, Edred, GHK and Martin How would go down into the Crypt on a Friday or Saturday night to say Compline. He also mentioned that students at Canterbury were allowed to perform prepared pieces on the cathedral organ as voluntaries after services but they had to be vetted and approved first.

Amongst the more illustrious students to pass through the College must be mentioned Michael Fleming, Arthur Wills, Eric Copperwheat, David Lepine, Russell Missin, Timothy Lawford and Edred Wright himself. Students from abroad formed a significant proportion of the resident students and this pattern continued into the Addington years.

The College of St Nicolas 1954-1974

On 28th September 1953 RSCM Council decided that 'from henceforth Fellows of the College of St Nicolas would be known as Fellows of the Royal School of Church Music.' The Annual Report of 1953 declared that 'At Addington all RSCM work will be integrated and treated as one. The 'College of St Nicolas' will lapse as a title but the work done there hitherto will continue at the RSCM and the word 'School' in the Founder's first name for our movement will be given its intended meaning after all these years.' Nevertheless there are numerous subsequent references in *ECM* to the College Choir, College choristers, etc. and in 1970 an application was made to the Department of Education and Science to have the College of St Nicolas recognised as an 'efficient independent establishment of further education' so that Addington study could be recognised and contribute to the degrees of other colleges and universities. The actual demise of the College was eventually to be in 1974 when termly resident students' courses ended and Lionel Dakers' new scheme of courses was instituted. On 18th July 1974, at the end of the final term, GHK gave an address in Chapel marking the closure of the College of St Nicolas. We speculate that this was probably a very sad occasion for him personally.

---

[111] Telephone conversation on 28th August 2014.

A) The teaching staff

The resident staff of Director, Warden, Clerical Commissioner and Headquarters Choirmaster were assisted in their teaching by part-time visiting tutors.

Visiting Tutors:

Gordon Phillips	1953-1955	Organ and paper-work
Dr John Henry Arnold	1953-1956	Plainsong[112]
Dr Sidney Campbell	1954-1956	(see Sub-Wardens)
A Robert Poole	1946-1964	Singing (also at Canterbury)
Norman Platt	1964-1974	Singing
Dr George Thalben-Ball	1960's	Choir-training skills
Ernest Warrell	1954-1959	Plainsong
Michael Fleming	1959-1973	Plainsong (see Wardens)
Martindale Sidwell	1959-1966	Assistant Tutor Organ
John Foster	1957-1967	Assistant Tutor Organ
Sir William Harris	1956-1961	(see Sub-Wardens)
Revd Dr Ronald C D Jasper	1964-1970	Liturgiology
Richard Popplewell	1964-1965	Organ
Barbara Hill[113]	1965-1966	Pianoforte
John Bigg	1966-1967	Pianoforte
Timothy Farrell	1966-1972	Organ
Carlina Carr	1968-1974	Pianoforte
Prof Noretta Conci-Leech	1969-1974	Pianoforte
Dr John Morehen	1969-1972	Organ
Robert Vincent	1969-1974	Organ
Fr Mark Tweedy	1970-1974	Liturgiology
Dr Anthony Greening	1972-1974	Paperwork
Simon Lindley	1973-1974	Organ
Stephen Roberts	1973-1974	Singing
Alfred Hepworth	1974-	Singing

Arnold, Dr John Henry, DMus(Lambeth), FRSCM: b. 1887; d.1956. Studied at Dulwich College with Martin Shaw and Harvey Grace. He was organist of St Alphege in Southwark from 1914 to 1920 and was assistant to Geoffrey Shaw at St Mary's, Primrose Hill from 1920 to 1930. An expert in plainsong, he published several books of plainsong accompaniment and was both on the executive of the Church Music Society and Hon Secretary of the Alcuin Club. He was made a Lambeth DMus in 1945 and FRSCM (ii)[114] in 1948.

---

[112] Unfortunately illness prevented regular visits.
[113] Barbara Hill was married to Martindale Sidwell.
[114] He was responsible for the plainsong accompaniments in the 1933 edition of *The English Hymnal*. See Appendix 8 for an explanation of the different categories of FRSCM.

Bigg, John, LRAM, ARCM: b. 1930, West Wickham; d.1997. Professor of piano at the Royal Academy of Music. He was Visiting Tutor in Pianoforte at Addington in 1966, but was absent 1967/68 whilst he was pianist-in-residence at the University of Cincinnati.

Carr, Carlina, ARCM, LRSM, LMus[115]: A Canadian-born pianist who graduated from the Royal Conservatory in Toronto and then studied further in London at the RCM and in Vienna at the Academy. She made her Proms debut in 1961 and in the late 1960's she taught at the Winchester School of Art, now part of Southampton University. Founder of the Cristofori Trio, she is still active on the concert platform.

Conci-Leech, Prof Noretta, MBE HonARAM: b. 1931, Rome. Concert pianist and teacher, pupil of Arturo Benedetti Michelangeli. She was piano tutor at AP from 1969 to 1974 and founder and former Artistic Director of the Keyboard Trust.

Farrell, Timothy Robert Warwick, FRCO, ARCM: b. 5th Oct 1943, Cape Town, South Africa. He studied at Diocesan College in Cape Town, in London at the RCM and at Addington from 1962 to 1966 before his appointment as a Visiting Tutor in organ from 1966 to 1973. He was assistant organist of St Paul's in Knightsbridge from 1962 to 1966, of St Paul's Cathedral from 1966 to 1967, sub-organist of Westminster Abbey from 1967 to 1974, organist of the Chapel Royal from 1974 to 1979 and organist of the Liberal Jewish Synagogue in London from 1975.

Foster, John, BMus, FRCO, ARCM: Organist of Beckenham Parish Church, he was Assistant Tutor (harmony and counterpoint), appointed 1957 to ease the pressure on Derek Holman when he had more students.

Greening, Dr Anthony: b. 10th Dec 1940; d. Mar 1996. From 1964 until 1966 he was assistant organist of Ely Cathedral. He was a skilled and enthusiastic editor of early music, publishing with the Oxford University Press as well as for the RSCM. He is remembered by several people as a 'quiet, humble academic'.

Hepworth, Alfred, ARAM, ARSCM: d.1987. Tenor in Hampstead Parish Church, then Lay Clerk at St Paul's Cathedral and Westminster Abbey. He was singing tutor including for the Overseas Summer Courses at Addington after the College closed. He was made ARSCM in 1981.

Hill, Barbara (Mrs Martindale Sidwell), GRSM, ARCM: b. 24th Oct 1920; d. 24th Sept 2008. Studied at the RCM with Kathleen Long and achieved the ARCM piano performance diploma in 1939. In 1961 she gave a piano recital in the Great Hall. A professor at the RCM from 1964 until retirement in 1990, she was visiting tutor in pianoforte at Addington for the academic year 1965/66.

Jasper, Revd Dr Ronald, CD, MA, DD: b. 17th Aug 1917; d. 11th Apr 1990. Succentor of Exeter Cathedral, Lecturer at King's College, London, and a Canon of Westminster, he was

---

[115] LMus Licentiate in Music at the Royal Conservatory in Toronto.

Tutor in Liturgiology from 1964 until 1970 and also Dean of York from 1975 until 1984. He was Chairman of the Church's Liturgical Commission.[116]

Lindley, Simon, LRAM, FRCO(CHM), FTCL, ARCM, GRSM, DUniv, FRSCM: b. 10th Oct 1948, London. Simon Lindley studied at Magdalen College School in Oxford and at the RCM in London. Secretary of the Church Music Society and past president of the RCO, he served as assistant organist of St Albans Cathedral from 1970 to 1975. Organist of Leeds Parish Church since 1975 and Leeds City Organist since 1976, he was made FRSCM in 2002.

Morehen, Prof John Manley, JP, MA, FRCO(CHM), ADCM, DLitt, PhD, FRCCO, HonFGCM,: b. 3rd Sept 1941, Gloucester, UK. Educated at Clifton College, Bristol, and Hymns A&M Scholar at Addington, he won an organ scholarship to New College, Oxford. Following completion of a doctorate at King's College, Cambridge, he was appointed sub-organist of St George's, Windsor, in 1968 and organ tutor at AP from 1969 to 1972. From 1973 he taught at Nottingham University becoming Professor there in 1989. His scholarly editions of 16/17C church music are widely used.

Phillips, Charles Gordon, FRCO, ARCM: b. 13th Oct 1908, Eton, Berks.; d. Oct 1991. (Charles) Gordon Phillips studied at Nottingham University and the RCM and was DOM at All Hallows-by-the-Tower in London from 1956, giving over 3100 lunchtime recitals there. He was a professor of organ and harpsichord at the London College of Music and visiting tutor at AP (1953-55).

Platt, Norman, BA: b. 1920, Bury, Lancashire, a singing teacher appointed at Robert Poole's retirement in 1964.

Poole, A Robert, LRAM, ARCM: d. 28th Jan 1968, Croydon, was a singing tutor at both Canterbury and Addington, attending once a week from the early 50's. He retired in 1964, and was succeeded by Norman Platt.

Popplewell, Richard, LVO, MA, FRCM: b. 1935, Halifax. He studied at the RCM and was organ scholar at King's, Cambridge. A professor at the RCM, he was assistant organist at St Paul's Cathedral from 1958 to 1966, of St Michael's, Cornhill from 1966 to 1979 and then at The Chapel Royal until retirement in 2000.

Roberts, Stephen, ARCM, GRSM: b. 1949, a former Addington 'London' student from 1968-1971 during which time he also studied at the RCM. He went on to be a Lay Clerk at Westminster Abbey until 1976 before embarking on a successful career as a solo baritone. During his Addington years he took major solo roles in the May concerts.

Sidwell, Martindale, FRCO, FRAM: b. 23rd Feb 1916, Little Packington, Warwickshire; d. 20th Feb 1998. Organist at Hampstead Church from 1946 to 1992, joined staff of AP as visiting organ tutor from 1958 to 1966. Also organist of St Clement Danes in London from 1957 to 1992, he founded and conducted the London Bach Orchestra from 1967 to 1981 and taught at TCL and RAM.

---

[116] See Roy Massey's note on p. 75.

Thalben-Ball, Sir George, CBE, MusD, FRCM, FRCO, FRSCM: b. 18th June 1896, Sydney, Australia; d. 18th Jan 1987, London. He was a visiting tutor at Addington, preparing students for the RCO's CHM diploma, with other college students forming a demonstration choir on which they could practise. MJRH recalls that he was a popular visitor at the Palace, and was always ready to quote Walford Davies, whom he had succeeded at the Temple Church, London. He was knighted in 1982.

Tweedy, Mark, CR, BD: d. 24th Aug 1989. A member of the Community of the Resurrection in Mirfield. Lecturer in liturgiology on Wednesdays from 1970 and then took plainsong Evensong.

Alan Snow (1972/73):

'Father Mark Tweedy visited Addington once a week to lecture on Liturgical Studies. He was an eminent theologian with a charismatic and personal charm. He invited a group of us to the community retreat he shared with nuns and monks. It was the most delightful haven sandwiched between the worst excesses of the East End at the time in Stepney running along Cable Street. I for one would not have been happy to have walked along that road at any time of the day!'

Robert Gower (1971):

'Clothed in his grey habit, with his prominent nose and teeth, and a strained tenor voice produced from the back of the throat, Mark cut a distinctive figure. But his sincerity won over the student body, who were full of admiration for his way of life and humility. Mark loved Bach (pronounced Baaaark) and would extol his works with a knowledge born of study.'

Vincent, Robert William, MA, FRCO: b. 14th Aug 1941, Medan, Sumatra. After a year at the GSM, Robert Vincent became organ scholar of Magdalen College, Oxford, from 1961 to 1964. He was organist of St Martin's-in-the-Fields from 1967 to 1977, during which time he taught at Addington. In 1977 he was appointed organist of Manchester Cathedral and then became DOM at Whitgift School in Croydon from 1980.

Warrell, Ernest Herbert, MBE, ARCO, ARCM, MA(Lambeth): b. 23rd June 1915, Camberwell, London; d.17th Aug 2010, Guy's Hospital. After study at Trinity College, London, he was articled to Tom Cook at Southwark Cathedral in 1937 and became assistant to him from 1946 until 1954. After serving at St Mary's, Primrose Hill, from 1954 to 1957 and at St John the Divine in Kennington, he was organist of Southwark Cathedral from 1968 to 1975. He was Secretary of the Plainsong and Mediæval Music Society, Musical Director of the Gregorian Association (1969-1982) and a lecturer at King's College, London (1953-1980). He was lecturer in plainsong at AP 1954-1959, and on Wednesdays would conduct the students in a plainsong evensong. He remained musically active until his death at age 95 in Guy's Hospital where he had been chapel organist for many years. He was made MBE in 1991 and Archbishop of Canterbury Rowan Williams awarded him a Lambeth MA in 2006.

B) Courses for the Residential Students 1954-1974

The teaching needs of the resident students were very varied. Some were young and inexperienced, needing theory lessons and organ-playing lessons as well as music history and choir-training lessons in order to pass the ARCO and other diplomas. Others, especially those from abroad, were already experienced musicians and choir directors in their own right, and were at Addington for more advanced study, perhaps for the ADCM, the FRCO or for liturgiological training.

Tailoring the specific educational needs of the students was generally not too difficult, but there were gaps in what was on offer and some students had to actively seek out tuition for their specific needs. Lionel Sawkins (1958/59) came from Brisbane Grammar School and writes:

> 'There was, to some extent, a mismatch between the expectations of mature overseas students (from Australia, Canada, New Zealand, the USA, South Africa and Japan) and the tuition available; it would have probably helped if we had each sent a CV detailing our previous experience together with our aims while in the UK. As it happened, the tutors found themselves facing a motley crew with widely varying abilities and experience. In my own case, I knew I needed to work on my keyboard skills (I had the ARCO in mind) and also to obtain the right British qualifications to enable me to teach in schools here. While both Martin and Derek quickly alerted me to the areas of my playing that needed improvement and were immensely helpful, I could not find anyone interested in my desire to acquire school-teaching qualifications. Fortunately, I had acted as page-turner for George Thalben-Ball when he was in Australia giving recitals, so I quickly made my way to the Temple Church. GTB saw my problem, and quickly put me in touch with William Lloyd-Webber; so it was to WLW I went each week and got the guidance I needed to get my ARCM (School Music Teaching).'

The 1960 Report to Council made the recommendation that 'in spite of the present shortage of full-course students, care should be taken to select only those who are of such a standard as to be capable of benefitting from the training provided at Addington.' This was a splendid ideal but, especially in the later years of full-time students at Addington, it became necessary to fill student places in order for the RSCM to survive financially. Unfortunately a number of students of low ability were admitted because their parents could afford the fees and the RSCM needed the money. Ironically the less able students took longer to achieve or attempt their ARCO and so were in residence for some time whilst the more able sometimes only needed one or two terms.

James Burchill (1961-62):

> 'When I finally arrived at Addington I was more than glad to have completed my basic study (including the Toronto MusBac. and the FRCCO) as this enabled me to get much more out of my two years in England.

At the University of Toronto some of my study was with the Canadian composer Godfrey Ridout and it amused me at one point to react to his frequent comment that he would have been a much better composer if he hadn't spent so much of his time with English FRCOs, by telling him that one of my ambitions was to achieve that qualification. He had no answer for that!'

The main lectures on music history were informative for both young and old. The organ lessons were tailored according to need with the more advanced students receiving tuition from Sidney Campbell and Sir William Harris ('Sir Bill') but with the majority of teaching from resident staff and the regular visiting tutors.

RSCM News October 1966 declared that 'Residential life is a very important part of any school, and perhaps particularly important to the music student, as it is here that he may exchange ideas on his subject, on people and places, and — most important of all — ideas concerning musical values, interpretation, and the merits and demerits of performers and composers. Students may find a willing hand to help them with problems arising in their work, whether written or practical. The experience of hearing the many different views and the reasons for them, also the experience of living with other students and helping them and serving them, proves a most valuable background for the tact and highly developed skill required of musicians in the world today.'

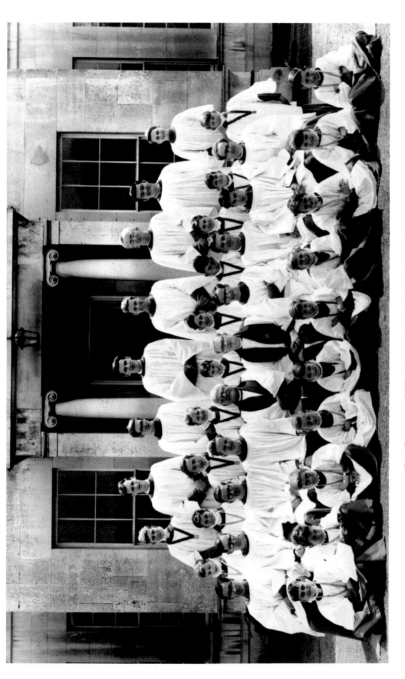

Students and Choristers in the Academic Year 1960/61

Back row (standing) L to R

Richard Barnes (chorister), Frank Carroll, Alan Miller, Martin Roberts, David Marsden, Russell Wheeler, Richard Hooi, A chorister

Third Row (choristers standing)

Graham Telfer (3rd from left), Peter Hood (extreme right)

Seated row L to R

Jerome Sawa, Gerald Milne, unknown, Martin How, Horace Spence, George Sage, Derek Holman, Godfrey Slatter, possibly Robin White, Jim Britton

Front row (choristers seated)

Peter Bennett (2nd from left), Graham Madeley (5th from left), Peter Wilson (4th from right)

121

College Students 1962

Back: (L to R) P Cousins, A Devadasen, D Williams, C Phelps, G Sadler, C Hughes, M Bailey, M Beynon

Middle: J Burchill, N Zelle, R Smith, D Price, B Law, D Langdon, C Smith, T Farrell, R Hooi

Front: F Carroll, M Godwin, St J Gadsden, D Holman, Rev G Sage, Rev H Spence, P White, Susan Hutton, M Roberts

C) Residential and Non-Residential courses for others 1954-1974

The first courses advertised for people other than the resident students during 1954 were:

Ordinands' Course	29th Mar-5th April
Instructional Course for Choirboys	20th-27th April
Choir-Training	7th-11th May
Lay Readers	May
Mirfield Ordinands	14th-21st June
Country Choirmasters	21st-26th June
[Royal Opening of Addington]	10th July]
Ordinands' Course	12th-19th July
Town Choirmasters	19th-24th July
Summer School for Adults	2nd-9th August
Instructional Course for Choirboys	2nd-9th August
Music in Worship (an ADCM course)	14th-21st September
Ordinands' Course	September/October
Ordinands' Course	December

No attendance figures are available for these courses except for the Easter Instructional Course for Choirboys (41 boys), the May Lay-Readers' course (6), the Summer School (35-21 Men and 14 Women) and its associated Choristers' course (53 boys). The adult Summer School was directed by GHK with Hubert Crook, Sidney Campbell, Dr Wilfrid Greenhouse Allt[117], Gordon Phillips and Charles Strafford[118] as staff, with Hubert Crook and Frederick Penny[119] directing the boys. During subsequent years a fairly regular pattern of study developed offering (per annum):

Four courses for Ordinands (and a special course for Mirfield Ordinands)

One or two courses for Lay Readers

Two courses for Junior Clergy

Three weekend courses for young (14-18) organists and choirmasters[120]

New Year, Easter and Summer one-week Instructional Course for Choirboys[121]

Summer School for Adults (coinciding with a boys' course)

A course for candidates taking RCO exams. The RSCM was especially well-equipped for candidates taking the RCO's (CHM) diploma in that there was a resident choir for the students to practise upon with expert guidance from the resident staff.

½ Day and One-day courses for organists, choirmasters and singers began in 1958.

---

[117] b.1889; d.1969. Organist of St Giles Cathedral in Edinburgh, Greenhouse Allt CVO, CBE, FRCO, FTCL was Principal of Trinity College London, from 1944 to 1965 and was made FRSCM in 1963 in the first batch of RSCM honorary awards.

[118] Major Charles E Strafford MBE, BA, FRCM, was an Inspector of Education.

[119] See Footnote 148 on p. 152.

[120] Looking through the Addington visitors' book, it is amazing how many present-day cathedral organists and well-known musicians were helped on their journey by attending these courses as teenagers.

[121] New Year and Easter courses averaged about 65 boys. There were fewer boys on the Summer course which was run alongside the adult Summer School and so accommodation was limited.

These were mostly outside student term time and contain a high proportion of courses for those being ordained. Just as at Canterbury, the training of ordinands, lay readers and clergy was seen as a vital part of the RSCM mission — to achieve excellence in choirs needed (and still needs) both training for choirmasters and also for clergy, in liturgy and music. Between the opening of AP and 1970, 76 courses were held for ordinands. Until the final few years when numbers fell off, there were usually 12-30 attendees. These courses ceased after 1970. LD wrote in *PCM* Jan 1976 that the courses previously held at AP for ordinands have given way to RSCM staff visiting the theological colleges and that during October 1975 he has visited St John's, Bramcote, and Wycliffe Hall, Oxford. The cost of sending ordinands to Addington was one of the factors blamed for this decline in training, and this at a time when liturgy and musical styles in church were beginning to diversify. Budget constraints and shorter training for ordination in recent years seem to have deprived many new clergy of any organised musical training apart from what they learn in their training parish, which may be very little.

According to the Annual Report of 1958, during the previous ten years 2458 students had attended external courses at Headquarters including 1000 ordinands, junior clergy and Lay Readers and, in the first four years at Addington Palace, 700 organists, choirmasters and singers had attended. During 1960 522 external students attended Addington together with 212 boys who attended Choristers' courses.

These early 1950's courses for Lay Readers, ordinands and clergy included instruction in public speaking. Cyril Taylor had worked for the BBC for some years and was fully conversant with the skills required in clear speaking and modern technology. He used tape-recorders, which had only recently become mass-produced, to allow the students to assess themselves.

Cyril Taylor (Left) instructing ordinands in public speaking with the help of a tape-recorder

A 1958 poster for the ordinands' course states that the fee is 'Five Guineas' (£113 today) and that 'these courses are designed to help the non-musical as well as the musical.'

From 1958 until 1967 a course was held for Prep School music teachers but attendance only averaged 16 and the cost of the external tutors could not be covered. Courses using the resident staff were always cheaper to run and smaller numbers could be tolerated.

Town vs Country

From 1947 the training offered to organists and choirmasters, both at Addington and in the provinces, was sub-divided into 'town' where a full SATB choir with a qualified organist was likely to be available and 'country' where the resources and ability of the choir and organist were more limited. This distinction continued until 1961 and then again sporadically from 1974 to 1983. The average attendance at these was about a dozen.

Saturday afternoon organ tuition

Early in 1956 the popular Saturday afternoon organists' classes began. *ECM* June 1959 recalled that 'Six organists participate in a class, each having two twenty minute spells at the console and remaining to profit from the instruction given to others.' The first session covered hymn playing and then, after tea, there was advice on accompaniment of psalms and canticles. Similar classes were held at Bitterne Park in Southampton and King Edward's School in Birmingham[122]. The tutors were Gordon Phillips, Alwyn Surplice and Willis Grant respectively. There is no record of when these classes ceased.

BNS wrote:

> 'This new venture was particularly invaluable in that the instruction was completely practical and concerned solely with the basic essentials required of a church musician in his weekly routine. Though its effect was limited by the small numbers that could be accommodated each time, this course was not confined to Addington but spread to the dioceses, where it provided an opportunity for the amateur to obtain limited and solely utilitarian organ tuition in a situation where he would be unable or unwilling to undertake regular organ lessons which would tend, in most cases, towards recital work rather than the basic requirements needed for service accompaniment.'

---

[122] Leslie Green's newsletter to Representatives in February 1956 mentioned that these courses would also be held in Manchester, but we have not yet found any evidence that this happened.

AP chorister instruction in progress with Geoffrey Barber (above) and Edred Wright (below)

D) Residential and Non-Residential courses 1974-1995

The New Scheme

On closure of the College to residential students, Lionel Dakers' 'New Scheme' of educational courses began in October 1974 with the aim of 20 varied courses in each term of the academic year (now renamed Periods A, B and C) to cover training for organists, choirmasters, singers and young people. Planning for the change had been in progress since before LD's arrival. Course No.1, on 5th October with David Willcocks 'Singing for All', was already oversubscribed by June of that year and Willcocks agreed to direct a second but shorter course the following day. Shorter because on the Sunday morning another course took precedence, he played golf on the course adjacent to AP! This 'Singing for All' course on the first Saturday of October with David Willcocks became an annual event until 1988 and regularly attracted more than 100 singers. Sir David was also involved in a regular autumn course to prepare choral scholars for scholarship trials at Oxbridge colleges, run alongside a similar course for potential organ scholars.

The first residential course was held the following week — 'The Church and Its Music Today' — led by Erik Routley with Allan Wicks, The Bishop of Leeds, The Bishop of London, Donald Swann and Prof Ivor Keys as speakers.

The important Young Organists' courses started in 1959, already mentioned, were continued at an increased rate from 3 to 4 per year and numbers were increased from 12 per course to 20, though the average attendance was around a dozen. In later years[123] these were sponsored by the Church Music Society. In addition to the resident staff, directors of these courses included many assistant cathedral organists whose names are now well-known at cathedrals and in recitals.

Specific courses of preparation for ARCO candidates replaced the on-going training formerly given to College students for this purpose. In the first year LD's attempt at ecumenism must have been disappointing as the first summer course advertised for Roman Catholics was cancelled due to lack of interest. Again in 1980, the first residential course for Free Church musicians[124] at Addington only attracted 10 attendees and even today the image of the RSCM is falsely perceived by many to be relevant only to the Anglican Church.

It was in 1974 that Janette Cooper began her Reluctant Organist courses, though the first two were actually titled 'Conversion Course' [from piano to organ — see Janette Cooper under 'Wardens'].

Following this usual Easter residential course for boys at AP, it was announced that the 1975 course would be, for the first time, for girls. However there is no evidence that a course was held the following year or subsequent years.

---

[123] From 1988 to 1994.

[124] There had been some one-day courses for Free Church musicians advertised, but no record of whether they took place or not and no entry in the Addington *Visitors' Book*.

In October 1975 *PCM* noted that, in the first full year of the new scheme of courses, there were 1300 participants. LD commented that the most popular courses were those for young organists, those featuring elite lecturers like David Willcocks and George Guest and the reluctant organist courses. Four years later the Annual Report of 1979 noted that in the previous year almost 1500 students had attended AP on the 60 courses and the Summer School. *CMQ* in 1982 noted that 2000 students attended courses in the previous year and so, by any standards, the 'New Scheme' was a success.

Cancelled Courses

In October 1980 *CMQ* noted that 'five years of New Style courses has now been completed. In the first year 1035 people attended and of the 60 courses, 11 were cancelled for lack of support. In the 5th year [1978/79] 1961 students attended [60 courses] and only one course was cancelled.' Apart from this, few figures are available for Addington course attendance from 1954 to 1973, figures are incomplete from 1974 to 1987 and so no accurate comparisons can be made, but from 1988 to 1996, 55 courses were cancelled due to lack of interest out of a total of 542 courses — roughly 10%.[125]

Plainsong

A few non-residential courses on plainsong were held in 1959 at Addington but it proved more convenient to London organists to hold these more centrally and for the next ten years these were held at All Saints', Margaret Street.[126] Lionel Dakers invited Dr Mary Berry[127] to lecture at Addington, usually at the same time as the Summer Overseas Course, and the twelve courses (some of them residential weekends) held up until 1994 were attended by between 30 and 70 participants.

Kneller Hall

The RSCM formed a link with The Royal Military School of Music at Kneller Hall, the home of Army music since 1857. In order to graduate from Kneller Hall, musicians had to learn and pass in choral conducting and Addington was the ideal place for them to learn this. These courses, attended by 6-12 bandmasters, ran from 1980 until 1992, mostly led by Martin How.[128]

---

[125] Cancellation figures for the last few years at Addington can be found in Appendix 5.

[126] See Chapter VI.

[127] Sister Mary Berry CBE, (1917-2008), was a pupil in Paris of Nadia Boulanger and then studied at Girton College in Cambridge. In 1945 she became Mother Thomas More and, after teaching at schools in Belgium, France and Italy, she developed an interest in Gregorian Chant which she taught in Paris. She was exclaustrated from her religious order and served as DOM at Girton and then Newnham colleges in Cambridge, serving until retirement from academia in 1984. Known worldwide as an authority on Gregorian Chant, she founded the Schola Gregoriana in 1975 and, with them, she continued to demonstrate plainchant for many years after her formal retirement. Her popular RSCM Handbook *Plainchant for Everyone*, published in 1979 and re-issued in 1987, was revised, re-published and expanded in 2015 as the *RSCM Guide to Plainchant*.

[128] John Cooke ran two of these.

128

The RSCM's relationship with Kneller Hall went back to 1968 with a visit to AP by Kneller Hall DOM elect Colonel C H 'Jiggs' Jaegar who directed the trumpeters at the *Jubilate Deo* 1970 Albert Hall festival.[129]

Martin How wrote:

'Colin Yorke and I well remember 'Jiggs' Jaegar visiting Addington Palace prior to his taking over his post at Kneller Hall, where he was to be in charge of music with the responsibility for training and conducting the Military Band. He was a great character — full of amusing remarks and anecdotes. He was also, in spite of appearances to the contrary, extremely modest. He travelled around many of the music colleges before he took over at Kneller Hall, to see what he could learn from their conducting classes. Needless to say, he visited us at the RSCM. We learnt far more from his visits than he would ever learn from us. Almost for the first time I was able to learn specific gestures and patterns of conducting styles. No one else had shown me certain tricks of the trade.'

Ecclesiastical Embroidery and Flower Arranging

The influence of Elisabeth Dakers could be found in the organising of these non-musical courses. 72 such courses (54 of these residential courses) ran between 1975 and 1995 with only the last one needing to be cancelled through lack of support. The average attendance was 16.

Elizabeth Elvin and Sylvia Green were the mainstay of the embroidery courses throughout these two decades. Elizabeth Elvin joined the Royal School of Needlework in 1961 specialising in the teaching of gold, silk and ecclesiastical embroidery. She became Principal of the RSN in 1987, retiring in 2007. In 1976 she designed a new altar fontal for AP Chapel. *PCM* October 1976 mentions that this was made possible by an anonymous donor. The design features St Nicolas and organ pipes. 'The theme is echoed in the design for 44 kneelers to be used in the chapel, each incorporating the coat-of-arms of a different diocese. The kneelers are being made by men and women on the Addington staff and by other kind helpers.'[130]

On 27th Oct 1982 a new RSCM Cope and Mitre were dedicated by RSCM Council Chairman, The Bishop of Bath and Wells at a special service in AP Chapel. They were made by 14 ladies from the ecclesiastical embroidery group and designed by Elizabeth Elvin and Sheila Berry based on the RSCM coat of arms and motto. The project was in memory of Dorothy Wigg, a founder member of the group. The Bishop wore these items for a BBC 'Songs of Praise' broadcast from Exeter Cathedral at Christmas 1982.

The 17 flower arranging courses often had a liturgical seasonal theme and Joan Thornton was the principal tutor.

---

[129] See footnote 235 on p. 218 for further information.
[130] See photograph on p. 21.

E) Addington Summer Schools

The Summer School has been a feature of RSCM education ever since the Chislehurst years but, whereas in the early days it was more directed at boy choristers who were on school holidays, throughout the Addington years the emphasis changed towards adult education. The Summer School was also invariably held at the same time as a choristers' instructional course, and indeed the boys of Choirmasters taking part in the Summer School were given priority places on the boys' course. The presence of the boys allowed not only for the course to sing SATB services, but also for the participants to see high quality choir training in action.

The 2nd Addington Summer School for Adults and Instructional Course for Choirboys
1st-8th Aug 1955 (51 boys, 34 men, 10 women and staff)

In the first ten Addington years the School was a one week course (average attendance 35[131]) directed by GHK or the Warden. In addition to RSCM staff and tutors (Sidney Campbell, Hubert Crook, Gordon Phillips, Robert Poole, Martindale Sidwell, Horace Spence, Cyril Taylor and Ernest Warrell) these years saw highly skilled church musicians as lecturers and specialist singing teachers from the London Colleges:

---

[131] AP could take about 40 residents and some people brought spouses, so this is a good number.

W Greenhouse Allt, Robert Ashfield, John Birch, Allan Blackall, Leonard Blake, John Brough, John Churchill, Arthur W Clarke, Charles Cleall, Lionel Dakers (then at Exeter), Harold Dexter, Willis Grant, Arthur Hutchings, Christopher Le Fleming, David Lepine, George Maybee, Sydney Northcote, Charles Proctor, Gordon Reynolds, Barry Rose, Erik Routley, John Rust, Watkins Shaw, Leo Sowerby, Laurence Swinyard, Stainton de B Taylor, Stanley Vann and Olga Watson.

In 1975, at the end of LD's first year of the 'new scheme', he arranged what would eventually become a regular six-week long residential course for overseas students, perhaps for those who would previously have considered attending the College of St Nicolas for a term or more. According to *CMQ* in July 1974 he initially intended this course to be three months in duration, but by *CMQ* October 1974 it was advertised as nine weeks and eventually it was run as two separate but complimentary courses of three weeks with a three-week break during which Addington was closed and students were encouraged to visit musical events such as the Southern Cathedrals Festival, the St Albans Festival, the Three Choirs Festival, the RSCM Cathedral courses and the IAO annual conference — at each of which they would receive a lecture by one of the musician's organising those events. The first course featured Peter Hurford, John Cooke and Francis Jackson and the second included Stephen Cleobury and Prof Ivor Keys. The following year there were also two three-week courses but with only one week in between. Thereafter it became a single six-week course with integral visits to cathedral, colleges and festivals. These courses were generally full to capacity (40 students), often a mix of amateur and professional musicians.

Reflections on the 1981 Summer School by Jenny Setchell, Christchurch NZ:

Allan Wicks — 'You won't forget him in a hurry' director of the RSCM, Lionel Dakers, told us.

'We' were the assembled students for the annual six-week summer course for overseas church musicians at Addington Palace, and word had it that Dr Wicks was THE person in the English church music scene. He was erudite, inspirational, exacting, an acclaimed recitalist with phenomenal skill and had been Organist and Master of the Choristers at Canterbury Cathedral since 1961. He was obviously brilliant. He was a God. I was terrified.

With all the innocence and gall of youth I wrote back home to New Zealand of my increasingly delighted impressions of this wonderful man and his effect on us during one week. And here they are, warts and all:

Monday, 3rd August, Dr Wicks bounced into Addington Palace for the first of his lectures which began with the subject *The Reality of Art*. I had imagined him to be a bit stuffy, uppity and limited to his only one sphere of interest, i.e. music. Just the opposite. In his 60's, Allan had the enquiring mind of a child and the wisdom to absorb and use information carefully — apart from that he was very human. He could talk on almost any subject but preferred to listen, and spent many hours with us just chatting in the common room or over a cup of tea on the landing, late into the night. The first lecture was a bonanza — so provocative that he upset one student who rudely stormed out in the middle of it, but that was the student's fault, not Allan's. We **were** in for a very vital and interesting week! After coffee it was back to singing, this time another full-scale Victoria mass in Latin. Years of coping with choirboys and men at Canterbury had armed Allan well for coping with a mixed bag of voices like ours and at the finish of just one session we even began to think that we weren't so bad after all.

Tuesday, 4th August: Allan set the ball rolling today with a routine lecture on *The Church Musician and Practical Theology*. He was as well-up in his theology as everything else, it appeared. He told us that he gives potential choirboys an official, expertly designed series of tests along with IQ tests and so on before admitting them to be personally auditioned for musical ability. One of these tests involved differentiating between sounds, and just for fun, Allan made himself and his wife do them. His wife fared fairly well, but Allan's results showed he had 'only some musical ability.' He thought this was enormously funny. He said it proved to him that tests only told so much, and for the rest, he always accepted choirboys who had a certain sparkle in their eyes — a gamble that always paid off.

Wednesday, 5th August: Morning off, spent in London. The bus back to Addington was full of stoically sweating 'poms' who looked thoroughly miserable in this intense and unusual heat wave. I was back just in time for Allan's lecture on *Tradition and the Great Composer*. It was so hot that the class had to be moved from the lecture room to the lawn outside, under the shade of the massive cedar tree, whose huge branches formed a canopy over us. Even there it was steaming hot but Allan ploughed on in fine style, tracing the development of music through the ages and through different countries. He could really cover a lot of ground in a short time, that man. But can I remember it?

If the Dakers family was a lively enough package, put them with Dr Allan Wicks and you had an explosion of activity. They decided some Scottish country dancing would help finish the day off nicely, now that evening was coming on and temperatures were dropping into the 20's. We learnt a kind of eightsome reel that night, using a tape recorder plugged in through a below-ground window. It was frenetic dancing and exhausting to the point where we feared for Fred's health. I took photos with my ailing camera, and in the twilight of 9.30pm we are barely visible, but by then we were also barely mobile — except for Allan. It was enormous fun, and others joined in from time to time to give the dancers a rest. All this lent itself to a very happy air in the Palace.

Allan Wicks (left, in blue) with Juliet Dakers (right, in white top) teach an eightsome reel

Thursday 6th August: The afternoon session was Allan on *Training and selecting choirboys for Canterbury Cathedral*. One of his methods of disciplining his boys if they misbehave is to throw rubber chickens at them from the organ loft. I wonder if any tourist has been alarmed by the sight of a flying rubber chicken in the hallowed confines of Canterbury Cathedral. He also dealt very sensibly with choirboys who got fidgety and restless: he would force march them, in line, to the West door, then shout 'Follow me' at the top of his lungs, and take off at full speed. It was up to the boys to follow — through gateways, under hedges, in and out of shops, until the boys were exhausted and he led them, running, back into their pews in the quire. They paid attention and sang superbly after a good work out like that, he claimed.

Allan said it was often tricky getting the right effect in sound with very small boys. Once he wanted them to sound terrified — scared to death in fact. Nothing he could do was getting the required effect, so he told them a long tale about a terrible, wicked man who had a hook for a right hand (Captain Hook comes to mind). Come the day for the performance of this scary work, Allan got up to conduct his boys wearing, as usual, his long-sleeved surplice. As he raised his arm for the down-beat, his sleeve fell away and the boys saw at once he had, not a right hand, but a HOOK! The resultant singing was marvellous and the boys sprang into action, scared out of their wits. But his care of the boys was genuine. No matter how a boy behaved, looked, sang or spoke, Allan always tried to remember that every boy was somebody's dearly loved son, and that Allan had no right to treat him as anything else. A most impressive man.

Saturday, 8th August: A 'Come and Meet Allan Wicks' public day began at 10am with a head-on tackle of Vaughan-Williams' *Dona Nobis Pacem* and a Stravinsky *Mass*. At sight — phew! It was possibly the hardest session of the whole course as both were pieces with peculiar harmonies and modulations that were hard to pitch correctly. To complicate matters, rhythms were extraordinary and there were up to eight parts going at the same time. I chose to be a second alto, hoping to hide in the middle of all the other voices around me, but it was even harder than being a mainline soprano. We often found ourselves having to pitch notes that were a semi-tone or tone away from notes in other parts on either side of us. Allan was fantastic and no-one could help but be impressed by his straight-forward control and musical leadership of this braying cacophony. He brought it all together for a final performance in the Great Hall which evoked no thunderclaps from the god of musical attainment. We were just relieved to have got through it. As we took to our beds, exhausted, Allan left quietly to return to his beloved Canterbury Cathedral and its choristers.'

Yes, you were right Lionel. We haven't forgotten him — and it certainly won't be in a hurry.

Jenny Setchell, March 2010

During the summer schools celebrity events were arranged on Saturdays and run as one-day courses open to non-residents. These would include organ recitals and organ master classes, usually run by Peter Hurford, 'Come and Sing' a major work type events[132] and specialist sessions such as Mary Berry on plainsong or Arthur Wills on composing. Some of the lecturers during the courses were very high profile such as Sir David Willcocks, George Guest, Simon Preston, John Rutter, Herbert Howells and William Mathias — the full list is impressive.

Harry Bramma recalls:

'In its heyday, the six-week Summer School was an attractive affair with structured courses and visits from many distinguished visitors and lecturers such as Sir David Willcocks, Herbert Howells, and John Rutter. Broadly speaking these courses were successful, but it was difficult to hold together membership of very varied ability. Some who came were not very advanced, whilst others were distinguished graduates of foreign universities. Some of these found the lack of structure and variety of ability distinctly irritating — there were some awkward moments! Further, by the 1980's the rather primitive arrangements — no en-suite facilities and all bathrooms and lavatories down a corridor — eventually were a factor which worked against Addington as a musical hotel. Additional income had been raised by letting out the facilities to organisations — particularly Church of England boards — but these gradually drifted away. The refurbishment of the bedrooms was quite beyond the means of the RSCM. Delegates to conferences became less willing to slum it — even in a Palace!

This having been said, the chance to stay in a country house with its elegant Norman Shaw interior, to share decent food and to enjoy the company of like-minded people in comfortable surroundings to some extent made up for the lack of creature comforts. The staff, and particularly Lionel and Elisabeth Dakers, acted as benevolent hosts, dispensing drinks at the bar, and generally taking a keen and friendly interest in those who had come to stay and learn.

By the late 1980's the idea was beginning to run out of steam. In fact, just before he retired, Lionel Dakers told me that I would probably have to cancel the 1989 Summer Course because of the insufficient number of applicants. This I eventually did and in its place Janette Cooper devised a plan of three one-week residential courses which appealed more to the home market. These were immediately very successful and ran from 1989 to 1995, just before the move to Cleveland Lodge in 1996. Indeed after the closure of the residential facility, it was found feasible to reopen the bedrooms and kitchen for these 3-week periods in 1994 and 1995.'

---

[132] See photo of Sir Charles Groves on p. 137.

Addington 1965 Summer School
Above: ball play on the back lawn; below: Roy Massey rehearsing in the Chapel

Overseas Summer School
students playing beer bottles
in Great Hall ca 1988

Horace Spence, GHK and MJRH with two
summer course chorister captains

Addington Summer
Course early 1990's,
relaxation on the back
lawn

Above: A comic-reading break on an Easter Course in the Common Room
Below: Sir Charles Groves' Brahms *Requiem* workshop in the Great Hall July 1983

Courses at Addington during the final years, by Harry Bramma

During my first 4½ years, I endeavoured to continue the pattern of courses set up by my predecessor. There were a number of well-established events which continued to attract considerable support including the long-running 'Reluctant Organist' courses which have already been mentioned. The Young Organists' weekends continued to flourish until 1993. The students arrived in time for dinner on Friday and left after lunch on Sunday. Many aspiring organists found help and inspiration and the courses were always full. A succession of talented young Directors came to teach on these weekends. I always tried to help at these courses as the teaching of young organists formed a very important part of my previous work, especially at Worcester, though I continued to teach choristers and young people the piano and the organ in my Southwark years.

The big singing days on Saturdays continued to be popular. Visits by John Rutter, Sir David Willcocks and many others continued to attract capacity (ca 100 people) to morning and afternoon sessions in the Great Hall at Addington. The walnut panelling and the high ceiling created a magnificent acoustic which encouraged people to sing. Sometimes these courses were for adult mixed groups e.g. 'Come and Sing the Bach *Magnificat* with .....' Others were for children, either mixed or for boys or girls alone. Such days usually finished with a service in the Chapel. All courses had the benefit of lunch between the sessions — either a picnic or a meal provided by the RSCM kitchens.

There continued to be one-day courses on Saturdays and weekdays on a variety of topics. These attracted smaller numbers on weekdays, but were much-appreciated by a dedicated body of students who came regularly.

The Closure of the Residential Facility at Addington 1993

Rising costs and falling numbers on residential courses led to the decision that maintaining staff to service the bedrooms and a full catering service were no longer economically viable. From then on, students brought packed lunches. But Michael Benson, the former full-time chef, did provide simple lunches for the staff on weekdays, which I thought important in encouraging good relationships amongst the workers at Addington. I was opposed in this view, but I'm glad to say that I prevailed! There were two exceptions to this shut-down of the residential facility. We decided that it would be possible to re-open the bedrooms for Summer Courses in 1993 and 1994. The two staff who had managed the first and second floor respectively agreed to come back for a short period and the catering was supplied by an 'imported' chef. This worked well and the courses attracted good numbers.

In the years 1994 and 1995, there were still successful day courses. I think the fact that the RSCM would be leaving the Palace encouraged people to come for a last look![133]

---

[133] Course statistics for the final years can be found in Appendix 5.

Chapter VI. Outreach from the Palace to Affiliates and Members

Introduction

The constant priority of raising money throughout the RSCM's existence led to a bewildering array of types of membership. From the earliest days there were, of course, the Affiliated Choirs with an annual membership fee together with personal subscribers, many of whom sent donations annually. There were also some 16 Diocesan Choral Associations who were 'Federated' rather than 'Affiliated' to the SECM.

Following informal discussions, the Archbishop of Canterbury wrote on 18th July 1952 to approve that the RSCM should offer help to choirs 'in the [other] recognised Christian Churches' but noted that 'I am quite clear that the Unitarians ought not to be admitted'[134]. RSCM Council subsequently decided to admit non-Anglican churches but call them 'Associated Choirs' rather than 'Affiliated Choirs.'

ECM July 1953 announced that:

> 'At the Annual General Meeting it was stated that the Council had decided on a change of emphasis in the School's objectives. Hitherto its efforts have tended to be concentrated mainly on church choirs and the technical improvement of their singing. Hereafter it will work on a broader basis by giving its attention to all musical aspects of public worship.'

> 'In future, encouragement and advice... will no longer be offered solely, or even mainly to organists and choirs but also to clergy and congregations.'

GHK wrote in *ECM* January 1953 that 'During the 25 years since the RSCM was founded this particular tension [between music for the skilled and music for the unskilled] has been a major preoccupation of church musicians and clergy alike ... practical work has been directed almost exclusively towards the skilled. The RSCM may be proud of its part in this work, but must also be conscious of having to that extent thrown its weight into one side of the balance and of the need in the next quarter of a century to meet the challenge of the unskilled.' He went on to say that 'Choirs have to learn that they are members of the congregation.'

The move to Addington marked the start of a decade of dramatic expansion following which RSCM headquarters, though important through the services provided by its paid staff, became the tip of the iceberg, with voluntary staff in the national and international areas doing the vast majority of the work in arranging courses and festivals. It had to be so, for there was no chance of finding funds to employ a whole network of paid staff. The talented and energetic trio of John Cooke (North), Martin How (South) and Bryan Anderson (Midlands and South West) was as much as could be afforded in the peak years of membership and activity even with substantial help from external grants. The vital work of clergy training

---

[134] He went on to explain why, but that is not relevant here.

had to be almost abandoned after the retirement of Clerical Commissioner Horace Spence. He was unsalaried and a replacement was not found.

Soon after the move to Addington, in September 1954, Captain Rivers was appointed as Appeals Secretary to 'find further means of achieving freedom from financial anxiety.' His first idea was to ask choirs to raise money by singing carols at Christmas 1954 and within a few months he had received £250. The following Christmas brought in £300 (from 90 choirs) and, following a special appeal by RSCM Chairman, the Bishop of Malmesbury, the 1959 carol singing brought in £501.

By 1971 (at the onset of decimal currency) there were also additional membership categories: Life Member (£50), Friend (£2.10 p/a i.e. two guineas), Personal Member (£1.05 i.e. one guinea) and Young Member (50p).

Diocesan Representatives

The original scheme of diocesan organisation was devised when membership was yet small. So, in the 1947 Annual Report, RSCM Council announced that 'For some time it has been trying to make its outside organisation more efficient, and it has come to the conclusion that the diocese, in most cases, is too big as a unit of organisation. From now on therefore, the unit will be the Archdeaconry.' The Council indicated that Area Representatives will be appointed for all the Archdeaconries which were to be the new 'Areas' and local Representatives will be appointed to look after groups of choirs within the areas at Rural Deanery level. They acknowledged that the success of the plan would depend on suitable individuals being available.

The 1951 Annual Report was combined with a complete listing of Affiliated Choirs and it is clear that some progress had been made. By then, the dioceses were each divided into Archdeaconry Areas and each in turn was divided into groups of choirs. Most dioceses had a Diocesan Representative (often joint reps, a cathedral musician and someone else) and many areas had managed to appoint Local Representatives but, being still thin on the ground, often they were responsible for several groups of churches, for instance the two Wells reps each had six groups of churches to look after. The Blackburn Diocese on the other hand, always a very keen RSCM Diocese with Tom Duerden at the helm, had enough local reps to provide one for each church grouping. It also shared with Southwark the record of having 46% of its 256 benefices affiliated, a figure we can only dream of today[135].

Diocesan Secretaries

By 1970 half of the English dioceses had a Diocesan Secretary to organise activities locally. Occasionally this was an official from the Cathedral but more often it was someone with business or administrative experience.

---

[135] A few years later they reached a staggering 51%.

Musical Representatives

From 1961 some dioceses appointed a separate Musical Representative 'to strengthen the means of serving the members.' His task was defined as 'When requested by the Diocesan Representative to undertake musical activities planned by the RSCM and after invitation by the parish to give help to individual choirs and congregations.' BNS summarises this well:

> 'There are three points worth emphasising here. The first is that the Musical Representative is not expected to undertake tasks requiring the specialised skills of a Special Commissioner. He may be asked to help with teaching a congregation a new setting, to take congregational practice, offer advice to the choirmaster or run a one-day school. The second is that 'his duties are confined to the diocese in which he is appointed', rather as a lay-reader is licensed in a parish. Thirdly, he is 'not authorised to visit churches except upon the invitation and with the official approval of the Diocesan Representative.' '

This all sounds very formal today and, of course, it was all laid down in the masculine gender. The job was pretty restricted and frustrating, for being dependent on being called upon by the Diocesan Representative it allowed for virtually no initiatives to be taken by the appointed person. Not surprisingly this post went into decline and disappeared. It was only in areas where there was a very active Committee that these general dogsbodies had much to do.

The Annual Report in 1984 indicates that the re-organisation of Area Committees is well advanced with 'their work based on a wider membership as a result of ecumenical policy now pursued by the Council.' In fact re-organisation and decentralisation were first mooted in 1947 in the Associate Directors' Report to Council, but had progressed very slowly. The change from Diocesan Committees to Area Committees sometimes only required a name change whereas some Dioceses needed to split into multiple Areas often according to Archdeaconries. In some cases the Diocesan Rep became the Area Rep and subsequently the Chairman of the Area Committee. It has always been the case that the main representatives, currently Chairman, Secretary and Treasurer, although perhaps offered as potential candidates by the Area Committee are appointments made at headquarters and approved by the Director. In some Dioceses the Bishop also has to approve the Chairman and/or Secretary.

A) The RSCM Chorister Training Scheme

Although working 'in the field' as Headquarters Commissioner from 1964 to 1968, Martin How was resident at AP and had his office there where, with the invaluable help of his secretary Mary Williamson, he worked at the details of his new initiative — the Chorister Training Scheme. Martin recalls that at the time of planning the CTS, he made constant visits to Alec Jackson's office in Publications during the day to discuss with him — or Mrs Fortune — the subject of the new medals and publications in connection with the scheme. Evenings would be spent making phone calls to choirmasters all over the country, to get their views and to draw on their experiences before finally devising the scheme. Martin added that it was a particularly exciting and creative time for him in his career.

The CTS was launched on Saturday 4th December 1965, at the St Nicolastide celebrations held at the Royal College of Music. The event was originally planned to be held at the Royal College of Organists, but the number due to attend required moving to a larger venue.

The basic element of the scheme was to do with organising, motivating and recruiting a lively set of choirboys. At the time of the scheme's inception, there were many choirs up and down the country with 14 or more boys as members. There was clearly a need for order and organisation in each choir set-up. Fundamental to the scheme was the use and development of the already established three grades of 'Chorister Progress' namely Junior Singing Boy (light blue ribbon), Senior Singing Boy (dark blue ribbon) and Chorister (red ribbon). The first move was to introduce training cards for each level which stated the exact requirements for attainment and promotion.

What follows is Martin How's carefully thought-out scheme, in considerable detail, and from this emerges a clear understanding of the psychology of the group — as well as the individual — in the choir situation, pointing out that no one chorister could successfully be in direct charge of more than seven others. Delegation and the training of leaders therefore become all-important. He goes on to stress that the principle behind any group activity has three areas of need, each of equal importance; namely individual needs, team needs and group needs:

> Individual needs: 'Where do I go (sit)? What do I have to do to be promoted?'
> Team needs: 'Best team? Tell/ask your Team Leader. Team Leader in charge.'
> Group needs: Visits to cathedrals to sing Evensong/Expeditions/tours/matches.

> 'Before any practice or service can be effectively started, order is necessary. Vestry drill provides for various stages e.g. 'Five minutes to go, two minutes to go, places, ready (silence)!' It is the aim that the Head Chorister, with the back-up of Team Leaders, can operate this system — in fact it is an important way of re-affirming his authority on each occasion. The secret is to enable the boys to establish their own order and 'readiness' without relying on some adult (e.g. the choirmaster).

> In the actual practice much would depend on responding to directions given once only, e.g. 'page No. 42, hymn No. 306.' The greatest emphasis would be laid on

acquiring the habit of 'listening and looking' i.e. following the music when it is played over or played through at rehearsals, with the inevitable question 'where have I stopped? – point to it in the music.' This would be the basis of learning to read music. The aim would be for each singer to build up an association between sound and symbol, in that order. Being able to sing at second-sight, after having first heard and followed the music is a useful aim for many singers. In other words it is all about building the correct habits in the young singers.

Team Leaders or senior singers (ex-trebles) can sometimes help in instructing the juniors in the requirements of the various tests on the cards. Often it will be enough for the choir director of a busy choir to simply tick off some of the tests as a result of 'general impression'. An important part of the regular motivation of each singer is the weekly standards chart. When the choir is well-established, the busy choir director will simply put two ticks against each name, on the basis that every boy has reached the generally expected standard of credit during the week and at the Sunday service(s) following. The choir director can then develop his or her own system for using the same chart to record attendance and level of effort at each previous practice.'

It will be seen from the above that the CTS was far more than simply a grade system for showing progress and status – with coloured ribbons. It was more to do with building an effective and responsive team. There were several early experiments with various features of the CTS. The key people here, and it is quite a list of the well-known in the church music world, were as follows:

Geoffrey Holdroyde, who had already published his own books on group psychology, and was the dynamic choirmaster at St Mary's in Warwick.
Geoffrey Barber, at St Paul's, Heaton Moor, see Appendix 4.
David Patrick, Director of Music at Barnet Parish Church.
Malcolm Cousins, from Mansfield Parish Church.
Russell Missin, from Nottingham, St Mary, and then Newcastle Cathedral.
Peter Morse, from Morden.
Peter Branker, from Southgate, London.
Keith Rhodes, from Bradford Cathedral.
David Squibb, from Sutton, later Trinity School, Croydon.

Other Directors of Music following the scheme and gaining excellent results were:

Anthony Pape at Rye, Alan Barber at Thornaby-on-Tees, Philip Liddicoat at St Andrew's, Plymouth, Henry Green at Squirrels Heath, James Ross in Scotland, Alan Baker at Wallingford, Harry Stubbs at Stoke-on-Trent, Bernard Cookman at St Giles' and St George's Ashtead, Ian Henderson at Bromley, Graham Brown at Bishops Waltham, Ray Thomas at Grimsby, John Clarke at St George the Martyr, Queen's Square, London, Geoff Hunnisett at St Mary, Beddington, Malcolm Bulcock at St John, Burnley, Russell Shepherd at St Mark's, Portsea, Leslie Mason at Stoneleigh and Walter Taylor at Merton.

Martin goes on to add:

'Perhaps my main partners and encouragers in all this were the indomitable John Bertalot of Blackburn Cathedral, to whom I owe so much, and the energetic and visionary Michael Nicholas at Louth Parish Church, who was such a friend and inspirer in my Grimsby days.'

Most of the above names were appointed Guild Advisors, whose role it was to help those choirs which wished to adopt the CTS. If choirs passed an inspection after adopting the scheme, they could become members of the newly-formed St Nicolas, or the St Cecilia Guild for girls.

Another innovation at that time was the introduction of Dean's and Bishop's Awards, the idea being to leave it to each RSCM Area to decide on their own syllabus and requirements. In addition, the more demanding St Nicolas award (boys) and the St Cecilia Award (girls) were established. In 1977 incentives and awards for seniors (ex-trebles) were put in place.

Martin concludes his account of the CTS scheme with a pertinent observation, surely still true today:

'The underlying principles of the whole scheme very much revolved around the difference (without apology) between boys and girls (sounds very politically incorrect today) in as much as there is the extra sense of urgency to lead boys to fruition with their treble voices before it breaks or changes at an early age, whereas in some ways the girls are just beginning. There is also the challenge with boys of leading them into singing with their broken voices. It is all very much a different growing-up process from the girls. A refusal to see the differences in these matters can lead to losing or never attracting the boys.'

The years 1964-1968 proved to be a particularly active time in a number of areas of training. Martin How's first choristers' course using the scheme as Master-in-Charge was the Easter course at Taunton School 1966 with 160 boys attending, divided up into houses of about 30, each house with a Housemaster and a Captain. A stalwart of those early years was Richard Barnes[136], a former Head Chorister in the Addington choir and, for many years, Housemaster on both instructional and cathedral courses. Martin established a Junior Demonstration Choir[137], made up of younger boys from local Croydon choirs, which became a kind of travelling choir and, perhaps most importantly, he set up the Cathedral Singers[138], with its first gathering on Saturday 8th January 1966 at Winchester Cathedral.

What was important here was establishing a regular programme of 'continuity of training' throughout the year, whereby it would be possible to offer a series of events and courses which would lead to a place on a summer cathedral course, if the young singer was in the

---

[136] Richard Barnes (d.2012) was Housemaster and Master-in-Charge at over 40 RSCM courses, latterly as Director of the Girls' Course at Kingswood School in Bath for ten years. He was made ARSCM in 1995. Photos on pp. 121 and 301.
[137] See p. 146.
[138] See p. 148.

end up to that standard. The result was a pattern of three-day courses during the Christmas holiday at various centres, week-long residential courses at Easter and one-day courses on Saturdays throughout the year. This was the means of spotting local talented youngsters who could be led towards follow-up events and courses. As a back-bone to the programme of events were the Cathedral Singers' gatherings in various cathedrals throughout the country. These days also formed essential training for the summer Cathedral Course. Later on there was the Monday Choir at Addington[139] — once a fortnight to begin with — which again trained up local boys to an acceptable standard for Cathedral Courses.

Following the launch of the CTS Martin toured the country doing demonstrations of the scheme in parish churches.

Martin How's CTS demonstration at St Paul's, Porth, Rhondda November 1966

The Chorister Training Scheme was re-launched as the 'Sing Aloud' scheme in 1989 and was replaced by the current 'Voice for Life' training programme in 1999.

---

[139] See p. 55.

The Junior Travelling Choir:

The Junior Travelling Choir, set up by Martin How and using boys from local choirs in the Croydon area, was a demonstration choir travelling locally and putting on a show called 'Choristers in Action'. The idea was originally conceived as an opportunity for junior boys to come to Addington Palace to sing and, importantly, enjoy themselves, whilst also giving their choirmasters the opportunity to get together to 'talk shop'. The choirs/choirmasters involved in this venture were: Elmers End, St James (Mr Markwell), Ashstead, St George (Bernard Cookman), Merton, St Mary (Walter Taylor), Beddington, St Mary (Geoffrey Hunnisett), Bromley, St Mary (Ian Henderson), Selhurst, Holy Trinity (Graham Bill), Sutton PC (David Squibb), Downside School (Derrick Herdman) and Addiscombe, St Mildred (Geoffrey Fraser). This demonstration choir became a useful tool for presenting and explaining the new Chorister Training Scheme. No regular practices were held; the choir met as arranged. This did mean that the repertoire was not extensive. A typical music list for these events would contain responses, two single chants, one double chant, two hymns and two anthems — not yet fully learnt. Linked to this was a show entitled 'Choristers Then and Now' loosely based on Nicholson's book *Peter — The Adventures of a Chorister (SPCK)* which gives the history of choirboys from Mediæval times, the press-ganging of choristers of the Chapel Royal at the Restoration, West Gallery choirs, the Oxford Movement, up to the twentieth century. This formed a potted history of the chorister movement, with musical slots along the way.

> 'Individual boys would have a specific part, a little act of their own to play... When it came to modern times, we would demonstrate aspects of the Chorister Training Scheme. Robert Prizeman... the imaginative and highly skilled Director of the boys' choir 'Libera' adapted the idea for his own choristers and developed the whole idea.'[140]

These lecture demonstrations were not meant as recitals, but a presentation of certain aspects of choir work which, as well as being entertaining, served as an introduction to the CTS.

Right:

'Choristers Then and Now'
ca 1967

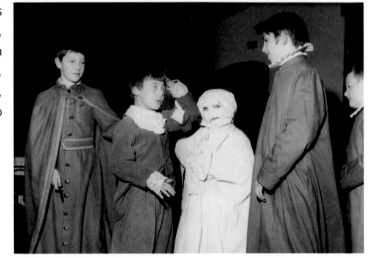

---

[140] *Unpublished Memoirs* Martin How.

Guild Choirs

Guild status choirs formed a higher level of attainment for choirs following the Chorister Training Scheme. Guild choirs were divided into St Nicolas Guild for boys' choirs and St Cecilia Guild for girls. The purpose of these guilds was to identify and recognise choirs which specialise in encouraging the training of boy or girl choristers, or both. To qualify for Guild status, a choir needed to have embraced the CTS and followed its principles, shown that the choir is able to work as an integrated team — feeling a sense of belonging to a wider fellowship (that of the RSCM and of the church as a whole) — and demonstrated that they are able to produce musical results which help the worship in their church. Choirs seeking election to the Guild were required to apply for adjudication by one of the Guild examiners, which took place in the applicant's church. The usual pattern was that the adjudicator would be present at a service, preceded by a short rehearsal of about 20 minutes. Then would follow a meeting with the choir trainer, the Head Chorister and Team Leaders and the incumbent or head teacher. The adjudicator would then submit a report to Addington who would either invite the choir to join the Guild, or advise them how they might reshape their set-up to conform to the requirements of membership. Each Guild Choir was expected to apply for re-adjudication every five years. Although we have no exact date when the scheme fell into abeyance, it was probably in the late 1980's.

Guild Advisors

Guild Advisors were appointed by the Director, in conjunction with the Headquarters Commissioner, applying a different set of criteria to the Special Commissioners. Their role was not to instruct choirs in RSCM ways, but to adjudicate choirs wishing to be elected to the Guild of St Nicolas and to give advice on the smooth operation of the Chorister Training Scheme, providing, if necessary, a demonstration of the scheme in action. It was therefore necessary for them to be choirmasters who had already demonstrated their own successful use of the CTS and been choirmasters of a Guild Choir themselves. As Sampson pointed out, 'successful Guild choirmasters are appointed rather than highly-skilled musicians though many, of course, are both; of the 35 appointed by 1967, ten were also Special Commissioners.'

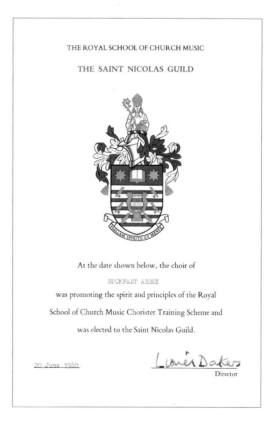

THE ROYAL SCHOOL OF CHURCH MUSIC

THE SAINT NICOLAS GUILD

At the date shown below, the choir of

BUCKFAST ABBEY

was promoting the spirit and principles of the Royal School of Church Music Chorister Training Scheme and was elected to the Saint Nicolas Guild.

20 June 1980

Director

Cathedral Singers

Cathedral Singers are first mentioned in Martin How's notebooks in September 1965, with a list of choirs to invite and the comment 'to be developed'. Saturday 8th January 1966 at Winchester Cathedral marked the first outing of CS.

Martin wrote in *RSCM News* in 1968:

'After two experimental seasons we are now able and keen to give more people the opportunity of taking part. If you are interested in furnishing a few singers (e.g. two trebles and your 'best' man) or if you would like to sing yourself, please write...

The main qualifications rest with the choirmaster concerned. He must be capable of teaching the singers the notes and of conveying the style of the music.'

It will be seen that the choice of singers and responsibility for training them fell upon the shoulders of the choir trainer. In these early days the CS sang around six times a year and in preparation for this they held three or four training days and a training weekend, much more preparation than in recent years.

Martin also wrote:

'The idea is to give an opportunity of really advanced work in a small group. Furthermore, we at the RSCM are enabled to locate talent through these events.'[141]

In 1974 singers were still auditioned annually and *PCM* in April 1974 notes that 200 singers were auditioned for the Cathedral Singers choirs 1974 season. It also noted that 'An increasing number of church music lovers have attended the cathedral services and, in a number of cases, entire choirs have travelled some distance to hear rehearsals and services. Observers at the cathedral rehearsals were welcomed.'

In May 1981 Bryan Anderson took over the Midlands Cathedral Singers begun by Martin How. It was then renamed Cathedral Singers (Midland and South West). Bryan continued to direct this until his retirement in 1996. His successor was Alan Harwood, DOM at Bishop Wordsworth's School in Salisbury who in turn was succeeded by David Ogden in 2003.

Martin How ran the Southern CS until retirement in 1992 when it was taken over by John Wardle. John Cooke ran the Northern CS until his retirement in 1993 when he was succeeded by Gordon Appleton, who, in turn, continued as Director until his own retirement in 2012.

Harry Bramma writes:

'When I arrived in 1989, the very successful Cathedral Singers, run by the Commissioners, were still for boys only. These flourished and were a much valued resource for those running boys' choirs. Though myself having long experience in running boys' choirs, I felt it was no longer possible to discriminate in this way. I therefore proposed that each of the three groups of singers should add an additional

---

[141] This was still the case around 2005 when David Ogden, Director of CS (M&SW) recruited and then 'stole' our best young singers for the RSCM's Millennium Youth Choir! [JH]

girls' section which could share the cathedral visits and actually increase the number of singing occasions. Girls could alternate with boys in the top line. During my ten years as Director this change worked well. The Regional Directors were able to search for talent when they were round their areas and enlist choir directors to take part in the scheme. The decline in boys-only choirs and the reluctance of some good boys' choirs to take part made for greater difficulty. Generally these were overcome, though some Regional Directors were, perhaps through lack of experience, less good at enthusing and training boy choristers. However, until 1998, the system was appreciated and generally was successful.'

B) Commissioners and Special Commissioners

The Chief Commissioner: Hubert Crook

The three Associate Directors appointed on the death of Sir Sydney were all busy men and although Gerald Knight extended his workload to act as both organist of Canterbury Cathedral and also Warden of the College of St Nicolas, none of the Associate Directors could possibly take on the immense task of visiting choirs formerly undertaken by Sir Sydney. In 1944 the Founder had appointed Hubert Crook as Chief Commissioner and, as Sir Sydney's health declined, Crook took on an increasing amount of the travelling to visit choirs. It was a natural consequence that, on the Founder's death, he took up the majority of this work, assisted by the appointment of Special Commissioners. He was such an important figure in RSCM history that we make no apology for presenting his life and career in some depth.

Hubert Crook was born[142] in High Wycombe, the son of a manager in the trade of furniture making, central at that time to the economy of High Wycombe. He seems to have had little formal training though he did study privately at the Tobias Matthay Pianoforte School in London. Little[143] else is known of his life until he was appointed as organist of High Wycombe Parish Church[144] in 1935, a post he held until he started work for the RSCM in 1944. By this time he had built the Wycombe choir into a skilled body of forty boys and sixteen men. He was already well-known to Sir Sydney having been a housemaster to the

---

[142] Various sources give either 1894 or 1897 as his birth year.

[143] Buckinghamshire newspapers around 1919/1920 give him as accompanist on piano and organ soloist in High Wycombe but by 1935, just prior to his move back to High Wycombe, he had a flourishing choir at St Paul's in Cliftonville, Margate.

[144] According to Bernarr Rainbow, Crook's successor at High Wycombe, the imposing church was known as 'The Cathedral of Bucks' [*Bernarr Rainbow on Music* p.54]. Rainbow also noted that the £250 p/a salary he was offered for the post was five times the average for a parish church at that time. Crook also instituted a music festival in High Wycombe which always featured the choir, ending with a Festival Evensong.

Director on every SECM course from Easter 1942 in Tenbury up to the large Durham Cathedral Course in 1944. It was shortly after this course that he was invited to leave his church and work full-time for the RSCM, though High Wycombe remained his home town and base until his death.

At Easter 1945 he returned to Tenbury to take his first course as Master-in-Charge. During the next fifteen years he would direct a further 70 courses, mostly week-long residential courses for boys, and a very large number of one-day courses. He clearly sided with Sir Sydney in the Director's view that gramophone recordings were a useful teaching aid, for the Yorkshire Evening Post for 1st December 1945 reported that he was 'using gramophone records to demonstrate points in church singing at a one-day school for choirboys held today in the St Peter's Hall of Leeds Parish Church.' Of the various RSCM residential courses he went on to make his mark, were those at St Elphin's School in Darley Dale (20 courses), at Rossall School (13) and also at the course for choirmasters and organists at Grantley Hall, Ripon (10).

In the many photographs of Crook in the RSCM archives, he appears as very severe and dour, but this belies the generosity and kindness which he bestowed upon choristers and choirs. Tony Cook[145] recalls that 'Hubert insisted on all boys wearing black shoes. In rare cases where he knew that they were not able to obtain these he would see that the boys complied by buying them shoes from his own pocket.'[146] Tony goes on to say that 'He lived at 'St Neots', Conningsby Road in High Wycombe with his sister who was a local Midwife. I remember one morning at 6.00.a.m. she rang me saying 'You have another chorister in the family Mr Cook!' ... he did have private pupils for piano and organ but certainly not enough to say that he could have lived on that. It was presumed that he had money of his own.'

In the RSCM Archive we have some of Crook's papers, lectures, correspondence and special Orders-of-Service, but not the records of his work as Chief Commissioner. Fortunately Barry Sampson's thesis helps out here.

'He made detailed records of his visits; the 75 choirs he visited from September to November 1949 contained 850 boys, 35 girls, 162 women and 475 men. Records and comments on each visit were made for filing at H.Q. [all now lost] and for the information of each choirmaster. Despite the amount of visits he made, it appears that he would have carried out even more if he had not been restricted during the summer months by refusals owing to holidays and other inconveniences. The ideal and most efficient use of his time was on such occasions when a visit was planned in minute details by the [RSCM] Representative on the spot. For example, Thomas Duerden[147] organised a visit [to Blackburn] in February 1950 and in fourteen days Crook was able to visit 44 choirs, address four Ruri-decanal Chapters and play at the

---

[145] Anthony E L Cook, Hon RSCM 1966, was Secretary of the RSCM Archdeaconry of Buckinghamshire and still lives in High Wycombe. Interview with JH 6th Dec 2014.

[146] Crook's generosity went further. Tony Cook also recalled that 'One or two of the poorer boys in the choir used to queue up for the 1d or 2d that he always gave them for their bus fares home. Not repayable!'

[147] Organist of Blackburn Cathedral from 1939 to 1965 and himself a Special Commissioner.

Diocesan Festival in the Cathedral, meeting during this time 458 boys, 38 girls, 169 women and 209 men. Late in 1950, during 53 visits to choirs ranging from Exeter to Sheffield, from Llandaff to Norwich and from Oxford to Northern Ireland, he came into contact with 632 boys, 31 girls, 125 women and 283 men, who, with the 820 who attended one gathering made a total of 1891 choristers. These figures give some idea of the enormous opportunities he had to influence choristers through his personal contact.'

Crook usually published lists of his visits in *ECM* though in later years they were not always printed depending on whether space in the magazine was tight. Between 1948 and 1950 he visited 556 choirs and then from 1951 to 1953, despite commitments at the Festival of Britain and Coronation, he managed 568 choir visits, 37 One-Day Schools, 15 Festivals and 17 addresses to clergy, organists and choirmasters. We don't know his exact date of birth, but this was certainly an enthusiastic and energetic 60 year-old in those days when most people would be considering retirement. As Tony Cook says 'Hubert Crook was a man of high principles, and single-minded regarding his aim in life. That was to train boys' voices and to forward the cause of church music

'Tommy' Duerden and Hubert Crook at AP ca 1955

in general.' This single mindedness continued until his death.

The move from Canterbury to Addington hardly affected his day-to-day work as this was mostly conducted in the provinces. He did however direct the first summer Instructional Course for Choirboys at Addington in 1954 (53 boys[148]), with Gerald Knight taking the adults on the concurrent Summer School (21 men and 14 women). In autumn 1954 he also reorganised the boys' choir at Addington, recruiting new boys for it from schools in the locality until in 1955 this task passed to Martin How on his appointment as Headquarters Choirmaster.

It was also noted by RSCM Council in 1955 that, unlike all other RSCM staff members, Crook had not received any salary increment since his appointment in 1944! This may give weight to the suggestion that he had a private income, though at Probate his effects were a mere £460. It is not widely known that, in addition to all the work already mentioned, he was

---

[148] He was assisted on this course by one housemaster, Frederick D L Penny FRCO, organist of Prittlewell Parish Church for over 50 years from 1921. Penny had been active with the SECM from 1929 and was made Hon Life RSCM in 1965.

the RSCM Advisor on organs[149]. Initially this service was provided free of charge by the RSCM to affiliated churches but churches were invited to give the collection at the opening recital or service to the RSCM. In late 1956 Council decided that the increasing number of requests for organ advice had reached a level where it would be necessary to make a charge and a scale of fees was issued.

In order to give a picture of how hard he drove himself in later years, it is worth examining just one year's activities: in 1956 Crook visited at least 159 choirs and heard four choirs at Addington, directed 19 One-Day Schools for singers, organists, choirmasters or clergy, three evening schools for boys, was master-in-charge at seven residential courses, conducted 13 festivals and gave seven lectures. This is an impressive and somewhat daunting list of engagements by any standard. However, in the spring of 1958 he suffered a heart attack in Blackburn, and as a consequence, took things a little easier for a while. By 1959[150] he had resumed his previous work load but in 1960 he had a further heart attack in March and died on September 13th 1960 aged (about) 65. Barry Sampson commented that:

> 'Sydney Nicholson used to claim that he probably knew more choirboys than did anyone else in this country. There is little doubt that Hubert Crook surpassed him, having visited more choirs, run more courses and conducted more One-Day Schools than anyone else. His choir-training was an inspiration to others and his efforts in spreading the influence of the RSCM everywhere was prodigious and he literally worked himself to a standstill, as Sir Sydney had done before him.'

Martin How recalls how much he, along with countless others, owed to Hubert Crook, after observing his special talent for working with youngsters, and also for his general kindness and encouragement. A memorial appeal was launched in 1961 which, by June of that year, had already reached £1,285[151].

There seemed to be no obvious 'successor in waiting' and, despite advertising the post of Staff Commissioner, no-one of sufficient calibre and vocation came forward and so RSCM Council decided in June 1961 that 'after careful consideration the Council has decided not to proceed with the appointment of a Staff Commissioner.' Though no precise reason was given for this, Sampson's suggestion that 'it is highly probable that the Council were unable to offer an adequate salary to a suitable candidate' seems credible.

Between Crook's death and 1964, when Martin How became Headquarters Commissioner, visits to choirs did not cease. Gerald Knight took on some, but the task was mainly devolved to the ever growing number of Special Commissioners.

---

[149] Following his death this role was taken on by the eminent authority Dr W L Sumner AKC, FLS, FIMIT, FRSCM of Nottingham University, who served as organ advisor to the RSCM from 1960 until 1972.
[150] During 1959 he took his 100th Choristers' Course, those being over 15 years of service.
[151] Originally intended for young musicians with talent, especially those who wanted to be organists and choirmasters, the fund later provided grants for students attending RSCM Residential Courses. With shrewd investment it stood at £66,000 by the end of 2000.

RSCM Special Commissioners

'Special' in the sense that they were part-time (like Special Constables in the police force) these Commissioners were either unpaid or received a small honorarium together with expenses. Considering that most of the Special Commissioners were eminent musicians in their own right, their remuneration was basically negligible, but their sense of vocation was strong.

The 'Warrant of Commission[152]' each received on appointment commissioned them to 'give assistance to members and to help them put into practice the Principles and Recommendations of the RSCM by giving advice, conducting festivals, lecturing, instructing choirs, congregations and individuals and by doing everything in accordance with the policy laid down by the Council.'

The first three were appointed in 1947: Thomas Duerden of Blackburn Cathedral, Leonard Blake, Director of Music at Malvern School, and Sidney Campbell, then organist of St Peter's in Wolverhampton and also Sub-Warden of the College of St Nicolas. Tommy Duerden was especially busy, averaging almost 70 choir visits a year for the next six years.

During this era it was expected that part of the role of a cathedral organist was to improve church music in his own diocese, and many did so with enthusiasm. However, it was not only cathedral organists and their assistants who took on this RSCM role for there were many organists and choirmasters of considerable standing, both in parishes and amongst school directors of music fully capable of shouldering the responsibility.

Records of commissioners' visits were kept at headquarters but sadly these are now lost. We know from *ECM* that by 1959, when there were 20 Special Commissioners active, 7,000 choir visits had taken place since these first began in 1935. By 1970, when there were 106[153] Special Commissioners (30 of them abroad[154]), the 11,000th choir visit was reached[155].

One snapshot of activity was given in a letter to Representatives by Leslie Green in July 1959:

> 'CHOIR VISITS. During the past twelve months (to 30th June 1959), 435 visits were paid by Special Commissioners and another 100 by the Director and Chief Commissioner. They were paid during thirty-six tours by Special Commissioners, as well as on a number of individual dates.'

---

[152] Printed warrants were only issued after 1964 and were also sent to all the different categories of Representatives setting out precisely what duties would be required of each holder. They were for three years in the first instance after which 'advice was taken about re-appointment' — an early example of peer-review.

[153] BNS reports that 'In 1970 of the 76 Special Commissioners in the United Kingdom, 54% held positions in Cathedrals, University Colleges or Royal Chapels, 25% were parish church organists and 23.7% held music posts in education. It will be appreciated that where Commissioners are known to fall into more than one category they have been included in both.'

[154] Canada 8, Australia 9, New Zealand 7 and South Africa 6.

[155] This was by GHK to St Mary Magdalene in Albrighton, near Wolverhampton.

These visits were spread over most of England. Some visits were in Wales and Scotland but none in Ireland during that year.

In addition to visiting choirs, the commissioners also conducted festivals, directed three-day, one-day and half-day courses as well as residential courses. After the introduction of the Chorister Training Scheme, several also used their own choirs to demonstrate how the scheme worked. Some also acted as St Nicolas Guild advisors making special assessment visits to choirs applying for Guild status.

Gerald Knight's criteria for appointing a Commissioner were four-fold. The candidate must:

1. Be a musician of some standing, having held a position and done the job well.
2. Be a man of tact, who understands other church musicians.
3. Be able to give encouragement to the choirs he visits.
4. Know clearly in his own mind the policy of the RSCM.

Sampson noted that:

'Without their help, often involving self-sacrifice to themselves and their families, the work of the RSCM in the field would collapse, for the School, without adequate numbers of permanent staff, relies on them to carry out the majority of its work outside Headquarters.'

Ian Henderson (staff 1961-65):

'My other main area of responsibility was [to organise] visits to choirs by 'Special Commissioners..' These were mostly cathedral organists and directors of music in public schools who generously gave time to the RSCM to conduct these visits. The affiliated choirs in the chosen area were invited to ask for such a visit to a practice or service, when the commissioner would hear them singing (whilst not forgetting the spoken parts of the service, deportment, etc.) and would give them helpful comments and advice for further improvement when that was felt to be needed. These visits were generally much appreciated, and choirs were often prepared to change from their usual practice evening in order for such a visit to be paid. Following the visit a written report was sent to the choir master (or choir mistress, though there were very few of them at the time) and a copy sent to Addington and kept in the choir's file. We often found that choirs were eager to invite a commissioner back for a further visit after a suitable period, to see if they had made any improvement.'

Clerical Representatives

The Clerical Representatives were appointed by Council 'where suitable men are available — clergymen to be spokesmen to their brethren in ruri-decanal chapters. Their duties are to make the work and activities of the RSCM known and to be a means of communication between the clergy and the RSCM and vice versa'[156]

From time to time before retirement, Spence wrote to all the other Clerical Representatives, sometimes with instruction and blessing, and occasionally mildly reprimanding them for not doing enough. In his July 1961 message he wrote:

'Dear Brethren,

Clerical Representatives now number about 150. They are spread rather unevenly over the dioceses of the two provinces of Canterbury and York, for no particular reason except that they are naturally more to be found where I have been able to make personal contacts...

One recently appointed Clerical Representative wrote to me a few weeks ago to say that he had visited every incumbent in his deanery to ask what they knew about the RSCM, and would they like to be linked with it. He was somewhat sad to learn that in almost every case the parish priests in his deanery of small scattered villages were not interested in our work, and saw no advantage in becoming affiliated, since there were no choirs to speak of in their churches.

I can well understand how such priests feel, but I am sure they are mistaken, and I hope that all our Clerical Representatives in such areas know enough about the work of the RSCM to be able to show how we can help them. It is important to point out that the RSCM is not solely interested in the fortunes of churches which have choirs. It is vitally concerned with the use of music in worship whatever the circumstances of the church may be.'

---

[156] *ECM* June 1959

The Clerical Commissioner: Horace Spence

Horace Spence takes Evensong in the Chapel in 1955, with his wife Marjorie kneeling

Gerald Knight wrote[157]: 'One day in 1952 I received a letter bearing the postmark Berkhamsted, Herts. It was from the Revd Horace Spence, Rector and Rural Dean of Berkhamsted, offering to serve the RSCM without payment in any way which would help the cause.' RSCM Council decided to appoint him as Clerical Commissioner and Assistant Chaplain at Addington Palace [158].

The Revd Horace Spence MA, BMus[159] began work shortly before his 60th birthday. His position was without salary, but with accommodation, storage space and services in kind supplied free of charge. He was a graduate of Christ Church, Oxford, and, in common with several other priests mentioned in these pages, he was also a music graduate before ordination training at Pusey House and Cuddesdon College in Oxford. Having served as a Vicar Choral and Chamberlain of York Minster from 1926 to 1933, he was then Vicar of St Martin's in Scarborough before moving to Berkhamsted.

[157] *PCM* Apr 1975.
[158] Appointed on 30th Sept 1952, he began work on 11th Apr 1953.
[159] b. 11th Nov 1893, Beckenham, Kent; d. December 1974, Canterbury.

He had served on the 1948 Archbishop's Committee on 'Music in Worship' and had also served on the RSCM's Musical Advisory Board since 1949. He was the author of two successful books published by the RSCM — *Decently and in Order* 1956 and *Praises with Understanding: A practical handbook for ordinands and the clergy* 1959. Not so well known are his four published musical compositions: a setting of the Evening Canticles published in 1915 before he went to university, *The Reproaches for Good Friday: A simple setting ... for singing in unison or harmony*, published shortly before he was ordained deacon in 1922, a carol: *A Cradle Song of Our Lady* published by Boosey in 1925 and the short anthem *O King most High*, published in 1947 by the RSCM in *Choir Book Ten*[160]. His other writings include *An Anglican Use, Five outlines of ceremonial*, 1930, SPCK and *Music in Children's Worship*, 1960, all from The Church Information Office.

In addition to his Addington chaplaincy work as lecturer and assisting the Warden with Chapel Services, his main outside role was 'to explain to clergy and congregations the aims and ideals of the RSCM' at deanery chapters, meetings, ruri-decanal conferences, parochial gatherings, theological colleges and at clergy refresher courses. He travelled widely in this work to far-flung corners of the Anglican Provinces of York and Canterbury with a special emphasis on areas where the RSCM's work was little known. Early on, in 1954, he had written that he had found 'A surprising lack of knowledge' about the RSCM. He also preached at Choral Festivals, both large and small. In *ECM* July 1954 he wrote about 'My First Year', with enthusiasm and missionary zeal and 'perceived the almost limitless opportunities for service which lie before the RSCM... [there is] a widespread need to secure an ever higher quality of worship.' In 1956 he wrote another report 'Two More Years' in which he said 'What is supremely encouraging is the undoubted fact that there is today a growing spirit of vitality and devotion in numberless parish churches, arising from the desire to improve their public worship — to make it more worthy, more free from unreal and old-fashioned trimmings, more reverent and seemly in outward form, more suited to the spiritual needs of present-day worshippers.' According to Sampson 'His most valuable asset was that he was a good speaker and he used this to good effect' and in Spence's obituary[161] Gerald Knight wrote:

> 'He was a man of striking presence and immense vitality, and it was not long [after appointment] before he was proclaiming far and wide the RSCM's message and advertising its wares up and down the length and breadth of the British Isles. It would be difficult to exaggerate the value of his work for church music, for members of the clergy and laity alike were quick to realise that here was one who spoke with authority and sincerity.'

---

[160] Also available separately.
[161] *PCM* Apr 1975.

In the first instance Council had offered Spence the post for five years, but they were naturally delighted when he agreed to a second five-year term in 1958. He was appointed Six Preacher[162] in Canterbury Cathedral in 1959 and the same year, recognising that his work was both valuable and impossible for one (gradually aging) person, Council decided to appoint Clerical Representatives to assist him. By 1960, in other words within one year, 60 had been appointed. In June 1962 he retired, was made Honorary Chaplain for the RSCM, and he and his wife Marjorie retired to a house in the Precincts of Canterbury Cathedral.

Martin How recalls two anecdotes about Horace Spence:

> 'Scene, Dining Hall at Addington Palace, and dinner had already started. 'Sorry to be late for dinner. Such a journey! There were two cars in front of me going so slowly. Eventually I managed to overtake the nearest one and pulled in behind the next one. It was only then that I saw the tow-rope.'

> Visiting choir of girls coming into the Palace, and Horace Spence was on the look-out for their choirmaster, to welcome them. Seeing a man with them, Horace says, 'Hello and welcome, we spoke on the phone this morning.' Marjorie (Spence) says, 'You fool Horace — that's the coach driver.'

> He also recalls that Horace had a very high-pitched voice, whereas Marjorie was very low pitched and this sometimes caused confusion when the Spence's received telephone calls.

> One person mentioned that Horace Spence could be somewhat humourless and would sometimes get the huff and become 'high church'.

> Marjorie chased him round the hall saying 'You fool Horace, you fool' if he had failed to do something and on one occasion he accidentally missed out the Benedictus in a Chapel service and she berated him — Why didn't you sing it? It's for my devotions.'

Mrs Marjorie Elizabeth Spence[163] was herself a key figure at the Palace in the organising of refreshments at the Summer Parties and November Fayres. On the Spences' departure *ECM* noted that:

> 'Several practical jobs [at Addington] she made her own. She ran the bookstall in the Great Hall and put herself out countless times in order to be at hand during a course or on occasions of an unusual influx of visitors so that the stall might be manned, publications supplied, and questions answered. Further, she was the model of a 'Choir Mother'; she kept the cassocks and surplices in tip-top order and saw that all the boys and students were fitted out properly, with the result that the choir was

---

[162] The college of Six Preachers of Canterbury Cathedral was created by Archbishop Thomas Cranmer as part of the reorganisation of the monastic Christ Church Priory into the new secular Cathedral. They were established by the Statutes of 1541 and were provided with houses in the Precincts but many became non-resident and rented out their properties. They had the right to dine with the Dean and Canons and to sit in the stalls in the quire with the canons during services. They were required to preach 20 sermons a year in their own parishes or in a church dependent on the Cathedral, as well as preaching in the Cathedral. There has been an unbroken succession of Six Preachers from 1544 to the present day. (Source: Wikipedia)

[163] Née Emson; b. 30 July 1897, Ditton Hill, Surrey; d.1st July 1981, Canterbury.

always turned out 'decently and in order'[164]. This was no mean task seeing that there were nearly one hundred boys and students to be dealt with. She also headed a small band of ladies who mended the music in the libraries at Addington.'

The *ECM* Appreciation goes on:

'The actual departure from Addington... was marked in the customary manner reserved for distinguished persons and well-loved friends. Every one available in the house takes station outside the main door of the Palace; after personal farewells and the departing friends have mounted into their vehicles, all bedlam breaks loose, each student smiting or blowing whatever musical or non-musical instrument comes to hand. The result is memorable for those who receive the treatment.'

Like the Founder, Spence had served the RSCM without a salary and the RSCM could not find funds for a paid successor. Despite advertising the post in 1963, no appointment was made.

Gerald Knight teaching in the Nicholson Practice Room ca 1956 with Horace Spence mid-picture

---

[164] It is not clear who wrote this appreciation of the Spences in *ECM* Oct 1962, but this play on words alludes to Horace Spence's book for Lay Readers with this same title.

Headquarters Commissioner: Martin How

How, Martin John Richard, MBE, MA, ARCM, LRAM, FRCO(CHM), LTCL, FGCM, FRSCM: b. 1931, Liverpool. The son of the ex-Primus of the Episcopal Church of Scotland, he was educated at Repton School and Clare College, Cambridge, where he was organ scholar. Martin then spent one term as a student at St Nicolas College in Canterbury before starting his National Service. Martin recalls that he was away at Sedgefield with the army when he was able to get special permission in the summer of 1954 to visit Addington Palace with a view to restarting his studies on completion of National Service. He arrived at Addington in January 1955, and clearly remembers the warm welcome he received, especially from Peter

White. By September of the same year he was invited to become a member of staff, taking over from Hubert Crook as Headquarters' Choirmaster. He was also organist of St John's, Selsdon, appointed in January 1958 (with the vicar acting as choirmaster) and then of St Mildred's in Addiscombe[165].

Martin started both the Chorister Training Scheme (launched in December 1965 during the St Nicolastide celebrations) and the Cathedral Singers in 1966. The CTS scheme, described in another chapter, obviously fulfilled a need, for, within a year, 2000 enquiries were received, but Martin recalls 'notwithstanding some scathing comments from senior colleagues, albeit retracted at a later date.' Ian Henderson, who worked in the RSCM office, also ran a local parish choir, and remembers that his choristers had been used as 'guinea pigs' to try out the record cards and charts which accompanied the scheme. Martin also started a Scout troop at the Palace, with Lindsay Colquhoun as Assistant Scout Master, very much following in the footsteps of Sydney Nicholson, who had recognised the value of scouting with his own choristers at the College of St Nicolas, Chislehurst. Martin then briefly sought pastures new, taking the post of Organist and Choirmaster at Grimsby Parish Church, which had a choir school attached, from the summer of 1961[166]. However, by August 1964, he was back at the Palace having been offered the post of Headquarters Commissioner, and then in January 1968, as Headquarters Choirmaster — once again. In September 1970 he was able to resume his duties as Headquarters Commissioner when Colin Yorke was appointed Resident Choirmaster. In 1971 Martin was appointed Commissioner for the South and he retired from this role at the end of August 1992, though continued in the part-time (3 days a week) role as Special Advisor. He had previously

---

[165] His last service there was Easter Day, 17th Apr 1960, but he continued a close relationship with the church in later years, using the church for concerts and RSCM courses.

[166] MJRH visited Grimsby on 1st/2nd September to see John Hoggett, the vicar, and Dennis Townhill, the [leaving] organist. He began work there in the following week.

moved out of AP in 1989 into his own flat. His final 'retirement' was in April 1994, but he still lives in his South Croydon flat and maintains strong links with Croydon Parish Church (now Croydon Minster). In his fulsome appreciation of Martin's contribution to the RSCM when he retired from being Southern Commissioner, Lionel Dakers — as well as detailing his skills as both choir trainer and composer — goes on to mention Martin's great sense of humour: ... many of us will particularly remember him as an accomplished mimic, especially over the bar at Addington when, after a drink or two, he would take off well-known church musicians, making them audibly and visually almost larger than life.'[167]

Paul Spicer (1970/71):

'I was very fortunate to travel with Martin How playing the organ for a number of his RSCM festivals in different parts of the country. I learned so much about choir training skills from observing his purposeful and always intensely musical rehearsals laced with his inimitable humour. How many times did we see him pretending to be in a lift at a door which had a window in it. Ducking down and gradually lifting himself up making wonderfully silly faces in the process. Childlike humour but infectious and, of course, wonderful with children.'

Michael Smith (1955/56) mentioned:

'Martin's lectures were always challenging and his choir training so effective: he would have us always play legato with that onward movement that he loved — and it has stuck with me. He crossed my path again later when I was in Lincoln and he was organist of St Mary's in Grimsby. He was a very generous Christian — I am sure he still is — and there will not be many of us who left his car open at nights to provide shelter for one or other of the men of the road!'

Martin Roberts (1960/62) recalled that Martin kindly lent him his Morris 8 car on more than one occasion.

Following his retirement in 1992, Her Majesty the Queen Mother wrote to congratulate and thank Martin How for his work and he was made MBE in the 1993 New Year Honours List for his 'Services to Church Music'.

Martin in the Robing Room with probationers ca 1956

---

[167] *CMQ* July 1992. Martin's skill in mimicry remains today and a CD exists with the 'voices' of Sir William Harris, Horace Spence, Gerald Knight and others telling tales of Addington.

C) External RSCM Courses 1954-1995

The external activities of the RSCM in the early post-war years were dominated by Festivals, but the Courses Register shows that 102 external courses were organised between 1940 and 1953 and that during this time several important regular venues were used which were to set a pattern for the future.

1) Residential

Courses for children were necessarily during school holidays and a scheme was soon developed whereby residential courses were held after Christmas or over the New Year, at Easter and in the summer. From the 1960's regular shorter weekend courses were also held at Whitsun and in the October half-term. *ECM* in 1949 summarised the aims of residential courses and these continued throughout the Addington years. They were: to develop a sense of leadership and of responsibility through self-discipline, and a system of House Captains who are responsible for the day-to-day running of the course. The houses consist of about 20 boys each and are in competition with each other. Each house has a 'duty' service giving the other boys the advantage of being able to listen critically. Each house also has a Housemaster who is an expert choir-trainer and who is chosen by the Master-in-Charge. A Chaplain is always attached to care for the boys' spiritual welfare, again generally one who understands boys. Perhaps the most characteristic feature of these courses is the aim to give intensive training in the practical work of a chorister. Pressure is applied for a considerable time during each day at practices, services and training periods, though for short lengths at a time. The day was long and tiring with a typical timetable of:

Morning		Afternoon & Evening	
7.30	Rise	2.00	Recreation
8.00	Breakfast	3.15	Instruction 4
8.35	Dorm inspection	4.15	Chapel practice in robes
8.50	Full assembly	5.30	Tea
9.30	Instruction 1	6.30	Evensong
10.10	Instruction 2	7.30	Recreation
11.10	Instruction 3	9.00	Snacks
11.45	Procession practice	9.30	Trebles' lights out
12.00	Full rehearsal in robes	10.15	Seniors' lights out
1.00	Lunch		

The difficulty of the work, the standards expected and the amount of music sung increases as the week goes by. Each chorister returns home with a written report for his choirmaster.

Gerald Knight considered the residential chorister courses very important and that 'More permanent and beneficial results have come from them than from any other RSCM activity.'

The cost of a 7 day residential course for a chorister in 1967 was £8-8-0 (about £140 today). In 1968 it was estimated that over 3000 boys and girls attended the residential and three-day courses (1584 at residential) and by 1970 course attendance had reached over 4000 (2261 residential). Several of the regular annual courses deserve special mention.

Rossall School, Fleetwood

By 1954, the annual Easter course at Rossall School in Fleetwood, Lancashire was well established. The first Rossall Course was held in 1947 with 125 boys directed by Sir Sydney and Hubert Crook with a staff consisting of Leonard Blake, Peter Burton, Edred Wright and J Escombe. It proved to be the last course directed by Sir Sydney. He was not well during that first week of April and, after driving to his home in Woodchurch, Kent, he suffered a minor stroke. He was well enough to attend two festival services in Canterbury Cathedral, but had a further stroke, was admitted to Ashford Hospital and died just six weeks after directing the Rossall Course.

For 14 of the Rossall courses (and also 14 of the Darley Dale courses below) Charles Bryars, Special Commissioner and organist of Chesterfield Parish, was either director or a housemaster. Sampson notes that:

'Part of its [the Rossall course] popularity was due to the personality of the master-in-charge... He was noted for his sense of humour which was guaranteed to make the difficult communal practices enjoyable. Without it many boys would probably have been depressed, especially in view of the icy weather often experienced at Easter. Mr Bryars was in charge [at Rossall] from 1962 to 1968 when GHK directed the largest course ever held up to that time.'

Procession at Rossall School in 1951

163

Above: Rossall Course with Hubert Crook. Below: Rossall Chapel, 1958 Course

Until 1956 the course attracted a similar number of boys, and then attendance began to slowly increase so that during the 15 year period between 1958 and 1972 a total of 3344 boys attended, an average of 223 boys (i.e. juniors and ex-trebles) each year, with a peak in 1968 of 285. Caring for, feeding, entertaining and teaching this number of boys, whose ages ranged from 10 to 20, was a major achievement. For this 1968 course GHK (the course director) enlisted the help of no less than 12 housemasters – Cecil Adams, Peter White, Martin How, Russell Missin, David Harding, Keith Rhodes, William Snowley, Keith Burton-Nickson, John Rippin, L G Fosdyke, Clifford Hartley and Philip Cooper. Some of the early Rossall Courses included a new feature which was a feature of some courses for a few years but did not subsequently catch on. This was a written test at the end of the course, adjudicated by an independent person. We doubt this was very popular with the boys!

The Director of Music of Rossall Junior School was Keith Burton-Nickson (1925-2014) who was also an RSCM Special Commissioner[168]. He only participated as housemaster on this, his home territory, on three occasions, but altogether he was housemaster on 18 RSCM courses and directed a further 18, notably establishing the Lincoln Cathedral Girls' Course mentioned below.

The Rossall courses continued[169] until 2001 when it was decided that the facilities there, apart from the marvellous great Chapel, were not ideal and numbers generally were falling. The following year this course moved to Pocklington, east of York. The demise of this 54-year enterprise was looked upon with sadness by many.

King's College, Taunton

At Easter in 1954 GHK directed an 'Instructional Course for Choirboys' at King's College in Taunton, little knowing that this would become a major and regular event until 1975[170]. Over 3000 boys attended these courses which, in the later years, attracted over 200 boys at a time. A senior house was present so a full repertoire of SATB music could be learnt. Directors of this course included GHK (twice), Frederic Waine (5 times), Martin How (6 times), Harold Dexter (twice) and Anthony Lewis (twice).

Dauntsey's School, Devizes

The large Easter Taunton course moved to Dauntsey's School in Market Lavington near Devizes in 1975 and continued there annually until 1982[171], directed each year by Martin How. As at Taunton, there was a senior house of 'ex-trebles' to provide for SATB singing.

Numbers at this course remained consistently high[172] peaking in 1979 when 247 boys attended. On all of these courses there were enough boys to warrant 8-10 housemasters.

---

[168] A former assistant organist at Carlisle Cathedral (1940-1945), he was made Hon RSCM in 1971.

[169] There were three years where the school was not available and the course moved elsewhere. During the time frame of this book, 1979 was one such year when the course was held at the Royal School in Wolverhampton.

[170] An outbreak of sickness at the Easter course caused them to look for an alternative venue.

[171] The school started to divide up the dormitory areas in preparation for admitting girls, which meant a drop in the numbers who could be accommodated and so another venue was sought.

Haileybury College, Hertford

In 1983 a 'big Easter Course' was held at Haileybury College near Hertford. This proved to be a successful and popular venue and thereafter became the main Easter course, continuing with Martin How as director until he retired and then with his successor John Wardle for 1993 and 1994.

In 1990 a Girls' Residential Easter Course was started at Addington under the direction of Karen Brown. With the Palace closing down, this moved to Bloxham School near Banbury in 1994. In 1995 the Haileybury boys' course also moved to Bloxham and the boys' and girls' courses ran side-by-side.

St Elphin's School, Darley Dale

Situated near Matlock (and so sometimes called the 'Matlock' course) St Elphin's School was founded in Warrington in 1844. In 1904 the school purchased a 50-acre parkland site on which was a hotel/spa known as the Darley Dale Hydropathic Establishment, which offered a 'Mild Water Cure'. The Hydro was effectively a high-class hotel, sumptuously furnished and with many facilities such as stables, golf, fishing, tennis, billiards and even an ice house. The school was originally a boarding school for girls, daughters of Anglican clergy, and amongst its more famous alumni was author Richmal Crompton (1890-1969) of *Just William* fame. It continued as a school until financial problems led to its closure in 2005. It is now a luxury retirement village.

Procession from the Chapel at St Elphin's School

The RSCM courses at Darley Dale began in 1950[173] and, from then until 1957, two courses a year were held (for boys), one at New Year and the other in the summer. Over this period 1490 boys (juniors and seniors) attended under the direction of Hubert Crook who was course

---

[172] 1977 208 boys; 1978 225; 1979 247; 1980 235 and 1982 224. In 1981 the Easter course was held at Sherborne School.

[173] According to Hubert Crook in *ECM* Apr 1950, this first course at St Elphin's School was arranged 'through the good offices of a friend of the RSCM' and the Headmistress, Miss Stopford, and her staff were clearly very helpful in what was presumably their own holiday.

director for all of these years. An experiment was tried in 1954 where a junior house (22 boys aged 10/11) was added to the usual treble house (86 boys aged 11+) and a senior house for ex-trebles (23 boys aged 14 to 20). By 1957 numbers at the New Year course were falling, and so from 1958 there were still two courses a year but they were both held 'back-to-back' in the summer. Over the next seven or eight years numbers held up with between 90 and 120 boys at each course. From 1960 a 'Summer School for Adults' was added to coincide with one of the boys' weeks and this gave extra ATB to the large number of boys attending. This Summer School, for choirmasters and with an emphasis on practical choir-training, was initiated because the regular summer Addington course for choirmasters was greatly oversubscribed. However numbers were small for the adult school (around 20 p/a) and it was discontinued after 1965.

1966 was to be a milestone for the RSCM in that the first ever 'Instructional Course for Choirgirls'[174] was held in place of one of the boys' courses. John Brough[175] was Master-in-Charge and his wife acted as Matron. 101 girls attended, so definitely a success, and the boys' numbers were up to 155 because they all had to be accommodated within a single one week's course instead of two courses. From 1967 therefore, it was decided to have three Darley Dale courses, two for the boys, as before, and a separate girls' course. This pattern continued until 1981 when the number of boys (123) was falling and one of the boys' courses was discontinued. The two other courses continued until 1989 and thereafter Kingswood School in Bath became the main summer venue for girls and boys. The two courses ran consecutively until such time as the number of boys was too small to make their own course viable and the two courses combined.

Anita Banbury (1963-66):

'In an extra 4th year I enrolled in two strands of the Addington course, choir training and organ accompaniment. In addition I walked up the hill each Friday to the 'Selsdon Afternoon Townswomens' Guild' (who rehearsed in the morning) and trained their choir. Another student came too to play the piano. It was at this stage I started my Chorister Course experiences — Bedford (3-day) and Darley Dale (residential). I was the youngest House Mistress on the first Darley Dale Course for girls. It was decided to run it exactly like the Boys' Courses until it needed altering! We learned that boys after a day of singing would let off steam outside with physical activity whereas girls tended to wilt visibly. I had a great House Captain (Marion Letter I think her name was) who had the ability to bring out the very best in every one she was with. House staff looked after the pocket money in those days; I remember sitting up late one night balancing the books and being 3d out. Finally I decided to call it a day, picked up the blue bag, and found a threepenny bit. I also (aged little more than the oldest on the course) escorted a party of choristers on the train from King's Cross (was it, or St Pancras?) and this involved a change at Matlock. I would

---

[174] There had been a non-residential 'Three Day Course' for boys and girls at Mansfield the previous December.
[175] A former Warden of the College of St Nicolas in Canterbury.

NOT do that in this day and age! Staff were served cups of tea several times a day, I think it was seven if you included meal times.'

Above: Darley Dale undated, boys taking written exams

Below: Darley Dale 1966, the first RSCM Girls' Residential Course

Cathedral Courses

For SHN and GHK the summer Cathedral Courses, from the very first in 1942 at Gloucester, were of great importance and represented the pinnacle of RSCM work each year. The 1949 Annual Report stated that 'These Cathedral Courses serve a definite purpose in that they are a natural climax to which all Instructional Courses lead. They provide the one occasion during the year when RSCM principles may be seen and heard in operation for a fortnight,[176] they prove that teenagers are capable of really excellent work in singing the underparts of the music, and solve the problem of providing Cathedrals with a competent choir during the holiday period.' The course members were selected by housemasters from other courses and also recommended by the Special Commissioners on their travels. The ATB in some of the earlier Cathedral courses were chosen from Public Schools but eventually most ATB were experienced ex-trebles who were also selected from courses. Starting during WWII it was the normal practice of the BBC to broadcast a Choral Evensong from these Cathedral Courses[177] and some of these we still have as recordings. Sometimes, as during the Canterbury Cathedral Course in 1984, two recordings of different Evensongs were made for transmission at a later date.

The first Cathedral Course organised from Addington was at Norwich in 1954. GHK was organist and housemaster to the seniors, while 8 altos, 9 tenors and 14 basses supported the 30 trebles. Edred Wright directed (his last Cathedral Course) and the Precentor of Norwich Cathedral remarked that it 'far surpassed 1945 in musical quality'.[178]

From 1955 GHK directed a course every summer until 1972[179] when Martin How, John Bertalot and Michael Fleming became regular directors. In 1966 both the summer Cathedral courses were held in succession at Westminster Abbey in their 900th Anniversary Year, thus providing high quality choral services for a whole month in the peak tourist season. After the appointment of John Cooke as Northern Commissioner he and Martin How, the Southern Commissioner, directed most of the Cathedral Courses from 1976 until the early 1990's. During most of this era one course was at Canterbury and the other in the North or West or Wales. The peak of these courses was during the years 1968 to 1981 when three Cathedral Courses were run each year except for 1973 when there were four courses and 1975 when

---

[176] The courses were of two weeks' duration except that the 1951 course at Westminster Abbey was extended to three weeks as part of the Festival of Britain. See Chapter VI (F).

[177] The Norwich course, held from 6th to 20th August in 1945, coincided with the end of the war in the East, and the choir, who had broadcast evensong on Tuesday, suddenly found themselves contributing to a Service of National Thanksgiving, broadcast nationwide by the BBC at 9.30 the following Sunday morning. Among the trebles taking part on this course was a young Martin How. Two days' VJ holiday had been declared, but not for the choir, who carried on with the cathedral services. The October issue of English Church Music records that 'It was not easy to enjoy a well-earned rest at night as loudspeakers just outside the dormitories relayed music for dancing in the streets which went on until the early hours punctuated by frequent fireworks and accompanied by displays of lamp-post acrobatics.' Cyril Taylor's annotated transcript of the service makes emotional reading even today.

[178] *ECM* Oct 1954.

[179] Except 1967 and 1970.

there were five[180]. In addition to BBC broadcasts from the Cathedral Courses, it was commonplace for the course choir to give recitals, often in local parish churches, but sometimes in more prestigious places, such as 1969 when the Norwich course with John Bertalot gave a recital in King's College, Cambridge.

PCM July 1972 mentions that the RSCM Cathedral Courses since 1942 have been populated by invited singers. 'The growing number of invitations from cathedrals means that there are extra places to be filled and that Martin How and Geoffrey Barber will for the first time be holding auditions in September 1972 for the 1973 courses.' The 1972 courses were held in Coventry, Wells and Canterbury during July and August. Note that in this era each of the three courses contributed a broadcast Evensong on Radio 3.

These summer courses invariably made a financial loss. It was thought imperative that the level of fees charged would not be too high to discourage the less well-off and, although bursaries (mostly funded through legacies) were, and still are, available for residential courses, some degree of subsidy was usually necessary. In 1976 Council provided a subsidy of £9517 for the external courses and from that time the Cathedral Courses were also slimmed down to 12 days[181]. From 1982, Rediffusion PLC (sponsor of the Chorister of the Year awards since 1975) gave a grant specifically for Cathedral Courses with a promise of similar sums in the next three years. Despite the disappearance of Rediffusion, the parent company BET expressed its intention of continuing the financial support of the Cathedral Courses and certainly, as late as 1992, £5000 p.a. was shown in the annual accounts.

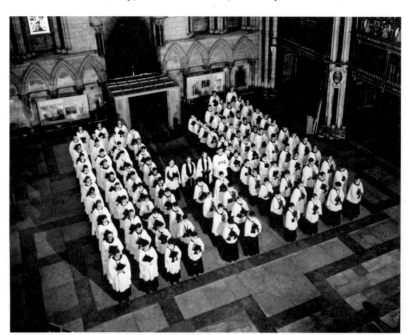

Precision line-up at the York Cathedral Course 1967

---

[180] 1973: Oxford, Ely, Exeter and Canterbury — 159 singers in total. 1975: Bath, Lincoln, Chichester, Canterbury and the new adult course at Salisbury — see below. No 1975 figures for attendance are available.

[181] They are now just one week.

GHK leads the Procession on the Lincoln Cathedral Course 1955

Rochester Cathedral Course 1960

Norwich Cathedral Course 1954

Durham Cathedral Course 1965

Toronto 1963

During 1963 the pattern of Cathedral Courses was broken. The Lambeth Conferences, convened by the Archbishop of Canterbury, have been held every ten years since 1948[182]. Mid-way between the 1958 and 1968 conferences an extra Anglican Congress was called from 13th to 23rd August in Toronto[183] with the theme 'The Church's Mission to the World.' In May 1962, the Bishop of Toronto (Rt Revd Frederick Wilkinson, 1896-1980), invited the RSCM to hold their summer Cathedral Course during the August Congress the following year. RSCM affiliations in North America and world-wide had been rising rapidly, indeed they had trebled from 500 to 1500 during the years 1955 to 1962, partly due to GHK's overseas trips. RSCM Council saw this as an excellent opportunity to publicise and strengthen the RSCM's work, especially with 16,000 Anglicans from 17 churches worldwide attending. It was decided to accept the offer. GHK would be the director, John Dykes Bower of St Paul's Cathedral, long-standing friend of the RSCM and Council member, would be the organist and RSCM Chairman of Council the Rt Revd Edward Roberts, Bishop of Kensington, would be the Chaplain and Precentor. John Bertalot and Martin How went as housemasters, staff member Ian Henderson went as choir librarian and the RSCM also took along a display of both publicity material and publications supervised by Captain Rivers and Dorothy Yorke. At Easter 1963 a three-day residential course for the 60 singers (boys and young men) to prepare was held at Addington. Each day was divided into eight practice sessions of 45-60 minutes, a tiring regime for adults let alone young boys.

Leslie Green organised the whole thing and Mrs Green would be going along as Matron. The idea was to charter a plane to transport the 60 strong choir, staff and nearly 40 relations and RSCM members across the Atlantic. Green visited Toronto in November 1962 to meet the committee responsible for looking after the choir[184]. It seems that chartering a plane was not a straightforward matter for both BOAC and IATA had rules and regulations about which kind of organisations might be 'charter-worthy', to use Green's terminology. He went on to report:

'I agreed that we should restrict membership of the charter party to personal subscribing members of the RSCM. When the question of boys was considered, any member of an affiliated choir was not considered to be a sufficiently identifiable part of the RSCM, and such a grouping might well take the acknowledged membership beyond the limit of 20,000 as laid down in IATA rules. There are five persons on our list of potential passengers whom we should all consider to be members of the RSCM but who do not satisfy the point made above. I propose that we treat them as it has been agreed to treat the boys who join the party — register them as members under Article 5h.'

---

[182] There have been 14 in total; the first was in 1867.
[183] It was the second Anglican Congress; the first was held in 1954 in Minneapolis, MN. An appropriate coincidence is that Toronto is an Indian name which means 'place of meeting'.
[184] In the accounts there was no mention of accommodation or meal costs. It seems likely that choir members were looked after through local generosity.

There were also insurance and coaches to arrange and so, after some shrewd negotiations, a BOAC Britannia was chartered for £7008 and 104 passengers (mostly paying £80 a ticket) set off in August. On arrival the choir joined up with twenty further singers, a mixture of choristers from the USA and Canada and former Addington students now living in Canada.

Gerald Knight rehearsing for the Toronto trip Easter 1963

Roy Massey also got to sing at the 1963 Toronto Anglican Congress:

'They [the RSCM] also invited anyone interested to go along as camp followers. I was interested and duly signed on as I relished the idea of a visit to Canada with some music thrown in. On arrival I discovered the hotel allocated to the camp followers was not particularly pleasant and somewhere along the line I bewailed this fact to Martin How. He, lovely man, came back shortly afterwards with the news that there was a spare bed available and would I like to sleep in it. More than that, would I like to be an extra bass in the choir? They found me a cassock and surplice and I jumped at the idea and had a wonderful time for the next three weeks.'

Above: Gerald Knight singing along in Toronto 1963

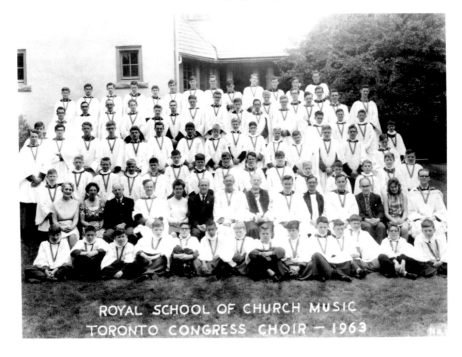

ROYAL SCHOOL OF CHURCH MUSIC
TORONTO CONGRESS CHOIR — 1963

In addition to participating in the opening and closing services of the Congress, the RSCM choir sang daily in St James' Cathedral on weekdays[185]. The UK singers also sang either services or recitals in St James' Cathedral in Hamilton, Ontario; St Paul's, London, Ontario; St George's Cathedral in Kingston, Ontario; at Christ Church Cathedral in Ottawa; St Matthew's Church in Ottawa and Christ Church Cathedral in Montréal. The repertoire was chosen to represent all periods of the English cathedral tradition including works by 20C composers — Howells and Britten as well as American Leo Sowerby and Canadian Healey Willan. In April 1963 Willan[186] suffered from a heart attack but he recovered to specially compose a newly-commissioned anthem *O Praise the Lord*, sung by a combined choir of 1000 voices at the opening service of the Congress on 13th August in Maple Leaf Gardens[187], Toronto. During the Congress, Willan occupied a seat of honour as 'Hon Director of the Music Council of the Anglican Congress.' The Archbishop of Canterbury Michael Ramsey wrote to the RSCM to say that 'those who attended the Congress would have amongst their most vivid and happy memories the services in St James' Cathedral. It is on occasions such as these that, with the accumulated expertise of many years, the RSCM excels itself and exerts an influence for good, which cannot be measured by ordinary standards.'

The trip was also a financial success in that the final balance sheet showed a surplus of just under £400.

Lincoln Courses

From 1965 to 1971 there was a boys' course (about 40 boys) held in Lincoln, based at the Old Palace and with some singing in the Cathedral. From 1972 to 1974 this was replaced with a general 'course for singers' but an important change was then made in 1975 when a Girls' Cathedral Course was inaugurated. Girls were recommended from other courses and from the Cathedral Singers groups. These courses were mainly directed by Keith Burton-Nickson, Mervyn Byers, Peter Smith and Martin Bussey. To begin with, adult TB were selected to support the girls, but from 1990 (male) adult ATB were sought. A further change after 1996 was to restrict all parts on the course to 'Young experienced male and female choristers aged 16-30.'

St David's College, Lampeter

St David's University College, to give its correct name in the 1970's, was opened in 1827 and received a charter to award degrees the following year. It functioned mainly as a theological college training clergy but gradually the proportion of ordination candidates to ordinary students declined until clergy training ceased in 1978. Now part of the University of Wales, an annual summer residential course for boys was started there in 1960 directed by Anthony Lewis, sub organist of Llandaff Cathedral[188]. This course continued until 1976

---

[185] The resident choir sang at the weekends.

[186] He was made FRSCM in May 1963, amongst the first batch to receive this honour.

[187] Maple Leaf Gardens was not an outdoor venue but a historic building built in 1907 as a 'cathedral' for ice hockey. In 1963 it could accommodate over 14,000 people.

[188] Vivian Anthony Lewis (1926-2006), known as 'V' or Tony to his friends, taught at the Welsh College of Music and Drama in Cardiff from 1950 to 1990 and was a leading light in the Llandaff Festival.

though the venue was used again for three years from 1985 to hold an adult course for organists, choirmasters and singers organised by Bryan Anderson.

Kingswood School, Bath

The first Bath Summer School was held at Kingswood School[189] in Lansdown, Bath during the summer of 1974 under the direction of Michael English and from then flourished annually[190]. After a peak in the 1980's with three courses p/a (one week for girls and one week for boys run simultaneously with an adult course) the numbers of choristers have slowly declined but a single joint summer course for boys and girls still continues to this day, with a strong emphasis on the young, including scholarships for young organists. Directors from the 1980's included Michael English, John Flower, Peter Smith, Bryan Anderson, Alan Harwood, Nigel Argust, Richard Barnes, Martin Schellenberg and Geoff Weaver. There are no early photographs of the Bath Course; below is the 2003 course.

Bath Course 2003 lined up for an outdoor vestry prayer with Director Geoff Weaver

Camping Courses

Sydney Nicholson promoted a number of camping opportunities both for scouts and choirboys, the latter camps including singing as well as outdoor activities. He had provided a camp at Rhyl in 1909 for his Manchester Cathedral choristers, and another at Bow Brickhill for his Westminster choristers and later used by SECM choristers[191]. The camping idea was resurrected in 1949 by the Vicar of Heacham, Revd R P Pott, in Norfolk who, with the collaboration of the RSCM, organised a summer camp on Heacham Beach, still a popular site for camping and caravans. The first camp ran through virtually the whole of the school summer holidays from 28th July to 6th September 1949. During that time around 500 boys attended in batches. The camp held 100 boys under canvas and groups attended for a period of a fortnight at a time. They sang regular services in St Mary's, Heacham, and

---

[189] The school was founded by John Wesley and was established to provide an education for the sons of Methodist clergymen.
[190] Apart from 1979 when the school was unavailable and The Royal School in Bath was used instead.
[191] Details and photographs of these in *SNCSN* and *SNMOM*.

others in the cathedrals at Norwich and Peterborough. The idea was repeated for two more years then seemed to run out of steam.

In 1953 the idea was tried again at Tarporley Camp near Chester catering for just 56 boys. It was organised by the Rector of Tarporley and musically directed by Hubert Crook with some services sung in Chester Cathedral. This project also ran for three years.

In the summer of 1961 a one-off Choir Camp was held at Broomlee Camp at West Linton just 14 miles from Edinburgh directed by Donald Leggat, but the following year at Whitsuntide a shorter (one week) camp was run at St Asaph Cathedral by Geoffrey Barber and this seemed to hit the spot, running annually until at least 1975 with numbers averaging about 80 boys. Services were sung in the cathedral, and other directors of the course include David Patrick and Roy Massey.

Tarporley Camping Course 1953

TARPORLEY CAMP COURSE
AUGUST 1953

'LET US WITH A GLADSOME MIND!"

Above: Hubert Crook and James Levett resting

Below: St Asaph camping course 1963, although some might suggest
that this does not appear like camping as we understand it today!

St Asaph Camping Course 1971. Graham Elliot (aka Rasputin!) fires a question

Dean Close School, Cheltenham

A one-week summer residential Instructional Course for Choirboys was held in Dean Close School in 1960 directed by Cecil Adams[192]. Initially with numbers of around 90, it slowly increased in size to 226 boys and ten Housemasters in 1972. Geoffrey Barber and Frederic Waine were also regular directors on this course. Latterly, a summer school for adults was held in conjunction with this course.

The 'Special Choir' on the 1970 course at Dean Close with Geoffrey Barber

---

[192] Cecil Sclanders Adams MRCVS (1913-1983), a vet by profession, was organist of Dursley Parish Church and Diocesan Organ Advisor to the Gloucester Diocese. He was a stalwart supporter of the RSCM and one of the first batch of musicians to be awarded the Hon RSCM when it was started in 1964.

Adult courses

Before the move to Addington, two regular adult courses had started at Dillington House in Ilminster, Somerset, and at Grantley Hall[193] near Ripon.

The Dillington House course was for all church musicians including singers and clergy. It was a more general musical training experience and at first was held in the summer. Advertising for this course tended to wax lyrical about enjoying a nice summer break in idyllic Somerset. Apart from the first three years with over 30 attendees, it was generally a small group of between 15 and 25. After a lapse, this course enjoyed a revival in the 1980's with Lionel Dakers taking the first one at Easter 1980. The then newly-appointed Commissioner for the Midlands and South West, Bryan Anderson, made this regular Easter course very much his own and developed it successfully until his retirement in 1996.

DILLINGTON HOUSE, SOMERSET

Dillington House, a 16C house, was the country residence of King George III's Prime Minister, Lord North, and was rebuilt in the late 19C. From 1950 it became a residential adult education centre run by Somerset District Council and the first RSCM course there was in 1952 directed by Leonard Blake. It is still open as a college, wedding venue and centre for the arts.

---

[193] Grantley Hall, so named after the family who built it in the 17C, was used as a convalescent hospital in WWII and then passed to West Riding County Council who used it as a residential adult education college. It changed hands in 1974 about the time the RSCM courses there ended and changed hands again in 2006 to become a private residence.

Hubert Crook and Gerald Knight at Grantley Hall 1955

Grantley Hall Adult College, Ripon

From 1950 until 1963 the Grantley Hall course, mainly aimed at organists and choirmasters, was held at Whitsun, but thereafter it was moved to the summer, continuing until 1975. Until 1964 it was usually directed by Hubert Crook or GHK but the latter was extremely busy during the summer with boys' and Cathedral Courses and so, after the change to the summer, a variety of different directors were used. From at least 1955 until 1971 there was also a concomitant small course for boys (varying in number from 10-35) so that there was a full quorum for singing and junior choir training opportunities available for the choirmasters attending.

Salisbury Cathedral Adult Course

In 1975 a new type of Cathedral Course was started, for auditioned adult singers alone. Until this time there were no Cathedral Courses for the adult soprano or contralto, especially those girls who had passed through other instructional courses or Cathedral Singers but had now passed the age limit for these. Experience in high quality cathedral-style singing was regarded as valuable for those considering a further study of music or singing. This new one week course was held in Salisbury with the singers resident in Sarum College and singing daily services in the cathedral for the week culminating with three services on the final Sunday (Eucharist, Matins and Evensong). During the Addington Years the directors of this course, who normally took charge for several years running, were successively Allen Ferns (5 courses), Alan Spedding (4), Peter Moorse (4), Lionel Dakers (2), Harry Bramma (4), David Dunnett (2) and Christopher Stokes (1). This adult course then continued regularly at Salisbury until 2002 after which the pattern changed and it moved to a different cathedral each year[194].

The final Sarum Adult Course directed by Tim Noon in 2002

---

[194] And still does today. Now called the RSCM Residentiary Choir, it held its first residency in Wells Cathedral during the summer of 2014.

Other Courses

From Easter 1969 Donald Leggat[195] ran a boys' residential course annually until about 1980. The first of these, which was also the first RSCM residential course in Northern Ireland, was attended by 60 boys.

In 1976 Northern Commissioner John Cooke initiated two autumn courses which became regular fixtures. At Ripon Diocesan House in Barrowby, near Harrogate, he held an annual course in choir training and organ accompaniment, each autumn until 1985. Between those same dates, though not annually, he ran a similar course at Carlisle Diocesan House in Rydal Hall, Ambleside.

Harry Bramma on residential courses:

> 'Of course there are factors in the last 15-20 years which have worked against residential courses. For example, the greater costs charged by schools and colleges and the overall decline in the number of children in church choirs.'

It is also the case that many more parish church choirs than previously visit cathedrals during the summer and sing the services whilst the cathedral choirs are on holiday. They are able to to enjoy some holiday themselves in a different location to home. This speaks well of the high standards being reached today at a parish church level.

---

[195] Donald Albert Leggatt (1914-1992) taught at St Edmund's School in Canterbury and was then Director of Music of St Bees School in Cumbria. An RSCM Special Commissioner, he was made Hon RSCM in 1965.

2) Non-residential

Three-Day Courses

The popular non-residential Three-Day Courses (TDC) were first held in the summer of 1949 in Birmingham, Bridgewater, Bury, Golders Green, Hull, Ilford, Taunton, Withington and Wolverhampton, together with two in Essex at New Year 1950. No attendance figures are available for these courses, but one can only assume they were either not well attended or made a financial loss because no further TDCs were organised from headquarters until 1959 when there were nine — New Year courses in Birmingham and Bedford, an Easter course in Grimsby, summer courses in Waddington, Rochester and Sunderland and an autumn course in Neath. The number of courses annually increased so that for most of the 1960's there were 20-22 p/a and by the early 1970's there were around 28 p/a.

These courses were more easily organised than week-long residential courses and cheaper for the participants. Larger numbers of singers could be accommodated and, as car ownership became increasingly widespread, the daily transport of children to non-residential venues became easier. Crucially however, these courses could be organised locally by RSCM area representatives and not (in some cases) at a great distance from headquarters and so it is not surprising that they flourished. In addition to the 600 or so TDCs in our database, there will be many others organised locally by RSCM Area Committees, and before that by Area Representatives, of which we are unaware.

During this 40 year period, only 20 courses arranged from Addington had to be cancelled due to insufficient support. Attendance figures are available for exactly 300 courses: almost 24,000 singers attended so an average of about 80 per course, the vast majority being children. One exceptional course in terms of numbers was the Heaton Moor New Year course run from 1961 by Geoffrey Barber in his home church of St Paul which usually also took 'ex-trebles' to provide ATB. Almost 2500 boys attended this popular course from 1961 to 1975 (with a peak of 226 in 1969). The course ran until 1985 but no attendance figures are available for the last decade.

The final day of a TDC was often also a half or full-day course for adults to enable SATB repertoire to be sung at the final Evensong, often in a nearby major church or cathedral. At some courses, adults would join the juniors daily for an afternoon rehearsal before Evensong.

The first Three-Day Course to mention girls was that directed by Malcolm Cousins in Mansfield (his own church) at New Year 1965/66. By the end of the decade girls' involvement was more frequent. Two of the longest running Easter TDCs are those in Bristol (1969 until recently) and Oxford (1974 and still going) and both the Bristol and Oxford TDCs included girls from the outset. Adult ATB were included at these two venues from around 1990.

1974 gives a good snapshot of TDCs:

New Year, 9 courses: Basingstoke, Bradford Cathedral, Addiscombe (Croydon), Eastbourne, Ecclesfield, Heaton (Bradford), Heaton Moor (Manchester), Southport and Watford.

Easter, 14 courses: Birmingham, Bolton, Bristol, Chester, Doncaster, Grimsby, Havant, Huddersfield, Leicester, Newcastle, Norwich, Oxford, Walsall and Southwell.

Whitsun, 2 courses: Ipswich and Leeds.

Summer, 2 courses: Guildford and Folkestone.

Autumn, 1 course Roker (Sunderland).

The places hosting TDCs and which held more than 10 such events were: Bedford (various churches), Birmingham Parish Church, Bradford Cathedral (with Keith Rhodes), Bristol Cathedral, Cambridge (St John's College Choir School and St John the Evangelist), Croydon (Parish Church and St Mildred's, Addiscombe), Doncaster (St James), Grimsby (St James' Parish Church and All Saints'), Guildford Cathedral, Heaton Moor (St Paul), Newcastle (St Gabriel, Heaton or St James URC), Oxford (various churches and Magdalen College School), Roker (Sunderland) and Southwell Minster (mostly with Minster organist Kenneth Beard).

Above: A Three-Day Course in Jesmond 1970

Right: These courses were hard work!

In October 1990, as part of National Learn-the-Organ Year, the first non-residential Three-Day Courses for organists were held in Birmingham and Leeds.

Two-Day Course

In 1967 a new type of course was tried locally in Newtown, Montgomeryshire. On the first day there was a choir practice at 10.00am. In the early afternoon there was a knockout football competition and other athletic activities followed by a further choir practice and dispersal at 5.45pm. The second day concluded with a service of Evensong. Whilst the RSCM magazines were full of reports of football tournaments arranged at a local level, and the RSCM has many photographs of choristers playing football from the 1950's to 1980's, this type of weekend course did not seem to catch on. In the Addington years only two Two-Day courses were organised from headquarters.

One and Half-Day Courses

Apart from courses held at Addington, all such courses were arranged locally. They had been a feature of RSCM training for some time. Hubert Crook reported in *ECM* January 1949 that in the previous autumn he had been to One-Day Schools at St Mary in Portsea (300 singers), St Barnabas in Gillingham (200 singers) and Christ Church in Dartford (160 singers) — significant numbers.

Sampson reported in 1971 that:

'The usual One-Day School was most frequently for the treble line only, but was often for the full choir as well, the alto, tenor and bass parts rehearsing in the afternoon. Other types included schools for ex-trebles (15-19 years of age) the course being designed to give the boys confidence in singing alto, tenor and bass; for Head Choristers; for organists and choirmasters; and village organists playing harmoniums... Variations added to One-Day Schools, which gave added incentives, were a barbecue and a football competition.'

In 1991 October *CMQ* notes that 555 boys, girls and adults attended the five summer courses — an increase of 12% over the previous year.

Hubert Crook at a One-Day Course in St Hilda's, Darlington 1958

Above: One-Day Course at Maidstone Parish Church directed by Peter Moorse in 1966

Below: John Cooke at a One-Day Course in Warrington, June 1977

Plainsong

In addition to the twenty or so plainsong days held at Addington, two plainsong experts in the form of Michael Fleming, then organist of All Saints', Margaret Street, in London and Ernest ('Ernie') Warrell, lecturer in plainsong at Addington and subsequently both Secretary of the Plainsong and Mediæval Music Society and Musical Director of the Gregorian Association, began a series of evening classes in the winter of 1959 which ran for ten years. There were two courses, one for singers and one for accompanists, each comprising six sessions either weekly or fortnightly with singers before Christmas and organists after Christmas.

St Mary, Woolnoth, London

From about 1957, and then for several years, a Singers' Workshop was held in St Mary, Woolnoth, Lombard Street. Held on a Friday lunch-time for city workers, Martin How (and later David Patrick) rehearsed service music for occasional performance. For example, Evensong using Noble in B-minor and anthems from the 1961/62 Festival Service book was sung by this group in St Clement's, Eastcheap, in July 1961.

Martin How rehearses *Blest pair of Sirens* by Parry in St Mary, Woolnoth, ca 1959

D) Communication

RSCM periodicals

From the outset there have always been house magazines, and the early SECM journals are itemised in *SNCSN*. During the Canterbury and into the Addington years the only magazines were *English Church Music* (edited by Leonard Blake) and the *Choristers' Leaflet* (edited by Hubert Crook), both quarterly, the latter a single sheet folded into four pages for junior choristers.

ECM was run according to criteria laid down by its first editor H C Colles in 1931. It was:

1. For the communication between the branches and headquarters.
2. To represent the RSCM, and all that it stands for, before the Church at large.
3. To provide a forum where Church Music can be examined in relation to the more general issues of worship and evangelism, the standards of secular composition and performance and the findings of liturgical and musical scholarship.

When these criteria were re-iterated in *ECM* January 1956, money was tight because of the heavy expense of moving to Addington and it was decided to cut *ECM* down to three issues a year for purely financial reasons. Many saw this as a retrograde step, for *ECM* was part of the public face of the organisation, which could not afford to pay for publicity or advertisements.

In September 1958 Leonard Blake resigned as editor of *ECM* after 10 years in the post. Cyril Taylor was invited to take over but declined and so the next issue was edited jointly by GHK and Leslie Green. There is no indication of who edited the magazine before the next major change was made in 1963[196] whereupon *ECM* split into two. One part, retaining the title *English Church Music*, became an annual collection of scholarly essays about church music matters, so fulfilling Criteria 3 above. This ran from 1963 until 1980 when the title changed to *The World of Church Music*, until cessation of publication in 1986. Criteria 1 and 2 above were fulfilled by a new magazine entitled *RSCM News*, back to a quarterly routine and of a rather lighter nature suited to the parish chorister. Unlike previous journals, which only rarely contained photographs, *RSCM News* was an illustrated magazine. Both adult and junior readers were catered for as the new magazine also incorporated *The Choristers' Leaflet* which had been started in 1941 by Sydney Nicholson. This junior part of the magazine, now called *Treble Clef*, occupied the centre pages and could be pulled out to pass around the choristers. How much this ever happened is uncertain, but the many contributions by choristers to *Treble Clef*[197] suggest that in the 70's and 80's at least there was some sharing of the magazine. It has been a perennial problem (and a worry) for the RSCM to place the magazines under the noses of anyone other than the church correspondent who actually receives it. Numerous pleas have been

---

[196] These changes were a direct result of the 1960 Confidential Report (see Appendix 11).
[197] *Treble Clef* was edited at various times by Peter White, Martin How and David Harding.

published to try and get the magazine away from the organist or incumbent's desk and into the choir vestry — and this battle continues today!

A third journal (also quarterly) was also initiated in 1963 entitled *Promoting Church Music*[198]. This was largely concerned with reviewing and, as the title suggests, promoting musical publications for the church musician. The RSCM Publications Department was rapidly developing a side-line in all kinds of material — postcards, diaries, badges, ties, key fobs etc — and this was a good platform from which to make them known in addition to the plans for publishing affordable choir music. In April 1964 the title page claimed 'Circulation 11,000 each issue' with this statistic increasing to 12,000 in January 1966 and 13,000 in July 1967 where it remained. The next change was made in January 1970 when *Promoting Church Music* combined with *RSCM News* but retained the title *Promoting Church Music*. From January 1977 this was further renamed *Church Music Quarterly* which continues today, changing to A4 format with the April 1988 issue.

Editors of *ECM/PCM/CMQ*

Leonard Blake	1948-1958
GHK and Leslie Green	1958-1962
Alec Jackson	1963-1968 (See Bursar)
Robert McDowall	1968-1982
John Ottley	1982-1988
Richard Morrison	1988/1989
Trevor Ford	1990-1999

Blake, Leonard James, MusB, FRCO, ARCM, Hon RSCM: b. 1907, Hendon; d. 2nd Aug 1989. Director of Music at Worksop and then Malvern College, he was one of the first Special Commissioners to be appointed when this post was introduced in 1947 and was a driving force behind the Public School Festivals held at Gloucester Cathedral. He was editor of *ECM* for ten years from 1948 to 1958.

McDowall, Robert: d. April 1999. He joined the office staff in February 1953 at Canterbury and married Geraldine Smith, one of the St Nicolas College students (1954/55). He was editor of *RSCM News* from its inception in 1963 and, on the retirement of Alec Jackson in 1968, he also took over editorship of *Promoting Church Music*. When these were replaced by a single journal (in larger format) in 1968, he continued as editor until retirement due to ill health in November 1982. He had latterly only been working three days a week. He was a long-standing and loyal member of the choir at St Michael's, Croydon, possessing a fine alto voice, and 'had a lovely sense of humour with which he enlivened choir practice.'[199] He was succeeded as editor by John Ottley.

---

[198] In 1963 *PCM* began with 24 pp. rising to 28 pp. in Apr 1966. There were just two 32 pp. issues — in Oct 1965 when Novello took out an extra 4 pp. of advertising and in Oct 1968.
[199] *CMQ* July 1999.

Ottley, John Richard BA, FRCO(CHM), ADCM:
b. 1947. Organ scholar at King Edward VI
Grammar School in Bury St Edmunds. Taught in
Cambridge and was Chairman to the Cambridge
Music Teachers Association. Came to AP as a
student (1973/74) and was appointed as a
general assistant in the secretarial office from
December 1974, also acting as Headquarters
Choirmaster from 1976[200]. In 1987 he moved
from the Secretary's office to the Publications Department working part-time under Noreen
Fortune. On the retirement of Robert McDowall in the autumn of 1982 he took over
editorship of *CMQ*. He retired to Suffolk in 1989 and was organist of Great Barton PC. He
was among the first to be awarded the Open University's Diploma in Music and gained his
BA(Hons) degree from the OU in 1996. He now works at BBC Radio Suffolk and is organist at
Rougham Church.

Morrison, Richard: b. 1946, a Cambridge graduate, was editor of *CMQ* from May 1988 until
mid-1989. A freelance musician, he joined *The Times* in 1990 and became chief music
critic. He writes a wide-ranging cultural column for *The Times* on Fridays. He also writes
for the monthly publication *BBC Music Magazine* for which he has won an award as
'columnist of the year'. Whilst he is better known as a writer rather than a performer, he
continues to perform music despite suffering serious cycling injuries[201] and is organist and
choirmaster of St Mary's Church in Hendon.

Ford, Trevor FRSCM, ARAM, HonRCM, HonRCO, FRSA,
FISM, DipRAM: b. 1951. After training as a chartered
accountant, Trevor studied flute at the RAM and became a
freelance orchestral musician. He was orchestral manager
of the English Sinfonia from 1979 until 2003 and also of the
Philomusica of London and the Midland Philharmonic
Orchestra. He is a professor at the GSM and is general
manager of the English Festival Orchestra, which he
founded in 1984. Trevor runs an accountancy practice for
freelance musicians and is Treasurer of the Incorporated Society of Musicians. He was DOM
at St John the Evangelist in Palmers Green, London for 17 years and became Chairman of
RSCM London in 2012. He has also served on the councils of both the RCO and the RSCM. He
was made ARSCM in 2000 and upgraded to FRSCM in 2010.

Asked by LD to be editor of *CMQ* in 1988, he was too busy and suggested Richard Morrison.
When Morrison was appointed to *The Times*, Trevor took over as editor of *CMQ* with the
April issue in 1990 and continued to the end of 1999.

---

[200] A somewhat diminished role as the boys' choir basically ceased in 1974.
[201] He has a titanium left elbow and a metal right ankle.

Church Music Quarterly

Harry Bramma writes:

'For me, the quarterly magazine of the RSCM was central to the work of the organisation. When I arrived the editor of *CMQ* was Richard Morrison of *The Times* but, for almost all of my time, the editor was Trevor Ford, who worked very closely with me to develop the publication. It was during the 1990's that rapid developments in digital technology gradually made it possible to introduce full colour and, in every respect, make the magazine more attractive. News of the members worldwide was, for me, always paramount, as were articles by distinguished writers on topical issues. The particular interest I took in the enterprise was the production of my quarterly articles over which I took much trouble, for I knew they were appreciated by the membership. It was a task that I enjoyed, giving me the opportunity to discuss in detail practical matters and issues of a musical, theological or philosophical nature — such as the one about the arguments for and against electronic organs; the introduction of girls into cathedral choirs and the payment of church musicians. Many of the articles were of a practical nature and I considered them to be a kind of manifesto for what the RSCM should be attempting to do. Sometimes I explored the theological and philosophical nature of our policy as well as subjects common to all spirituality such as the human need for silence.

I also very much approved of the 'parish magazine' element of *CMQ*. One must not forget that the RSCM is a 'movement' as well as an advice bureau. The members liked to read accounts of events and initiatives worldwide, as well as to see photographs of the members in action. This was important for building up the essential 'esprit de corps' of the organisation.

One should never under-estimate the galvanising power of an informed, interesting and newsworthy quarterly publication. It is not an exaggeration to say that *CMQ* binds and holds the membership together. The continued development of the publication throughout the Addington years was a crucial factor regarding the health and vigour of the RSCM.'

RSCM News-Notes

In March 1961 the first issue of *RSCM News-Notes* was published: 'An occasional paper intended to fill the gaps between issues of our official magazine. There is no mailing list; a copy is slipped into any letter which comes from the office.' At this time *ECM* was only published three times a year and this informal single sheet was able to provide dates that were not available when *ECM* went to press and to publish minor local items of news that might not find a place in the main journal. With no extra postal costs and being only a single stencilled sheet, this was a very inexpensive way to communicate with affiliates.

Agreeing with the Revd Horace Spence who last week condemned children's hymns as 'childish, sentimental or of introspective character.' I offer the above illustration of some of the hymns he refers to.

A. 'All things bright and beautiful'   C. 'Fight the Good Fight'   E. 'Peace, perfect peace'
B. 'You in your small corner'   D. 'We are but little children weak'   F. 'Like a little candle'

The first issue mentions the gift, by the artist[202], of the original cartoon by Giles of choristers wreaking havoc, which still hangs in the Director's office with the caption above. It was published in the Sunday Express on 7th August 1960[203] in response to a comment by Horace Spence.

With the re-organisation of the Lincolnshire area in 1962, a separate edition of *RSCM News-Notes* began in October 1962 which ran for 18 issues until October 1964.

---

[202] Ronald (k/a Carl) Giles OBE (1916-1995), cartoonist, best known for his work for the Daily Express newspaper.
[203] The cartoon is reproduced by permission of Giles/Express Newspapers.

Administrative Communication

The RSCM magazines served as a channel of information, news and encouragement from headquarters to members, affiliates and also to the general public[204]. Despite the frequent call for letters, photographs and news from choirs and choristers (especially in later *PCM* and *CMQ* years) this was effectively a one-way channel. It was necessary however for headquarters to communicate with the various representatives in each diocese in a more administrative way. Mention has been made of Horace Spence's regular newsletters to the Clerical Representatives, but there was also a regular letter from Secretary Leslie Green to the Local and Diocesan Representatives, a tradition that extended back to SECM days. Generally he wrote to all reps six times a year and, although much of his writing consisted of exhortations to raise money and attract new members or affiliates, he gave news of courses and representative conferences in various dioceses, he encouraged reps to send reports of activities arranged locally, he could give advance notice of when the various Special Commissioners were touring certain areas and, above all, he promoted the idea of the RSCM being a family. The reps were encouraged to meet and get to know one another and to personally become acquainted with the affiliated choirs in their area. He said 'The need is for the organisation [i.e. local reps] to become a centre of RSCM life and activity in each Diocese, and to make certain that each affiliated choir, and each personal member, knew the reality of the RSCM in and around the choir or individual.' Then (as now) some dioceses were very active at a local level, but others were inward-looking and merely arranged a Diocesan Choral Festival and a few local events without actually engaging with individual choirs and organists.

In his letters to reps, the Secretary was able to respond quickly to events, unlike the magazines which were generally a month or two behind with their news. For example, if the Easter courses at various venues were fully booked, but places were available on other courses, Green could react within a few days to inform the reps. These letters, however, were a considerable expense and one cannot help thinking that Leslie Green would have been in his element with email. On Green's retirement, Gerald Knight continued to write to reps, but only sporadically.

The Saturday organ accompaniment tuition sessions have already been mentioned[205] and there are many references to these in Green's letters where he encourages local areas to set up such schemes offering headquarters' help. GHK also said in one of his letters to reps in 1967 that:

> 'Of all the problems facing us in the church today I would put the improvement of organ accompaniment very high on the list. The imagination boggles at the thought of the number of churches whose services can never be musically bearable until their organists learn to improve their accompaniment of choir and congregation. Things are not getting better here; they're getting worse.'

---

[204] It is not generally known that *ECM* had a notional cover price and was sold to any interested parties.
[205] See p. 125.

E) International Outreach

The authors do not have material available to attempt any detailed assessment of the RSCM's work overseas during the Addington era, and the few pages here devoted to overseas work does not reflect the remarkable achievements undertaken overseas. Examination of the list of church musicians from overseas who have been awarded RSCM Honours gives a more realistic idea of the important work done by them.[206]

RSCM influence overseas was a vision of Sydney Nicholson and was spearheaded by his international tours to Australia, New Zealand, Canada and the USA in 1934 and again to North America in 1938.[207] From December 1955 until retirement as Overseas Commissioner in 1978, Gerald Knight travelled worldwide and, as with the overseas visits by Sir Sydney, each trip was followed by an increase of affiliate applications from the countries visited.

GHK's Overseas Travels

In 1947 the Proprietors of *Hymns A&M* had given £1000 (£37,000 today) in memory of SHN with the caveat that it be used to send someone to visit RSCM members overseas. Following his appointment as Director, GHK felt that he could undertake an overseas tour until 'we were fully established at Addington'.[208] In 1955 he briefly visited Gibraltar, Malta and Ireland and, in the December of that year, embarked on a major seven-month tour of India, Ceylon, Burma, Thailand, Hong Kong, Singapore, Malaya, Australia, New Zealand, Fiji, the USA and Canada. In *The First Forty Years* he wrote:

> 'Sir Sydney had made his first tour before the days when flying was not the everyday affair that it now is. He had journeyed round the world at a pace the leisure of which makes me envious. He was able, for example, to write the whole of his opera for boys' voices *The Children of the Chapel* during the sea voyages. I for my part had to be content during my first world tour to travel by air with very few periods of leisure to make recovery possible from the inevitable fatigue of long flights.
>
> It was a real thrill to find myself following in the footsteps of the Founder; to stand as I did in Wellington, on the very same spot as my predecessor had stood twenty years before to conduct a One-Day School; to see the head chorister of a church wearing the SECM badge presented to one of his predecessors in office by Sir Sydney himself; and to meet adults who as boys had seen him at work in Australia and New Zealand.'

Following this 1955/56 tour, RSCM Council formulated a constitution under which branches were formed in each of the States of the Commonwealth of Australia and among suitable groupings of members in New Zealand. In 1967 GHK revisited these branches to see how they were getting on and most, if not all, have flourished to this day. His travels continued:

---

[206] This can be found on the RSCM web page www.rscm.com [follow links — 'about us' — 'honorary awards'].
[207] See *SNMOM* for details and photographs.
[208] *The First Forty Years*.

'In 1958 I did something which Sir Sydney had intended to do but for World War II — to visit the African continent. From the Gambia in the west, via Sierra Leone, Ghana and Nigeria across to the Sudan, down to Uganda and Kenya, over the water to Zanzibar, back to the mainland in Tanzania, Rhodesia, Zambia, and finally to South Africa. This, though the shortest [3½ months] was one of the most interesting of all my tours. To see church music developing in very un-English conditions was fascinating.'

He went on to say:

'It was distressing to find that some of the habits taken to Africa from England in all innocence by early missionaries were regarded in many places as correct, indeed, as an integral part of Anglicanism. Conservatism is at least as strong in African church circles as it is in England, and RSCM principles will have to be adopted cautiously and gingerly if they are to prove acceptable. Perhaps the most difficult task in black Africa is to get people to see the value of using African music — so many think of Dykes and Barnby as the high priests of Anglican music, and that no church can be loyal to the Anglican tradition unless it uses their music.'

From 1964 he made overseas tours almost annually, except for 1965, when he was acting as General Secretary in the interregnum between Leslie Green and Commander West-Byng.

These overseas tours by SHN, GHK, subsequent RSCM Directors and others, including Martin How, Arthur Wills, David Willcocks and John Bertalot, helped to strengthen the bond between far-flung church musicians and RSCM headquarters in an era when internet and telecommunications had not shrunk the world as it has today. Most overseas visits were followed by a flurry of new affiliations and an increase in One-Day Schools, diocesan and regional choir festivals in the various countries. Annual Summer Schools were established in Australia, South Africa and New Zealand, usually based in varied locations because of the vast size of those countries.

Two simple examples of the effect the tours had on membership can be gleaned from the Affiliation lists of 1955 and 1957. They show that, following GHK's 1955/56 tour, the number of affiliates in New Zealand rose from 59 to 101 in 1957 and in Australia from 156 to 247. This, together with opening of local branches mentioned above, was a real achievement. Interest from New Zealand choirs was also given a boost when extracts from the 1951 Festival of Britain service, along with other RSCM recordings, were broadcast several times on the New Zealand Broadcasting Service during 1953.

The Wa-Li-Ro summer choir camp in the USA was founded in 1933 by Dr Paul Beymer ARSCM (1893-1965), organist of Christ Church in Shaker Heights, Ohio and a former student of SHN at Chislehurst.[209] Located at the wonderfully named Put-in-Bay on South Bass Island, Ohio, the name Wa-Li-Ro was derived from the Bishop of Northern Ohio in office that year, The Rt Revd Warren Lincoln Rogers, who conceived the idea. From 1937 the camp was held

---

[209] See SNCSN.

annually with Healey Willan (in his retirement) as a regular lecturer, Leo Sowerby[210] as a regular tutor and with the participation of many visiting British church musicians including GHK.[211] Paul Beymer was succeeded as Director at Wa-Li-Ro by Warren Miller, organist of Grace Church in Sandusky, Ohio, who was made Hon RSCM in 1986.

The boys lived in a building originally used as a summer hotel, the cost (in 1970) being $18 per week. The clergy and choirmasters were accommodated in the Guest House at $25 per week. The boys practised daily for two hours each morning in St Paul's Episcopal Church and returned for a short rehearsal before an evening service in the church. The rest of the day was spent in outdoor activities including boating. By the 30th anniversary of the camp in 1963, it was estimated that 12,000 boys had stayed at the camp — with 50 to 60 attending at any one time.

The Work Abroad 1989-1998

Harry Bramma writes:

'It was during the early Addington years that RSCM work began to develop in the USA and Canada — built up after the visit of Gerald Knight. There was no attempt to organise nationally at this stage, but there were pockets of enthusiasm in the Episcopal Church in the USA and the Anglican Church in Canada. That this country was part of the British Empire was very much a factor in post-war years. The arrival of Lionel Dakers gave considerable impetus to an attempt to organise more thoroughly in North America. Up till then it had been rather piecemeal.'

Harry Bramma goes on to give an account of his work in Australia (first visited in 1990), New Zealand (1991), South Africa, USA and Canada, commenting that he felt his work overseas was both successful and historically significant, mainly because Australia and the USA had been contemplating breaking away from the RSCM's UK base. There was some resentment in Australia being ruled from Addington, to the extent that the Director of the RSCM chose the conductors for the annual Australian summer school. This HB changed, henceforth expecting them to choose their own course directors.

'I enjoyed my visits, made many friends and worked through an exceedingly hectic schedule — talking to local committees, conducting events, giving organ recitals, many talks and exchanging ideas in continuous social engagements!

After a further visit to Australia and New Zealand in 1994 to commemorate the 60th anniversary of Sir Sydney Nicholson's visit in 1934, it was obvious that there was beginning to be a change of opinion. We discussed these matters informally, and gradually it seemed that some sort of devolved arrangement might be a preferred option. This being so, a 'summit' meeting of all the Area Chairmen and Secretaries from the seven Branches was proposed for early 1995. Charles King and I went

---

[210] Sowerby actually became ill and died during the 1968 camp.
[211] Also including Francis Jackson, Sidney Campbell, Stanley Vann, Christopher Dearnley, John Bertalot and a young George Guest, who was somewhat taken aback when GHK, over a meal, casually suggested/told him to go in 1958!

together and at a meeting in Sydney under the Chairmanship of William Clark (NSW Chairman [later FRSCM]) it was unanimously agreed to draft a constitution for RSCM Australia — as it was to be known. It then took almost three years to agree to the form of the constitution, much helped by the advice of a member of the UK RSCM Council, Mark Bridges, who gave valuable legal advice and monitored the development of the new constitution.'

On his third visit to New Zealand in 1998, Harry discussed the proposals which were about to be adopted in Australia, and which New Zealand then agreed to adopt, under a similar arrangement. Throughout his visit, he received a warm welcome, and was involved in a multitude of activities.

'I remember being much impressed by the girls' choir at a school in Marton where they gave a wonderful account of a motet by Casals. I must also not forget my encounter with the 4-manual Norman & Beard organ in the Town Hall at Wellington, a veritable leviathan.'

During Lionel Dakers' Directorship, an RSCM office had been opened in Litchfield, Connecticut. Initially it had made quite a difference and membership had increased. However, it all went wrong and the RSCM lost a great deal of money. Council minutes in June 1985 mention that RSCM America had been in serious financial difficulty for some time, but this came to a head and the American Office in Litchfield was closed and staff paid off. Several courses were already planned and financial help for these was promised from the UK. A continuation of courses in America was considered essential and a Training Courses Committee was set up. It was decided that US affiliation fees would henceforth be collected by AP and RSCM Council accepted responsibility to pay the debts of the American RSCM 'not-for-profit' corporation (some $40,000) 'to preserve the good name of the RSCM Worldwide.'

A bank account was opened in New York. With the grants already made to establish the American operation, and therefore lost, the total damage to RSCM funds would eventually exceed £100,000.

The Annual Report in July 1986 mentions that:

'Council is encouraged to see that, in spite of the changes which the US Board of Directors had to make in the work there following the closure of the office at Litchfield, Connecticut, the majority of members have retained their links with the RSCM. During the summer, the US Training Courses Committee promoted three successful courses for choristers, and Lionel Dakers and Martin How each visited a number of centres.'

Harry recounts the aftermath.

'On my visit to the country in 1990, we held a meeting at St Thomas's Church, 5th Avenue in New York, presided over by the Revd John Andrew, the Vicar and also President of the RSCM in America. At this meeting (to which I was accompanied by Vincent Waterhouse) it was resolved to re-open an American office, but this time with much stronger safeguards. Robert Quade, organist of St Paul's, Akron, in Ohio, agreed to set this up at his church, aided by a member of his choir and others from his church. Gradually things started to move and bases were set up in other States, North to South on the Eastern side of the country. Gradually this led to much new life, under the responsibility of the American Board of Directors. The number of residential courses in the summer has increased and, at the time of writing [2015], has expanded to around 12 courses per annum. The RSCM has many devoted workers in The States [and] there is no doubt that the reopening of an office in the USA has made a huge impact in the RSCM's activities and influence.'

The main problems in Canada are that it is a vast but thinly-populated country. The most active area in HB's time was that of Niagara and SW Ontario — a long corridor stretching from near the Niagara Falls to the American border at Port Huron. Harry recalls:

'There was good leadership and much activity in towns like Burlington, Stratford and London and I conducted many successful events in this area over several visits. Elsewhere, activity was more sporadic. The Toronto Branch organised events from time to time; and I visited Vancouver and Vancouver Islands, but in many places, the organised events depended on the work of dedicated RSCM supporters.'

Moving on to the work of the RSCM in South Africa, Harry makes the point that with the strong musical tradition in the white, black and mixed race communities, the South African Summer School moving around the country has been an important feature. Some of the larger branches of the RSCM in Johannesburg, Natal and Cape Town had been very active — receiving much support from leading musicians like Barry Smith FRSCM in Cape Town, Richard Cock FRSCM in Johannesburg, Errol Slatter ARSCM in Durban, and many others.

'I had visited South Africa before I became Director to direct the Summer School in Grahamstown in 1985. At this time apartheid was still in force, and the RSCM managed to house all ethnic groups under one roof — I suppose because it was church organised — it was quite contrary to the prevailing practice in the country. When I returned seven years later as Director in 1992, apartheid had largely gone. I visited again in 1996 and have many good memories of music in churches of all types where I was kept busy conducting, speaking, playing the organ and meeting the committees. There were many able people working in the various regions doing a great deal of useful work. I visited the Drakensburg Choir School set high in the mountains where the choir master, 'Bunny' Ashley-Botha had the choir sing for me. I particularly remember a remarkable 11 year-old boy who sang, with great élan, the tenor solo from the Sanctus of Gounod's *Messe Solennelle* at the correct pitch! There were a good many enthusiasts in Durban and Pietermaritzburg and, right out in the middle of the Orange Free State, there was a choir at the cathedral in Kimberley. A memorable visit to a Roman Catholic basilica near Kimberley also remains firmly in my mind. A young choir of men and women in their 20's and 30's met daily after work at 4.30pm to rehearse for an hour. Their voices and performances were stunning.

Money was always a problem in South Africa. The exchange rate in those days was even more disastrous 25 years ago than it is today. Financial relationships with Addington were difficult, and a considerable brake on progress, but the visits I made assured me of the very great life and commitment in the RSCM Branches, which was heart-warming.'

RSCM Summer School, Johannesburg, January 1978
directed by Martin How

F) Commercial and music publishing activities

In the SECM era, the Musical Advisory Committee was set up in 1929 by Sydney Nicholson inviting members of the Church Music Society (of which he was chairman) to provide reviews of suitable music to be recommended in the magazine — suitable for both large and small choirs. The committee also gave specialist replies to queries from affiliates about the choice of music. In 1946 RSCM Council formally re-launched the committee as the Musical Advisory Board. It was initially defined as 'Ten musicians, representing interests within the RSCM, to assist Council in providing for the future musical policy and continuity of the RSCM.'

Board members served for three years at a time, a mix of cathedral musicians from old and new cathedral foundations, parish musicians and school directors of music. From 1947 until 1967 the chairman and then vice-chairman (to GHK) of this committee, which met three or four times a year, was Sir John Dykes Bower[212]. The remit of the Board was not only the choice of music for publication and the production of recommended lists of music; they also debated matters relating to instructional courses, festivals, liturgy and ways of developing RSCM activities. It was the MAB who suggested in 1948 that a trial be made in the following year of the first non-residential three-day courses. They also considered matters such as organist recruitment and remuneration; and even the problems of choirboys' homework and book-rests on choir-stalls.

Recommended Music

In 1946 the MAB issued a list of *Recommended Church Music*, based on a 1935 list drawn up by the Musical Advisory Committee of the Church Music Society. During the Addington years this was followed up with 'recommended lists' of organ voluntaries, easy organ voluntaries, piano music, music for treble voices, anthems for men's voices, anthems for SATB, music for the ASB and carols for Christmas, Epiphany and Easter. These lists were revised from time to time and the compilers had no hesitation about recommending music that was out of print hoping that good music would be reprinted if there was a demand.

RSCM Music Publishing

Many of the publishing and marketing endeavours mentioned later in this chapter are sideshows to Sydney Nicholson's original purpose of providing quality church music suitable for parish use at affordable prices. We do not intend to cover this important area of RSCM activity in any great or critical detail in this book, but will provide an overview.

The selection and editing of music to bear the RSCM imprint has largely been in the hands of the Director and the MAB. In general terms Gerald Knight's musical taste was very conservative and as there was no money available to commission new works, the majority of publications in his time were either older music, newly edited, or new music written for special RSCM occasions. Publications during the Canterbury years included a number of musical items from pre-war service books reprinted as single copies because they had

---

[212] See Chapter I.

proved valuable; however, anthologies were always seen as the most practical way of providing music more cheaply. *Service Book Two* was issued in 1947 and the series continued to *Service Book Ten* in 1958. The *Choral Service Book* series started in 1955 and was followed by a series of 33 devotional services published between 1956 and 1989 beginning with the well-known *Cross of Christ*. The *Music for Courses* series started in 1961 and the series of ten *Festival Service Books* was published between 1967 and 1979. The majority of these service books were intended for use at diocesan festivals, both small and large, but the musical content was always designed so that some music would be simple enough for parish choirs to use in their own church after the festivals. Most of the service books sold well, indeed many sold out and had to be reprinted, and the affiliated choirs seemed to have confidence in publications from the RSCM.

In addition to the Chorister Training Scheme[213], another major project of 1965 was the issue of two books of music for Holy Communion. Book I (56 pages) contained five communion settings[214] together with 15 hymns suitable for use during the administration of communion and Book 2 (80 pages) contained 22 motets (mainly unaccompanied) of varying length and difficulty. The novel aspect of this latter publication was that it only included very few items edited or arranged by the RSCM, but was mainly copyright material from other publishers and, priced at 6/6d, it was indeed good value for in today's money 6/6d would be equivalent to £5.75 for the 22 anthems. 5000 of the 'Motets' book were sold and it was reprinted in 1969.

A best-seller — blank service sheets

Although not much used by choirs today, numerically one of the biggest selling items was the blank service sheets introduced in 1958. After just nine months they had sold 71,000 and by the following year 230,000 had been sold. By July 1963 a million had been sold and

---

[213] See Chapter VI.
[214] The (plainsong) *Coventry Mass* ed GHK, The (Plainsong) *Missa de Angelis* ed Francis Burgess, *Missa de Sancta Maria Magdalena* by Healey Willan, *A Short Communion Service in D* by John Beck and *An Octave Communion Service* by Alan Gibbs.

in 1965 a second design was added: 'Form B' which omitted Matins — a service already in decline.

In addition to sheet music, teaching guides also formed part of the RSCM's core publishing effort. Between 1956 and 1969 a series of *Study Notes* were published, beginning with *Chanting for Beginners* by Hubert Crook and ending with two reprints of articles by Bairstow and Nicholson from Nicholson's *A Manual of English Church Music*.

Lionel Dakers was also fairly conservative in his musical tastes, but he was keen to anticipate the needs of member churches and took a close personal control of RSCM publishing during his era.

Harry Bramma comments on publishing in the 1970's:

'The transformation of the Publications Department during Lionel Dakers' time was one of the great success stories of Addington. He seized opportunities as they arose — he was a considerable entrepreneur as well as being a fine administrator. He responded quickly to the new liturgies being devised by the Church of England in the late 1970's, commissioning new music for the modern English texts, particularly of the Eucharist. Many of these were best-sellers, composers like Martin How, Richard Shephard and many others. Much written then has become well-established in the musical life of the Church. There were so many new things — Mary Berry's *Introduction to Plainsong* amongst the many handbooks[215], an abundance of new anthems suitable for churches with modest resources and a number of special Service Books designed for use at great choral festivals. All this provided welcome resources for the church and considerable financial underpinning for the RSCM.

Dakers was a prodigious worker. He undertook the task of music editor asking composers to write to fulfil particular needs, but he always coped with the massive job of adjudicating all the manuscripts which came in unsolicited. Much could be discarded quickly, but this source did yield some gems. Often Dakers would send out manuscripts asking for an opinion from other musicians — but much of the editing was done by himself.

During this period the selling of other publishers' music became big business. The RSCM held a large stock of the core repertoire and was able to order, at short notice, requests for music not in stock. This all generated considerable business, needing a Publications Manager (notably John Sansom) and assistant (Dorothy Nicholls). They organised the despatch of orders by the workers, usually about four, in the parcel room. Many members, out of loyalty, sent large orders to the RSCM including many cathedrals. The whole venture throughout the Addington years, and for a time at Cleveland Lodge, was an important and profitable service.

Dakers was a good business man and was always on the lookout for an opportunity to make money. A particularly successful move was to take over as Publishers to the

---

[215] Eleven Handbooks were issued between 1979 and 1989.

Church Music Society from Oxford University Press who were beginning to find the work more trouble than it was worth. New music was added including both scholarly editions of older music or the publication of excellent new music like the Leighton *Second Service*. At the time of the move from Addington, the Publications Department was still a much-used and profitable service.'

One of Harry Bramma's initiatives beginning in the Addington years was to provide anthologies of music to satisfy the growing need for music in the more contemporary 'worship song' style; these were duly published with the help of William Llewellyn, James Whitbourn, Noel Tredinnick and Robin Sheldon, alongside more traditional fare of books of liturgical plainsong for seasonal use and an anthology of music by Purcell.

The Addington Press

GPC minutes in October 1977 mention an approach by publisher A R Mowbray to set up a joint publishing company with the RSCM, and in April 1978 the launch of the Addington Press was announced in *CMQ*. A formal agreement was signed between the RSCM and A R Mowbray in June 1978 and the official launch was in November 1978. Ivor Keys, professor of music successively at Belfast, Nottingham and Birmingham universities, was music editor for the Press. In the summer of 1979 The Faith Press ceased its printing and publishing activities and the Addington Press took over (and purchased the stock) of *The Parish Psalter*. In October 1988 the firm of A R Mowbray was taken over and the new owners did not wish to be part of the Addington Press. The RSCM agreed to pay £25,000 for the Mowbray share and £6829 for existing stock, thus bringing all the titles, including the *Parish Psalter* which was the single best-selling item, into the RSCM catalogue. These sums were allocated from a large bequest by a Mr H G Jakins of Wells. During its 11 years the Addington Press published two books, two communion settings and nine anthems and a book of plainsong Psalms. Apart from three editions of Buxtehude, Mendelssohn and Stanford, all the editions were of newly-composed music.

Walford Davies and Basil Harwood

In 1975 it was announced that, 'at the request of the Trustees of the late Sir Walford Davies, the RSCM will publish his choral works.' Much of the stock of Walford Davies' music held by Messrs Novello was transferred to the RSCM. As the W-D repertoire included some part songs, this represented a change for the RSCM which had never before published secular choral music.

In the autumn of 1990 the Trustees of Basil Harwood's estate authorised the RSCM to offer an 'on-demand' printing service for Harwood's choral music. For many years the RSCM has housed the archive of Harwood's music presented by the Executors. This archive contains many autograph manuscripts in addition to printed copies and an annotated catalogue of his complete works. Some of the hymn tunes and chants, and at least one organ work, remain unpublished.

Both of these agreements remain in force.

Church Music Society Publishing

In April 1982 *CMQ* announced that the RSCM would publish on behalf of The Church Music Society in succession to the Oxford University Press. Two years later, the GPC minuted that the first two years of publishing with the CMS had been successful and that 'A cordial working relationship had been established with Dr Watkins Shaw, the Society's Chairman, and the Executive Committee, and the link with a highly-regarded organisation must be of benefit to the RSCM.' In April 1994 it was decided not to renew the contract with CMS for publishing their music. The original contract was thought to be 'too tight for comfort' in commercial terms. CMS were unwilling to re-negotiate hence the parting of the ways though the RSCM remained as a principal retailer of CMS music.

St Martin's Publications

In 1968 the RSCM took over St Martin's Publications, one of a number of music publishers for the Roman Catholic liturgy that flourished in the 1960's and which were given a boost by the Second Vatican Council which required (in *Sacrosanctum Concilium* 1963) that settings of the liturgy in English replace the traditional Latin. Some publishers had over-extended themselves with too many new editions and, being unable to sell their old stock of Latin church music, they failed. In February 1968 the entire stock of St Martin's Publications was moved to Addington and administered by RSCM staff, though under the control of the Trustees and a committee. GHK was a trustee and Vincent Waterhouse was on the committee. In May 1970 however it was reported that the changes in Catholic liturgy had adversely affected sales and, in 1974, St Martin's Publications was fully absorbed into the RSCM.

Organ Music

Between 1981 and 1987 the RSCM had a brief foray into the publishing of organ music, all newly-composed (by Barry Ferguson, Jack Hawes, Martin How, Philip Moore, Harrison Oxley and Arthur Wills), of an easy-to-moderate standard with some being 2-stave. Nine editions were published. The only previous organ edition had been the excellent book of *Accompaniments for Unison Hymn Singing* edited by Gerald Knight in 1971 and still in print, although many of the settings are in keys rather higher than are generally sung today.

RSCM Artefacts

It is not certain when the first RSCM Christmas Cards were produced, although postcards had been available ever since the Chislehurst days of the SECM; however, it was noted that during 1960 1500 choir badges and 28,000 Christmas Cards were sold.

Sadly few RSCM Diaries survive, but they were probably first published around 1960. Each year there were different articles aimed to interest young choristers, often with a celebrity foreword — in 1964 the Primate of all Canada, 1966 Sir Malcolm Sargent, 1967 Arthur Askey, 1969 Derek Nimmo, 1970 the Archbishop of Cape Town and in later years comedian Cyril Fletcher, Alf Ramsay (England Football manager), Violet Carson from 'Coronation

Street' and so on. They were very popular — in 1966 the 6250 print-run sold out before Christmas — and, for 1967, 6750 were printed but again all were sold before Christmas.

The Blazer Badge was available as a machine-made version at 10/6d or a hand-embroidered version for 50/3d.

One of the popular older artefacts was a small lapel badge bearing the notes C and B, representing the word 'ChoirBoy'. The idea for this was suggested to SHN in 1935 by Richard Bush, a chorister from Folkestone Parish Church[216].

The 1960's marketing boom

A whole host of RSCM artefacts were offered during the 1960's in response to the 1960 Confidential Report which suggested 'That the production and sale of music, books and other articles be steadily increased.' Some of these can be seen on this and subsequent pages.

In 1963 new items included — a new shield shape lapel badge, a silkscreen badge for coats, football shirts and luggage, a metal car badge, key fob, tie clip, a book of *Prayers for the Church's Music and Church Musicians* edited by Horace Spence and book labels. These of course added to a long list of items available since the mid 1950's including a wall shield, scarves, pencils and a variety of badges.

In 1964 there followed a long-service certificate, cuff-links, a reprint of Sydney Nicholson's book *Peter The Chorister* by SPCK (with a new foreword by GHK), a pocket wallet and the choir members' badges in bronze, which were also then made available in chromium.

In 1965 the Certificates of Affiliation and Association were redesigned in colour, RSCM music manuscript books were issued along with LP records of the 1965 Festival Service.

In 1966 the CTS materials were introduced and *PCM* January 1966 notes that 'The three badges (shield type) specially designed for the CTS are supplied only to choirs which have been elected as members of the new St Nicolas Guild.'[217] In the same year an RSCM ball-point pen was introduced and the RSCM pencils were revamped. An LP record *The People's Parish Communion Service* (OLY 129) made by the College Choir directed by Peter White was issued with Merbecke on one side and communion music by Peter Burton and Martin Shaw on the other. In 1966 it was noted that 10,658 RSCM ties, introduced in September 1955, had been sold.

In 1967 a bookmark, plastic covers for hymn books and (choir) transfer cards were introduced and the whole stock of 1000 pocket comb and cases announced in July 1967 were sold in four weeks. Ladies' medals (Singing-Girl, Leader and Head Choirgirl) were

---

[216] Richard Bush (1918-1990) had written to SHN suggesting that choristers should take up instruments and that an RSCM Orchestra be formed. Nicholson's letter of reply to Richard (November 1935) indicates that a motif from the *Halleluiah Chorus* was also suggested. SHN preferred the 'CB' motif and provided a draft drawing. The original badge had SECM lettering, later changing to RSCM. As girl choristers became more prevalent, this design was superseded by the shield shaped unisex badge illustrated on a subsequent page.

[217] They also had to be worn with the appropriate coloured ribbon.

introduced in October 1967 along with girls' versions of all the CTS material and a St Cecilia Award medallion. Initially there was some confusion about the medals and many orders had to be declined because the same rules applied as with the boys' badges i.e. to be eligible, 'the choir must not only use the CTS but be members of the St Cecilia Guild.'

From January 1968 the College of Church Musicians at Washington Cathedral became agents for (selected) RSCM publications, and *PCM* that month noted that 38,000 RSCM music folders had been sold. A year later this figure was 40,000, at which time the folders were also offered with pockets. In 1969 an attempt was also made to bring in a uniform for choristers, a blue gabardine jacket with cloth badge and a plain blue tie. The idea barely lasted a year and was discontinued on the grounds that the jacket was 'out of fashion.'

In 1969 the cap-badge was replaced with a colourfast version; prior to this washing boys' caps had been a problem. In the same year the RSCM tie was re-designed with a single crest rather than multiple crests.

The Palace Kitchen

In the summer of 1976, redecoration of the dining room was made possible by the sales of *The Palace Kitchen*, a collection of 220 recipes, compiled by Christine Meekison, wife of the Bursar, and published at the end of 1974. It proved to be very popular and by 1980 had undergone four reprints and had sold 5000 copies.

Whilst thinking of food and drink, *CMQ* in 1977 (see below) noted that RSCM South Australia had commissioned two wines from well-known winemakers Thomas Hardy (est 1853), thus anticipating the current boom in New World wine sales. And to think that the RSCM is often accused of being behind the times!

WE REJOICE to hear that the RSCM is deriving some benefit from the sale of two South Australian wines that have been produced and bottled specifically on behalf of the RSCM. The two labels are shown above. "Cantoris Claret" is described as a "smooth dry red wine" grown at McLaren Vale, while "Decani Riesling" is a "crisp, delicate, dry white with a pronounced Riesling bouquet" grown in the Barossa Valley.

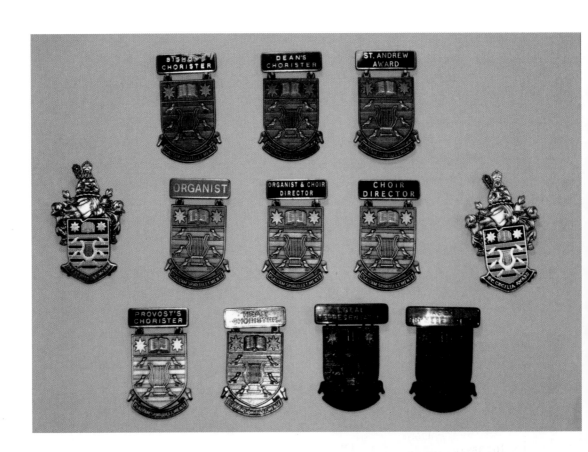

Hymns for Celebration

In May 1974 the RSCM launched a new hymn book — *Hymns for Celebration*. This was designed as an ecumenical supplement of 28 hymns to be used at the celebration of Holy Communion. The hymns were selected, arranged and edited by Erik Routley and John Wilson. A number of contemporary tunes, including some composed by the editors, were included and an LP recording was issued, recorded by Birmingham Cathedral Choir, directed by Roy Massey with John Pryor at the organ. The collection had a moderate reception and seven of the new hymns found their way into the 1983 *Hymns A&M New Standard* edition.

Recordings

In addition to the 1965 Festival and Communion settings recordings mentioned above, further RSCM recordings were made during the Canterbury and Addington years.

		Record Label	Ref. Number	
1948	RSCM 21st Birthday Recording: 6th Dec 1948, St Sepulchre's, Holborn.	Levy	S277-281	78
1949	Lichfield Cathedral Course: Choral Evensong	(private recording)	n/a	78
1949	Canterbury Cathedral Course: Choral Evensong	Revd W L George	RF1-RF6	78
1950	St Sepulchre, Holborn: St Nicolas Day Service 6th Dec 1950	MSS	n/a	
1950	Canterbury Cathedral Course: Choral Evensong 22nd July 1950	MSS	n/a	78
1950	York Cathedral Course: Choral Evensong 22nd Aug 1950	MSS/Drury	n/a	78
1951	Rossall Course: Choral Evensong	(private recording)	n/a	78
1953	St Paul's Cathedral Course: BC Choral Evensong 25th Aug 1953	MSS	n/a	78
1954	RSCM Courses: Darley Dale Jan 1954	(private recording)	n/a	LP
1954	Norwich Cathedral Course: BBC Choral Evensong 25th Aug 1954	MSS	n/a	LP
1955	Lincoln Cathedral Course: BBC Choral Evensong 24th Aug 1955	Sound News	n/a	LP
1957	St Paul's Cathedral Course: BBC Choral Evensong 28th Aug 1957	Sound News	n/a	LP
1957	St Paul's Cathedral Boys' Course: 12th Oct 1957	Sound News	n/a	LP
1958	RAH Triennial Festival	Olympic	OLY112-115	LP
1958	Southwell Minster Course: BBC Choral Evensong 20th Aug 1958	Olympic	OLY127/128	LP
1960	Rochester Cathedral Course: BBC Choral Evensong 24th Aug 1960	Sound News	n/a	LP

1961	RSCM Liverpool Cathedral Course: BBC Broadcast 16th Aug 1961	(private recording)	n/a	LP
1962	Coventry Cathedral Course: BBC Choral Evensong 8th Aug 1962	Sound News	n/a	LP
1965	Truro Cathedral Course: BBC Choral Evensong 18th Aug 1965	Sound News	n/a	LP
1965	RAH Festival Service	RSCM	RRM 1/2	LP
1966	The People's Parish Communion Service	Olympic	OLY129	LP
1968	St Paul's Boys' Course: BBC Choral Evensong 21st Aug 1968	Sound News	n/a	LP
1969/71	The Royal Banners: Plainsong College Students with Michael Fleming	Welkyn	OLY130	LP
1970	RAH 'Jubilate Deo' Festival	RSCM	RRS4/5	LP
1974	Hymns for Celebration	Strobe	OLY133	LP
1975[218]	Rutter and Shephard Series 3 Communion Services	Counterpoint	OLY131	EP
1975	Wicks Series 3 Communion and Psalms 42, 97, 122, 130 [New Translation]	Counterpoint	OLY132	EP
1977	RAH 'Rejoice' Festival	Abbey Records	LPB781	LP
1977	RSCM Stoke on Trent 50th Anniversary Festival	Deroy	1416	LP
1982	Lionel Dakers Lecture on Choir Training	RSCM	OLY134	Tape
1987	RAH 'Let all the World' Festival	Decca/Argo	421418	LP
1990	U-Sing, two compilations of hymn accompaniments for use in churches without a keyboard player. Performed by Noel Tredinnick.	RSCM	U1/U2	Tape

The Chorister's Pocketbook

In 1934, shortly after Canon Lowther Clarke[219] (Editorial Secretary of SPCK) joined RSCM Council, he published the *Choirboy's Pocket Book*, 'designed to give choristers something that will help them both on the religious and musical side of their work.' Reprinted the following year, it was renamed the *Chorister's Pocket Book* in 1937 and was so popular that it underwent a total of eight reprints by the time that the RSCM became established in Canterbury. In 1967, after 18 reprints, it underwent a revision with the help of Cyril Taylor, Horace Spence, John Dykes Bower, Bernarr Rainbow and Derek Holman.

The book contained short biographies of church musicians, musical terms, an explanation of 'Difficult words in the Prayer Book', the Church's Calendar with Saints' days, articles on church architecture, the organ, the CTS and 'how to read music' — quite a mine of information within 110 pages. So much so that the authors of this book learnt for the first

---

[218] The two recordings of Series 3 liturgical music featuring students of the College, directed by Michael Fleming with Simon Lindley at the organ, were recorded in 1974 in St John's, Upper Norwood, but a shortage of plastic and the 'three-day week' (i.e. firms were only allowed electric power three days a week) caused by the coal miners' strike, meant they were not issued until 1975.

[219] See Appendix 2 - Council Members.

time that the well-known aerial photograph of Addington Palace and Golf Course was taken by resident student Michael Carnegie, 'one of the few church musicians qualified to pilot an aeroplane.'[220]

In 1980 the book was revised again by Lionel Dakers into the bright red format familiar to many who read this and with the new title *The Chorister's Companion*. This edition noted that 140,000 copies were sold since the original 1934 edition. One aim of the revision and title change was to make the book suitable 'for the enjoyment and edification of choristers and church musicians of all ages' and it was of course 'unisex'. A second edition was published in 1989, further revised by Harry Bramma and illustrated with photographs.

The last revision, an expansion to over 200 pages with a completely new design, was in 2009 as *The Voice for Life Chorister's Companion*. New features in this edition include advice on voice production, a composer timeline relating composers' lifetimes to contemporary events from 1066 onwards and colour photographs.

Harry Bramma comments that:

'The RSCM was very much a 'cottage industry' where many dedicated people worked tirelessly on very modest incomes. The working practices to us now seem Dickensian. Everything was 'manual' — computers arrived only towards the end of Dakers' time, masterminded by the Accountant Michael Kerrigan, and the arrival of a fax machine only came in my early days as Director. Much has been superseded by emails and the internet speeding up the working — but at the same time putting people out of work. The camaraderie of a sizeable workforce working closely together creates a special atmosphere. So did the lunches provided for the staff, the morning tea at 10.00am and the tea and cake at 3.00pm. I always thought the morning refreshment was rather early, but it could not be altered as it was a relic of the timetable of the College of St Nicolas. There were also set places at lunch and I was seriously in trouble with Vincent Waterhouse if I moved from the Director's seat at the end of the table when fewer people were lunching and I was marooned in solitude at the end of the table. It was inevitable that these very conservative working practices should change. It did not make sense that an employee only had one job and could sit and read the paper when their particular tasks were finished. Flexible working was not on the agenda, but technological change did bring about a different atmosphere which worked against the friendships which developed in the work place.'

---

[220] Now in 2015, there are quite a few — including professional airline pilots.

The Harold Smart Competition

In 1988 the first annual anthem competition in memory of Dr Harold Smart for composers was announced, with a cash prize of £100 and the possibility of the winning composition being published. This competition still runs today and usually attracts between 30 and 70 entries. There is usually a defining brief, different each year, to indicate the kind of composition required, the forces to be employed, the level of difficulty expected and perhaps suggesting a specific text or source of text. Each competition is announced in the autumn, with adjudication after Christmas and prizes announced in the spring.

That first competition in 1988 attracted 70 entries with one winner (Ronald Watson with *Confirm the hope thy word allows*) together with three commended compositions, all of which were published. In subsequent years there have sometimes been joint-winners, other years where none of the submitted works came up to expectation and also years when prizes were awarded but publication of the winning work did not go ahead[221].

The competition was set up in the memory of Dr Harold Smart, a General Practitioner and ENT surgeon with a love of church music, but not himself an organist. The aim was to encourage the composition of anthems within the context of a church service.

Footnote

As a footnote to RSCM Publications, it should be added that, of the (approximately) 1500 RSCM titles published over the years, all are held in the RSCM archive. They can be found in the online catalogue of the RSCM Library at www.rscm.com, and, with the miracle of modern technology, on-demand copies of almost anything the RSCM has ever published can be supplied, subject to copyright rules.

---

[221] These failures of publication were usually at times when the RSCM did not have sufficient funds for publication, rather than suggesting the works themselves were not worthy enough to be printed.

G) Festivals

Triennial Festivals and the Festival of Britain

With Sir Sydney Nicholson's first Royal Albert Hall Festival in 1930 began a tradition of major triennial RSCM festivals[222], halted by WWII but restarting again with the Festival of Britain in 1951. In the previous year the Arts Council had invited the RSCM to organise church music for the Festival of Britain, proposing a large festival for choirs in the Royal Albert Hall on Wednesday 20th June and five regional festivals[223]. Following the established practice, these were to be services and not concerts.

At the Royal Albert Hall The Lord Archbishop of Canterbury, President of the RSCM was the preacher, John Dykes Bower of St Paul's Cathedral was the conductor, William McKie of Westminster Abbey was the organist and HRH Princess Elizabeth was present, together with a choir of 1000 singers from RSCM affiliated parish, cathedral and school choirs.[224] Amongst all these eminent people, the Precentor for the service was to be a parish priest, Joseph Poole, Rector of Merstham in Kent. But the Revd Canon Joseph Weston Poole was no ordinary parish priest. He had already served as Precentor and Sacrist at Canterbury Cathedral and would have not only a notable personal career but would also fulfil an important role devising special liturgies for the RSCM.[225]

The two special festival music books were devised by the Musical Advisory Board to take into account the needs of smaller choirs. The service was essentially the same, but the larger Albert Hall Festival book included three more difficult anthems less suited to small choirs[226]. Before the service Henry Ley played music by Purcell, Charles Macpherson, Stanford, Harwood and Parry. William McKie played for the service, including the 'Middle Voluntary' — *Rhosymedre* by Vaughan Williams — and after the service William Harris played S S Wesley's *Choral Song and Fugue* and his own *Flourish for an Occasion*.

Although the service was not broadcast live, the BBC did broadcast extracts on the following weekend, introduced by Ernest Lough, once the famous boy soprano from the Temple Church.

Whilst these festivals gave the RSCM widespread publicity, a little-remembered further activity gave a wider public the chance to witness RSCM principles in practice throughout the summer at the Church of St John the Evangelist in the Waterloo Road. This was rebuilt

---

[222] 1930 Royal Albert Hall: 1,200 voices from 182 choirs; 1933 Crystal Palace: 4000 singers from 216 choirs; 1936 Crystal Palace; 1939 Royal Albert Hall.

[223] In the end, seven Regional Festivals took place. In Bath Abbey, 340 singers dir. Hubert Crook; Peterborough Cathedral, 17 choirs dir. Douglas Hopkins; Durham Cathedral, Brangwyn Hall, Swansea, 800 singers dir. Eric Coningsby; Wakefield Cathedral, 900 singers dir. Percy Saunders; Canterbury Cathedral, 500 singers dir. Sir Ernest Bullock and Chester Cathedral, 600 singers dir. Sir Ernest Bullock.

[224] From 150 affiliated choirs. Altogether 2600 singers had applied for places, but there was only space allocated for 1000 singers.

[225] For further biographical details of Joseph Poole see Appendix 4.

[226] Charles Wood *Hail, gladdening light*; Edward Bairstow *Blessed City* and Vaughan Williams *Te Deum in G*. The music common to both books was: Tye *O come ye servants*; Canticles *Walmisley in D-minor*; The Ferial Responses; Weelkes *Hosanna to the Son of David*; Purcell *Thou knowest, Lord*; Travers *O worship the Lord*; S S Wesley *Blessed be the God and Father* and Wood *Jesu, the very thought*.

and re-dedicated on 24th April 1951 with HRH Princess Elizabeth in attendance and became the official Festival Church. Altogether 116 RSCM choirs[227] sang the services there in a 5-day rota with the church's resident choir singing at the weekends.

Festival of Britain Service Albert Hall 1951

Although much RSCM administrative energy was then put into planning and executing the move to Addington, there was energy enough to plan a 1954 Triennial Festival. GHK wrote of festivals that:

> 'While we must not disregard the excellent work done at smaller gatherings and in more intimate surroundings than are provided by these larger [1930-1939] Festivals, there can be no doubt that the pre-war festivals and those in 1951 acted as a stimulus to greater effort on the part of choirs, and evoked an enthusiasm from the singers which was of immense value to them in the work which they do in their own churches.'

The 1954 Albert Hall Festival did not follow the pattern of its predecessors, namely Evensong with extra anthems, but was based instead on the 'Office of the Guild of St Nicolas' followed by the story of Man's Salvation told in readings and music[228], all as before

---

[227] 135 choirs had applied.

[228] Bach *Zion hears her watchmen's voices*; H C Stewart *On this day, earth shall ring*; Byrd *Ave verum corpus*; Stanford *Ye choirs of new Jerusalem* and Finzi *God is gone up*.

216

selected by the RSCM Musical Advisory Board. A notable inclusion in this FSB was Martin Shaw's own uplifting descant to his tune 'Little Cornard', not published anywhere else.

It would be four years, and not three, before the next festival, the reason being that the 1957 festival was postponed for a year to coincide with the 1958 Lambeth Conference. It reverted to the form of Evensong plus anthems[229] and readings on various themes. Also held in the Royal Albert Hall and in the presence of HM Queen Elizabeth, The Queen Mother and 150 Archbishops and Bishops, the music was chosen in the hope that 'churches in the many parts of the Anglican Communion will find the contents of this book useful.'

Guyon Wells (1957-1959) wrote:

'While the hall was filling [Joseph Poole] was rehearsing the congregation. Meantime the students with allotted tasks were in the bowels of the building helping the dignitaries into their academic regalia with much difficulty. I had been assigned to Sir William when suddenly he became aware of the music from above. It was his large scale Anthem, *Oh What Their Joy* that was being rehearsed.

'What is that music?' he exclaimed.

'It is your anthem' I naively explained. Whereupon he was overcome with joy and began to hum along with the rehearsing audience. What a treasure was Sir William.'

In 1959 RSCM Council policy began to change as it was thought that the festivals held in London touched only a small part of the RSCM's membership, and laid a considerable burden of extra work upon the choirs[230]. Also the London festivals tended to be supported mainly by choirs in the South. They felt that other parts of the country should have the opportunity to experience large festivals. The *Festival Book 1961-62*[231] was devised for a festival in each Province. The first, in the Province of York, was held at Leeds Town Hall in the presence of HRH The Princess Royal in July 1961 and the second, in the Province of Wales, was held in October 1962.

The London festival, for the Province of Canterbury and in the presence of HM Queen Elizabeth The Queen Mother, was delayed until July 1965 and by this time a new *Choral Festival Service 1965* book was published. This was however text and hymn tunes only; singers had to buy the choral items, which, for the first time, contained only 20C music, indeed the hymns and anthems[232] were all composed since 1924. GHK and Martin How conducted the 800 singers, and the four organists were John Morehen, Roy Massey, Peter

---

[229] Canticles: *Stanford in C*; Anthems: Weelkes *Gloria in excelsis*; Batten *O praise the Lord*; Battishill *O Lord, look down from heaven*; S S Wesley *The Lord has been mindful* and Harris *O what their joy*.

[230] *ECM* Oct 1959.

[231] Contained Canticles: *Noble in B-minor*; Anthems: Byrd *Prevent us, O Lord*; Handel *With cheerful notes*; S S Wesley *Thou judge of quick and dead*; Bairstow *Let all mortal flesh*; Hutchings *God is gone up* and Joubert *O Lorde, the maker of al thing*.

[232] Gelineau *Psalm 122*; Bernard Rose *Responses*; Wills *Behold now praise the Lord*; Chants by GHK and Sydney Nicholson; Canticles: *Sumsion in A* (composed for the RSCM); Tony Hewitt-Jones *Bring unto the Lord*; Bairstow *Jesu, the very thought*; Thorpe-Davie *Come, Holy Ghost*; Vaughan Williams *Te Deum in G*.

White and also Gillian Weir[233] who played Messiaen's *Alleluias Sereins* from *L'Ascension* as a 'Middle Voluntary'[234] and the *Final* from Vierne's *Premier Symphonie* as a final voluntary, published 1899 and so probably the oldest piece of music heard that day apart from the National Anthem! Four of the composers represented, Dr Sumsion, Dr Wills, Dr Rose and Mr Tony Hewitt-Jones were all present on the platform. The BBC recorded the whole service and broadcast an edited 45-minute version on the Home Service on 4th August in the Choral Evensong slot. It was also available as a two-LP record set in both mono and stereo. No special music book was published. Instead *Choral Service Book 5* was used in conjunction with other items. The whole set was sold for 10/1d. It was noted in *PCM* that 'The photographs taken at this service were found to be disappointing and are therefore not offered for sale.'

The next major Albert Hall festival was *Jubilate Deo* held in 1970 and this demonstrated the ever increasing ecumenism of the RSCM, with representatives of the Free Churches and the Roman Catholic Cardinal Archbishop of Westminster represented, and in the presence of HM The Queen. The military trumpeters from Kneller Hall were memorably directed by Lt-Col CH 'Jiggs' Jaeger OBE[235]. GHK was to direct and Roy Massey to play the organ, but both were sadly indisposed and so Martin How conducted with John Jordan at the organ. Unfortunately GHK was in hospital for five weeks and was then expected to take six months to recuperate. The choir consisted of 850 singers from affiliated choirs in the Province of Canterbury, and the programme included a descant by Herbert Howells for his hymn tune 'Michael', especially composed for this service[236].

Subsequent major RSCM Festivals were arranged on special RSCM Anniversaries: *Rejoice* (50th Jubilee, Royal Albert Hall) 1977, *Let all the World* (60th anniversary, Royal Albert Hall) 1987 and *The Light of Life* (75th anniversary, Westminster Cathedral) 2002.

---

[233] Now, of course, an internationally-known recitalist and teacher, Dame Gillian Weir had been a London student at Addington and had graduated from the Royal Academy of Music in the previous year. For Dame Gillian's own recollections of Addington see p. 80.

[234] Several festivals used 'middle voluntaries' to separate groups of reading and anthems. Middle voluntaries were common until the mid 19C and were usually played after the Psalm, a space for reflection upon the text just heard. There were many criticisms of players being too exuberant and not dignified enough, and so the practice lapsed.

[235] C H 'Jiggs' Jaeger OBE, Mus Bac, LRAM, ARCM, 1913-1970. In 1937, he was a Kneller Hall Trumpeter in Westminster Abbey, at the Coronation of King George VI, when he played the fanfare at the moment of crowning. He was appointed Bandmaster of the 4th Hussars in 1942, Director of Music of the Irish Guards in 1949. He was Director of Music at Kneller Hall for just two years before his premature death.

[236] The other music was: Psalm 122 (Faux-bourdons by Sydney Nicholson); Parry *I was glad*; Hubert Middleton *Let my prayer*; Gibbons *O clap your hands*; Thorpe-Davie *Come, Holy Ghost* and Handel *Let the bright seraphim*.

The 1977 Golden Jubilee[237] service was again attended by HM Queen Elizabeth The Queen Mother, who throughout her life took an interest in the RSCM, both as a Patron and as a practical supporter[238]. Sydney Nicholson had arranged her wedding music at Westminster Abbey back in 1923 when she was Lady Elizabeth Bowes-Lyon and, though they were never close friends, she remained his constant supporter long after he left the Abbey. Lionel Dakers and John Cooke were the conductors and the organists were Francis Jackson, Martin How and Arthur Wills. On this occasion there was an orchestra present, from the Royal College of Music, a sign of the increasing ties between the RSCM and the London Colleges. The hymns were skilfully orchestrated by David Willcocks and a semi-chorus in the service was drawn from members of the three Cathedral Singers groups. The service, according to the introductory notes by Canon Joseph Poole[239], 'looked both backwards, with gratitude for what the RSCM has already accomplished: and forwards, with resolution to meet the tasks of tomorrow.'

1977 Festival recording engineers

1977 Festival: a chorister's view

---

[237] Psalm 24 Antiphons by Bernard Rose; Parry *I was glad* (including the *'Vivats'*, as it was performed in the presence of Royalty); Byrd *Sing joyfully*; Elgar *Give unto the Lord*: The Middle Voluntary was *Symphony No 4 in F* by William Boyce; Vaughan Williams *Rise heart*; a newly composed anthem by Peter Aston — *The True Glory*; Psalm 121 set by Walford Davies was sung by the Cathedral Singers' semi-chorus who also sang Henry Ley's *Evening Hymn of King Charles I*.

[238] She sent gifts for the Addington Fayre raffle.

[239] See Appendix 4.

1977 Golden Jubilee Festival Service at the Royal Albert Hall

It is not widely-known that the *RSCM50* logo used in 1977 was designed by Herbert Norman (1903-2001), who had recently retired as senior partner of pipe organ builders Hill, Norman & Beard.

The RSCM50 Jubilee was widely-celebrated by affiliates at home and overseas, both with special services and with Jubilee Dinners. There are too many to mention in detail but Lionel Dakers, Gerald Knight, David Willcocks and Meredith Davies (conductor of the Royal Choral Society) all directed Jubilee festivals whilst on their travels in North America, Tasmania, Australia and South Africa respectively. Even in remote places such as Mauritius at St James' Cathedral in Port Louis there was a Jubilee service singing a Nicholson Psalm, Rose Responses, Harris in A-minor Canticles together with anthems by Purcell and Vaughan Williams.

Above: RSCM Jubilee service in Cape Town City Hall conducted by Meredith Davies 1977

Below: Jubilee Banner made by the RSCM West Australia Branch

The 1987 Diamond Jubilee Service *Let all the World* in the Albert Hall was attended by HM the Queen and HRH The Duke of Edinburgh, with the Archbishop of Canterbury. A choir of 850 and congregation of 7000 were conducted by Lionel Dakers with Martin How at the organ. LD reported[240] that it had taken three years to plan, that he had asked Michael Perham[241] to devise the service and that he regarded this as a good occasion to commission new works. So the *ASB Responses* were set for choir with brass, percussion and organ by Paul Patterson, Richard Shephard contributed a restrained setting of *O for a thousand tongues to sing* and William Mathias' brief was to end the service with all forces at his disposal with *Let all the world in every corner sing* leading to everyone singing Basil Harwood's tune 'Luckington'[242]. John Barrow, RSCM Assistant Secretary, was responsible for assembling a balanced choir, no mean feat as UK applications greatly exceeded the space available. It was also decided to leave 150 of the 850 available singing places to singers from overseas RSCM affiliates. Nineteen regional rehearsals were held, all directed by LD and accompanied by Martin How who was to be service organist[243]. On the day before the festival LD took a rehearsal of the overseas singers in St George's, Hanover Square. Afterwards he wrote of the service in *CMQ*:

> 'From my bird's eye view on the rostrum I would put first the extraordinary, almost uncanny, sense of atmosphere which was somehow generated. With not a seat to be had well in advance of the day, it was like a vast family converging from the four corners of the earth intent on celebration and, as someone remarked, making the aura more like that of a great cathedral than a concert hall.
>
> Then there was the superb brass and organ playing, even if Gillian Weir and Gerre Hancock, representing Australasia and North America, could hardly be heard because of the noise of the talking before the service.
>
> Pride of place must go to the hymns so spaciously arranged and orchestrated by David Willcocks[244] and placed at five focal points in the service.'

Gillian Weir played the *Final* from Vierne's *Premier Symphonie* as a final voluntary, just as she had for the 1965 Festival.

Because of the packed hall, ticket revenue was excellent and, after expenses, the event made a profit of £6882. From this were taken subsidies for the London and Leeds Jubilee Dinners, expenses for the Westminster Abbey service in December and a party for RSCM staff, thus leaving £3571 which was put in the AP repairs fund. The service was recorded by

---

[240] *CMQ* Oct 1987.

[241] Bishop Michael Perham (b. 1947), a former Curate of St Mary's, Addington, from 1976 to 1981, served on the Church of England Liturgical Commission from 1982 to 2001 and was one of the architects of *Common Worship*. Bishop of Gloucester from 2004 to 2014, he was also Chairman of SPCK from 2007 to 2011.

[242] The other music was Haydn *The heavens are telling*; Alan Wilson *ASB Magnificat*; Bairstow *Let my prayer come up*; Middle Voluntary Howells *Rhapsody No 1* (played by Roy Massey) Wood *Glorious and powerful God*; Stanford *Agnus Dei in F*; Psalm 96 Chant by GHK and Elgar *The Spirit of the Lord*.

[243] Roy Massey, Gillian Weir and Gerre Hancock also played.

[244] These arrangements are still available from the Oxford University Press.

the BBC and by Decca Records. It was broadcast on BBC1 TV on 28th June at 10.30am and issued on twin 12' LP records and CD under the Argo label.

Sadly the Royal Albert Hall has become too expensive to risk mounting major festivals there without financial backing of some kind. When the 70th anniversary came in 1997, at a time of RSCM financial problems following the expense of moving from Addington to Dorking, the celebrations were small though no less joyful or celebratory. On 31st May 1997, the 50th anniversary of Sir Sydney Nicholson's death, Evensong was sung in Westminster Abbey by the Abbey Choir supplemented by 150 choristers from RSCM affiliated choirs and conducted by Abbey organist Martin Neary with assistant Martin Baker at the organ. On 5th July later that year in York Minster there was a 70th anniversary celebration sung by a choir of 250 singers drawn from affiliated choirs in the North and directed by Gordon Appleton with Minster organist Philip Moore at the organ.

One other major joint event deserves a mention, that of 26th May 1990 – the 'The Glory of the Psalms' which was held at the Albert Hall. It was to mark the publication of *Songs from the Psalms* and *Psalms for Today* just published by Jubilate Hymns (Hodder and Stoughton) and was arranged by the RSCM and Langham Arts in association with the publisher. It was neither a concert nor a service, but more of an audience-participation lecture recital. Harry Bramma recalls:

> 'I chose 550 singers from affiliated churches with flourishing choirs. Many singers travelled great distances, including a contingent from Liverpool. The congregation also came from London and much further afield. The hall was sold out, with every seat taken. It was a unique occasion – 550 robed choristers on the stage, including many boys and girls, accompanied by the All Souls' Orchestra conducted by Noël Tredinnick and myself, with Martin How at the organ. There were also some small instrumental ensembles to add variety[245]. The concert was compered by the Bishop of Chester (The Rt Revd Michael Baughan) formerly Vicar at All Souls', Langham Place.
>
> The idea behind this act of worship was to present as many different settings of Psalm texts – ranging from Parry's *I was glad* to plainsong; metrical Psalms such as the 'Old 100th' sung by all; and a variety of modern settings. It worked very well musically and demonstrated that there need be no conflict between different styles of music if the music is done well. In fact I had actively argued that many revivalist hymns and folk melodies have more in common with classical music than has some of the more staid and stilted music 'in good taste' in the Anglican Tradition.'

During the course of the evening the 3000 or so members of the audience had a chance to try some 'Psalmody Ancient & Modern' themselves and to listen to actor David Suchet ('Hercule Poirot') bring to life some Psalm texts. The event was a great success and the

---

[245] Including a more contemporary worship group led by Chris Rolinson, more used to playing to 60,000 at Spring Harvest than at the Albert Hall.

RAH was packed so that, although under-written by Hodder & Stoughton, it made a profit, largely because the orchestra and most of the musicians gave their services without fee.

Harry Bramma:

'When the possibility of another Festival in 1997 was considered, RSCM Council were adamant that the recent move to Cleveland Lodge had put great pressure on the RSCM and it was not the time to be side-tracked by organising another great RAH event. I now feel that this was a great mistake occasioned by a considerable failure of nerve. In a way, this was understandable; but a great public show of strength would have propelled the RSCM forward and overcome the sense of instability felt by members of the Council. That meant that the last great RSCM event was the service to launch the [Sing with the Spirit] Appeal on 3rd June 1994 at Westminster Abbey which I organised.'[246]

Diocesan Festivals

Whilst the major RSCM festivals gave excellent publicity and provided many participants with a once-in-a-lifetime experience, the total number of singers attending was small compared to the vast legion of RSCM and other singers who took part in the many regular Diocesan Choral Festivals arranged by Diocesan Choral or Church Choir Associations or by the RSCM, either at a local diocesan level or centrally. The tradition of parish choirs gathering in cathedrals for communal singing has a history much longer than that of the RSCM, with some diocesan choral associations, such as Canterbury, Ely and Salisbury, having been founded as early as 1860.

Not that the major London festivals were numerically even the largest of their kind, because, of the many provincial DCFs arranged locally, some had support that we can only envy today — Chelmsford in 1952 boasted 1700 singers with 1300 the following year, Worcester in 1953 drew 1000 singers, in 1952/53 Canterbury, Chester and Bristol each attracted 800 singers.

The level of activity through the 1950's and 60's was high. In a letter from Leslie Green to RSCM Representatives in October 1957, he lists 20 provincial DCFs in October and nine in November. *RSCM News-Notes* in April 1966 listed 36 festivals planned for England and Wales. The official Register of Festivals gives figures for the autumn of 1961 showing that the Festivals Nos 175-184 had the following attendance:

Autumn Festivals arranged from HQ in 1961

Place	Singers	Choirs	Conductor	Organist
St Mary's Portsea	400	28	Derek Holman	F B Coley
King's College, Cambridge	300	19	David Willcocks	(unknown)
Brighton PC	590	28	V Bradley	Gavin Brown
All Saints', Ealing Common	93	7	Dr Geoffrey Leeds	(unknown)

---

[246] See Appeals p.344.

Southwark Cathedral 'A' Festival	424	27	Harold Dexter	(unknown)
London DCF	480	24	Dr A J Pritchard	J Dykes Bower
Christ Church, St Marylebone	112	7	Dr A J Pritchard	Mr J Burchill
Canterbury Cathedral DCF A	556	25	Dr R J Ashfield	R Adams
Canterbury Cathedral DCF B	592	29	J S Brough	G Isaac
Aylesbury PC	326	21	Dr D Lumsden	R G Kalton
Chichester Cathedral	740	34	John Birch	Richard Seal
Totals	**4613**	**249**		

The music for these 1961 festivals was mostly taken from RSCM publications — *Festival Service Book 1961-62, Music for Courses, Choral Service Book 2, Choir Book 10, Service Books 5, 8 & 9*, together with various extra loose anthems and canticles such as *Brewer in D* and *Walmisley in D-minor*. The two large DCFs in Canterbury (usually held one week apart[247]) accounted for ¼ of the total singers and at the remaining nine festivals each choir sent an average of 17 or 18 singers. Whilst courses are of more educational value than festivals, the experience of singing in large groups can be inspiring for members of small choirs. A report in *RSCM News* April 1966 given by Mr Lees, the choirmaster of Holy Trinity and St Mary in Dodford near Bromsgrove, whose choir consisted of one bass, four tenors, three altos, seven girls and four boys, after attending the Worcester Cathedral DCF reads:

> 'It was a wonderful experience to join with so vast a body of singers, especially when you find that everyone has found difficulties in the same place... Then there is the marvellous improvement which a conductor like Christopher Robinson can make in a short time.'

In addition to large local choral festivals it was commonplace for a handful of RSCM choirs to meet locally for some special service.

The vast majority of all the festivals mentioned so far took the form of Evensong, but there was a gradual move towards special themed services (notably the Devotions and FSBs published by the RSCM) and even the occasional Eucharist. In *ECM* October 1959 Gerald Knight gave vent to a frustration which is still true today for those of us who arrange choir festivals:

> 'There was only one thing that I regretted: the absence of the choirs of some of the larger churches. This is unfortunately a feature which is met with in other dioceses; there is a superior attitude displayed which seems to say 'we are the choir of St Blank's and can't waste our time on the simple stuff which those other choirs are doing.' Or else they say 'We have our own festival and can't alter the date of that.' **The larger and more successful choir has a duty to the less fortunate ones**[248]; by

---

[247] There is a note for the previous year that the two Canterbury festivals were attended by 509 and 527 singers respectively. Applications could not be accepted from a further 260 singers from 14 choirs.
[248] The emphasis here is editorial, but this attitude is still sadly prevalent today.

their presence at festivals they can give not only practical help to those who are struggling, but also provide powerful encouragement.'

Harry Bramma recalls:

'Up to 1998 when I retired, it was assumed that a great deal of the Director's work would be musical. It was considered important for the Director to be seen and known in the areas working closely with the Chairmen and Area Committees. Visits around the UK could take many forms. They might be simply meeting with committees to discuss RSCM policy; or it might be a social occasion when the Director would speak of plans for the future. Some of these were highly organised affairs with sumptuous buffet suppers and much conviviality. Winifred Sibley, Wife of Eric who was organist of Sleaford Parish Church was notable for her catering. Her husband went back to the days of Sydney Nicholson who had visited Lincolnshire in his early days. I mention this to demonstrate the tenacious loyalty which had been engendered by successive Directors.

By far the most important events the Director was called upon to conduct were the great Area Festivals. Up to my time these were enormous occasions — and still are in some places. I remember the festival at Exeter where the whole Nave of the cathedral was filled with singers; similarly at Durham where the massed choir of 700 stretched right to the West end of the cathedral. It required much effort to weld these massed forces into a musical unit, but in terms of morale it was worth it; singers went home with a spring in their step, feeling themselves to be an important part of a greater whole. It would be tedious to list all these great occasions — at places like King's College, Cambridge; the Octagon at Ely and the Choir of Canterbury. They left a very great impression on me personally and they were indeed a great show of strength.

Boys only Festivals

The first boys' festivals were organised by Sydney Nicholson at Westminster Abbey during WWII[249] each involving around 600 boys. The idea was revived on 12th October 1957 when 250 boys from all round the UK were selected from those best known to the Special Commissioners and from residential chorister courses. Altogether 140 choirs were represented. 1957 should have been a 'triennial festival' year, but this was deferred until 1958 to coincide with the Lambeth Conference and this boys' festival arranged instead — GHK directed with Derek Holman at the organ. 'It was intended that this event shall be a demonstration of boys' singing at its best.' Boys were required to attend at least one regional rehearsal and Martin How travelled round the country to take these. A great deal of work went into making the standard of the Festival as high as possible. The music was Canticles: Sumsion in G, Anthems: Walmisley *Ponder my words*, Greene *O praise the Lord*, Boyce *Turn thee unto me* and GHK's own *Christ whose glory fills the skies*.

The similar Boys' Festival was held in St Paul's on 15th October 1960 when the music was Canticles: Sumsion in G, Anthems: Purcell *Evening Hymn*, Nares *Rejoice in the Lord* and

---

[249] See *SNMOM*.

Harris *Behold now, praise the Lord* — with *Music for Evensong Set E*. The service included a specially composed anthem by Alan Gibbs. Again Martin How took the rehearsals, GHK directed the 250 boys with John Dykes Bower at the organ and, for the service, the cathedral was packed full.

In the mid 60's two further Boys' Festivals were held, one at York Minster and one at St Paul's where John Dykes-Bower was the organist. Martin How took the rehearsals and conducted both. Martin recalls the day he arrived at St Paul's to be met by a verger who clearly wasn't expecting them. 'You can't rehearse in the cathedral', they were told, 'there's a wedding.' It seems this kind of welcome was not uncommon from vergers in those days and Martin's stock reply was — 'Oh dear, have you got a railway timetable?' A blank look from the verger was followed up by Martin adding 'We have XXX boys here — we can't let them wander around London — we must send them home at once.' The verger departs to consult superiors and then returns usually with good news. Martin used this approach a number of times. On this occasion the happy couple were married in a side chapel with the background musical accompaniment to their wedding, the boys rehearsing, as planned, in the Quire.

Public School and Prep School Festivals

The very first festival entered in the RSCM Festival Register was for public school boys in Gloucester Cathedral, held in 1941 with boys from Malvern College, St Michael's, Tenbury, and from the public schools at Felstead, Betteshanger, Repton, Monkton Combe and Westminster. There were 307 singers present — 163 trebles and 144 ATB. This festival continued annually through WWII and Gloucester as a venue remained popular. The Festival Register ends in 1965 by which time there were 709 singers from 16 schools. Throughout most of these two decades, Leonard Blake[250], DOM at Malvern College, RSCM Special Commissioner and Editor of *ECM*, was in charge and Herbert Sumsion was organist. In 1947 an attempt was made to expand the idea to Peterborough and Canterbury cathedrals. This failed — partly due to lack of support but also due to late delivery of music from the printers. Another expansion attempt was made the following year when festivals were also planned for Salisbury as well as Peterborough and Canterbury. This time 187 voices were tempted to Canterbury but Salisbury and Peterborough were again cancelled. Not to be deterred 1949 saw festivals planned at Gloucester, Leicester, Canterbury and Eton College, all of which took place, with 970 boys attending. From this time forwards these festivals grew to five in number in 1958 when 1380 boys and girls attended.

On 7th June 1959 the first Preparatory Schools Festival was held in Tonbridge School Chapel directed by Dr Allan Bunney with 283 trebles from 14 schools present, and by 1965 3439 singers from 110 affiliated schools attended the nine festivals held that year. Many festivals were held during the summer term when examinations and other school commitments were considerable, and the RSCM did well to make them so successful. In 1983 *CMQ* noted for the 25th anniversary of the RSCM Festivals for Preparatory Schools

---

[250] See Chapter VI (D).

that, during those 25 years, there had been 114 festivals with over 20,000 singers participating. It was also noted that the seven and eight festivals held during 1982 and 1983 attracted 1200 and 1300 singers respectively, a significant fall from the 1965 figures above and a decline in attendance which was to continue.

From 1967 the RSCM began to publish dedicated books of music especially for these festivals. The Public School festivals were renamed 'Senior Schools' Festivals until 1984, when the festival had settled in Ripon, it was thereafter known as the Ripon Schools Festivals. These music books continued to be published (along with Prep School FSBs) until 1996 from which time a 'themed' service book for school or young voices festivals was produced. These are still published annually by the RSCM, but are now intended for upper-voices only.

Above: Public School Festival at Hurstpierpoint College in June 1958 with 126 voices

Below: Stoke on Trent Archdeaconry Festival in the Victoria Hall, Hanley, in 1959;
1000 voices from 44 choirs were directed by GHK with Melville Cook at the organ

Annual British Legion Festival of Remembrance

From about 1955 the RSCM was asked by the British Legion to provide a choir for the Festival of Remembrance held in the Royal Albert Hall each year on the Saturday before Remembrance Day. A choir of 30 boys and men was supplied by inviting five affiliated choirs to provide singers.

Ian Henderson (staff 1961-65):

'There were many occasions when I was able to visit some of the Festivals which I had helped arrange, as well as some rather special events. One of these was the annual British Legion Festival of Remembrance in the Royal Albert Hall. The RSCM was asked to provide the choir for the service which formed an important part of the ceremony. Representatives from affiliated choirs were invited to send a small number of singers, the choirs concerned were those that had supported the RSCM over the years, and were selected by the Director. They had to attend a rehearsal on the morning of the Festival [at 10.30am], and there were then two performances[251]; in the afternoon and the evening one which was attended by HM the Queen and the Duke of Edinburgh and was invariably televised[252]. It was not only a privilege to be a part of this event; it also enabled me to meet several of the personalities who took part.'

Trevor Jarvis recalls:

'My choir, Buckfast Abbey, was invited to sing in 1983, 4 trebles, and one alto, tenor and bass. The letter, from Vincent Waterhouse stated: 'Regrettably, we cannot invite women or girls to take part on this occasion.'

The guidelines were strict regarding turn-out. Surplices and ruffs were to be freshly laundered, all cassocks should be well-fitting and of the correct length! Black shoes should be well-polished and everybody's appearance should be neat and tidy. Each boy should bring a comb and hoods should not be worn, but those entitled to wear war medals are asked to do so.'

Four well-turned out choristers at the 1968 Festival of Remembrance

---

[251] The matinee is open to any member of the public. The evening event is open only to members of the Legion and their families, and is attended by senior members of the Royal Family.
[252] The day finished at 9.00pm. Both lunch and tea were provided by the British Legion.

H) St Nicolastide Festivals and Fayres

From the earliest days of the SECM a special service of thanksgiving was sung annually at St Nicolastide (6th December)[253], generally at St Sepulchre in Holborn. It was also common for affiliated churches around the country to celebrate the day with special services or festivals. In 1948, for the RSCM's 21st Birthday, 200 singers from twelve choirs were gathered in St Sepulchre; a private recording was made by Levy's Recording Studios of New Bond Street and issued on five double-sided 78rpm records. The combined choirs sang an introit: Tye *O come ye servants of the Lord*; Canticles: *Stanford in B-flat*; Anthems: Nicholson *Let us with a gladsome mind*; Nicholson *Teach us, good Lord*; Purcell *Rejoice in the Lord alway* and Wood *O thou the central orb*. The service concluded with Psalm 150 using Stanford's setting.

An RSCM Council meeting was usually also held at St Nicolastide, together with the public AGM and presentation of Council's Annual Report. A typical day in the post-war period would be:

Morning:	Celebration of the Eucharist at the College, after which staff and students migrate to Central London.
Late Morning:	Council Meeting (and lunch) held in London.
Afternoon:	Rehearsal for singers from affiliated choirs in St Sepulchre.
	Everyone attend Evensong at Westminster Abbey followed by AGM at Church House.
	Evensong at St Sepulchre.

In the first year at Addington a new format was tried. The AGM was held at the Palace and was followed by tea in the Great Hall, after which Evensong was sung by the students. *ECM* noted that 'members showed their appreciation of this by being present in larger numbers than ever before.' No doubt they were also eager to have a look at the RSCM's new home. On this occasion there was also an address entitled 'A producer looks at some problems of public worship' by Mr E Martin Browne, Director of the British Drama League. *ECM* reported that 'the printed word cannot convey the varied tone-colouring, the clear enunciation, or the (apparently) artless phrasing of Mr Martin Browne's spoken extracts...'

In 1956 the first St Nicolas Fayre[254] was held at AP and was to have been opened by BBC personality Brian Johnston, but he was admitted to hospital and could not attend. Lady Swan, wife of Council member Sir Kenneth Swan and herself an organist, opened the Fayre. The AGM of the RSCM was held just prior to the Fayre and HM The Queen Mother, Patron of the RSCM, sent a gift of half a dozen fish knives in an oak case for the raffle. In several subsequent years she also sent gifts. This Fayre was so successful that it became an annual event, organised by an enthusiastic committee and executed by ladies from RSCM staff and

---

[253] 6th Dec is the anniversary of the meeting convened in 1927 by Sir Sydney Nicholson in the Jerusalem Chamber of Westminster Abbey which led to the founding of the SECM/RSCM. St Nicolas is the Patron Saint of choristers (amongst others) and in RSCM usage is always spelt Nicolas without an 'h'.

[254] The Fayres/Fairs were invariably held on the last weekend of November.

from the local community. The first Fayre was an afternoon event, but in subsequent years it became an all-day event and spread through the whole ground floor of the Palace.

The Fayre was more than just a vehicle for the AGM and Annual Report, for it was a source of significant funding. The first Fayre raised over £400 (£10,000 today) and in subsequent years the amount raised slowly rose. In 1961 the Fayre was opened by Mrs Kettle, Mayor of Croydon and the prizes were given by Lady Marshall. Her husband, Alderman Sir James Marshall, had recently received the Freedom of the County Borough of Croydon. *ECM* notes that it was 'his advocacy in the Croydon Council Chamber that resulted in the RSCM being installed in AP. Since then he and his wife have been staunch supporters of the RSCM. Lady Marshall was a driving force in the annual Fayres' — indeed she had been chairman of the organising committee from the beginning. In 1961 £700 was raised (£13,000 today), in 1964 it broke the £1000 barrier and in 1968 reached £1727 (£27,000 today). In 1969 the Fayre was curtailed by a violent snowstorm[255] and receipts fell to £1422. In 1971 it was announced that there would be no more Fayres as Billy Rivers, who was by then the driving force behind them, was retiring (aged 71). There was such dismay that Mrs Mary Williamson, Martin How's secretary, organised a mini-fayre. Mr Harold King, a local businessman and RSCM supporter stepped in and a full Fayre was reinstated in 1972 raising £1407. In this year there was a special appeal for Green Shield Stamps[256]. Mr King died in May 1976 and Elisabeth Dakers took over organisation of the Fayre.

The 20th RSCM Christmas Fayre in 1975 raised £2007 which was used to redecorate the Norman Shaw Room (previously used by the Colles Library) into a fully-equipped lecture room. The Fayre also provided serendipitous income for special projects which otherwise would have been difficult to provide in the general budget. These included:

1970: The Peter Collins organ was largely funded from the Fayre proceeds.
1978: £2872 for restoration work on the H&H Chapel organ, its first overhaul for 25 years.
1980: £3366 for redecoration of the staircase and new curtains for the dining-room.
1981: £4513 used to decorate and renew the lighting in the Chapel.
1982: £4859 to be used for renovation of the Great Hall.
1983: £5218 raised towards redecoration of the Great Hall.
1984: £6000 used towards the purchase of a Blüthner grand piano for the Great Hall. [Further donations were subsequently made which allowed for the purchase without the necessity of using RSCM funds.]
1985: £4005 to be used to help in refurnishing the Chapel and also to buy video equipment for use by courses.
1986: £5082 allowing new chairs to be ordered for the Chapel.
1990: Profits were used to provide Bursaries for boy and girl choristers to attend summer residential courses. 13 bursaries of £75 were made available for 1992 courses.

---

[255] See photograph taken by Therese the cook in Appendix 3.
[256] Green Shield Stamps (1958-1991) were a loyalty scheme using trading stamps designed to encourage or reward shopping, by being able to buy gifts.

From 1979 the antiquated spelling 'Fayre' was dropped. In 1991 there was no Fair, but the following year RSCM Council member Christopher Field organised one, opened by Prunella Scales and raising £4631. In 1993 the Fair included organ recitals in the Chapel by Martin How and Richard Pilliner, and a recital was given by Croydon Parish Church Girls' Choir directed by Christine Phillis along with 'Choirgirl of the Year' Fiona Wright. The last Fair at Addington was held in 1994.

The committee sometimes sought to find a celebrity or local personality to open the annual Fayre.

This photograph shows popular singer Michael Holliday at the 1959 Fayre. He lived in Croydon at the time. 1959 also saw the introduction of sit-down lunches at the Fayre.

St Nicolas Fayre 1958: Choristers Graham Bill and Roger Durston present flowers to Lady Scott

Moving back to the more formal side of St Nicolastide, in 1958 the AGM and celebrations returned to St Sepulchre's in Holborn. Choirs who were unable to be offered places at the 1957 RAH festival were invited to take part. GHK directed and Derek Holman played the organ. In this year the AGM was also back in London, at the Cutler's Hall, but held a week later. Through the following decade a new general pattern for the day was established:

Late Morning: Celebration of the Eucharist at St Sepulchre.

Afternoon: AGM or lecture at Cutlers' Hall.

Tea followed by Evensong or lectures at St Sepulchre or Holy Trinity, South Kensington.

The services were often sung by the College choir and students and the lectures included:

John Joubert on 'Church Music Today'.

Bernard Rose on 'The Interpretation of 16C Church Music'.

John Whitworth on 'The Counter–Tenor voice'.

Erik Routley on 'Hymns probable and improbable'.

St Nicolastide in 1965 was dominated by the launch of the CTS.[257]

40th Birthday Evensong Westminster Abbey December 1967

---

[257] See Chapter VI.

Being the 40th Anniversary of the RSCM, 1967 saw somewhat more elaborate celebrations. The new Practice Block had been opened that year and Addington was warm at last with new boilers, the Chorister Training Scheme was a roaring success, residential courses for girls had been started and the Cathedral Singers were fully established. There was plenty to celebrate.

The day began with a Morning Eucharist in St Sepulchre's, Holborn, sung by the students. Evensong in Westminster Abbey was sung by invited RSCM choirs conducted by Martin How [music by Nicholson, Stanford, Weelkes, Purcell and Leighton], followed by tea in Church House and a talk by GHK on the 'First Forty Years' illustrated with recordings. His talk was subsequently published as the booklet *RSCM: The First Forty Years*.

Giving thanks at the memorial to Sir Sydney Nicholson in the Cloisters during the 40th Birthday Evensong Westminster Abbey December 1967

The 1974 Nicolastide celebrations were at Addington and began with the usual Sung Eucharist in the morning celebrated by RSCM Chairman, the Bishop of Ely, in the Chapel. During the afternoon the AGM was held followed by the 'first annual' Nicholson Lecture: 'Two Modern Renaissance Men — The contribution of Sydney Nicholson and Martin Shaw to the progress of English Church Music', given by Erik Routley. The lectures did indeed become annual but, because of poor attendance, only for a total of four years, with the following speakers:

1975 – Colin Mawby: 'Liturgy Today – Catholic or Anglican'.

1976 – Donald Swann: 'Church Music as I see it'.

1977 – Dr Arthur Wills: 'Composing for the Church today – its challenges and its problems'.

There is then no mention in *CMQ* of any St Nicolastide events until Diamond Jubilee year in 1987 when, for the 60th Anniversary, Evensong was sung in Westminster Abbey by the Nicholson Singers under Michael Fleming with Martin How at the organ.

The AGM moved back into London to the RCO Headquarters in Kensington Gore for 1975 and 1976, and then in Jubilee year 1977 appropriately back to the Jerusalem Chamber of Westminster Abbey, where the SECM/RSCM was born, and the AGM remained here annually until the 1990's. Producing the annual report and accounts booklet and the distribution of this to members was a costly business, but legally necessary. On taking over as Director, Lionel Dakers ensured that the report and accounts were slimmed down to be as minimalist as possible – just eight A5-sized pages, cheap to print and distribute. Unfortunately for us today this means that there are no longer full accounts of those years' activities to indicate what Council regarded as significant achievements and to give any indications of changes in Council policy.

Celebration Days

The tradition of using St Nicolastide to both remember the origins of the RSCM and to celebrate its work was superseded in the 1990's by Harry Bramma's initiative of an annual Celebration Day. Harry writes:

'Early in my time as Director, I felt there should be an annual national festival when RSCM Choirs could be invited to form a large choir for a great service of thanksgiving. I originally thought of calling it 'Commemoration Day' but John Cooke rightly commented that this was rather stuffy and suggested 'Celebration Day' instead. This was an inspired suggestion which has come to characterize an event which has continued to flourish under my three successors. I rather liked to add lustre to the occasion by inviting a distinguished speaker – a practice which has now lapsed – but a grand musical occasion, in my day organised by the local regional director, continues to be popular.

An important component of these days is the conferment of Honorary RSCM Awards by the Chairman. For the first three years we had a separate meeting after lunch where a distinguished guest gave an address: at Southwark – David Mellor MP; at York – Dame Janet Baker and at Worcester – Sir John Tooley. After that, on the very sensible suggestion of Richard Lawrence, the award ceremony was incorporated into the service itself.

I felt the occasion should showcase fine pieces — always including a Te Deum, and small pieces which would be suitable for small choirs in their home churches. Full accounts of these services can be found within the pages of CMQ. The events were successful because they gave inspiration and enjoyment to RSCM Choirs and members in the regions, and encouraged a feeling of corporate belonging.'

RSCM Celebration Days during the Addington Years

	Cathedral	Preacher
1991	Southwark	Rt Revd Donald Coggan, former AOC
1992	York	Rt Revd Nigel McCullogh, Bishop of Wakefield
1993	Worcester	Prof Peter Gomes, Minister of Harvard Memorial Church, USA
1994	Guildford	Very Revd Nicholas Frayling, Rector of Our Lady and St Nicholas, Liverpool
1995	Edinburgh (St Giles)	Very Revd Gilleasbuig McMillan, Minister of St Giles
1996	Gloucester	Rt Revd David Bentley, Bishop of Gloucester

Chapter VII. The Directors

Gerald Knight

For the many choristers, students and visitors who passed through the doors of Addington Palace between the years 1953 to 1972, the dominant figure was that of the Director, Gerald Knight.

Background

Gerald Hocken Knight CBE, FRCO, MA, DMus(Lambeth), FRSCM, was born at Par, Cornwall on 27th July 1908, and attended the Truro Cathedral School where he also sang in the Cathedral choir. As a boy he must have shown considerable aptitude since the Cathedral Organist, Hubert Middleton, appointed him Assistant Organist at the age of 14 — a post he held for the next four years. In 1926 he went up to

Peterhouse, Cambridge as a Choral Exhibitioner where he read English, and also studied music, winning the John Rannoch Scholarship in Sacred Music. After Cambridge he enrolled as a student at the newly-formed College of St Nicolas at Chislehurst in 1930, which had been set up by Sydney Nicholson as the centre for the School of English Church Music the year before. This brought him into direct contact with the Founder who, in Knight's own words, 'dominated our lives'; and, in the space of two years, he was invited to join the staff there as Tutor in Plainsong, whilst simultaneously holding the position of organist at St Augustine's, Queen's Gate in London. Christopher le Fleming, who was a student at the College at the same time, observed in his autobiography[258], with some perception, that Knight was 'already the Anointed Heir Apparent.' He goes on to say that the students had divided themselves into two groups — 'either for the Establishment or in Opposition. For the Establishment; Gerald Knight … was chief spokesman. He would gently chide us when he felt we needed to become a little more decorous in our general bearing.' The 'Opposition' students were referred to as being 'less dedicated to the prevailing total addiction to the mystique of the organ loft.'[259] It would appear that Knight was already cast in the role of a future Director although two others were invited to interview for the post — Dr Henry Havergal of Winchester and Dr Gordon Slater of Lincoln.

In what may have seemed by some to be an act of faith, and certainly of perspicacity on the part of Dean Hewlett Johnson, Knight was appointed Organist of Canterbury Cathedral in 1937 at the comparatively young age of twenty-eight. Working closely with Clive Pare the Headmaster, he transformed the choir, moving the boarder choristers into new

[258] *Journey into Music*, Bristol, 1982.
[259] *ibid.*

premises at No 18 The Close and reorganised the choristers' singing duties so that by using day-boy choristers as well, he was able to cover holiday periods, and sing all the year round. Here, he may well have been influenced by Sydney Nicholson's similar innovation whilst at Manchester Cathedral and latterly at Westminster Abbey (see *Sydney Nicholson and his 'Musings of a Musician'* RSCM 2013 for more details). He also replaced the Old Cathedral Psalter with Nicholson's recently published Parish Psalter. However, the outbreak of the Second World War in September 1939 forced the evacuation of the boarder choristers from Canterbury. The St Austell area of Cornwall was chosen, largely at the suggestion of Knight who, having grown up at the nearby village of Tywardreath, arranged for the boys to stay at a guest house in St Blazey and sing weekday services in the parish church there. A period in the RAF followed, first as an airman (1942-1943), and then as an education officer (1943-1945). This did not prevent him from making hurried trips back to Canterbury – very often in uniform – for special events, notably the enthronement of William Temple, followed two and a half years later by his funeral, and the enthronement service for Geoffrey Fisher. In 1945 he returned to Canterbury, resuming his duties as Organist and Choirmaster.

Gerald Knight: The Director

After the death of the Founder in 1947 the RSCM Council, as an interim measure, appointed a team of three Honorary Associate Directors to take the work of the organisation forward. They were John Dykes Bower (Organist of St Paul's Cathedral), William McKie (Organist of Westminster Abbey) and Gerald Knight. This was a strong team indeed. However, the main work-load was carried by Knight, chiefly because he was on the door-step of the RSCM which had relocated to Canterbury in 1946 and who had also been engaged as Warden of the College of St Nicolas. And so in 1953, when the RSCM moved to their new home at Addington Palace, Knight was the obvious choice as the next full-time Director. Accordingly he resigned his post as Organist at Canterbury at the end of 1952.

His self-declared aim on taking up his new role was to visit as many choirs as possible, both home and abroad, 'to see for myself the state of music in churches... so that future policy may be firmly based on first-hand knowledge and experience.'[260] In 1954 alone he travelled a total of 20,000 miles across the UK. In December of the following year he embarked on the first of many overseas tours. Under his leadership, the years that followed were of considerable expansion both nationally and internationally, albeit with the long-continuing financial problems which have beset the organisation since its inception.

He retired as Director in 1972, handing over the reins to Lionel Dakers. However, he maintained his strong links with the RSCM when Council appointed him Overseas Commissioner, a post he held until July 1978, when he finally retired and moved out of Addington Palace to a flat in Maida Vale, London, to enjoy what turned out to be a short-lived retirement. He had served the RSCM for nearly 50 years. During that time he had made 21 overseas tours and visited 90 countries, 45 of them 'on duty'. Lionel Dakers recalls

---

[260] *ECM* July 1954.

in his memoirs[261] that Gerald would be gently teased by the Palace staff for planning his overseas tours to coincide with the most favourable weather abroad 'so that he could indulge to the full in his beloved swimming.' Bishop Roberts, past Chairman of Council, remembered that 'Gerald's itineraries were worked out and kept to with meticulous care, and long before he started out on a tour he knew precisely in whose house (and usually of course near which beach!) he would be staying at any given time.'[262] Dakers adds, somewhat wryly I suspect, that in consequence he [Dakers] would encounter some very cold weather on his foreign tours. Of his many overseas visits, it may be said that Gerald had friends on every page of the atlas. The considerable growth of overseas affiliates and members during his directorate can be largely attributed to his missionary work on these trips.

He died on 16th September 1979, after a short final illness, and following a simple funeral service, at the wish of his sister, in the Chapel at Addington Palace, his ashes were interred just outside the north transept of the chapel in the churchyard at St Michael's College, Tenbury, where Gerald had been a Fellow of the College for a number of years. Lionel Dakers, who had been delegated to convey his ashes to their final resting place, spent the night before travelling to Tenbury at The Athenaeum, and noted in his memoirs '… his remains rather aptly spent their last night above earth [on the mantelpiece] in my bedroom, in a building he so loved and habitually inhabited.'[263] The interment took place on 29th September which, being the Feast of St Michael and All Angels, coincided with the College's annual Commemoration, and was attended by the Fellows. The College choir sang Purcell's *Thou knowest Lord* at the graveside. Subsequently, a Service of Thanksgiving with address by CVT was held at the Church of the Holy Sepulchre, Holborn on 11th October, attended by many friends and colleagues. It was entirely appropriate that this was the church chosen, not only because it is the Musicians' Church, but also because of the long association with Sydney Nicholson and the early days of the School of English Church Music. It was fitting that the music on that occasion included Knight's anthem *Now the God of peace* and his chant for the 23rd psalm.

Gerald Knight: The Musician

Over a period of many years, Knight, working closely with Canon Joseph Poole[264], Precentor of Canterbury and latterly Coventry Cathedrals, produced many of the RSCM Festival Service Books and devotional services. He also made many arrangements and editions of simple anthems for use by parish church choirs, notably those by the Tudor composers Tye and Farrant, but he wrote very little in the way of original compositions. Worthy of mention here, however, is his anthem for boys' voices *Christ whose glory fills the skies* and the Easter SATB anthem *Now the God of peace*. He was a perfectionist in all aspects of his

---

[261] *Places where they Sing*, Canterbury Press, 1995.
[262] *CMQ* Jan 1980.
[263] *ibid*.
[264] See Appendix 4.

life, his appearance, his manners and even his musical manuscripts are written in an immaculate hand.

He composed for Joseph Poole a set of Final Responses which, to this day, have been sung daily after Evensong at Coventry Cathedral from manuscript copies. These are now typeset and available from the RSCM.

At Poole's request in 1939, GHK composed and assembled a short sequence for use in funeral and memorial services in Canterbury Cathedral according to the Book of Common Prayer 1928. In a letter dated Feb 1981 Poole said: 'The music is planned for use with Psalms 90 and 23.'

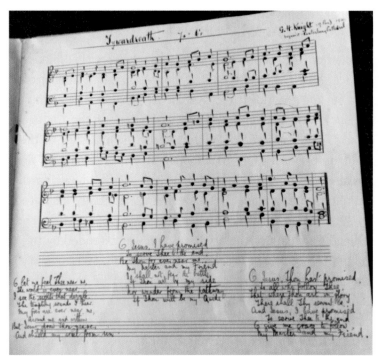

A hymn tune of Gerald's, named Tywardreath (the village where Gerald lived as a boy), set to the words *O Jesus I have promised* has recently come to light in an old manuscript book.

Gerald was an 'Assessor' for *Hymns Ancient & Modern* becoming a Proprietor along with Sir Sydney Nicholson in 1943. When the constitution of *A&M* changed in 1975 he continued as a member of the 'Council of Management'. He was joint musical editor for *Hymns Ancient & Modern (Revised)* 1950, a task he took over and completed following the death of Sydney Nicholson, and also of the two supplement *100 Hymns for Today* and *More Hymns for Today*, barely completing the latter just before his death.

He provided incidental music for Dorothy Sayers' plays *The Zeal of Thy House* (1937) and *The Devil to Pay* (1939) both of which were performed at Canterbury. He was also joint editor (with Dr William Reed) of Vols.4 and 5 of *The Treasury of English Church Music* (1965), of the *Revised Psalter* pointed for singing to Anglican Chant (1966), *A Manual of Plainsong — Revised Psalter* (1969) and of the RSCM best-selling book of *Accompaniments for Unison Hymn-Singing* (1971).

Regarding performance, Gerald was a perfectionist, and his insistence on the highest standards of musicianship applied equally to his Canterbury choristers, who would earn the epithet 'duffer' if they fell short of his expectation, and later to his Addington students, who would be the recipients of his wrath when anything less than perfect was offered. A former Canterbury Cathedral chorister (Desmond Franks[265]), recalling his days as a boy in the choir under Knight, commented that 'he [Gerald] always wanted what was best; and of course he was impatient if he didn't get it.' He goes on to make the observation that 'Men like these are either disliked or greatly admired by those they teach' and adds, with devastating honesty... 'Gerald was disliked by some... greatly admired by most... and respected by everyone.' He was particularly fastidious over clarity of diction in singing, and would insist that every consonant and syllable be clearly heard in every corner of the building. This seeking of musical perfection in execution was impressed on the students at Addington. James Burchill, a student in the early sixties, remembered 'One Monday morning, after playing for Morning Prayer, I was waiting with the rest of the students in the rehearsal room for our first class when Gerald Knight came in and, without mentioning any names, made it quite clear that I had played [the hymn tune] St Stephen much too fast.' He goes on to recall a particular lecture given by Gerald, which obviously left a lasting impression on him, on the accompaniment of psalms, using subtle and imaginative organ registrations and varying the chant with the addition of descants. He stressed the importance of always being aware of the text, and mentioned [disparagingly] 'the organist who was unable to 'smite his enemies in the hinder parts' with nothing more potent than a four foot flute!'[266] Another student, who observes that GHK 'seemed rather impervious to the liberalising climate of the early seventies', goes on to say of the students that '... if they joked about his perceived propensity for musical austerity (rehearsing ferial responses was a house speciality) then, equally, his 10.00 am Tuesday morning seminars on Church Music History, held in the capacious sitting room of his flat, were a mine of information for his charges.' [RG]

Such was Knight's reputation in insisting on the highest standards of performance, that any flying visit he made during an RSCM course could cause quite a flutter amongst the staff. Roy Massey recalls:

'Also about this time I was invited to take part in a course at St David's College, Lampeter, where we found the chapel organ to be well on its last legs. I think Tony Lewis, sub organist of Llandaff Cathedral was in charge and suddenly we heard that the Director would be visiting us one day. This caused some flutterings in the staff room and, as luck would have it, it was my turn to play for Evensong on the day of the visitation. At this period I was organist of St Alban's, Conybere Street, in Birmingham which was the leading Anglo-Catholic church in the Diocese. Consequently, I always borrowed a surplice from St Martin's when going on RSCM events as, for some strange reason, I didn't think the School of English Church Music would appreciate the rather Romish cotta I wore back home. I duly wore my borrowed surplice and played for Evensong in the presence of the great man and

---

[265] In *The Old Chorister*, the journal of the Federation of Cathedral Old Choristers' Associations, April 1979.
[266] Psalm 78 v.66.

turned the miserable organ inside out as best I could — up an octave — down an octave, and other subterfuges — and survived the service. On descending the organ loft stairs, I found GHK waiting for me. 'Were you playing the organ?'; 'Yes sir.' 'My dear, your surplice is dirrrty.' in that delightful west-country brogue of his. Not a word about the performance.'

Martin How recalls the time when he heard the Canterbury boys [under Gerald] singing *Angels ever bright and fair* by Handel at a weekday evensong '... the most lovely singing ... so calm and well blended. This was after attending a boys' practice, where again everything was done so easily and without effort. Gerald Knight sat at the piano, and you could see his own enjoyment.'[267] Martin goes on to relate a similar instance on a Taunton boys' course with about 300 boys on it. 'Gerald sat at the piano in the hall — and from his seat directed and controlled all the boys as they sang exquisitely *O Worship the Lord* by Travers. Immediately there came forth this beautifully relaxed tone — utterly different from what most of us [Housemasters] had been experiencing in our houses.' There seems little doubt that he was able to engender a particularly relaxed tone, with his generally quiet manner and the restrained cantabile style of his piano playing at rehearsal.

However, like so many choir-trainers, he did have certain foibles — one of these was an insistence that quaver movement should not be hurried, and he made a point of warning singers about 'not hurrying the passing notes, you see.' This led, on one famous occasion during a rehearsal in St Paul's Cathedral when, after Gerald had given this warning, the passing notes were taken so slowly that the music simply came to a halt. Gerald, in a masterly statement of the obvious, then said 'now it's stopped, you see.'[268] [MJRH] adds 'he [Gerald] was a fine choir trainer and, if not of the 'inspired sort' certainly achieved 'neat and tidy' performances, with everything in its place.'

Gerald Knight: The Man

Knight was the epitome of the perfect English gentleman, and his well-groomed appearance and charming, albeit somewhat old-fashioned, manners endeared him to many. He was renowned for his precision and exactitude in all things — a maxim he applied to himself as well as expecting it of others. This precision extended even to the particular way in which tea should be served — 'tea, milk, water, my dear' (from a former student). Knight was generous by nature: over big issues such as the changes made at Addington by his successor, Lionel Dakers, which he recognised as being the characteristics of the next chapter in the RSCM's history. The most significant change, and probably the hardest to bear, was undoubtedly the closing of the College of resident students — an action compelled by economic necessity. Canon Cyril Taylor recalled that in the many conversations he had with Gerald over these changes, he never heard a word of criticism. In fact he showed support for everything that his successor was doing as a necessary consequence. It was not always plain sailing. Vincent Waterhouse, who was Secretary from

---

[267] Martin How, *Unpublished Memoirs*.
[268] *ibid.*

242

1965, noted that there were, inevitably, occasional differences between them, and at times the relationship became strained '...but Gerald always remained the same; kind, courteous, never bearing ill-will' (*from a personal tribute*). Knight was generous over small things as well: a former student (Robert Hunter Bell) recalls 'Gerald Knight heard me practising Stanford in B flat Magnificat one day and stopped in his tracks to give me a lesson on it. It was a typically generous act on his part for which I was grateful.' He goes on to say that Knight, who also held the post of Organist at Lambeth Palace, offered him the opportunity to play for a funeral there: 'What an experience that was!' Another student recalls that Gerald was '... always out in front with his keen sharp wit — he made a lasting impression. His ability to score points over others was renowned.' [AS]

Knight was renowned for his direct way of approaching a problem. George Guest remembered the occasion when he was sat next to Knight at tea, probably in the Empire Room (a drawing room situated on the first floor of Addington Palace overlooking the forecourt where Knight usually took afternoon tea), Gerald said — without any preliminaries — 'By the way can you go to the USA and Canada next year?'[269] Gerald had a flat on the first floor of the Palace, and the Empire Room served as Gerald's sitting room. As well as containing some elegant furniture, it housed his two grand pianos. Roy Massey recalls that 'he much enjoyed playing two-piano music, and I was often invited to join him in this capacity after dinner. We played some interesting stuff, but anything fast was usually prefaced with the words 'nice and steady, my dear' in order to slow down my exuberance at the keyboard.'

Canon Cyril Taylor, a former Warden at Addington, in his address given at Knight's memorial service, recalled 'the quick brain reflected in the quick movements and the quick response.... and the remarkable and not always convenient vanishing trick — 'Gerald.... Where *is* Gerald? He was here a moment ago.' Yes, but a moment later he wasn't!' Incidentally, Gerald's habit of beginning sentences with 'Now you see, dear [most were addressed thus] ....' or ending with '....don't you see?' — together with his gentle Cornish accent — made him the subject of much affectionate impersonation. Like the BBC, Gerald's nickname was 'Auntie', and, just as with the BBC, it was sometimes held that 'Auntie knows best', so the same could be said about Gerald, usually with some considerable justification, given his long experience in church music together with a remarkable memory.

He was considered by some to be somewhat dry, and in consequence did come in for a little gentle leg-pulling. The following anecdote recounted by Martin How, which enjoyed wide circulation at the time, well-illustrates this, but also shows that Gerald was not without a sense of humour.

'Scene: Summer Party at Addington Palace, on the steps down to the garden. Gerald, who had only recently been awarded an honorary Lambeth D Mus degree, was standing with Derek Holman who had worked assiduously for a D Mus (London).

---

[269] *ECM* Oct 1957.

Gerald, wearing his pure silk Lambeth hood and somewhat finicky about detail, touches Derek's hood and says 'Now, artificial silk you see dear.' Derek, fingering Gerald's hood in turn and imitating Gerald's voice, replies 'Artificial degree you see dear.' To his credit, Gerald took the teasing in good part, and laughed. Incidentally, he used to refer to his doctoral robes as 'my pink dressing gown'.'

John Eagles (1971/72) tells this same story about hoods and explains that:

'At the summer Garden Parties held at Addington Palace it was customary for the staff to be robed in academic dress as they mingled with guests on the lawns surrounding the palace.'

In a personal tribute, Watkins Shaw wrote: 'Knight was continuously and intimately connected with the music of the church from boyhood until his last illness and death, and he served it conspicuously in three posts of distinction and responsibility ... it ought to be said that he viewed church music not in isolation, but in the context of his religious convictions and of the Church of England, to which he was devoted.'[270] He was widely regarded as the 'Ambassador of Church Music', and two significant honours that marked his long service, a Lambeth Doctorate of Music in 1961, and a CBE in 1971, served as fitting tributes.

Martin How on GHK:

'I remember well how when I first joined the staff at Addington, as Headquarters' Choirmaster in the mid 1950's, I always had the Director, Gerald Knight lurking in the background, and he would not hesitate to make comments which were apt — and to the point (i.e. not 'wrapped up'). Sometimes these comments would be in the presence of other people, other students even. When I was taking a boys' practice, Gerald Knight could not help but hear it if he were in the building, and he would say 'Now Martin over-stimulates the boys, you see', meaning that I was always anxious to 'wake them up' and get them excited by the music.

I could not see my own fault, but all I know is that I used to be amazed how beautifully calm, and indeed effective, was the approach of say Robert Prizeman (now Director of Libera — the internationally famous boys' choir). He produced quickly the loveliest sounds because he didn't 'stimulate' his singers but 'calmed' them.

GHK also said to me when I started: 'Now, my dear, there are two things I require of you — one is an FRCO and the other is a pair of black shoes.''[271]

Roy Massey on GHK:

'The benign all-seeing presence around the place was GHK who took a warm interest in the students and the activities of the college, and I found his advice most helpful

---

[270] *CMQ* Jan 1980.
[271] Martin had obtained the ARCO whilst in the army and had passed the playing part of the FRCO, but found the paperwork requirements for FRCO beyond him. Private lessons with 'Sir Bill' enabled him to achieve this goal.

as I was finding my way around the new job. He lived in a pleasant flat on the first floor and had as a sitting room the magnificent Empire Room at the front of the palace which accommodated some elegant furniture and his two grand pianos. One night the boot was on the other foot when John Birch came up from Chichester and GHK paired me off with him at the pianos. As well as being a consummate organist and choirtrainer, John was also a superlative pianist and sight reader and it was my turn to plead for a more merciful tempo.'

GHK was, of course, a very busy man and, as a member of numerous councils and committees, he was away very regularly and, periodically, he would go abroad for a more extended period visiting RSCM affiliated choirs in various parts of the world. I think he much enjoyed this side of his work and on these trips he would often recommend a promising youngster to come to Addington as a student, and some of them did eventually join us. He was basically a rather shy person who, in the early part of his career, probably found mixing and relating to ordinary people quite difficult, but he improved with age and experience, eventually becoming adept at relating to singers, old and young, as he conducted choral festivals and also very assured in his addresses to the RSCM membership. I found him a most kind and caring individual, genuinely interested in my welfare and happiness and we became great friends. In my early days I heard that he had a reputation for being very critical of anyone playing the organ for him on a course as they could be given a rough passage if the playing fell short of what he required. Consequently, I was slightly nervous the first time I played for him, but found his beat was clear and his instructions straightforward and all went well. Over the years I was his organist on many prestigious occasions in such places as the Albert Hall, Westminster Abbey, St Paul's Cathedral and Lambeth Palace. I always very much enjoyed the experience and without fail, after a big event there would be a little note of appreciation in my letter box afterwards. One Christmas I persuaded him to play for the Carol service at the Parish Church and it was lovely to discover that all his old Canterbury accompanimental skills were still there – and he watched the beat! He played very beautifully and it was then my turn to write the little note. Years later, in 1991 after I had been awarded a Lambeth Doctorate by Archbishop Robert Runcie, I had a letter from Vincent Waterhouse, GHK's executor, offering me his two D Mus hoods, saying that he felt sure that Gerald would have liked me to have them. I was delighted and moved at this – they were in excellent condition and I have worn them regularly ever since.'

Anita Banbury (1963-66):

'I remember his Armstrong Sidley, i.e. the 'Auntie-Mobile', and his particular way of pouring his tea – it had to be 'tea, milk, water, my dear.' There was one day he walked through the Common Room, in shirt sleeves plus black waistcoat carrying a coal scuttle, and we said 'where are you going my pretty maid?' he graciously laughed with us.

George Fletcher-Baker (chorister in Sittingbourne PC) recalls:

'In June 1950 I attended a choral festival to be held in Canterbury Cathedral. A rehearsal was held in the morning, and Gerald Knight's voiced introduction to everyone was this 'Please forget what all your choir-masters have taught you, I want you to sing everything my way.' There were so many affiliated choirs involved that they had to split us into two choirs, one to process in from the Cloisters, and the other one from the Crypt. So to enable him to conduct us, he had to dash through the Choir Screen and conduct one choir, and then the other. I'm sure his antics must have caused a few chuckles amongst the boys.'

William French (1963-65) recalls:

'Gerald was very fastidious and would often approach a student and say 'you don't mind my dear' as he removed a loose thread from a jacket. A couple of us were naughty and put a spool of white thread in the front pocket of our jackets and allowed a bit of thread to be visible on the lapel. Gerald took the prank with amusement and in the right spirit.'

James Burchill (1960-62):

'Gerald Knight often used to talk about imaginative psalm accompaniments: descants, subtle and suggestive registrations, always being aware of the text. My many visits to Cathedrals in recent years suggest that few congregations today have the opportunity to enjoy this style of imaginative psalm accompaniment and in addition half notes/minims often tend to be played in fairly strict time. This may possibly be because in the 60's the Psalm was likely accompanied by the Cathedral organist, a man of years and experience, whereas today it is probably the assistant organist, a young man or woman who is still finding their way around the Psalter.'[272]

John Morehen (1960/61):

'Dr Gerald Knight, the Director, was a slightly aloof figure so far as Addington students were concerned. After we had left Addington, however, he followed our careers with interest. He was very helpful to me in later years. While at Addington he would invite some of us, as a great privilege, to play bridge with him in the wonderful Empire Room. At the appointed hour — 9.30 pm, I think — he made us all a cup of tea, and brought out the tin of biscuits: 'One plain, one fancy', he used to say!'

Alan Snow (1972/73):

I didn't get to know Gerald Knight for some time. He had been recovering from an illness and was for a while very much in the shadows. Always out front with his keen

---

[272] The authors venture to suggest that, at least at a cathedral level, the art of psalm accompaniment is still alive and well in the 21C and that possibly both Sir Sydney and Gerald Knight would be impressed by the cathedral choirs and assistant organists of today compared to those in the 1930's.

sharp wit, he made a lasting impression and friend. His ability to score points over others was renowned with the usual approach of 'Now you see my dear.' '

Harry Bramma:

'Gerald Knight loved to visit overseas and seems to have been fond of California. I remarked to an RSCM member there that Knight seemed to have found much to do in the relatively small number of affiliated churches there. 'Oh', he said, 'he loved to visit the RSCM swimming pools'.'

Peter Jewkes[273] wrote:

'... there were also innumerable trips in Gerald's Rover, including the Three Choirs' Festival that year. There I heard my first live performance of Gerontius, and on telling Gerald how moved I had been by it, recall feeling both awestruck and patronised by him replying that 'Yes it was quite good my dear, but I preferred it in 1927 when Elgar was conducting it, and he had the brass on the other side of the platform!'

London student Violet Chang (1963-66) mentioned[274] that Gerald Knight had agreed to be accompanist for her solo graduation recital. She felt honoured and wondered why she should receive such special treatment by the Director. GHK replied that no-one had ever asked him before! Terence Allbright, another London student, recalls GHK's kindness:

I was a 'Londoner', studying at the Royal College of Music and living at Addington Palace. Northampton Education Authority generously gave me full tuition and maintenance grants – my mother was struggling valiantly on her own, and I hadn't saved much from my £50 a year village organist job. I arrived at Addington with just a few pounds, and not only had those all gone after two weeks but my maintenance cheque hadn't arrived at the RCM in Prince Consort Road. I had never borrowed money before, but before dinner one evening, as we were all gathering in the great hall, I went up to Dr Knight with my heart in my mouth and said 'Dr Knight, I wonder if I could have a word with you after dinner?' He put his hand on my arm and said 'How much do you need my dear?' (And the cheque duly turned up at the RCM.)

---

[273] Australian organ builder, attended the 1976 Summer Course for overseas students in 1976 when he acted as sub-organist at St Bride's, Fleet Street. Now a highly respected Sydney organ builder servicing a vast area of NSW churches (and Sydney Town Hall), he has been organist of Sydney's legendary Anglo-Catholic Christchurch St Lawrence in Sydney since 1997.

[274] Conversation with [JH] 19th June 2015.

Lionel Dakers

Lionel Frederick Dakers CBE, FRCO, FRSCM, DMus, DMus(Lambeth), b. 24th Feb 1924, Rochester, Kent; d. 10th Mar 2003, Salisbury, Wiltshire, studied at Rochester Cathedral with H A Bennett and at York Minster with E Bairstow. He was assistant organist of St George's Chapel, Windsor, organist of All Saints' Church, Frindsbury in Rochester from 1939 until 1942, of the Cathedral of Our Lady of Fatima in Cairo from 1945 until 1947, of Finchley PC 1948 until 1950, of Ripon Cathedral 1954 until 1957 and of Exeter Cathedral from 1957 until 1972. He was a Special Commissioner from 1958 before his appointment as Director in 1972. He was made FRSCM in 1969, received a Lambeth Doctorate in 1979 and was appointed CBE in 1983.

Arrival at Addington — The Challenge.

Harry Bramma writes of the Dakers Years:

'When Lionel Dakers arrived at Addington Palace at the beginning of 1974, he was faced with an immediate and major problem — the closure of the residential college of St Nicolas which was half-way through its final year. When he was appointed, the RSCM Council left him in no doubt that the College had to close. It was difficult to sustain financially; but it was also difficult in changed times to attract students of the right calibre. In post war years, musicians of ability were drawn strongly to the greater opportunities of musical conservatories and the increasing number of universities, many of which were offering organ and choral scholarships in association with local cathedrals.

The college had been at the heart of the RSCM for 46 years since it was inaugurated at Chislehurst, and continued at both Canterbury and Addington. Gerald Knight, the Director, a protégé of Sir Sydney Nicholson, had been associated with it since its foundation and Leslie Green, the first Secretary, who played such a major role in the move to Addington were but two of the many persons who felt continually involved in the College — but in the case of Leslie Green he was no longer around, having been asked to leave by the Council in 1964. He and Gerald never got on. The idea of closure was a highly emotive issue with staff and students alike, and particularly so with Gerald Knight who had been asked to stand down at the age of 65 in 1974, but who had been allowed to stay on for five years as Overseas Commissioner still living at Addington Palace. Naturally this made life difficult for Lionel Dakers, working next to his aggrieved predecessor.

There can be no doubt that the new Director rose to the challenge magnificently. He was a first-rate administrator and a very good entrepreneur. He found a way of breathing new life into the RSCM. His many new initiatives compensated for what had been lost and were probably more in tune with changing times in the 1970's.

New Scheme of Courses[275]:

i) Short residential courses.

In place of the residential college, new courses were planned which utilised the facilities at Addington. Improvements were made to the accommodation and visits to the Palace very much caught the imagination of the membership. Some were run at weekends (Friday to Sunday) attracting considerable numbers. The long-running courses for young organists were particularly successful right up to the time in 1993 when maintenance of rooms and catering became increasingly uneconomic.

Then there were the weekday courses of three or four days on a variety of subjects such as composing for choirs or choosing the music for the liturgy. But, by a long way, the most successful midweek courses were those for 'reluctant organists' — an idea thought up by Janette Cooper (subsequently Warden from 1982 until 1990) which really met a need. Dozens of people with little organ training, who had been dragooned into service because they played the piano, found great help and encouragement in these courses. Janette Cooper had just the right touch, managing to build up a community of persons who got to know one another. It became a highly successful 'club' and people returned frequently for follow-up sessions. After the closure of the residential resource, Janette returned to take day courses, building on what had been achieved in the longer sessions.

ii) Day courses.

Alongside the short residential courses, there were many one day events which covered a wide field. Sometimes the teaching took place once a week on, say, four successive Tuesdays. These courses attracted perhaps a dozen to twenty participants. Michael Fleming's sessions on an aspect of English Church Music might run for four individual days exploring, for instance, the sacred music of the Elizabethan Period. This was an attractive option for retired people living within striking distance of Addington.

Saturdays at Addington

A particular feature of the Dakers Era, and later, were the large Saturday gatherings in the Great Hall. A visit by John Rutter or the Christmas Carol 'sing-along' brought capacity numbers. The Hall had wonderful acoustics which made people want to sing. There was a great variety of events, some particularly for children and others to introduce members to new repertoire. A glance at the programmes for the year shows how wide a range of events was on offer. It also records the many distinguished musicians who were prepared to support the RSCM by leading courses, often without a fee.

Saturdays at Addington were very popular and showed how useful a dedicated headquarters was in building an affection and 'esprit-de-corps'. Michael Benson, the chef, was adept at

---

[275] See also Chapter V.

putting on simple tasty lunches for up to a 100 people. These were much enjoyed along with an aperitif in the bar! But they also had the important 'spin-off' of raising considerable sums for the work of the RSCM. Even the reasonable fees charged generated a good deal of income. This was enhanced when participants were able to make purchases downstairs in the Publications Department over the lunch period.

Work in the field

This RSCM term, used much by Lionel Dakers, spoke of the importance of getting around the membership. This was central to Sydney Nicholson's agenda — he famously visited 350 affiliated churches in his first year! He appeared regularly throughout the UK at events in the period 1927 to 1939 — and even during the war-time when he continued to organise festivals. This work was continued by Gerald Knight and Lionel Dakers and was a major factor in the continued growth in membership for forty years up to Dakers' retirement. Though he was busy abroad and with all kind of administrative matters, he found time for much work in the RSCM in the UK. He had an avuncular manner which served him well when moving round a room full of members. He made many friends and was a good ambassador for the cause. He liked meeting people and superficially was very good with people but he did not like penetrating questions or going too deeply into things. So long as the occasion only required 'bonhomie' he was first-class at the job.

It was assumed during the time of the first four Directors, including myself, that visits would be made and that there would be musical events conducted by the Director together with training and teaching sessions headed by him. In order to supplement his work, there were the RSCM Special Commissioners. At first there was one — Hubert Crook, who travelled constantly round the UK mainly to visit choirs giving encouragement and advice. He even visited me in 1955 when I was Choirmaster of All Saints' in Bingley, West Yorkshire, just before I left for university. I found him rather formidable. The work of Hubert Crook was augmented by Special Commissioners and the Clerical Commissioner Horace Spence. Many Special Commissioners were cathedral organists who made visits to choirs. I remember as a very young chorister at St Paul's Church, Shipley, about 1946 when we had a visit from Conrad Eden, organist of Durham Cathedral. He was the first person I had seen with a beard! He heard us sing and then commented on our performance. I remember we sang *Nearer my God to Thee* to the tune which prompted him to speak of his fondness for Dykes and how he thought Dykes was unjustly criticised for being Victorian and sentimental!

The ultimate phasing out of the 'work in the field' and the position of Commissioner [Regional Director] has dealt a serious blow to the influence that could be exerted through regular personal contact.'

Changes to Canon Law

It was rare for Directors to become involved in the politics of the Church. Sampson noted in 1970 that 'For many years the position of the organist and choirmaster had not fully been recognised and in very few cases was there any security of tenure even for a Cathedral organist who depended on the position for his livelihood.' The conditions and status of musicians in the Anglican Communion is governed by Canon B20 'Of the musicians and music of the Church'.

Lionel Dakers made a rare foray into politics, together with former RSCM Council member Dame Betty Ridley, by making recommendations and giving evidence to the General Synod Revision Committee in 1984 and 1985. Dame Betty reported on the General Synod discussions regarding 'Security of tenure for parish church organists' in *CMQ* Oct 1985, but it would be 1987 before a revision of Canon B20 received Royal Assent. The effect of the change was to make the appointment and dismissal of parish organists no longer the sole prerogative of the incumbent, but must also involve a decision by the PCC. This was seen at the time as an important change with the 'back-stop' of the PCC being introduced to prevent a summary dismissal of musicians by the incumbent.

The use of the organ, which parts of the service shall be sung and choice of music do, however, still remain the ultimate responsibility of the incumbent but, if there is an organist, choir director or Director of Music, the incumbent should 'pay due heed to his [or her] advice and assistance in the choosing of chants, hymns, anthems, and other settings, and in the ordering of the music of the church.'

Elisabeth Dakers

Harry Bramma writes:

'At this point some special mention must be made of Elisabeth Dakers. She was a key factor in the success of Addington Palace. Early on in 1974, she took on the job of Housekeeper, a very great commitment in the days when residential courses were frequent. She organised the domestic staff who did cleaning and laundry, and worked with chef Michael Benson, ensuring that imaginative food was always on the menu.

When her husband was away on foreign visits, sometimes for as long as six months, she had to hold the fort, working with Vincent Waterhouse, the Secretary and Administrator, to make sure all went well. She had much to offer personally, was a person good to get to know and was, in fact, a first-rate musician, having been trained at the RCM. When the Dakers were first at Exeter she was much appreciated by the Exeter Choral Society which she took when her husband was away. In another age, I often imagined she would have been a Director of Music in a well-known school or perhaps a Headmistress of a girls' Public School.

Such thoughts as these came to me very strongly in the autumn of 1988 when she came to Southwark Cathedral to collect a leaving present for her husband who was in bed with 'flu. After the gift had been presented, she made an excellent speech of thanks. She was fluent, amusing and came across as a person of real substance. The RSCM should continue to be grateful for all she did to support and enliven those days at Addington in the 70's and 80's — working ceaselessly with very modest financial reward.'

Elisabeth Dakers died in March 1997.

The Dakers family (and dog Dominic) on Lionel's appointment as Director in 1973

Harry Bramma

Bramma, Harry Wakefield MA, FRCO, DLitt, FRSCM, b. 11th Nov 1936, Shipley, West Yorkshire; Harry Bramma was educated at Bradford Grammar School, was a pupil of Melville Cook (Leeds Parish Church) and read theology and music at Oxford University where he was organ scholar of Pembroke College. He was DOM at King Edward VI School in Retford from 1961 to 1963 and then assistant organist at Worcester Cathedral and DOM of the King's School in Worcester. In 1976 he was appointed DOM at Southwark Cathedral before becoming Director of the RSCM in 1989 where he served until 1998. He was DOM at All Saints', Margaret Street, from 1989 until 2004.

Geoff Weaver writes of Harry's achievements:

'Harry Bramma came to the RSCM as Director at a time of immense change, both within society at large and more particularly within the Church, and perhaps his main challenge, apart from turning around the finances and declining membership of the organisation, was to make the RSCM more relevant in a changing world.

When he took up the reins, the RSCM was perceived by many, with some justification, to be a resource for Anglican churches that still maintained a thriving choral tradition. In one of his early editorials in *CMQ*, he listed seven myths about the RSCM — that the RSCM is:

    a) only interested in churches with the choirs,

    b) too Anglican,

    c) only interested in larger churches,

    d) too 'middle of the road',

    e) only interested in organs,

    f) only interested in music and

    g) only interested in Choral Evensong.

During the course of his nine years as Director, Harry Bramma strove to change these perceptions, and it is interesting to follow the course of those changes through his editorials in *CMQ*.

From the outset, he made it clear that one of the RSCM's responsibilities was to maintain the great English choral tradition — and to that end the RSCM would always aim for high standards, offering the very best in worship. He wrote of the importance of striving for beauty in worship, recognising that music, poetic language and visual beauty can touch the heart of the worshipper, and can help to bring spiritual renewal and healing to the wounded soul.

However, in many of his editorials, Harry wrestled with the challenge of embracing stylistic diversity in order to meet the different needs of the people of God. A number of times he affirmed the role that 'popular' music had played within the Church, and how composers such as Bach and Vaughan Williams had taken popular tunes and folk melodies and incorporated them into their works. He also affirmed the imaginative use of orchestral instruments in worship, enabling young people to offer their skills in worship.

A key challenge came in 1996 when, following the report of the Archbishops' Commission on Church Music *In Tune With Heaven*, the RSCM was appointed as the official church music body to serve the Church of England. It was clearly a challenge to fulfil this role and, at the same time, offer its services as an ecumenical resource. However, Harry had set an important precedent, calling together a meeting of church musicians from right across the theological and stylistic spectrum to discuss ways in which they might devise a common syllabus for the comprehensive training of church musicians. From this remarkable, ground-breaking initiative came CHIME (The Churches Initiative in Music Education) which set itself the task of drawing up guidelines for training in key areas, guidelines which were subsequently used by a number of denominations in their own training programmes.

Harry Bramma took other key initiatives in building bridges with the Evangelicals, who had always felt that the RSCM had little to offer them. In 1991, for example, there was a festival in the Royal Albert Hall in which 550 singers came together, accompanied by the orchestra of All Souls', Langham Place, one of the leading Evangelical churches, to sing a varied programme of church music. Alongside these initiatives, Harry himself built strong relationships, based on mutual respect, with Christian musicians from across the spectrum.

In his editorials, Harry often pleaded for a deeper understanding of worship and liturgy on the part of church musicians and clergy — thereby touching on the age-old issue of clergy-musician relationships. He saw the role of music in worship as foundational, always at the service of the liturgy. Indeed, he saw worship and music as key to the mission of the Church in an increasingly secular society. Music in worship could prepare the heart, could enable the expression of emotion and could carry, in memorable melodies, the truths of Scripture, thus enabling the worshippers to offer their deepest, creative selves to God. The importance of enabling people to be creative was another of Harry's key concerns — giving opportunities for people to create something beautiful for God in music, poetry or the visual arts.

Always, at the heart of the RSCM's mission, as Harry saw it, was the task of enabling the Church to be a Singing Church — and, more particularly, a Church that encouraged young people to sing. He believed that it was vital that boys should continue to be encouraged and enabled to sing — but he also affirmed the development of girls' choirs from the 1990's onwards. Singing in a choir, Harry believed, often brought spiritual awakening to a young person — and, in a memorable phrase in one of his editorials, he wrote of our responsibility to 'discover the divine within the child'.

Within the organisation itself, Harry took important initiatives, appointing new regional staff in the UK, and visiting Australia, New Zealand and the USA to enable the development of new structures, more appropriate for a post-colonial age.

In 1994 the 'Sing with a Spirit' Appeal was launched with a magnificent service in Westminster Abbey, at which Bishop Tim Bavin preached, John Rutter's new anthem *I will sing with the Spirit* (dedicated to the RSCM) was sung for the first time and the Westminster Abbey Choir sang Walton's *Coronation Te Deum*. Harry was deeply moved to see a packed congregation of RSCM members who had travelled from far and wide to be present — and to show their support.

In his final editorial in *CMQ*, Harry reflected on the importance of continuity within a changing world, but also of the need to be open to new approaches. He concluded with a prayer of Sir Francis Drake which had meant a lot to him throughout his life:

'There must be a beginning of any great matter, but the continuing unto the end until it be thoroughly finished yields the true glory'.'

Chapter VIII. Students of the College of St Nicolas

No register of students exists, and so the following list, compiled from RSCM magazines and personal communications from former students, may be incomplete, especially in respect of the 'London' students. Despite invaluable help from 'Mr Google', it has not been possible to locate and contact all the College students listed below and a number did not reply to our approach. Our apologies for any serious errors and omissions, but there is only room in these pages for very brief shorthand biographical annotations which take the form:

Name, Degrees if known, (AP Years), Birth/death dates if known, Nationality; Brief biographical notes.

Adams, Adrian ARSCM, (1967-1970), b.Croydon, UK; a former chorister at St Philip's Church, Norbury, was organist of St Martin's in Croydon at age 17, then of St James' in West Croydon. After Addington he taught at Dulwich College Preparatory School and has been organist of St John's, Upper Norwood, for forty years. He was the first Hon Treasurer of 'The Society of St Nicolas' in 1971. In 2012 he was made ARSCM.

Aiken, Ian Richard (1967/68), Australia; from Daglish, W Australia, to King's School, Ely. Author of *The Organs of Bourne Abbey 1834-1977.*

Allbright, Terence James BMus, FRCO, (1965-68), b 1946, Northampton, UK; Head Student 1967, organ scholar Jesus College, Cambridge, 1968, studied at RCM.

Allcoat, Nigel (1969-71), b. 1950, Hinckley, Leicestershire, UK; International recitalist, won second place in the St Albans Improvisation competition and has taught at the RNCM, Oxford and Cambridge universities as well as European conservatories.

Allen, Roger, BA, BMus, DPhil(Oxon), (1970/71), UK; a pupil of Noel Rawsthorne in Liverpool, organist of Ellesmere College. From 1989 DOM at New College School in Oxford, Dean, Fellow and tutor at St Peter's College, Oxford, and noted authority on Richard Wagner.

Allwardt, Dr Paul, (1961, two terms only), b. 1906; d. 1986, USA; studied at Capitol University and the Union Theological Seminary, New York. After war service, came to AP from Gustavus Adolphus College MN.

Anderson, John, MBE, TCL, LLB GTCL LRAM, (1973/74), Northern Ireland; a London Student at TCL, later a prominent lawyer but still, from 2014, organist at Duddingston Kirk in Edinburgh.

Ashcroft, Michael, GRSM, LRAM, ARCO(CHM), (1965/66), UK; at the RNCM 1962-65, A&M Scholar at AP, Assistant DOM at Giggleswick School, DOM at Dulwich College for 18 years until retirement in 2004.

Asher, Christine, (1972/73); married Julian Drewett (1970-73), contralto and singing teacher in Nottingham, now living in Scotland.

Ashley-Botha, Christian (k/a Bunny), ARCM BMusEd, ARSCM, (1964-66) b. 1944, Mossel Bay; d. 2014, South Africa; Director of the Drakensberg Boys' Choir School from 1980 for 27 years.

Askew, John, (1973/74).

Bailey, Michael H. FRCO, GRSM, ARCM, (1960-63), UK; was formerly DOM Bromley Parish Church 1966-1997 and DOM Eltham College 1984-1992.

Baker, Michael, MA, FRCO(CHM), (1965/66), UK; organ scholar Jesus College, Cambridge, 1968. Organist of Chesterfield Parish Church 1977-2005.

Baker, Paul C, FRCO, ARCM, (1965-67), Canada; studied at RCM, in London, Ontario, in 1972.

Banbury, Anita, ARSCM, ARCO(CHM), LRAM, ARCM, GRSM, AIRMT, (1963-66), UK; studied at RAM, to New Zealand to teach at St Mary's School, Stratford. Was Chair of RSCM Auckland and awarded ARSCM in 2003, currently Director of the mixed voice St Mary's Singers at Auckland Cathedral.

Barber, Ian A M, FRCO(CHM), ARCM, GRSM, ARSCM, (1960-65), UK; from Belfast, went to the RCM, then to Canada as organist in Ottawa and St Catharine's, Ontario. On returning to Northern Ireland he served at St Columb's Cathedral in Londonderry, Ballywalter Parish Church and as both assistant and full organist to St Anne's Cathedral, Belfast. The new chamber organ at the cathedral is named the 'Barber Organ' in his honour.

Barlow, Brian G, MA, FRCO, ARCM, (1957/58), UK; organ scholar Jesus College, Oxford. DOM Yardley Grammar School, Birmingham, Trent College, Organist of Wisbech Parish Church and Lecturer at King's Lynn, County Technical College in 1971 and organist of All Saints', King's Lynn.

Baseley, Pauline, (1972-74); now an auditor.

Batten, Shirley, (1954/55), UK; of Culverhayes, Chard in Somerset. Director of Chapel Music at Downe House School, Newbury then of Upper Chine School in Shanklin, IOW.

Bebbington, Peter, (1966/67), South Africa; ex-Johannesburg Cathedral.

Bell, Robert Hunter, MusB, ARCO(CHM), ARCCO, ARSCM, DMus(Lambeth), (1958/59), b. 1932, Canada; returned to Calgary to be organist of the cathedral there. President of the RCCO 1973, he also served at St Mary Magdalene in Toronto from 1975 and at St George's Cathedral, Kingston, Ontario from 1996.

Benny, Dr William, (1967/68), South Africa; worked at a Government Hospital in South Africa.

Berriman, Christopher, (1967-69); He assisted Martin How by running the 'Reserve Choir' of Addington choristers. DOM at Northbourne Park School in Deal, Kent, until retirement in 2009.

Best, Hubert, (1973/74), b. 1952, Durban, South Africa; studied at Rhodes University. He was assistant and then full organist at Birmingham Cathedral from 1978 to 1985 and an organist in Jerusalem before training as a solicitor. In 2006 he founded Best & Soames, a media law firm.

Beverley, Elizabeth, LRSM, ARCO, (1962/63), New Zealand; a pupil of Peter Godfrey, she was DOM at Epsom Girls' Grammar School and Kuranui College in Auckland and organist of St Patrick's Cathedral in Auckland.

Beynon, Michael, (1962), from South Wales; One student mentioned that he had a 'devilish sense of humour.' He was still an examiner for ABRSM in 2011.

Birch, John, (1973/74); [not John Birch, former organist of Chichester Cathedral].

Bird, Revd J O, (1958/59), USA, d. 1985, Johnstown, PA.

Birrell, Sydney, FRCO, GRSM, ARCM, (1973/74), b. Sarnia, Ontario, Canada; former chorister at St George's Anglican Church in Montreal. Founder and conductor of the Peterborough Singers, he was Director of the Ministry of Music at Murray Street Baptist Church for many years and long-term organist at Lakefield College School. Studied at the RCM and on returning to Canada in 1975 was organist at St John's Anglican Church in Peterborough until 1984.

Blake, Ann, (1960/61); One student recalls her as 'a pretty London student who always waited breathlessly for Sir William Harris's chauffeured arrival from Windsor on late Evensong Mondays, who was never so frail and wobbly as when Ann was there to help him up the long grand staircase ascent, each clinging to the other for dear life!'

Boughton, Stephen, (1972-74).

Bowen, Bill, (1973/74).

Bowen, P B C, (1959), British Guiana; organist of St George's Cathedral in Georgetown, Guyana from before 1942 until 1962.

Bowen, Ronald, (1966 or 1967), British Guiana; son of P B C Bowen above, spent one term of his European vacation at AP as English Hymnal Scholar.

Bowkley, Vivien, ATCL, (1956-58), UK; came to the RSCM as a mature student, stayed on as Resident Assistant Domestic Supervisor and was temporarily promoted to full Housekeeper on the departure of Mrs Audrey Taylor in 1958. She was organist of Mathon Parish Church, Worcestershire, in 1971 and lived in Malvern.

Bracewell, Chris, (1972/73); organist of St Peter's in Hammersmith ca 1983.

Bridge, Ian F, LRAM, FRCO, (1956/57), Australia; was organist of City Congregational Church in Brisbane at the age of 16 in 1954. Organist of St Mildred's in Addiscombe, whilst a student and also there in 1958. Organist of Ballarat Cathedral in 1971, director of the chapel choir at Brighton Grammar School in Melbourne 1977.

Brimer, Michael, (1954/55) — see Headquarters Choirmaster.

Briton, James, ARCM, (1958-60), b. 1926, Sydney, Australia; (name variously spelled by former students but is certainly Briton and not Britton or Britten), he studied piano at the Sydney Conservatorium. He left AP to teach at Copthorne School in Sussex. He returned to Australia to teach at schools in Queensland, and serving as organist of Perth Cathedral 1968-1970, in succession to Bruce Naylor. On leaving the cathedral he married and taught Arts at Scotch College in Swanbourne.

Broman, John, (1967/68), USA; from Staunton, VA.

Brooks, Roger, (1967/68); DOM in a Midlands Public School.

Brown, Norman, (1966-68), Bermuda.

Brown, Robert D, (1968, one term), UK; from Ross-on-Wye, read Classics at Corpus Christi, Oxford.

Brydon, Russell John, (1959/60), b. 1924, Dallas, TX; d. 2012, Dallas, TX, USA; was organist and choirmaster at the Episcopal Church of the Incarnation in Dallas for more than 44 years and often played for services at Temple Emanu-El and Temple Shalom.

Burchill, Dr James Frederick, PhD, FRCCO, FRCO(CHM), (1960-62), Canada; has served for most of his life at the Cathedral Church of All Saints in Halifax, Nova Scotia — first as a chorister, then as organist and choirmaster from 1971 to 1977 and from 1994 to 2006, and then in retirement as a member of the Cathedral choir.

Burtenshaw, Dr Leonard John, PhD, DMA, MMus, DSCM, (1963), b. 1931, Sydney, NSW, Australia; head of Music Education at the Sydney Conservatorium 1971-1994, Organist of St Stephen's Presbyterian and Uniting Church in Sydney 1972-1981, Director of the Adelaide Singers.

Bush, Sharon, (1973/74).

Butchard, Kirstin, (ca 1968/69), UK.

Callaghan, Mervyn Arthur, BMus, LRAM, ARCM, ARCO(CHM), ARSCM (1957/58), d. 2008, Australian; in 1959 he ran the Easter AP Choristers' course and was assistant organist of Wells Cathedral at that time. A Special Commissioner from 1963 he was awarded the ARSCM in 1966, DOM of Geelong Grammar School 1966-74, organist of Trinity College Chapel, Parkville, VIC, 1980-1982.

Campbell, Susan, (1967/68), was a soprano soloist in the 'May Concerts'.

Candasamy, Yves, (1965/66), Mauritius, at St James' Cathedral, Port Louis in 1960 and still there in 1979, he was Chief Commissioner in Mauritius for Boy Scouting in 1970.

Carnegie, Michael, FRCO (1960/61), Jersey. Taught at St Michael's School in Jersey. A qualified pilot, it was he who took the aerial photograph of Addington and the photograph used as the Frontispiece to this book.

Carroll, Frank G, ARCO(CHM), (1959-62), (deceased), Australian; organist Holy Trinity in Dubbo, NSW and of St James' Cathedral in Townville, Queensland, from 1966-1994. One student recalled: 'At first he needed GHK's help, who described his choral conducting as 'like pulling a lavatory chain.' ' Despite this inauspicious start, he won the Brook Prize with his ARCO(CHM) diploma in 1961.

Cassidy, Geoffrey, FRCO(CHM), BA, LRAM, (1972/73), UK; from Derby, DOM at Rossall School in 2004, choirmaster at Lytham Parish Church.

Charity, Andrew, FRCO(CHM), BMus,(ca 1967/68), UK; went on to teach at King's College School in Wimbledon, Choral director at the Royal Academy of Dramatic Art, organist of

St Faith's, Wandsworth, directed the Barnes Choir from 2000-2013 and conductor of the New London Opera Players.

Cleverdon, Faith, ARCM, GRSM, (1958-61), UK.

Cock, Richard Charles Alan, FRSCM, (1972/73), b. 1949, Port Elizabeth, South Africa; from Cape Town, an alto lay vicar at Chichester Cathedral before becoming Assistant Organist in 1978 and DOM at the choir school. Returned to South Africa in 1980 to work for the South African Broadcasting Corporation. He was organist of St Mary's Cathedral in Johannesburg, and, according to Wikipedia, he was South Africa's 'first professional countertenor.' He was made ARSCM in 1986 and upgraded to FRSCM in 1994.

Cockerham, Michael, (1973/74, one term), b. Yorkshire, UK; educated at King Edward's School in Birmingham where he studied organ with Roy Massey, alto choral scholar at King's College, Cambridge, DOM Monkton Combe School in Bath, then taught at Cheltenham College, finally DOM at The Royal High School in Bath, retiring in 2009. Director of Wells Cathedral Voluntary Choir since 1998.

Colquhoun, Lindsay Talbot, BDS, FRSCM, (1958-61), b. 1931, Australia; known at Addington as 'Coco', he was a dental surgeon by profession and had studied at the University of Adelaide before attending the RSCM. He married Anne, one of the cooks at AP, assisted in inaugurating the Addington Scout Troop and subsequently became organist of St George's, Norton. A past President of The Organ Club from 1989-91, he was a member of the St Alban's Diocesan Synod from 1970 to 1987 and Chairman of the RSCM St Albans Area Committee. He served on RSCM Council 1992-2000 and was made FRSCM on retirement.

Coltman, Bridget, (ca 1968-69), UK.

Cooper, Philip Lindsay, BMus, LRAM, FRCO(CHM), ARSCM, (1956-58), d. 1971 in the UK, Australian by birth; organist of St Andrew's in Walkerville, Adelaide in 1953, he was awarded (the first) English Hymnal Scholarship in October 1956. Head Student 1957-58, during his time at AP he was organist of Holy Trinity, South Kensington, and from 1958 he was at Emmanuel School, Wandsworth and Coulsdon Parish Church. He later taught at St Dunstan's in Catford and was an RSCM Special Commissioner.

Cotterill, Rowland, MA, FRCO, LRAM, ARCM, (c.1964); went on to be organ scholar at Jesus College, Cambridge. Author of a book about Wagner, he has been a lecturer in English at Warwick University.

Cousins, Malcolm Ernest, LRAM, FRCO(CHM), ARSCM, (1953-56), b. 1932, St Neots, Huntingdonshire, UK; Head Student 1955, he was assistant organist at Peterborough Cathedral 1956-59. Organist of Mansfield Parish Church for 34 years from 1959 to 1993, he directed many RSCM courses.

Cousins, Peter J., ARCO (1961/62); was sub-organist of St Bride's Fleet Street. He did not continue with music as a career but taught in Hitchin.

Cowley, Russell Euston, ARSCM (1966/67), b. 1928, Invercargill; d. 2009, Invercargill, New Zealand; was organist of St John's in Invercargill, New Zealand for most of his life and worked actively for RSCM New Zealand.

Cridland, Revd Anthony, (1969-71), UK; the second R/C priest to study at AP. He was priest at St Thomas the Apostle in Nunhead from 1982 and at St Finbarr in Aylesham until retirement.

Cruden, Robert J, ARCO (1954-55), UK; taught at Stockwell College, organist of St Andrew, Undershaft, in London in 1971 and published a book about the Renatus Harris organ there.

Dacey, Richard, (1972/73), UK; from Cardiff. Briefly at Malvern Priory and in Canada at St Matthew's in Ottawa before returning to the UK in 1980 to teach at Shrewsbury School. He was DOM at Repton School from 1994 to 2006, Director of Leicester Philharmonic and Derby Choral Union.

Dance, Alan I, ARCO, (1955 & 1959), UK; assistant organist at Southwark Cathedral ca 1960 and at Ripon Cathedral 1963-74, he was organist of Holy Trinity in Hull 1991-99, DOM Bridlington Choral Society and organist of St Martin's on the Hill, Scarborough, and organist of Howden Minster.

Date, David, GRSM, ARCM, ARCO, (1956/57), b. ca 1928, UK; DOM at Monkton Combe Prep School in Somerset until retirement.

Davies, Jennifer, ARCO, (1965-67), UK; studied at RAM, private music teacher in Lymington, Hampshire.

Davis, Godfrey, (1973/74).

Deasey, Revd Michael Keith, OAM, ARCO, BEd, ARSCM (1969-71), b. 1947, Sydney, NSW, Australia; from Carlingford, NSW, married Antonia Harman (1970-74), was organist of St Andrew's Cathedral in Sydney for 25 years. He was ordained deacon in All Saints Cathedral, Bathurst, in July 2004, after which he took up his role as Precentor and DOM there until retirement in 2015. He was Regional RSCM Representative for Western Australia.

Dellow, Ronald Graeme, MBE, FRCO(CHM), ARSCM, (1958), b. 1924, Auckland; d. 2004, Auckland, New Zealand; was organist of Pitt Street Methodist Church and All Saints', Ponsonby, both in Auckland. He was president of the Auckland Organists' Association twice and was a lecturer at the university there.

Devadasen, Abraham, (1962, one term only), India; organist of Madras Cathedral attended AP for the Easter Term 1962 with a bursary from the British Council. Also Principal of Christ Church School in Madras.

Dewdney, Eric S, ARCO (1964/65), Canada; organist emeritus of Trinity Anglican Church, in Cambridge, Ontario.

Dickinson, Stephen, (1967-69), UK.

Diehl, Foster, ARCM, FTCL (1958-61), USA; was organist of Holy Name Cathedral in Chicago from 1964, in 1976 he moved to St Petronille in Glen Ellyn, Illinois, retiring in 1991. In retirement he has been organist of Highland Presbyterian Church in Largo, FL.

Diehl, Revd John Henry III, (1972-74), b. 1934, Lancaster, PA; d. 2004, Asheville, NC, USA; he was offered the post of Chaplain at AP after the death of Revd Leslie Katin, but declined it. Rector of St Mark's, Lehigh Valley, KY, until January 1976, then Canon Rector of St Stephen's Cathedral, Harrisburg, Rector of St John's Episcopal Church, Hagerstown, from 1979 to 1991.

Dixon, Nigel, (1967/68), UK; to Durham University, taught at Stamford School, Lincolnshire.

Dod, Kenneth, (1965), USA.

Doran, David, (1973/74), USA.

Drewett, Julian, (1970-73), UK; was assistant to Michael Fleming at Croydon Parish Church in 1972-76, then organist in Tenterden, Kent. Now General Secretary of the Churches' Fellowship for Psychical and Spiritual Studies. He married Christine Asher (1972/73).

[AH] recalls:

> 'Their wedding was in the chapel at Addington Palace and the reception in the grounds on a glorious summer day — Felicity Dakers, Wendy Pearce and I were bridesmaids.'

Driedger, E Alan, (1963-66), Canada; from Ottawa, went on to the Goethe Institute in Germany before settling in the UK.

Duthie, Howard A, FRCO, (1967/68), UK; studied at the RCM and was organ scholar at Christ's College, Cambridge. He was DOM at George Heriot's School and organist at Greyfriars Kirk in Edinburgh. From 2001 he was DOM at Morrison's Academy in Crieff until retirement in 2010. The following year he was appointed DOM at St John's Kirk in Perth.

Dyer, Michael George, LTCL, LRAM, ARCM, ARCO (1959/60), b. 1930, Sydney; d. 2011, Dural, Australia; was assistant organist of St Bride's Fleet Street in 1959, preceding Robert F. Smith. Was organist of St Philip's Anglican Church in Church Hill, Sydney, from 1967, taught at the Nepean College of Advanced Education.

Eagles, John, FRCO, MMus, (1971/72), UK; was organist of St Andrew's and then St Mark's in Bromley.

Eggington, John, (1964/65), Australia; gave a recital at Melbourne Town Hall in 1953 at age 26. He was assistant at Manchester Cathedral in 1967.

Erwin, Joseph, (1966, one term), b. 1923, Huntsville, AL, USA; was organist of the Congregational Church in Tryon, NC, 1978-2010. He was a pianist and student of Carl Friedberg at the Juilliard School in New York and became a professor there. Also head of the Dwight School in New Jersey for 30 years.

Everhart, Charles, (1964-66), USA; from Christ Church Cathedral in Indianapolis, at Trinity Episcopal Church in Cranford, NJ in 1966.

Farrell, Timothy, (1962-66) see Visiting Tutors.

Faulkner, Duncan, (1972-74) b. 1951, Northampton, UK; also studied at the RCM with Richard Latham and Herbert Howells, was organist of St Anne's in Wandsworth. Married Wendy Pearce (1969-1972).

Felton, Carol, (1968-70), UK.

Ferris, Derek FRCO, (1954-55/1956-57), b. 1937, USA; resident in Westerly, Rhode Island, came to AP Jan 1954 as one of the first students. Went to Boston with a scholarship from the New England Conservatory. After ten years as a church musician he made a complete career switch to Engineering and retired as an electrical engineer in 2001 in Pawcatuck, Connecticut.

Finnamore, David J, FRCO(CHM), FTCL, LRAM, ARCM, (1956-58), UK; organist of Westerham Parish Church, Assistant at Chapel Royal, Assistant DOM at Oxted County Grammar School, organist of Frome Parish Church 1965-68, DOM at Gillingham Comprehensive School. Also a Senior Trinity College Examiner.

Fisher, D E, ARCO (ca 1967).

Flood, David, FRCO(CHM), MA, DMus, FGCM, (1973/74), b. 1955, Guildford, Surrey, UK; assistant (1978-86) and then full Organist and Master of the Choristers (since 1988) of Canterbury Cathedral having been Organist of Lincoln Cathedral in between.

Flower, A John, (1959/60), UK; assistant organist of Southwark Cathedral from 1959 whilst at AP where he was Head Student. Taught at Solihull School 1963-67, St Edward's School in Oxford from 1967. Assistant organist of All Saints' in Ryde, IOW, 1977-95. While in Oxford he established RSCM courses there.

Foad, Michael J L, MA, ARCM, LLCM, (1952-54), b. 1937, UK; Hymns A&M Scholar at Canterbury and then AP from 1952, went on to Gonville and Caius Cambridge, taught and was organist at Eastbourne College from 1959 to 1965 and then taught at Bootham School in York for 12 years, before moving back to Kent. From 1988-2005 he conducted both the Dover Choral Society and the Folkestone & Hythe Orchestra. He plays the organ at Folkestone United Reformed Church.

Ford, Rodney, FTCL, LRAM, ARCO, ARCM, AdvStdCert(RCM, Lond), Australia; DOM at Brighton Grammar School, Victoria, retired 2012.

Forrester, Fiona, (1967/68), UK; from Sutton Coldfield, later in Selsdon, Surrey. A piano teacher.

Fowler, Ivan, (1973/74), UK; from Gravesend, held organist posts in London at St Columba's Pont Street, St Mary the Virgin Primrose Hill from 1975 and in Bristol.

Foy, Aubrey, FRCO, (1956/57), b. ca 1943; d. 2003, Quebec, Canada; was Head Student, in September 1963 he became choirmaster at St Mark's Anglican Church in Ottawa, then to St James Cathedral in Toronto, at St Andrew's College in Aurora 1976-93.

Freeman, Eric, (1967-69), UK.

French, William C, (1963-65), b. 1944, USA; from Woburn, MA, and writes: 'I soon discovered almost everyone was more talented at the keyboard than I, so I returned to

262

Boston and worked in the management of the Boston Symphony Orchestra. Later, I ventured into the Real Estate Business for better economic survival. I have been a member of Trinity Church Copley Square in Boston, Massachusetts for many years.'

Fricker, Paul (1965, two terms), UK; studied Theology at Durham University and was a choral scholar in the cathedral choir. He taught at St Stephen's College, Hong Kong for six years. On returning to England, he taught at Norwich School and then became Head of Religious Studies and Lay Chaplain at Bedford High School until retirement.

Frodsham, Prof Olaf M, (1962, one term only), b. 1915; UK, d. 2005, Pasadena, CA, Anglo-American; from Occidental College, Los Angeles, CA, then professor emeritus there.

Furusawa, Kasei, (1965/66), b. 1929, Japan; studied at Seinan Gakuin University, Southern Baptist Theological Seminary, the Royal School of Church Music, King's College, London and Cambridge University. Was professor of sacred music and organist at Seinan Gakuin University in Fukuoka, Japan.

Fysh, David, (1967-69), b. 1935, UK; Hon Secretary of the newly-formed 'Society of St Nicolas' in 1971, organist of Saint Silas Church in Kentish Town from 1969, then DOM at Wycliffe College Junior School, Stonehouse, Gloucestershire for 25 years, ordained priest 1992 and Parish Priest at St Mary's, West Walton in Wisbech, Cambridgeshire from 1995 and Priest-Vicar at Ely Cathedral. Now retired and resident at the College of St Barnabas in Surrey.

Gadsden, St John, FRCO(CHM), LTCL, (1960-62) d. 2005, UK; Lady Mary Trefusis Scholar at AP and senior student in 1962, organist Ashford Parish Church from 1962, director of Ashford Choral Society 1964-1970.

Gallienne, John, (1965-67), b. 1945, Guernsey; studied at the GSM and went to Canada. Was organist of St George's Cathedral in Kingston, Ontario, for 20 years.

Gatward, David, ARCM, LTCL, FRCO, LRAM, (1953-1957), b. 1934; d. 2010, Rugby, UK; one of the last students at Canterbury, Head Student 1956, taught first at Summerfield Prep School in Oxford, and then at Rugby School. Married Moira Teesdale (1955-57).

George, Michael, (1969); a former chorister at King's College, Cambridge, studied singing at the RCM and is now an internationally-known singer.

Gilfillian, Geoffrey, MusBac, (1969), Australia.

Girdlestone, Errol Nelson Richey, ARCO, (1963/64), b. 1945, UK; to Keble College, Oxford. A founder member of the Hilliard Ensemble in 1974.

Godwin, Duncan, GTCL, ARCM, AMusTCL, (1956-60), UK; studied at TCL, taught in Banbury.

Godwin, Miranda, LRAM (1960-62), UK; Duncan's sister, studied at RAM, became Mrs Peter Hutchings, deceased.

Goss, John, FRCO, FRCCO, (1962-64), b. 1943, London; d. 1986, Barbados, Anglo-Canadian; became a choral exhibitioner at Christ Church, Oxford. Also studied at the Royal Conservatory in Toronto and then joined the National Ballet orchestra eventually becoming associate conductor. He took Canadian citizenship. Related to Sir John Goss, he died in a car accident whilst on holiday in Barbados.

Gower, Robert, MA, FRCO(CHM), LRAM, ARCM, FRSA, (1971), b. 1952, UK; A&M Scholar at AP to Organ Scholarship Lincoln College, Oxford, DOM of Radley College and Glenalmond School, Perthshire until retirement in 2012. Organist of the Cathedral Church of St Barnabas in Nottingham since May 2014, he is an editor and compiler for The Oxford University Press and Chairman of both the Gerald Finzi Trust and the Percy Whitlock Trust.

Graham, Fred Kimball, MusBac, MM, PhD, FRCO, (1965, one term only), b. 1946, Oshawa, Ontario, Canada; organist of All Saints' Cathedral in Halifax, NS 1978-1985 and taught at the Atlantic School of Theology and Dalhousie University. He was involved with the production of the United Church Hymn Book (1996) and Service Book (2000). In retirement he is organist of Egglington St George's United Church.

Green, Carver, (1973/74).

Gregory, Jonathan T, FRCO, MA, (ca 1968-1971), UK; to organ scholar Clare College, Cambridge, then DOM Leicester Cathedral from 1994 until 2010.

Griffiths, Keith Charles, BA, MusB, ARCM, FRCO(CHM), (1960/61), b. Worcester, UK; Hymns A&M Scholar at AP, to organ scholarship at Emmanuel, Cambridge, assistant organist at St Mary's Episcopal Cathedral in Edinburgh, then DOM of Ipswich School in Suffolk, then for 21 years DOM at Merchant Taylors' School in Northwood, Middlesex.

Griswell, Geoffrey, (1957-60), was Sacristan of AP Chapel.

Groome, Nigel, ARSCM (1978-1982) b. Bournemouth; and, no, the dates for Nigel's residence at Addington as a 'London' student at the LCM and RCM are not incorrect. He was resident at AP <u>after</u> the college had closed. In exchange for his subsidised accommodation Nigel accompanied services in the Chapel, at courses and even did the washing up! He has served the RSCM as Regional Coordinator for the South-East and as Regional Music Advisor for the South and South-West. He has been Music Advisor to the Rochester Diocese and, since 1980, DOM at Beckenham Parish Church. He was made ARSCM in 2008.

Groves, Anthony, (1967/68), UK.

Guðjónsson, Guðjón, (1970, one term), Iceland.

Hagger, Dorothy, LRAM, BMus, (1963-65); became Mrs Charles Everhart.

Hales, ARCO(CHM) (1964).

Hall, R, (ca 1959), New Zealand.

Hamilton, Ann, LRAM, (1956/57), Australia; became Mrs Walter Sutcliffe and his assistant organist.

Hamilton, Daphne, (1972/73), Northern Ireland.

Hamilton, Robert Jerald, (1955, one term only), b. 1927, Wichita, KS; d. 2009, Edgewood, NM, USA; from Grace Cathedral in Topeka, KS.

Harding, David; was organist of St Mark's, Surbiton and All Saint's, Banstead, and became DOM of Dover Grammar School. He was sometime editor of the *Treble Clef*, section of *RSCM New*.

Harman, Antonia, AGSM, CertEd, (1970-74); from Cornwall, studied piano and violin at the GSM, married Michael Deasey (1969-71) and moved to teach and sing in Australia.

Harris Tom, (1972/73), USA; from Durham, NC.

Harrison, David, ARCM, FRCO, (1955/56 & 1958/59), UK, studied at RCM, taught at Brambletyre School in East Grinstead, at Sandroyd School in Salisbury, DOM at Craigflower School in Torryburn, Fife in 1971.

Harrison, Richard, (1962-67), UK; London Student from Stevenage.

Hartley, Pamela, (1966/67), studied at RCM. Became Mrs Rodney Vaughan.

Harvey, Geoffrey, ARCO, (1964), b. 1944; d. 2009 UK; organ scholarship to Brasenose College, Oxford. Organist and DOM of St John's School in Leatherhead for 40 years.

Heath, Susan, GRSM, ARCM, LRAM, ARCO, (married name Heath-Downey) (1972/73), UK; was Artistic Director and Organiser of the IAO's annual 'London Organ Days', now DOM Rotherhithe & Bermondsey Choral Society and of The Elizabethan Singers of London, organist of St Paul's Deptford (since 2010).

Hedley, Michael, (1969), UK; studied organ with Nicholas Danby in London and attended master classes with André Marchal, Michael Schneider and Luigi Tagliavini. In 1978 he studied at the Sweelinck Conservatory in Amsterdam and has been organist of the Basilica of St Nicholas in Amsterdam since 2000.

Henesy, Father Michael, CSsR, (1968/69); the first R/C Priest to study at AP, became a Redemptorist priest in Edinburgh and then Middlesbrough.

Henry, Frederick W, BMus, (1955/56), USA; from Irwin, PA.

Higgins, John, ARCO, (1971/72); went on to be organist of St Barnabas, Purley.

Hilton, Michael, LRAM, (1957/58), UK; taught at Ardingly College, organist of Uckfield Parish Church.

Hinton, Cecilia, (1964/65), UK; London Student at the RCM.

Ho Sze-Nang, Revd Edward, BA, MMus, FTCL, LRSM, (1964), b. 1939, Hong Kong; also studied at TCL, Lecturer in Music at the Chinese University in Hong Kong, Head of Music at the University of Singapore in 1973.

Holder, S Donald, LTCL, LRAM, (1964/65), Australia; pupil and then DOM at Friends' School, Hobart, from 1959, after leaving AP was DOM Trinity Grammar School Chapel, Summer Hill, Sydney and still there 1985.

Holman, Michael, ARCM, (1954-57), UK; studied at RCM, taught at Uppingham School, was a housemaster on several RSCM courses from 1957 to 1969.

Hooi, Richard, ARCM, LRAM, (1959-62), Malaya; a bass-baritone, supported by a senior Anglican cleric in Singapore, he returned to Kuala Lumpur after AP. He also lived in

Canada. [MR] recalls 'I think he did a bit of film-extra work during his holidays, during which he managed to travel around Europe.'

Hooper, John D, (1954/55), Canada; organist of Trinity Presbyterian Church, Peterborough, Ontario. Was one of the Last Canterbury Students who transferred to Croydon and before this was organist of St James' Cathedral in Toronto from 1951.

Hoskins, Graham J Douglas, ARCO, (1964-66), UK; A&M Scholar at AP, organist of Esher PC, DOM Reed's School in Cobham, Surrey, and Gresham's School.

Houlton, Neil, (1969), Canada; He received a loan for his study but defaulted on repayments. Despite letters from the RSCM solicitors and a Canadian firm of solicitors, the £72.80 was written off by RSCM Council as a bad debt.

How, Martin, (1955/56), UK; see Headquarters Commissioner.

Howard, Colin M, FRCO, GRSM, (1964-66 & 1967/68), b. 1944; d. 2008, Cape Town, South Africa; studied at the RCM, organist and choirmaster of St Mary's Church, Hitchin, and Director of Music at Hitchin Boys' School in the 1970's. He returned to South Africa, was active in the Cape Town Branch of RSCM South Africa, he was awarded the Cert Special Service 2004.

Howe, Dr Mark, PhD, (19??), USA; studied at Westminster Choir College and Yale University before AP, DOM at the Cathedral Church of St Paul (Episcopal) in Burlington, Vermont since 1999.

Hughes, G Campbell, BMus, ARCO(CHM), (1961/62); became a recording engineer with the BBC and eventually BBC Senior Music Studio Manager. He worked with John Rutter at Collegium Records and retired to Dorset.

Hume, John M, MA, BMus, FRCO(CHM), (1966-68), d. 2013, North Shore, New Zealand; organist of St Aidan's in Remuera, President of the Society of Recorder Players and organist for the Parish of Devonport before his sudden death. Awarded an Hon RSCM in 2010.

Hunt, Chris, (1968/69).

Hurrle, Norman William, ARCT, ARCM, ARCO, FTCL, (1958/59), b. 1927, Peterborough, ON; d. 1989, Saskatoon, Canada; organist of St Matthias's in Westmount, Montreal after AP. Was organist at St James' Cathedral in Toronto (1965-69), at Christ Church Cathedral in Vancouver (1970-73), at Christ Church Cathedral in Victoria (1981-83) and latterly at All Saints' Anglican Church in Saskatoon.

Hutton, Susan Margaret, LGSM, ARCO(CHM), (1960-62), b. 1934, London, UK; She wrote: 'While at Addington, the director received a letter asking if there was a student who would like to go to New Zealand and teach in a C of E girls' school there. I was asked and the rest is history!' This was in Stratford and was followed by six years at the Diocesan School in Auckland. She returned to the UK in 1985.

Jackson, Sir Nicholas Fane St George (Bart.), (1954/55), b. 1934, London, UK; at the RAM he was an organ pupil of C H Trevor and harpsichord pupil of George Malcolm. In 1971 he became organist in London of St James's in Piccadilly, and then of St Lawrence Jewry, before becoming organist of St David's Cathedral from 1977 to 1984.

Jan, Elaine, B.Ed., ATCL, (1957-59), Canada; from Vancouver.

Jenkins, John, (19??), Trinidad; one term only, from Holy Trinity Cathedral in Port of Spain, Trinidad.

Jenkins, Lindsay, (1966), Australia; two terms only, from North Melbourne.

Jewell, Susan, (1972/73).

Johnson, John, (1968).

Jones, Elwyn, ARCO, (ca 1955), UK; organist of Oldbury Grammar School in Birmingham, Llandeilo PC and was County Music Organiser for Carmarthenshire in 1971.

Jones, Jonathan Hellyer, (1969), b. 1951, UK; is Precentor and DOM at Magdalene College, Cambridge.

Kaizi Lwasa, Eriya, (1952-54), b. 1901; d. 1980, Uganda; from Kampala, A chorister at Namirembe Cathedral from 1915 and organist there from 1935. An uncle of King Edward Mutesa II of Buganda and originally taught the organ by missionaries.

Kalule, Michael, (1962), b. 1927; d. 1982, Namirembe, Uganda; a chorister at Namirembe Cathedral from 1935, he became assistant organist and choirmaster working with Eriya Kaizi until the latter's death in 1980. In 1976 he returned to AP as a tutor to the summer course for overseas students. He was robbed and murdered by an armed gang in December 1982. His *CMQ* obituary records 'He had worked hard for our cause in East Africa and latterly, during the difficult times being experienced in Uganda, we were able through the kindness of the Bishop of Winchester to send music to him for use at Namirembe Cathedral.'[276]

Kantz, Joseph A, ARCM, (1963-64), USA; organist of St Augustine's by the Sea Episcopal Church in Santa Monica, CA in 1971.

Karashani, Joseph, (1961, Summer Term only), Uganda; a medical student from Makerere College on a British Council Bursary.

Keefe, Robin J W, (19??).

Kellner, Michael, ARCM, (1970/71), USA; counter-tenor and organist, from Baltimore, MD. Organist St John's Church in Huntingdon, Baltimore, from 1998.

Kerr, Leslie, (1966/67), Australia; living in Melbourne.

Kilian, Ivan, ARCM, LRAM, LTCL, LRSM, (1957-59), South Africa; DOM St Andrew's College in Grahamstown. Examiner for UNISA in 2005.

Kim, David [Chang Hwan David], (1963-65), Korea; Kim was talent-spotted by GHK on his 1962 trip to Korea[277]. An appeal was made for £1000 to fund his two years at AP. GHK

---

[276] *CMQ* April 1983. The Bishop of Winchester was a CMS missionary in Uganda for several years and had visited again in 1982.
[277] *ECM* Oct 1962.

thought Kim could do a great deal for church music in Korea. He was a choirmaster and language teacher in Seoul.

King, Geoffrey, b. 1949, Croydon, UK; studied at the RCM with Humphrey Searle and Alexander Goehr. From 1976 he taught at St Mary's Music School in Edinburgh. In 1988 he moved to Amsterdam.

King, Larry Peyton, LRAM, (1957/58), b. 1932; d. 1990, Fullerton CA, USA; was assistant organist at the Cathedral of St John the Divine in New York, organist of St Paul's in San Diego, California, and organist of Trinity Episcopal Church in New York from 1968 to 1989. He studied at the University of Redlands in California and at the Union Theological Seminary in New York.

King, Michael J, ARCO, (1956), South Africa; from Grahamstown, organist of St Michael and All Angels, Queenstown, SA in 1971.

Kirk, J Allan, BMus, (1967/68), Canada; from Barrie, Ontario, a Divinity graduate of Trinity College in Toronto and a music graduate of University of Toronto. Taught at the Royal Conservatory in Toronto. Was the Dean of Saskatoon and Rector of St John's Cathedral in Saskatoon.

Knowles, Geoffrey, ARCO, ARCM, FRCO, (1964/65), UK; organist of St Mary the Virgin in Mold.

Kursinski, E Robert, (1962, one term only), b. 1921, Los Angeles, CA; d. 2011 Tucson, AZ, USA; was organist of many churches in the Los Angeles/Pasadena area and taught in public schools.

Lancelot, James, MA, MusB, HonFGSM, ARCM, FRCO, FRSCM, (1970/71), b. 1952, UK; gap-year student at AP between Ardingly School and organ scholar at Kings, Cambridge. Organist of Durham Cathedral since 1985.

Langdon, J David, ARCM, FRCO, GRSM, (1961-65), UK; DOM at Summerfields Prep School in Oxford until retirement.

Langdon, Rupert, (1973/74).

Law, Brian John, LRAM, FRCO(CHM), ARSCM, (1961-64), b. 1943, UK; former chorister at Brighton PC and was Head Student at AP. [RS] recalled that he was a 'Very personable and capable musician. Keen on the new fashions, emigrated from London to Canada in 1965 to be Director of Music and Organist at St Matthews, Ottawa, and then went to New Zealand in 1991 to be Director of Music of Christchurch City Choir.' He became DOM at Christchurch Cathedral in 2004, retiring in 2014.

Lawford, Janet, (1956-58), UK; a London student.

Leek, John C, (1969/70), Canada; Master of Choristers at Viscount Montgomery School in Hamilton, Ontario, the first Boy Choir in Canada, founded by him in 1970.

Leigh, David, LTCL, (1955-57), Hong Kong; his father was an Archdeacon whose family built a well-known Chinese church in Kowloon City. Ordained priest on his return to Hong Kong, he was Vicar of St Mark's, Hunghom, Chaplain of All Saints' School, Homantia, and RSCM

268

Representative for Hong Kong. He was made HonRSCM in 1986. Much respected among the Chinese speakers, he worked into his 80's because they needed him. He also produced a new Hymn Book for the Chinese church.

Leigh, Elizabeth, ARCM, LTCL, (1956), Hong Kong; David Leigh's sister.

Le Roux, Mark, GTCL, LTCL, ARCM, (1960/61), from St Helier, Jersey; Director of the Arts Centre, Charlottetown in Canada in 1974, taught at Shawnigan Lake School ca 1980, organist of St Mary the Virgin in Oak Bay, from 1984, RFS recalled 'Highly entertaining character! Life of any party!'

Lester, John, (1972-74), b. 1952, Grays; d. 2007, Chepstow.

Lim, Bek Neo, ARCO, (1954/55), b. 1931, Singapore; Mrs Lim Bek Neo became organist of St Andrew's Cathedral in Singapore. She won a scholarship to study at RCM in 1953 and combined this with study at AP.

Linton, Elizabeth, (1973/74).

Ludlum, W Douglas, (1973/74), USA; organist of First Baptist Church, Salisbury, NC. After AP he was at St Mark's Lutheran Church, NC, in the late 1970's and from 1981 at St Matthew's in Charleston, SC.

Lyne, Richard C, BMus, MA, GRSM, FRSA, ARCM, ARCO, FRSA, (1966/67), UK; Society of Faith Scholar at AP, a graduate of London and Nottingham universities, he studied at the RCM with John Birch and subsequently taught there. DOM at St Michael's in Barnes, founder and conductor of the Howells Singers, he is Hon General Editor of the Church Music Society.

Ma, Marina, LTCL, GTCL, ARCM, (1958-61), Hong Kong; now Mrs Marina Lau resident in Vermont, Victoria, Australia.

Mahinder, Arthur, (1963, one term only), India; organist of The Cathedral of the Redemption in Delhi for 32 years.

Mahon, Christopher M, FRCO, (1964-67), UK; to Durham University, in Reading 1971, came from Grimsby where Martin How was organist, now in Somerset.

Marsden, J David, ARCM, LRAM, ARCO(CHM), (1959-61), b. 1938; d. 1990, Canada; Head Student, from St John's, Sandwich, Ontario, to Christ Church, Elbow Park, Calgary, then St Thomas's in St Catherine's, Ontario in 1975.

Maskell, Elizabeth, (1967/68), Canada, from Ottawa, Ontario.

Mason, Paul, (1967/68), UK.

Matthew, John, (1969), UK; from Sherborne School.

Matthew, Glynis, (1973/74).

Matthias, Philip V, ARCO(CHM), (1977-79), Australia; from Brisbane.

Mayo, Graham J D, MA, FRCO(CHM), ARCM, (1957, two terms only), d. 2004, UK; studied at the RCM, to organ scholarship at Corpus Christi Cambridge, conductor of Northampton Symphony Orchestra 1964-1985 and of Northampton Philharmonic Choir 1963-2004, organist of All Saints' Northampton 1962-1972.

McClurg, Catherine, (1969/70), Northern Ireland; organist of Holy Cross Church, Durley near Winchester in 2014.

McGrath, Hume, (1966/67), Tasmania; at Anglican Parish of the Parks, St Silas & St Anselm Albert Park.

McIvor, Donald William, (19??), New Zealand; organist of Nelson Cathedral, New Zealand, made Hon RSCM in 1986.

McKinley, Ian William, MA, ARCM, (1958/59), b. 1929, MacKay, Queensland, Australia; studied at the University of Queensland, He was a foundation member and later National Secretary and Treasurer of the Australian Society for Music Education. He taught at Mt Gravatt College of Advanced Education until retirement in 1987. He was DOM of the Queensland Bach Choir from 1977 to 1987, organist of St Andrew's Anglican Church, South Brisbane for 13 years then DOM at Christ Church, St Lucia until retirement in 1993.

McLearon, Frederick Lionel, (1965, one term), b. 1911, d. 1999, Victoria, B C, Canada; from Montreal, DOM of Lachine High School and organist of First Baptist Church in Montreal in 1954.

Meakins, Vaughan, (1968-71); DOM at the Royal Ballet School.

Miller, Allan B, BA, ARCO, (1959-61); UK, awarded an Alto Choral Scholarship to St John's Cambridge in 1961, Taught music at Cheltenham College Junior School, Assistant DOM at St Peter's School, York.

Milne, Gerald A, LRAM, ARCO, (1958-60), UK; English Hymnal Scholar at AP, went to teach at Bretton Hall Teacher Training College in Leeds, then taught at St Matthew's School in Rugby and at Haileybury Junior School. In 1971 he was organist of Holy Trinity Garrison Church in Windsor.

Milner, John W, (19??).

Moore, Christopher, BA, FRCO(CHM), FTCL, ADCM, LRAM, HonFGCM, (1970/71), UK; from Durham. He was DOM at the University Church of Great St Mary in Cambridge, taught at schools in Cambridge and was DOM of the St Ives Choral Society. From 2004 to 2011 he was organist of the Cathedral of St Michael and St George in Grahamstown, South Africa. Retired and living in Bury St Edmunds.

Morehen, Prof John Manley, MA, FRCO(CHM), ADCM, DLitt, PhD, FRCCO, HonFGCM, (1960/61) – see Visiting Tutors.

Morley, Oliver, FRCO, ARCM, (1952-54), UK; assistant organist Chester Cathedral from July 1954, organist of All Hallows in Twickenham.

Morris, John, (1972/73).

Moss, D Britten, (19??).

Naylor, Revd Bruce Alan, MMus, ARSCM, ARCM, (1957/58), Australia; a chorister at St Paul's Cathedral in Melbourne, returned to Australia in 1960 and became organist of St George's Cathedral in Perth, Australia, in 1961, ordained deacon in 1965, moved to Adelaide in 1967, ordained priest in 1979.

Newberry, Andrew Robert, FRCO(CHM), ADCM, (1967/68), b. 1949, London, d. 2000, UK; organ scholar at Selwyn College, Cambridge, assistant organist Peterborough Cathedral 1971-1979, then organist of St Peter's Collegiate Church in Wolverhampton 1979-1983.

Newton, Michael, (1967/68), UK.

Nichols, David M, FRCO, GGSM, ARCM, LGSM, (1956/57), UK; also studied at GSM, appointed DOM of Blackpool Grammar School on leaving AP, then DOM at Warwick School, sometime organist in Great Yarmouth.

Nittinger, Carl E, (1969-71), b. 1946, USA; acted as Sacristan and Choir Librarian at AP, organist of the Church of the Resurrection in Baltimore, MD, 1965/66, assistant organist St Luke's Church in Germantown 1972/3, organist at Grace Church in Merchantville, NJ 1975-1985 and St Alban's Church in Olney PA 1985-1999. Now resident in Haddonfield, NJ.

Noake, Keith Alexander, MMus (Dunelm), (1965/66), b. 1915; d. 1968, Australia; studied at St Andrew's Cathedral in Sydney and with Edgar Bainton. He taught at the conservatory in Newcastle NSW and was cathedral organist there from 1950 until his death.

O'Donnell, John David, BMus, LTCL, FRCO(CHM), ADCM, (1969), b. 1948, Sydney, NSW, Australia; a musicologist at the University of Melbourne.

Old, David, LGSM, (1972/73); According to Google 'He combines his musical activities with a career in Television and Feature Films Sound Post-production, and has been awarded no fewer than seven BAFTAs so far!' He was organist of Easthampstead PC in 2013.

Olsen, Sheila, (1969), UK.

Omideyi, Olaolu (k/a James), ARCO, (1954/55), b. 1918, Ibadan; d. 2003, Ibadan, Nigeria; organist of St James-the-Less in London until 1957 (succeeded by Ayo Bankole), founded the Ecumenical School of Church Music in Ibadan and was organist of St James Cathedral in Ibadan. He had studied at the Pratt School of Music in Lagos in the early 1940's. He was assistant DOM to the Nigerian Broadcasting Corporation.

Omideyi, Segun, (1973/74).

O'Neill, Lindsay, FRCO(CHM), Hon RSCM, (1958, one term, & 1963-65), Tasmania; to St John's in Launceston, Tasmania in 1958. Head Student when he returned in 1963, organist of St Andrew's in Brighton, Victoria, and RSCM Special Commissioner.

Oni, Emmanuel Kayode, (1969), b. 1943, Ibadan, Nigeria; known at AP as 'Oni', pupil of the Bankoles, father and son, organist at the Chapel of the Resurrection at the University of Ibadan then organist at Our Saviour's Church, Ikenne from 1982. Also organist for the Radio Nigeria Choir and retired as Controller of Music for Radio Nigeria in 1995.

Osgood, Graham, (1962/63).

Ottley, John Richard, (1973/74); see Editors of *CMQ*.

Oversby, Peter, (1970/71), UK; CMS Scholar at AP, to organ scholar at Gonville & Caius College Cambridge.

Packman, Allan, ATCL, (1958), New Zealand; from Ashburton, New Zealand, organist of St Mary's Merivale in Christchurch.

Parkes, Revd David, ARCO, HonFGCM, (1956-59), b. 1937, d. 1990, UK; acted as Sacristan at AP Chapel, [RS] recalls that he was 'Another St Bride's sub-organist where the organ copy of *Parish Psalter* was labelled 'The Psalms of David Parkes.' ' To Exeter College, Oxford in 1959 and organist of St Mary's in Kidlington. Ordained Deacon 1964 in Durham, at Christchurch in Gateshead 1970-1977 and then organist of St Margaret's in Durham City. He also acted as an organ consultant. Vicar of St Michael in Aylsham, Norfolk, at the time of his death.

[LS] remembers when the late Denis Stevens, musicologist, was the guest of the then Warden, Cyril Taylor. David Parkes, genial but ungainly, got up to help himself to the 'extra' chops put out by Harry Blacktin, the steward. Sadly, Harry had managed to drop the tray of chops, then, having retrieved them, spread the grease over an area of the floor. David slipped on his way back, sending his extra chop cartwheeling through the air to land on Denis Stevens's chest, thereby eliciting the casual remark from the Warden, 'We do this every Tuesday'. This somewhat belies the suggestion that Cyril Taylor had little sense of humour.

Partridge, Peter Muir, ARCO, (1961/62), b. 1941, Canada; was assistant to George Maybee at St George's Cathedral in Kingston, Ontario, in 1960, at St Catharines in Ontario, Canada in 1971, now Vice President & Portfolio Manager at RBC Dominion Securities.

Paul, James E, DMA (1958/59), USA; non-resident student from the University of Washington in Seattle. Became a professor at San Diego State University.

Pearce, Sally, (1973/74).

Pearce, Wendy, (1969-72); married Duncan Faulkner (1972-74).

Pearson, S Martin, (1967-69), UK; was assistant to Martin How in running the Chapel Choir. He went on to teach at Betteshanger School in Deal, then to Norway.

Perkins, E Adrian, BMus, FRCO(CHM), (1960/61), UK; English Hymnal Scholarship at AP, DOM St Lawrence College in Ramsgate in 1971, organist of Holy Trinity Church in Broadstairs in 2009.

Phelps, (Eric) Christopher, FRCO(CHM), LRAM, GRSM, (1961-65), b. 1943, Cheltenham, UK; to Ireland then in Colchester, [RS] commented 'ex-head chorister of Gloucester Cathedral under Sumsion. A happy, entertaining character.'

Phillips, Charles, (1968, one term); from Lagos, Nigeria.

Phillips, Harold, (1954, one term); from Johannesburg, South Africa.

Phillips, Peter, (1972, two terms), b. 1953, Southampton, UK; founded and directed the Tallis Scholars.

Pierce, William, FRSCM, (1955/56), d. 1996, Australia; organist of Louth PC, and teacher at King Edward VI Grammar School, Louth. Became chairman of the RSCM Tasmania Branch in

Australia, sometime organist of St John's in Launceston and Launceston City Organist for many years.

Pinock, James R L, (1959-61).

Pipes, Robert, (1972-74); was assistant organist at St John the Divine in Selsdon 1972/73.

Powell, A John, MBE. (19??), b. Abergavenny, Wales; taught at Davenant Foundation School from 1971 to retirement in 2012. He was made MBE in 2009.

Powell, W J D, (19??).

Price, David, FRCO, (1961-63), UK; studied at Stockport School with Geoffrey Barber before attending full-time at AP. He was DOM at Taverham School, Norwich, for 24 years from 1969 and also served as organist of St Nicholas in Great Yarmouth. Since 1979 he has been an ABRSM examiner both in the UK and abroad.

Pugh, Revd Peter, (1972).

Pugh, Roger, (1963-65); studied at the RAM, pupil of George Malcom and assistant organist at Westminster Cathedral until at least 1977.

Rawlings (Hinder), Margaret (Maggie), (1966-69).

Riley, Donald H, ARCM, LRAM, (1956-58), b. 1936; d. 2013, UK; taught at Saint Ivo School and then Soham Grammar School from 1966 to 1972.

Roberts, John, (1966), West Africa.

Roberts, Martin, BA, BMus, ARCO(CHM), (1960-62), UK; to alto Choral Scholarship at St John's, Cambridge, then to a one-year alto Academical Clerkship at Magdalen College, Oxford, and then into teaching in 1965. Sang professionally with the 'Clerkes of Oxenford'. He became DOM at Bloxham School near Banbury.

Roberts, Stephen Pritchard, (1968-71), b. 1949, UK; studied at the RCM and was a soloist in some of the 'May Concerts..' Now a well-known solo singer.

Roberts, William, (1967/68), Barbados.

Rogers, David, ARCCO, (1964/65), Canada; assistant organist of Vancouver Cathedral in the late 1950's, Now retired, living in Somerset and organist of East Coker church since 2005.

Royse, Anthony P H, ATCL, (1957-60), b. 1939, UK; 'k/a Tony' DOM of Appleby College in Oakville, Ontario 1973 until at least 1979, conductor of the Oakville Symphony Orchestra 1976-83, back in Kent UK in 1996. Has been DOM at a number of other Schools including Beechwood Park School in Herts., Wellesley House School in Broadstairs, The Dragon School in Oxford and Hilton College in Natal, S. Africa.

Russell, Anthony M T, LTCL, (1957-59); A&M Scholar at AP, DOM Pinewood School in Bourton, Shrivenham in 1971.

Russell, Bill, LTCL, (1957); educated at Lancing, organist of St Edwards in New Addington whilst a student. Then at St Philips, Norbury, and taught at Winton House School.

Sadler, A Graham, BMus, PhD, (1961/62), UK; to Nottingham University, a Professor at the Birmingham Conservatoire and visiting professor at the University of Oxford, now Emeritus

Professor of Music at the University of Hull. He is an authority on the composer Rameau. One student recalled that he had a 'Great sense of humour.'

Sandberg, Christine, (ca 1962).

Sandquist, Carl E, (1973/74).

Saruta, John Nagaharu, (1954/55 & 1965/66), Japan; a student from The School of Church Music in Tokyo, started at the RSCM in Canterbury then returned to AP for the year 1965/66. He was DOM at St Paul's University in Tokyo.

Saunders, Lindon Charles Mansell, ARSCM, New Zealand; DOM at King's College in Otahuhu, New Zealand, also Music Critic for the NZ Herald (an Auckland newspaper) for many years. RSCM Special Commissioner for Australia from 1995.

Sawa, Revd Jerome, (1959/60), Japan; from Tokyo,

Robert Hunter Bell (1958/59) wrote:

> 'Father Jerome Sawa from Japan arrived for two years of study knowing little or no English. What a fine, brave man he was. When baffled and exasperated, he would cry 'too much enough!' '

Martin Roberts (1960-62) recalls that he:

> 'practised Stanford in C repeatedly until he couldn't play it other than correctly.'

Sawkins, Lionel, ARCM, (1958/59), Australia; from Brisbane Grammar School, organist of St Mark's in Bromley and Lecturer at Whitelands College in London in 1971.

Schofield, Revd Tim, (1972/73), b. 1954; studied music at Durham, taught music in Exeter, trained for ordination at Lincoln Theological College, 23 years of parish ministry in the dioceses of St Albans and Exeter, Precentor of Chichester Cathedral since 2006.

Sefton, Alfred, LRAM, LTCL, FRCO, (1956), UK; Hymns A&M Scholar at AP, organist of St Michael's in Dumfries in 1971.

Sever, Allen J, MSM, (1955/56), b. 1929, Kansas City, USA; studied at Northwestern University and, after US military service in Korea, at the Union Theological Seminary in New York. He was organist of the Stephen Wise Free Synagogue in New York for over 40 years and he has taught at the Manhattan School of Music.

Shore, Timothy, (1973/74); DOM at Laleham Lea Prep School in Purley ca 1981.

Simmons, Morgan F, (1955/56), b. 1929, Andalusia, AL, USA; studied at De Pauw University in Indiana and the Union Theological Seminary in New York. He was organist of First Methodist Church in Evanston, Illinois, and then of Fourth Presbyterian Church in Chicago from 1968 until retirement in 1996. One student recalls him as '[an] American whose feet never became at home on the pedalboard!'

Slatter, Godfrey W, FTCL, GTCL, ARCM, LRAM, FRCO, (1957-60), UK; married Elizabeth White (1957-60), DOM of Cheltenham College Junior School, DOM Exeter School in 1971, an examiner for TCL, retired to Cornwall.

Small, Andrew Robert, BMus, (1969-1971), UK; organist of St Barnabas in Tunbridge Wells whilst at AP.

Smith, Barry, MA, FTCL, ARCO, LRSM, FRSCM, HonFGCM, (1960-61), b. 1939, Port Elizabeth, South Africa; organist of St George's Cathedral in Cape Town, South Africa, and taught at the University of Cape Town. Special Commissioner from 1967, awarded the ARSCM in 1972, upgraded to FRSCM in 1994.

Smith, Craig E, BA, MSM, (1961/62), USA; from Painsville, OH, Choirmaster of Groton School 1977-2005.

Smith, Geraldine, (1954/55), USA; from Honolulu, married Robert McDowall (AP Staff).

Smith, Michael J, ARCM, ARCO, (1955/56), UK; from Berkhamsted, Hymns A&M Scholarship to AP, organ scholar Queen's College, Cambridge, to Cuddesdon College 1960 and then ordained in York Minster to serve in Redcar. Retired as a priest in 2003.

Smith, Dr Michael John, MA, DMus, LRAM, FRCO(CHM), LTCL, ADCM, (1963), b. 1937, Wanstead, Essex, UK; was organ scholar at Christ Church, Oxford, has served as organist at Louth PC, assistant organist at Salisbury Cathedral and as organist at Llandaff Cathedral from 1974 until retirement.

Smith, Nicholas, ARCM, LRAM, (1969-71), UK; from Fareham, English Hymnal Scholar at AP.

Smith, Robert Frank, BMus, FRCO(CHM), (1961-63), Australia; from Sydney, DOM at St Bride's Fleet Street in 1968, DOM at Francis Holland School in Clarence Gate, London in 1971.

Smith, Stuart Marston, ARCO, GTCL, (1954-56), UK; was Lady Mary Trefusis Scholar at AP, to Exeter Cathedral as assistant organist and Alto Lay Vicar 1956 to 1961, and director of the Voluntary Choir. By 1971 he was DOM at Bearwood College in Winnersh, Berkshire.

Snow, Alan Michael, ARCO, GTCL, (1972/73), UK; DOM of Royal Wolverhampton School 1979. DOM at St Nicholas in Great Yarmouth in 1997.

Snowden, Martin, (1964-66), b. Boston, Lincs, UK; came from Grimsby when Martin How was there. Studied at TCL and the RCM. Solo singer in London until retirement.

Soper, Bob, (1971-73); was a former chorister at AP from 1966 to 1968 and then, from 1971, a London student, studying flute. Subsequently DOM at two local Croydon churches.

Souza, Yucema Torres de, (1966/67), Brazil; from Rio de Janeiro.

Spencer, R Michael, MA, ARCM, LTCL, ARCO, (1963-66), UK; organist of St John's, Upper Norwood, 1966-1972, also organist of St Paul's in Beckenham and DOM at Dulwich College Prep School. His nickname at AP was 'Rossini'.

Spicer, Paul, BMus, ARCO, (1970/71); a former chorister of New College, Oxford, he studied with Herbert Howells and Richard Popplewell at the RCM and himself taught there from 1995 to 2008. An internationally known choral director, especially of the Finzi Singers, he is also a composer and author of acclaimed biographies of Herbert Howells and George Dyson. He was also DOM at Ellesmere College from 1974 to 1984.

Steele, Terence, (1969-71), UK; Alto.

Sutcliffe, Walter, FRCO, (1956-59), b. Yorkshire, UK to Australia 1965; organist of St James, King Street, in Sydney from 1966 to 1994 and of All Saints' Church in Woollahra from 1994 to 2004. He became an RSCM Special Commissioner in 1970. Principal Double Bass in the Sydney Symphony Orchestra for many years.

[AH] comments in 2015 that: 'He now sings and plays the organ part time in our current Cathedral choir in Bathurst; he is 79!'

Sykes, Nicholas, (1973/74).

Synder, Peter, (1965-??), Canada.

Tang, Agnes, (1965), Penang; in 1998 was organist of Christ Church, Peckham. Composer of hymn tunes.

Tattersall, David W, MEd, LRAM, ARCM, ARCO, (1955-58), New Zealand; became DOM at the Auckland School of Music in Remuera, and DOM at University of Canberra.

Taylor, Anthony, ARCO, (1967-69); DOM at Scott Lidgett Boys' Comprehensive School in Rotherhithe, London, by 1971.

Taylor, H Naughton, (1958/59), b. 1924; d. 2002, USA; from Watertown NY, spent four terms at AP, in 1966 he was in Topeka, Kansas, in 1991 he was organist of Holy Trinity Episcopal Church in Ukiah, CA. He retired back to Watertown, NY.

Taylor, Jeryl E, BMus, FRCO, (1970-73), Canada; from Mississauga, Ontario, blind from birth, studied at the Royal Conservatory in Toronto and the University of Toronto before coming to AP. Latterly organist of Holy Trinity Anglican Church in Vancouver.

Taylor, Michael L, (1962/63), UK; organ scholar at Christ's College, Cambridge.

Tchao (née Chang), Violet, (1963-66), China/USA; studied at the GSM and was known at AP as 'Blossom'. Now resident in Philadelphia and a US Citizen, in her international career she has made a speciality of singing arrangements of ethnic songs and can sing in 20 languages.

Teague, Michael, (1966), USA.

Teesdale, Moira, (1955-57), UK. Married David Gatward (1953-57).

Thomasson, Revd Harold Frederich, (1962, one term only), b. 1924; d. 2000, Guelph, Canada; from Niagara, he studied at the University of Western Ontario and Huron College. Ordained in 1951 at Christ's Church Cathedral, Hamilton. Went from UK to be Rector of St David's in Welland, Ontario. Made Honorary Canon of Christ's Church Cathedral in 1972.

Thorne, David John Moncrieff, BA, FRCO(CHM), LRAM, (1969-), UK; A&M Scholarship at AP, chorister at Exeter Cathedral, assistant organist of Portsmouth Anglican Cathedal, organist of Portsmouth R/C Cathedral.

Tinker, Christopher, (1968-1970); DOM at Whitgift School, Croydon.

Toll, John, FRCO, (1965/66), b. 1947, Little Wymondley, d. 2001, UK; A&M Scholarship at AP. Became organ scholar at Magdalen College, Oxford, was keyboard player to the

Bournemouth Sinfonietta in the early 1970s and became a passionate harpsichord player and early music specialist.

Tomlins, Shirley, (1969), UK; choirmaster of St Peter's, Brockley.

Towler, Janet, (1967/68), a singer.

Tsukioka, Gregory M, (1964/65), Japan/Canada; from Tokyo, to Preston, Ontario.

Uttley, Revd John R, BSc, ARCO, (1963/64), Canada; organist and associate priest of St Thomas Belleville, Ontario, 1981-2013, also organist at Albert College and St Michael's R/C Church for many years and Choir Director for the Belleville Choral Society, Trenton, Ontario.

Vaughn, Rodney L, (1966/67, two terms), USA; remained in UK and now an active member of Croydon Minster. Married Pamela Hartley (1966/67).

Voss, Gail De, (1968/69).

Walker, Robert, BA, (1964/65), b. 1946, Northampton, UK; former chorister at St Matthews, Northampton, with John Bertalot, organ scholar of Jesus College, Cambridge, was organist of Grimsby Parish Church from 1968 to 1973. After working for Novello, teaching at the London College of Music, working in Bali and teaching at Silpakorn University in Bangkok, Thailand, he returned to England.

Wallace, Edward A, MusD, (1964, one term), USA; from St Thomas, New York, (assistant organist there 1952-1964), was organist of the Church of St Michael and St George in St Louis, MO, from 1966 to 2001.

Walsh, Michael, ThD, DMus, FTCL, GTCL, ACertCM, FGMS, FASC, HonFNMSM, (1968-70), UK; he assisted Martin How in running the Junior Choir and went on to be an Alto Lay Clerk at Chichester Cathedral and a composer, possibly best-known for his *Preces and Responses*.

Wambugu, Railton D, (1965/66), d. 1999, Uganda.

Waring, Prof Michael, MA, PhD, ScD, (1972/73), UK; a fellow in Biochemistry at Jesus College, Cambridge, from 1965 and since 1999 Professor of Chemotherapy at Cambridge. Also an organist, he studied at AP on sabbatical from the university.

Waswa-Sentanda, Geoffrey, (1967, one term), Uganda; stood as a candidate for Parliament in the 2011 Uganda Elections but was not elected.

Watson, Fr Charles James, (1972/73), b. 1919; Plymouth, d. 2007, Prinknash Abbey, UK; former chorister at Exeter Cathedral and a monk at Prinknash Benedictine Abbey, Gloucestershire, for 57 years from 1949. Ordained priest in 1955. He built all three organs at the Abbey.

Weir, Dame Gillian, DBE, HonFRCO, DMus, (1962-64), b. 1941, Martinborough, New Zealand; studied with Ralph Downes at the RCM, her career as an outstanding and internationally respected recitalist and teacher, took off after she won the St Albans Organ Competition in 1964. She was appointed DBE in 1996 and has honorary doctorates from many universities. She retired from the concert world in December 2012.

Weir, Kenneth, (1963/64); a part-time student, born in Scotland but family moved to New Zealand in 1951. Studied at University of Otago, then studied piano in London with Cyril Smith and organ with James Dalton and Marie-Claire Alain. He was a prize-winner at the St Albans Organ Competition in 1967, took a Masters degree in piano at the University of Indiana in Bloomington and from 1972 was back in New Zealand teaching at the University of Canterbury. After teaching at the University of Melbourne in Australia he returned to the UK in 1987 where he taught at Sherborne School until retirement in 1995. He is not related to Gillian Weir.

Wells, Guyon Russell, OBE, BSc, MusB, ARCO(CHM), ARSCM, (1957-60), b. 1931, Ashburton, New Zealand; awarded the Lady Mary Trefusis Scholarship in 1958, left AP to teach at St Peter's School in Cambridge, New Zealand. An RSCM Special Commissioner, he was conductor of the Hamilton Civic Choir from 1987 and taught at the University of Waikato.

Wheeler, David, (1968/69).

Wheeler, Russell, (1960/61), USA.

White, Elizabeth, ARCM, GRSM, (1957-60), UK; from Hove, married Godfrey Slatter (1957-60).

White, Maurice J, ATCL, ARCCO, ARCO(CHM), (1960/61), Canada; DOM at St John's Anglican Church in York Mills, Toronto, from 1964 until retirement in 2001. Also served as Choirmaster at Royal St George's College 1965-1988 and taught at The Royal Conservatory of Music 1969-1999.

White, Peter Gilbert – see Headquarters Choirmasters.

White, Raymond Eric, ARCO, ARSCM, (1966/67), b. 1944, Wyndham, New Zealand; from Invercargill, Organist of St Paul's Cathedral, Dunedin, New Zealand.

White, Robin Leonard Woolford, BMus, MEd, LGSM, GGSM, ARCO, (1957-60), b. 1938, Winnersh; d. 2012, Winnersh, UK; studied at the GSM, taught in Berwick-on-Tweed from 1963, then DOM at the Forest School in Wokingham.

Wilks, Derwent, (19??); organist Faversham PC 1956.

Williams, Derrick R, ARCO, (1961-64), UK; Society of Faith Scholar at AP, organist of St Augustine's in Edgbaston and taught at King Edwards Five Ways School. Later DOM at West Bromwich Grammar School.

Williams, John Edward, FRCO(CHM), (1954/55, two terms), b. 1919 Columbus, NM; d. 2007, Spartanburg, SC, USA; a graduate of Illinois Wesleyan College in 1941, he joined the US Navy, and served throughout World War II in London where he played for American servicemen. After WWII he trained at the Union Theological Seminary in New York. organist of First Presbyterian Church in Spartenburg for 43 years retiring in 1991. It was during this latter appointment that he came to AP.

Wilmot, Brian, (1967-69), UK.

Wisnener, Malcom, (1973/74).

Wrightson, James, (1973/74).

Wyatt, David, (1969), UK; from Kilburn, organist of St Mark's, Harlesden.

Wyckoff, Raymond, (1974), d. 1975 or 1976, soon after leaving AP.

Yorke, Colin, MMus, LRAM, (1967/68); — see Headquarters Choirmasters.

Zelle, Nicholas J, GRSM, LRAM, ARCO(CHM), (1961-65), b. 1943; d. 2013, Malta, UK; was educated at, taught at, was organist and finally ran the Old Boys' Society of Clayesmore School.

One student recalled that Nick 'Claimed that his ambition was to have three sons in each of the choirs of Westminster Abbey, St Paul's and King's Cambridge!'

Miscellaneous Photographs of Students

Students 1961: (L to R) John Morehen, Barry Smith, Miranda Godwin, Marina Ma, Mark le Roux and Keith Griffiths

James Omideyi (1954/55) with wife and his two assistants at their pharmacy in Nigeria around 1957

Legend on the back reads: 'Group Photo taken in first-floor flat (Choirmaster's Quarters)
December 1961

Viewed L to R: Back Row: MR (Blue pullover)[Martin Roberts], Brian Law, name forgotten (short visit North American), James Burchill, Robert Smith

Centre Row: David Langdon, Miranda Godwin, Michael Bailey, Michael Beynon, Richard Hooi, name forgotten (Canadian)

Front Row on floor: John Gadsden, Michael Brimer (Choirmaster), Harold Thomasson, Susan Hutton, David Price'

Right: GHK with David and Elizabeth Leigh (L)
and Marina Ma (R)

280

Chapter IX. The Palace Organs

The number of organs at Addington has varied from three on arrival (though effectively two as the Chamber organ was not functional) to seven[278]. Between 18th and 22nd October 1993 the last adult residential organists' course took place at the Palace. On the penultimate day there was a celebration of the seven organs in a service with readings, organ music and plainsong sung in procession from room to room. Martin How gave a demonstration of the stops of each organ and this was recorded and issued as an audiotape by PH Music[279]. It is a valuable and probably unique audio record of all the Palace organs.

The Cleverley Organ

The first organ owned by the RSCM was a small two-manual organ, presented by Mrs Cleverley of Wallington, Surrey, being the property of her late husband. The Cleverley organ was originally built by William Hill (date unknown, probably 1860's) and, upon donation to the College in 1928, it was restored and revoiced by Harrison & Harrison free of charge, though the College provided an electric blower at a cost of £87. It was used in the chapel of the College of St Nicolas in Chislehurst for the first time at Evensong on 13th Mar 1929. Arthur Harrison later suggested that further work was needed and this was carried out by Messrs. Cousans of Lincoln in 1936[280].

The 1928 specification is unknown but the 1936 specification included two manuals of 58 notes and a pedalboard of 30 notes.

Swell	Hohl Flute	8'
	Gemshorn	4'
	Oboe	8' (to tenor C)
Great	Dulciana	8'
	Clarabella	8'
	Open Diapason	8' (to tenor C)
	Principal	4'
	Double Dulciana	16' (to tenor C)
Pedal	Bourdon	16'

Swell to Great, Swell to Pedal and Great to Pedal couplers. Reversible Great to Pedal composition pedal. The action was mechanical to the manuals and drawstops, but the pedal division was tubular pneumatic.

Following closure of the College in 1939, the organ was removed to Canterbury and served in the small Chapel in No 17 The Precincts. To make it fit, the top of the 'Churchwarden' Gothic case had to be removed. In 1954 it was removed to Addington Palace (where George

---

[278] As a curiosity we mention that in 1965 Gerald Knight informed RSCM Council that, for £100, he was intending to purchase an Apollo reed organ manufactured by Rushworth & Dreaper between the wars and that he would place this in the basement. It had an electric blower and standard RCO 2 manual and pedal console, but there is no evidence that this ever happened.

[279] By the time this is in print, it is hoped that some of these recordings may be available to hear online.

[280] The reconstruction of the organ cost £150 and was paid for with a donation of £100 from Prebendary L A Phillips (of *Hymns A&M*) and £50 from the profit of the 1936 Crystal Palace Festival.

Thalben-Ball gave a recital upon it) and where it was initially placed in the Nicholson Practice Room[281]. This room later became a Common Room and when the organ was removed, a bar for the students was put in its place. In 1955 a new blower was provided at a cost of £79. It underwent a transformative rebuild by Kenneth James in 1974 and was installed in the Octagon — part of the Practice Block at Addington that was a former Summer House and called the Octagon due to the similarity in shape to the well-known feature of Ely Cathedral. The 1974 specification also had two manuals of 58 notes and a pedalboard of 30 notes but the swell box was removed, though the actual balanced swell pedal was left in situ.

Manual I	Clarabella	8' (Extension from Pedal Bourdon)
	Principal	4'
	Twelfth	2⅔'
	Open Flute	2'
	Nineteenth	1⅓' (Extension from the Twelfth)
Manual II	Hohl Flute	8'
	Oboe	4'
	Gemshorn	2'
Pedal	Bourdon	16'
	Bass Flute	8' (Extension)
	Flute	4' (Extension)

The couplers and composition pedal remained unchanged at this rebuild.

On leaving Addington Palace in 1996, the organ was transferred to St Clement's Church in Turnford, Hertfordshire, where it is still in use. After the various rebuilds there is little of the original pipework remaining.

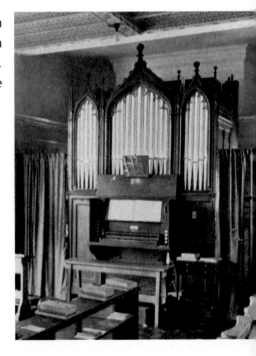

The Cleverley Organ in the Chapel at Chislehurst

---

[281] See photograph of GHK teaching on p. 159.

The Chapel Organ

The printed College Syllabus of 1934 notes that 'On St Nicolas Day 1931, the new organ presented[282] for the [Chislehurst] chapel by Mrs Helen Man Stuart, in memory of her husband (Col John Alexander Man Stuart, CB, CMG) was dedicated by the Bishop of Rochester. This instrument was built by Harrison and Harrison of Durham, and every pipe was finished in the Chapel by Arthur Harrison himself. It has two manuals and pedals, and consists of eleven speaking stops and seven couplers, with four composition pedals and balanced swell, and exemplifies the builders' pneumatic action. The specification makes it possible to use a great variety of combinations in spite of the small number of speaking stops. The organ originally in the chapel [the Cleverley Organ], was removed to another room. It was of a more simple specification than the chapel organ. Both organs are electrically blown.'

This organ has two manuals of 61 notes and a pedalboard of 30 notes.

Swell	Lieblich Gedeckt	8'	
	Gemshorn	4'	
	Twelfth	$2\frac{2}{3}$'	
	Fifteenth	2'	
	Contra Oboe	16'	
Great	Open Diapason	8'	
	Claribel Flute	8'	The Claribel and Salicional have a
	Salicional	8'	common bass (wood)
	Dulcet	4'	
Pedal	Sub Bass	16' (wood)	
	Flute	8' (Extension)	

Swell to Great, Swell to Pedal, Swell Octave, Swell Suboctave, Swell Unison off, Great to Pedal and Great to Swell couplers.

There are two composition pedals to each manual and a balanced Swell pedal. The composition pedals and drawstops have mechanical action; the manuals have tubular pneumatic action.

The specification was regarded as most unusual at the time, especially the provision of a Great to Swell coupler, and a Swell division which, by use of the various couplers, could also be used as a solo division. Over the years many players have been impressed by the versatility of this instrument. The original casework of the organ was by Sir Charles Nicholson, Sir Sydney's elder brother. During the war this organ was transferred to the Crypt of Canterbury Cathedral where it was used for services until, in 1954, it was moved to Addington Palace. In 1996 it accompanied the RSCM on its move to Cleveland Lodge in Dorking — Harry Bramma writes:

---

[282] Interestingly this was not a gift to the SECM but a personal one to SHN. He then gifted the organ (together with all the other chapel furniture and fittings) to the SECM in February 1943 when the instrument was transferred to Canterbury.

'I felt it must go with us. It fitted perfectly in the large music room at Cleveland Lodge. I was able to get the Livanos Trust to pay for its move and refurbishment.'

In 2006, when the RSCM Head Office relocated to Salisbury, it was given on long term loan to St Alkmund's Church in Shrewsbury.

Organ events noted in Magazines and Council Minutes

1953 16th July It was noted that a suitable organ case to house the Harrison organ was available and that Mr Chadwyck-Healey had offered to pay for this.

1956 October *ECM* reports that the Harrison organ in the Chapel had been decorated to a design by Mr Stephen Dykes Bower paid for by the generosity of Mr Cuthbert Harrison.

1957 July Minutes The Chapel organ blower keeps breaking down. The motor was replaced at a cost of £26 of which £11 was paid by the insurer.

1958 October *ECM* notes that few organs get as much use as the Chapel organ. Except for meal times, it is played from 9.00am to 10.30pm daily and as a result the lettering on the stop knobs has almost worn off. Cuthbert Harrison refilled them at his own expense.

1964 Easter The worn out Chapel organ pedal-board was replaced.

Paul Spicer:

'The little Harrison organ in the chapel was a marvel of its type. It had a tiny number of speaking stops but, and this was the key to its success, it had a 16' reed on the Swell. It was this that gave it the gravitas which helped make accompaniment colourful and which gave the organ the feel of a much more substantial instrument. In the lovely warm acoustic of the conservatory which served at the chapel it was a real success.'

It is hard to believe, when listening to the final improvisation on the CD issued with this book, that Martin How had only 10 ranks of pipes at his disposal.

Harry Bramma at the Chapel Organ

The Chamber Organ

A small chamber organ rebuilt by Coleman & Willis in the 19C was acquired at Canterbury around 1949 with the intention of restoration. The bottom key is stamped *3 1777* which is a possible original builder's date. According to organ builders Goetze & Gwynn: 'physical evidence suggests the Georgian organ builder used an earlier wind chest and some of its wooden pipes (ca 1680-1700) within a new case and with a new mechanism.' The firm of Coleman & Willis were active around 1860 and it is thought that they only added the Keraulophon.

CHAMBER ORGAN,
ADDINGTON PALACE

ECM in June 1957 noted that the chamber organ in the Great Hall was unplayable and appealed for £70 for its restoration and installation of an electric blower. On 17th October 1957 a concert was held in the Great Hall at which the newly-restored chamber organ was heard for the first time in a concert with the Morley Chamber Orchestra conducted by David Gedge. The restoration was done by a Mr Applegate of Selsdon (local to Addington Palace) and presumably paid for by Mrs Grace Greany as the organ bears a plate which reads:

In thankfulness to God for the memory of
Peter Mawe Greany, late I.C.S.
This organ was restored by his widow, Grace
1957
KHUDA HAFIZ

Maurice Peter Mawe Greany (1894-1954) served in three wars and was a member of the International Chamber of Shipping. His father was a policeman in India and the Persian inscription KHUDA HAFIZ means literally 'May God be your Guardian' or, in the vernacular, 'Goodbye'.

The organ has one manual of 54 notes from low GG to high e

Open Diapason	8'	from middle C
Stop Diapason	8'	
Keraulophon	8'	
Principal	4'	front pipes
Twelfth	2⅔'	
Fifteenth	2'	

The organ was purchased from the RSCM for his home in 1975 by Dr Peter Caudle (1927-2002), a Cambridge Chemical Engineering graduate who was Economics Director of the Chemical Industries Association.

Durham Room Organ (1)

In November 1957 Council agreed to buy a Bevington organ from St Edmund's Church in New Addington. The costs were £100 for the organ and £120 for removal, repair, installation[283] and electrical work. When Dr Waters' Hunter organ arrived in 1978 the Bevington was moved to the Music School at Christ's Hospital in Sussex.

The organ had two manuals with 54 notes from low C to high f3.

Swell	Stop Diapason	8'	
	Gamba	8'	
	Principal	4'	
Great	Open Diapason	8'	
	Dulciana	8'	bottom octave from Swell
	Flute	4'	to tenor C
Pedal	Bourdon	16'	

Robing Room Organ (1) then the Dungeon Organ

In 1966 this 1907 Norman & Beard organ from Coloma Convent in Croydon was installed in the Robing Room. It was moved to the basement in 1970 when the Harrison organ from Denver Mill in Norfolk arrived. In 1970 it was also rebuilt by Harrison & Harrison along classical lines. The original specification was mainly 8' stops and after rebuild the new specification was:

Manual I	Claribel	8'	
	Spitz Principal	4'	
	Blockflute	2'	
	[spare hole]		
Manual II	Gedackt	8'	
	Open Flute	4'	
	Nazard	2⅔'	to tenor C
	Fifteenth	2'	
Pedal	Bourdon	16'	
	Flute	8'	
	Flute	4'	

---

[283] *ECM* stated that the organ was 'repaired and re-erected by our neighbour Mr Appelgate of Selsdon.'

Both manuals were unenclosed with 58 notes from low C to high a3; the concave radiating pedals were 30 notes from C to f1. Tubular pneumatic action with mechanical stop action to the two manuals. Tuning Kirnberger II.[284]

Couplers: Manual I/Pedal, Manual II/Pedal, Manual II/Manual I

In 1995 the pipework of this organ went to Cape Town in South Africa, for use in the enlargement of another instrument by Norman & Beard which had an incomplete Choir division.

Robing Room Organ (3)

This 1919 Harrison & Harrison organ was built for F B Eastwood of Woodyates Manor in Dorset. In 1935 it was purchased by Tom Harris of Denver Mill near Downham Market. At that point it was enlarged with voicing completed personally by Arthur Harrison 'who, as Tom Harris proudly proclaimed, told him that he had never left anything better'[285]. On Harris's death in 1969, his widow bequeathed it to the RSCM. It was installed in the Robing Room at a cost of £1750 by Harrison & Harrison and a further £355 was also needed for a new blower. Many staff and students have found this instrument particularly gratifying to play and Martin How spent many happy hours improvising upon it. The instrument bore the legend:

To the Glory of God
and in memory of Thomas Edwin Harris of Denver Mill, Norfolk this
organ is given by his widow Ethel Rebecca Harris 1970.

This organ, the largest and most 'romantic' at Addington had two manuals with 58 notes from low C to high a3.

Swell	Lieblich Gedeckt	8'	
	Salicional	8'	
	Vox Angelica	8'	to tenor C
	Viole d'Orchestre	8'	
	Harmonic Flute	4'	
	Contra Oboe	16'	
	Trumpet	8'	
Great Lieblich	Double Salicional	16	bottom 24 pipes from Pedal
	Open Diapason	8'	
	Claribel Flute	8'	common bass with Rohr Flute
	Rohr Flute	8'	common bass with Claribel Flute
	Dulciana	8'	
	Octave	4'	
	Octave Quint	2⅔'	
	Super Octave	2'	

---

[284] One source gives the temperament as Werckmeister III.
[285] Letter from John Belcher in *CMQ* July 1994.

Pedal	Sub Bass	16'
	Lieblich Bourdon	16'
	Flute	8'

Concave radiating pedals — 30 notes from C to f1 Tubular pneumatic action throughout.

Couplers & Accessories: Swell/Pedal, Swell/Great, Swell Octave, Great/Pedal

Balanced Swell pedal, three composition pedals to Swell, three composition pedals to Great.

Harry Bramma:

'The best of the remaining organs was the large two-manual Harrison & Harrison organ in the Robing Room. This found a very good home at Stoke Gabriel Parish Church on the Dart Estuary. It fitted perfectly into the South Transept. I played the organ for the Dedication by the Bishop of Exeter in 1999.'

Peter Collins Chamber Organ

In March 1970 RSCM Council approved that 'the Director may order a two manual and pedal organ from Peter Collins at a cost of £2478.' The organ had two manuals with 56 notes from low C to high g3. The lower 19 notes of the 8' stops have a common bass.

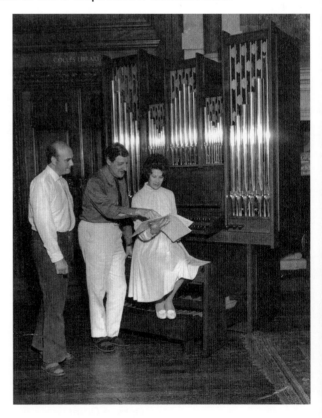

Upper Manual	Wood Gedact	8'
	Gedact Flute	4'
Lower Man	Rohr Flute	8'
	Principal	4'
	Gemshorn	2'
Pedal	Dulzian	16'

Unenclosed, mechanical action throughout, pedalboard radiating concave, black naturals 30 notes from Low C to high f1. Couplers: Lower Manual/Pedal, Upper Manual/Pedal, Upper Manual/Lower Manual.

Peter Collins, Lionel Dakers and Gillian Weir with the Collins Organ in the Great Hall, 1975

On 28th June 1975 at the Addington Summer party and presentation of Diplomas there was a 'preview' informal recital on the Peter Collins organ given by Michael Fleming before the official Inaugural Recital by Gillian Weir a few days later on 2nd July. Further recitals that year were by Francis Jackson on 18th July and Margaret Phillips on 9th Oct, a recital which included a *Toccata* by Alan Ridout specially composed for her and for the organ[286]. The following spring on 9th March Peter Hurford gave a recital which was recorded by the BBC and broadcast on BBC Radio 3[287]. The programme was Bach *Prelude and Fugue in G* BWV 541, Pescetti *Sonata in C-minor,* Buxtehude *Chorale Fantasia on 'Wie schön leuchtet'* BuxWV 223, Bach *Seven Fughette* BWV 696-704 and Chorale Preludes on Christmas Chorales. In July recitals were given by Martin Neary and Arthur Wills, and from this time summer recitals became a regular feature, especially during the years of the Summer Overseas Course[288]. Not many attendance figures are available, but in July 1992 Peter Hurford gave an all-Bach recital which 134 attended. In July 1993 his recital attracted an audience of 107. Hurford's last recital was 22nd June 1994. The organ went to Cleveland Lodge and is now in the Choir School of Salisbury Cathedral.

Peter Hurford OBE, MA, FRCO(CHM), DMus, HonRAM, HonRCO, FRSCM, b. 1930, Minehead, Somerset, was not a staff member at Addington, but, in addition to the many organ recitals he gave there, he played such a significant role in teaching that he deserves a mention here. Peter studied music (and law) at Jesus College in Cambridge, and then in Paris with André Marchal. He served as organist of St Albans Cathedral from 1958 until 1978 before embarking upon a free-lance career as a recitalist and teacher. Renowned for his interpretation of the organ music of J S Bach and founder of the St Albans International Organ Festival, he was made FRSCM in 1977 and OBE in 1984.

Peter Hurford

Peter gave organ masterclasses and taught at the Addington summer courses from 1975 until 1994.

---

[286] It remains unpublished.
[287] 13th Sept 1976 at 16.30.
[288] Mostly given by Peter Hurford.

Durham Room Organ (2)

Most sources say that this organ was originally built by A Hunter of London in 1893 for a private house and was moved to Ewell Congregational (later URC) Church in 1913. It was presented by well-wishers to Charles Waters in recognition of his 'exceptional musical talent and as an incentive to further progress.' This was at the age of 18 and so at some point it must have then been moved to his house. Possibly this was in 1938 when Ewell URC was demolished and a new church built on another site.

Dr Charles Frederick Waters CBE, Mus D. (London), FRCO, (1895-1975) was a professional civil servant at the Ministry of Labour and National Service until retirement in 1955 when he was made CBE. He was organist of St Philip in North Cheam (at the age of 15), St Saviour in Croydon (1928-1948), Epsom Parish Church (1948-1957), St James's in Malden and finally at All Saints' & St Barnabas in Lambeth from 1966. He was the author of a useful book *The Growth of Organ Music: An Historical Survey* published by the journal *Musical Opinion* in 1931. He was made Hon RSCM in 1966 and had served on the Musical Advisory Board for some years. Following his death in 1975, the family donated his organ to the RSCM and *CMQ* July 1978 announced that it 'was to be installed in the Durham Room.' The pamphlet *The Organs of Addington Palace* commented that 'In spite of its rather antiquated appearance, much of the pipework is of very good quality, and the widespread use of spotted metal will be observed; the tone is sweet and gentle, and it is reminiscent of the best work done by this notable firm.'

The organ had two manuals with 56 notes from low C to high g3. Pedal compass 29 notes, low C to high e1.

Swell	Open Diapason	8'	bottom 12 pipes from Gedact
	Lieblich Gedact	8'	
	Salicional	8'	bottom 13 pipes from Gedact
	Voix Celeste	8'	to tenor C
	Principal	4'	
	Oboe	8'	
	Tremulant		
Great	Open Diapason	8'	
	Stopped Diapason	8'	
	Dulciana	8'	
	Flute	4'	
	Harmonic Flute	4'	changed to 2' in the 1990's
Pedal	Bourdon	16'	

Mechanical action throughout. Two composition pedals to Great. Couplers: Great/Pedal, Swell/Pedal, Swell/Great.

This organ moved in 1995 to Hammerwood Park[289] in East Grinstead, Sussex, and is still in use.

---

[289] Hammerwood Park was built in 1792 by Latrobe, architect of both the White House and the Capitol in Washington DC. It was converted into flats in the 1960's, was purchased by Led Zeppelin in the 1970's

Hill, Norman & Beard Chester Organ in the Resource Centre and Lower Library

The autumn of 1982 saw the installation of a new extension organ with electronic playback facility in the Lecture Room. An Opening Recital was given by Michael Fleming on 1st December for representatives of the grant-giving bodies who had funded the organ, which at the time increased the numbers of organs at AP to seven.

The organ had two manuals with 61 notes from low C to high c4.

Upper Man	Gemshorn	8'
	Flute	8'
	Gemshorn	4'
	Flute	4'
	Nazard	2⅔'
	Piccolo	2'
	Tierce	1⅗'
Lower Man	Bourdon	16'
	Flute	8'
	Gemshorn	8'
	Flute	4'
	Gemshorn	4'
	Twelfth	2⅔'
	Gemshorn	2'
	Nineteenth	1⅓'
Pedal	Bourdon	16'
	Flute	8'
	Quint	5⅓'
	Gemshorn	4'
	Flute	4'
	Gemshorn	2'
	Nineteenth	1⅓'
	Twenty Second	1'

Pedal compass 32 notes, low C to high g1. Electric action throughout. Two ranks, extended, but the bottom octave of the Flute is electronic,

Couplers: Lower Manual to Pedal. Upper Manual to Pedal.

Accessories: Manual reverse button.

This organ was transferred to the residence of Philip Smith in Ruthin, and on his appointment as organist of Holy Trinity Cathedral in Auckland, NZ in 2008, he took it with him.

---

and was rescued from dereliction by the Pinnegar family in 1982. Regular concerts are held there in the summer using the many instruments available at the house.

Chapter X. The Final Years: 'Leaving the Palace' by Harry Bramma

The final years at Addington were dominated by the question of the move. Vincent Waterhouse came into my office early in my time to explain that the lease from Croydon Council, who owned the Palace, expired in 2003 — fifty years after the RSCM's arrival in Croydon. This lease was extremely favourable to the RSCM who had a peppercorn rent of £1000 per annum. The upkeep of the building was divided between the Croydon Council and the RSCM. The Council were responsible for the structure and exterior of the building; the RSCM were to maintain the interior in a decent state. Peppercorn rents are of a former age and it was certain that the arrangement could not be repeated if the RSCM were to renegotiate a new lease from 2003. The rent would have been greatly increased and the upkeep of the building might have fallen more substantially on the RSCM. The financial implications would have been quite unmanageable and therefore a move had to be contemplated and thought through.

My personal view was that the RSCM needed a home where people could meet and where music and teaching could happen. My experience as Hon Treasurer of the Royal College of Organists in the late 1980's, where we negotiated a surrender value for the remaining 13 years of the lease (for which we paid £1 per annum!) was that moving into much smaller premises in Holborn in 1990 much diminished the work of the College. I wished to prevent a similar occurrence at the RSCM.

We knew that moving would be expensive and that it might not be possible to find the ideal HQ, however a door opened which presented to us the possibility of taking over the home of Lady Jeans at Cleveland Lodge in Box Hill. Michael Hockney, a member of RSCM Council, initiated this idea. After much discussion, Lady Jeans decided to give the house to the RSCM and, though she died before the transfer could be legally formulated, the family decided to honour their mother's intentions. They had misgivings, not surprisingly, but in the end they decided on an act of amazing generosity. There were also misgivings within the RSCM Council, some making alternative proposals.

However, in some ways, Cleveland Lodge seemed right. It was next to the railway station and very close to the M25 — in fact much more accessible than Addington. It was the right size and set in the most idyllic countryside with breath-taking views of Box Hill. Unfortunately it was in a bad condition and the building needed much work to make it fit for use. We eventually moved in during July 1996 when the building work was only half completed. The refurbishment was not completed until after I retired and the subsequent history of the RSCM at Cleveland Lodge is beyond the remit of this volume.

The final two years at Addington were for me a time of enormous activity. In addition to maintaining my normal work as Director and taking a leading part in the RSCM Appeal, I had the job of deciding how to retain or dispose of the contents of the Palace. All agreed that the Colles Library must move to Cleveland Lodge. It did so, and subsequently has found a home in Salisbury. It is a valuable collection with much manuscript material and remains a considerable resource. Caring for the Library and moving it twice, fell to the lot of the Hon Librarian, Dr John Henderson.

My role in all this centred on three areas — organs, pianos and valuable antique furniture.

i) **Organs** — the fate of the seven Addington organs is described in Chapter IX.

ii) **Pianos**

There were about 20 upright pianos ranging from good to mediocre. Incredibly, we managed to sell or place all of those.

There were four grand pianos. The best, a Blüthner in the Great Hall, moved to the Music Room at Cleveland Lodge. The very pleasant small Bechstein, originally owned by Gerald Knight, found a home in my office at Cleveland Lodge. The other two grand pianos were sold — the walnut-cased Broadwood in the Great Hall to a private buyer. The black serviceable piano in the Lecture Room went to a school in Croydon.

iii) **Furniture**

There was a great deal of fine furniture at Addington which belonged to Sir Sydney Nicholson, originally in the family home at Totteridge. Some of this was spread around the Palace. The major part of it furnished the Empire Room, a grand sitting room over the front door at Addington.

It was not possible to take all the pieces, some had to be sold, but I collected together a good number of items which we fitted into Cleveland Lodge. I felt it was important that this link with Nicholson should be maintained — that we should be good custodians of his legacy.

There had to be frantic activity at Addington finding all this valuable material. I made sure the Palace was searched from the cellars to the attics. An amazing archive of printed material emerged from every nook and cranny in the building. I was determined, against some opposition, that the archive should go with us[290].

Farewell Events at Addington — Spring 1996 by Harry Bramma

The series of events was fully subscribed and a particular highlight was Sir David Willcocks' Saturday 'Come and Sing the Bach *Magnificat*'. This achieved a remarkable standard of performance with ca 100 singers. A Former Students' Dinner and a Candlelit Dinner were other attractions, but I felt it was right to close our association with Addington with a service in the Great Hall on a Sunday afternoon. I was responsible for the organisation of this.

I persuaded Ernest Hart (of Copeman Hart) to install an electronic organ which was played by Martin How. The choral singing was by the Nicholson Singers under the direction of Michael Fleming. I invited Canon Anthony Caesar (a former Warden) to take the service and I gave a short address.

---

[290] Sadly, much of this did not survive the subsequent move to Salisbury.

I was particularly anxious to put right a grievous omission by conferring, at the service, the FRSCM on Edred Wright, one of the most distinguished of RSCM alumni. As a former Nicholson Chorister at Westminster Abbey, he sang at the opening service at Chislehurst in 1928 and helped Sir Sydney at weekly services in the Chapel. He was an outstanding Director of Music at the King's School, Canterbury, for many years, he trained the RSCM choristers for the Coronation Service in 1953 — the first event to be held at Addington; and around this time he directed memorable cathedral courses. People still speak of the excellence of the course at St Paul's in 1953. Christopher Robinson, now retired from St John's College, Cambridge, then a boy at Rugby School, attended this course and is adamant that Edred Wright was one of the finest of choirmasters. How appropriate that Edred should be honoured at the 1996 Closing Service, 68 years after singing in the Chislehurst Opening Service!

210 people attended the final service in the Great Hall

Farewell Dinner in the Great Hall

Appendix 1. Miscellaneous Palace Photographs

Above: Addington Palace frontage ca 1960, the Bungalow far left.

Below: MJRH with Senior Choristers at the front entrance of AP in 1959
Left to Right: Brian Weller, Martin How, Peter Hood, Richard Barnes, Graham Madeley, Peter
Bennett, Chris Chambers; The Scout in the window is Adrian Crowley

Addington Palace taken from the Fountain on the Summer School 1962

An Aerial view of Addington Palace and Golf Course taken by resident student (and pilot) Michael Carnegie

Appendix 2. RSCM Patrons, Presidents, Chairmen and Council Members

Royal Patrons

In July 1946 Their Majesties the King and Queen visited the College in Canterbury and met with the Warden and Staff. Sir Sydney had arranged the music for their wedding in Westminster Abbey in 1923 and had also organised the choir for the 1937 Coronation of George VI. This was followed in 1947 by a further royal visit, when HRH The Princess Royal also visited the College. In 1950 GHK was able to announce, during the garden party celebrating the 21st Anniversary of the opening of Chislehurst, that the King and Queen had been graciously pleased to grant their Patronage to the RSCM.

On the death of the King, Her Majesty Queen Elizabeth II consented to be a Patron with the Queen Mother remaining as Patron until her death in 2002.

Presidents and Vice-Presidents

Until 2005, the President of the RSCM was always the current Archbishop of Canterbury. On their retirement as Archbishop each then became a Vice-President.

1928-1942	Cosmo Gordon Lang	Translated from York; retired; died 5th December 1945.
1942-1944	William Temple	Translated from York; died in office.
1945-1961	Geoffrey Fisher	Translated from London; retired; died 1972.
1961-1974	Michael Ramsey	Translated from York; retired; died 23rd April 1988.
1974-1980	Donald Coggan	Translated from York; retired; died 17th May 2000.
1980-1991	Robert Runcie	Translated from St Albans; retired; died 11th July 2000.
1991-2002	George Carey	Translated from Bath & Wells; retired.
2002-2012	Rowan Williams	Translated from Monmouth; resigned.
2013-	Justin Welby	Translated from Durham.

Further Vice-Presidents have been (ex officio) The Archbishops of York and Wales. In 1953 the Primus of the Episcopal Church of Scotland was added. In the same year Council members Dame Grace Kimmins and Hilary Chadwyck-Healey were elected, *honoris causa*. Others elected, *honoris causa*, include Bishop Walter Frere (in the 1930's), The Rt Hon Lord Kennet GBE, DSO[291] and Council Member Fred Martin-Smith. In 1960 the Archbishop of Cape Town was elected, followed in 1962 by the Primates of Canada, Australia and New Zealand. Since 1964 all Primates of the Anglican Communion have been offered Vice-Presidency and most have accepted. Ecumenism within the RSCM was advanced in 1971 when the Roman Catholic Cardinal Archbishop of Westminster, the Moderator of the General Assembly of the Church of Scotland and the Moderator of the Free Church Federal Council were added to the list of Vice-Presidents. Changes were made in 2005 whereby Her Majesty The Queen became Royal Patron, the various Primates become Patrons, the AOC remained as President and the Vice-Presidents were elected[292].

---

[291] Lord Kennet of the Dene (1879-1960) was a former journalist and politician. He assisted RSCM Council in financial planning around 1955/56.

[292] At that time (2005) they were: the Bishop of Salisbury, The Rt Revd David Stancliffe and Mr Brian Kay, choral conductor and founder member of the King's Singers.

RSCM Council

What is the RSCM Council? Many RSCM affiliates and members have little idea of who they are and what they do. The RSCM, as a registered Charity and also a Limited Company,[293] has a *Memorandum of Association*[294] which states that 'The business of the Association shall be managed by the Council.' In other words, Council have a legal requirement to oversee all the RSCM's work and watch over its administration and monies in accordance with the strict rules as laid down for all charities. Some members of Council are also directors and officers of the RSCM Limited Company. The Council was to consist of a minimum of five and a maximum of 24 members, with one-third retiring from office each year, though they are eligible for re-election at the AGM.

The Council was 15 in number in the early days, increasing in size to 16 in 1956, to 24 in 1957 and then to 30 in 1994. This ultimately proved unwieldy and in 2000 it was decided to slim down to 12 Trustees plus a Chairman with the other council members stepping sideways to become an Advisory Board. Council originally met three times a year and this proved to be insufficient to supervise day-to-day management and so, following the 1960 'Confidential Report', a General Purposes Committee was established to meet regularly, in an effort to streamline routine administration.

Council meetings in 1928 were of the 'Provisional Council', the first full Council meeting being held on 11th April 1929 in the Jerusalem Chamber at Westminster Abbey. During Sir Sydney's lifetime the Council largely followed his lead. Fred Martin-Smith, friend and former chorister of SHN at Barnet Church, served on the Council for 32 years. He said that SHN usually brought up topics for discussion at meetings and he aptly summed up the relationship between Director and Council as:

'He was the comet and the others the tail.'[295]

---

[293] In the early days this was known as an 'Incorporated Company'.
[294] The *Memorandum of Association* has been slightly modified from time-to-time, the last change being in 2007.
[295] From a conversation between Fred Martin-Smith and BNS.

SECM/RSCM Chairmen of Council

Julius Arthur Brewin (chair of Provisional Council)	1928
Sir Arthur Somervell	1930-1937
Sir Walter Alcock	1937-1947
Sir Stanley Marchant	1947-1949
Dr Ernest Bullock	1949-1952
Rt Revd John Leonard Wilson, Bishop of Birmingham	1952-1957
Rt Revd Edward Roberts, Bishop of Malmesbury, Kensington and Ely	1957-1977
Rt Revd John Bickersteth, Bishop of Bath & Wells	1977-1987
Sir John Margetson	1987-1994
[Roger Butler Vice-Chairman as acting Chairman[296]	1994-1996]
Sir David Harrison	1996-2004
Mark Williams	2004-2010
Rt Hon Lord Brian Gill	2010-

RSCM Chairmen during the Addington years

Rt Revd John Leonard Wilson KCMG, BA (1897-1970), Bishop of Birmingham

Bishop Wilson studied at Queen's College in Oxford and trained at Wycliffe Hall for ordination. Dean of Hong Kong and then Bishop of Singapore from 1941, he was interned in Changi Prison after the Japanese occupation of Singapore and during this time he managed to convert not only internees but also some of the Japanese soldiers to Christianity. He was Dean of Manchester from 1949 to 1953, Bishop of Birmingham from 1953 to 1969 and Chairman of RSCM Council from 1952 to 1957.

Rt Revd Edward Roberts (1908-2001), Bishop of Malmesbury, Kensington and Ely

Whilst all the Chairmen of RSCM Council have been good or outstanding in various ways, it is worth dwelling briefly on the longest-serving holder of the post, Bishop 'Ted' Roberts, Chairman from 1957 to 1977. At his retirement, the RSCM was forty years old and he had been chairman for fully half of this time. Suffragan Bishop of Malmesbury when appointed, he was educated at Marlborough and Corpus Christi College, Cambridge and was ordained from Cuddesdon College in 1931. After serving a curacy at All Saints', Margaret Street, he returned four years later as Vice Principal of Cuddesdon College before appointment in 1940 as vicar of St Matthew's in Southsea. In 1949 he became Archdeacon of the Isle of Wight before elevation to the Episcopacy in 1956 as Bishop of Malmesbury. He translated to Kensington in 1962 and to Ely in 1964, retiring in 1977.

---

[296] Sir Angus Stirling was appointed to be Chairman of Council in 1996 on his retirement as Director-General of the National Trust, but withdrew after it became apparent that major fundraising was necessary and he felt that he could not give enough time to this. He did however serve on Council from 1996 to 1998.

Sampson noted that 'Immediately on his appointment, he visited Headquarters and made himself known to all the staff, asking countless, searching questions.' He occasionally joined in as a choir member on the Cathedral Courses and he was Chaplain and Precentor for the Toronto trip. He was a frequent contributor to *ECM* and *PCM*, usually in an encouraging tone to the membership, and he rarely missed any important RSCM event.

His obituary in *The Daily Telegraph* commented 'Essentially a pastoral bishop, and in his day one of the most highly-regarded members of the episcopal bench, Roberts combined deep spirituality with great wisdom. Archbishops and senior bishops frequently turned to him for advice when faced with knotty problems, and his views were always heard with great respect in the Church Assembly and the General Synod.'[297] He may have spoken out to Synod on important issues, such as pro-ordination of women (in 1972), but he commented on retiring that 'he had never once spoken during his four years in the House of Lords.'

A tower of strength to the RSCM, his hand was on the tiller through some major initiatives: the establishment of the 1960 Report on the RSCM's management and work[298], the re-vamping of the RSCM magazine in 1963, the expansion of Addington in 1964, the opening of membership to other denominations in 1967, the development appeal in 1970, a change of Director in 1974 and the instigation of the new scheme of courses thereafter.

He was a competent musician and was fully able to weigh up both the musical and the liturgical aspects of policy that arose. All this in addition to the duties of his Bishopric.

Rt Revd John Bickersteth KCVO (b. 1921), Bishop of Bath & Wells

Educated at Rugby School and Christ Church, Oxford, he was ordained in 1951. After serving as Vicar of St Stephen's Church in Chatham, he was elevated to the Episcopate in 1970 as Suffragan Bishop of Warrington, and after five years was translated to Bath and Wells in 1975, retiring in 1987. He was also Clerk of the Closet 1979-1989 and he served as Chairman of RSCM Council from 1977 until 1987.

Sir John Margetson KCMG FRSCM (b. 1927)

Educated at Blundell's School and St John's College, Cambridge, he was a former British Ambassador to Vietnam, the United Nations and the Netherlands. Made KCMG in 1986, he served as Chairman of RSCM Council from 1987 to 1994 when he retired due to ill-health.

---

[297] *Daily Telegraph* 3rd July 2001.
[298] Of which he was Chairman.

Harry Bramma writes:

'Sir John Margetson was the first non-bishop to be RSCM Chairman [since Ernest Bullock at Canterbury]. He took office in 1988 just before I arrived and he had been present at the interviews for Director at the end of 1987 whilst he was still British Ambassador to The Hague.

I soon formed a close rapport with him and we became great friends. He supported me wonderfully and was very much an active Chairman and constantly had ideas from which the RSCM benefited. For instance, he organised the fund-raising Gala Dinner and Concert at the Guildhall in November 1992, attended by the Duchess of Kent and at which the Choir of St Paul's Cathedral sang. For this, he set up an amazing organising committee of which he was an active member.

He also felt strongly that the RSCM should widen its scope to make the RSCM more acceptable to churches in the evangelical tradition. He was also a key figure in the negotiations leading to the move to Cleveland Lodge and in setting up the RSCM 'Sing with the Spirit' Appeal. It was a great sadness that he missed the launch of the Appeal owing to illness which necessitated his retirement as Chairman in 1994, after barely six years in post. It was a particular sadness for me to lose him so early, but happily our friendship has survived strongly to this day and he retains a keen interest in the affairs of the RSCM.'

Roger Butler (1937-2000), Vice-Chairman/Acting Chairman

Roger Butler, a Banker, was on Council from 1981 until his unexpected and premature death. He was Chair of GPC from 1984, Vice-Chairman in 1992 and then acting Chairman from 1994 to 1996 during the interregnum between Sir John Margetson and Sir David Harrison. His widow Margaret was awarded the FRSCM in 2000 on his behalf.

Harry Bramma writes:

'The two years without a Chairman were very difficult for me and for the RSCM — particularly as so many crucial decisions had to be made about the future at Cleveland Lodge. Acting Chairman Roger Butler had been a senior manager at the Bank of England; he also, as a boy, had been a Chorister at New College, Oxford. He gave himself without stint during these two years and he believed deeply in the RSCM. He was a genial man and of great integrity. He was however hindered by the fact that he imagined others were as kindly as himself. In short, he found it difficult to be tough when occasion demanded, and some members of the Council treated him with a lack of respect he did not deserve.'

Harrison, Sir David, CBE, FREng, FRSCM (b. 1930)

A research chemist and academic, he was Master of Selwyn College, Cambridge, when appointed Chairman of Council. He had previously served as Vice-Chancellor of the University of Keele (1979-1984) and Vice Chancellor of the University of Exeter (1984-1994). Harry Bramma writes:

> 'The appointment of Sir David Harrison, brought a degree of stability. He had a distinguished career as Vice-Chancellor of Exeter University; he was used to the rough and tumble of institutional life and had the ability to take tough decisions, whether right or wrong. He came in at a difficult time, just as we had moved to Cleveland Lodge, and he gave himself fully to try to sort the many problems facing the RSCM — not least those of finance. He had a genuine love of church music. I always maintained a cordial relationship with him and there were times when his support was crucial.'

Sir David Harrison at the Addington Farewell Dinner in 1996

Council Members of the SECM and RSCM from 1928 until 1996

Mr Harry Vincent Abbott (1911-2009) 1970 to 1987	Architect by profession working for London County Council projects, including the Royal Festival Hall. In later life he lived in Kingsdown near Deal and then in Canterbury. Further information in *SNCSN*.
Col Alfred Dyke Acland CBE (1858-1937) 1928 to 1937	Hon Treasurer from 1929, see *SNCSN*.
Lady Beatrice Acland (1864-1942) 1932 to 1938	Dame Justice of the Order of St John of Jerusalem, see *SNCSN*.
Sir Walter Galpin Alcock (1861-1947) 1937 to 1947	Chairman of Council from 1937-1947 after Sir Arthur Somervell. Further information in *SNCSN*.
Dr Thomas Henry Wait Armstrong FRSCM (1898-1994) 1956 to 1957	Principal of RAM in succession to Sir Reginald Thatcher.
Ralph Bailey (b 1925) 1985 to 1995	Research scientist, was resident in Cheltenham.
The Very Revd Albert Victor Baillie (1864-1955) 1929 to 1937	Dean of Windsor. Further information in *SNCSN*.
Mr Edward John Balderson (1937 to 1947)	A Company Secretary.
Rt Revd Cuthbert Killick Norman Bardsley CBE (1907-1991) 1952 to 1956	Provost of Southwark Cathedral in 1944, Suffragan Bishop of Croydon in 1947, translated to Bishop of Coventry from 1956, serving until 1976.
Canon John Harrison Barrow Hon Life RSCM (1881-1981) 1933 to 1978	A graduate of Pembroke College, Oxford, he was ordained priest in 1905. After serving as Precentor of Chelmsford Cathedral from 1914 to 1917, before parish appointments and acting as organising secretary to the SPCK in the London area from 1922 to 1932. From 1932 to 1954 he was vicar of Stanstead Mountfichet. In 1935 he was made an honorary Canon of Chelmsford Cathedral and from 1957 he acted as Chapter Clerk. He was a member of RSCM Council from 1934 and Vice-Chairman 1945-1976, retiring from membership in 1978. He was made a life member of the RSCM in 1965 and died just before his 100th birthday. He was the father of John Barrow FRCO (Administrative Staff).
Revd John Lamberton Bell (b 1949) 1994 to 1995	Church of Scotland minister, hymn writer and composer. A member of the Iona Community.
Rt Revd John Monier Bickersteth KCVO (b 1921) 1976 to 1988	Chairman of Council (see above).
Venerable Kenneth Julian Faithful Bickersteth (1885-1962) 1943 to 1952	Educated at Rugby, Christchurch, Oxford and Wells Theological College, he was ordained in 1909. He became Archdeacon of Maidstone in 1943 serving until retirement in 1958.

Mr Edgar William Bishop Hon Life RSCM (b 1893) 1953 to 1973	An accountant by profession. Financial Secretary of the SPCK and then assessor to the Proprietors (of whom he was one) of *Hymns Ancient & Modern*. He was one of the editors of *100 Hymns for Today*.
Mr John W Blair-Fish (d 1957) 1952 to 1957	A retired engineer.
Sir Edward Charles Gurney Boyle (1923-1981) 1957 to 1960	Baron Boyle of Handsworth was educated at Eton and Christ Church, Oxford. He worked at Bletchley Park in intelligence and in 1950 he entered Parliament as MP for Birmingham Handsworth, a seat he would hold until his retirement in 1970.
Mr Julius Arthur Brewin (1875-1937) 1928 to 1936	A member of the Stock Exchange was the first Chairman of the (Provisional) Council. Further information in *SNCSN*.
The Hon Mark Thomas Bridges MA (b 1954) 1990 to 1997	A solicitor and partner in Farrer & Co., he was a Choral Scholar at Corpus Christi in Cambridge and a member of the London Bach Choir.
Dr Lee Hastings Bristol Jr FRSCM (1923-1979) 1971 to 1979	Lee Hastings Bristol (Jr.) was born into the Bristol-Myers Corporation and in addition to working in the family business he was an organist in New Jersey. From 1962 he was head of Westminster Choir College.
Miss Gina Buckle 1933 to 1935	A spinster in Chislehurst.
Sir Ernest Bullock (1890-1979) 1949 to 1952	Sir Ernest Bullock studied at Durham University and was assistant organist to Edward Bairstow at Leeds Parish Church and then to Sydney Nicholson at Manchester Cathedral. Organist of Exeter Cathedral from 1919 to 1927 and then of Westminster Abbey from 1928 to 1941, he was then Professor of Music at Glasgow University and finally George Dyson's successor as Director of the RCM. During his time at Westminster Abbey his home and all of his belongings were destroyed in the 'Blitz' of 1940. Knighted in 1951, he composed much church music and many songs.
Mr Roger Butler (1937-2000) 1981 to 2000	Acting Chairman of Council (see above).
Mr David Charles Calcutt MA, LLB, Mus B QC (1930-2004) 1966 to 1986	Barrister and musician, he was a former chorister at Christ Church, Oxford, and held a choral scholarship at King's College, Cambridge. Founder of the Eddington Festival, which he directed from 1956 to 1964, he was Master of Magdalene College, Cambridge from 1985 until 1994. He was responsible for the creation of the Press Complaints Commission.
Mr Moir Carnegie FSA, Hon FRAM (d 1949) 1947 to 1949	The Register of RSCM Directors [of the company] gives his occupation as 'Gentleman'. He taught at the RAM.
Mr Hilary Philip Chadwyck-Healey (1888-1976) 1928 to 1953	Hon Treasurer from 1940-1950, he was made a Vice-President (honoris causa) of the RSCM in 1954. Further information in *SNCSN*.
Dorothy Chatterley (b 1932) 1996 to 2004	General Synod Appointee.

Revd Dr William Kemp Lowther Clarke (1879-1968) 1933 to 1945	Deputy Chairman from 1936 to 1944. Rector of All Saints' in Dulwich from 1921 to 1945 and thereafter Canon Residentiary of Chichester Cathedral. He was a prolific author of books on liturgy, theology, morality and history including the histories of Hymns A&M and the SPCK (he was on the board of the SPCK and was Editorial Secretary).
Mr Stephen Cleobury MA, MusB, FRCO, FRCM, FRSCM (b 1948) 1982 to 2000	Was organ scholar at St John's College, Cambridge, sub-organist of Westminster Abbey before becoming Master of Music at Westminster Cathedral in 1979. Organist of King's College, Cambridge, from 1982, he was also Conductor of the BBC Singers from 1995 to 2007.
Mr Lancelot Kenneth (k/a Lance) Cock (1906-1993) 1950 to 1988	He was a member of RSCM Council for 38 years from 1950, retiring in 1988. He served on the Finance Committee from Feb 1951 and was Chairman of the General Purposes Committee from its establishment in 1965 until 1976 and again from 1982 to 1984. The GPC Minutes note that 'his record of attendance at meetings had been exemplary.' It is quite clear reading the GPC Minutes that he was a major and enthusiastic force within that committee. During the period 1952-1954 he was the member of the Finance Committee who effectively acted as Publications Manager. He also had a residence in Oporto, Portugal and was in the wine (Port) importing trade (MW = Master of Wine).
Mr Henry Cope (k/a Harry) Colles DMus (1879-1943) 1928 to 1943	Gave his occupation as 'Journalist' in the Register of Directors. Further information in *SNCSN*.
Lindsay Talbot Colquhoun BDS, FRSCM (b 1931) 1970 to 2000	A dental surgeon by profession, he was organist of St George's, Norton. A past President of The Organ Club, he was a member of the St Alban's Diocesan Synod from 1970 to 1987 and he was Chairman of RSCM St Albans Area.
Rt Revd David Stewart Cross (1928-1989) 1983 to 1989	Precentor of St Albans before elevation to the episcopate, he was Bishop of Doncaster from 1976 to 1982 and was then translated to Bishop of Blackburn serving from 1982 until his death.
Mr Benjamin James Dale (1885-1943) 1939 to 1943	A professor at and Warden of the RAM, composed in the mainstream. As a young man, however, he was an organ recitalist (and one of the few pupils of E H Lemare) and organist of St Stephen's in Ealing,
Revd Francis Noel Davey (1904-1973) 1945 to 1953	Taught at Pembroke College, Cambridge, and joined SPCK as Editorial Secretary in 1944. In 1955 he became Director of the Society, retiring in 1970.
Mr Albert Meredith Davies CBE (1922-2005) 1957 to 1962	Organist of Hereford Cathedral 1949-1956 and of New College Oxford 1956-1958. He was conductor of the City of Birmingham Choir from 1957 and conducted the premier of Britten's *War Requiem* in Coventry jointly with the composer.
Christopher Hugh Dearnley LVO, FRSCM (1930-2000) 1970 to 1977	He was a former organ scholar of Worcester College, Oxford, and a pupil of H K Andrews and E Rubbra there. He served as organist of Salisbury Cathedral from 1957 to 1968 and of St Paul's Cathedral from 1968. On retirement in 1989 he moved to Australia and served as a locum in several churches and cathedrals there.

Mr Walter Dixon Hon Life RSCM (d 2002) 1965 to 1971	Of Newcastle-on-Tyne
Mrs Ethel Margaret (Mrs H J Dolan) Dolan (b 1915) 1935 to 1941	Hon Sec to the Friends of the College of St Nicolas, Further information in *SNCSN*.
Revd Dr Alan Campbell Don KCVO DD (1885-1966) 1957 to 1965	Editor of the Scottish Book of Common Prayer, he was chaplain and secretary to Cosmo Lang, Archbishop of Canterbury, from 1931 to 1941. Rector of St Margaret's, Westminster, from 1941 to 1946, Chaplain to the Speaker of the House of Commons from 1936 to 1946 and Dean of Westminster from 1946 to 1959.
Philip Edmund Duffy KSG, GRSM, ARMCM, PGCE, Hon FGCM, FHEA, FRSCM (b 1943) 1992 to 2000	Master of the Music at Liverpool Metropolitan Cathedral from 1966 to 1996 and lecturer at Liverpool Hope University from 2000 to 2013.
Mr Cecil Montague George (Monty) Durston ARSCM (d 2009) 1965 to 1991	Chairman of GPC from 1977. Vice-Chairman of Council 1984 to 1991, he continued to attend the AGM as a Member for several years after leaving Council.
Sir John Dykes Bower CVO DMus (1905-1981) 1944 to 1975	See Chapter 1.
Sir George Dyson MA FRICS FAI (1883-1964) 1958 to 1961	He studied at the RCM with Sir Charles Stanford and was director of music at Marlborough, Wellington and Winchester Colleges and he also taught at the RCM becoming its director from 1938 to 1952 in succession to Sir Hugh Allen.
Sir Seymour John Louis Egerton GCVO (1915-1998) 1962 to 1979	Educated at Eton, Chairman of Coutts Bank from 1951 to 1976. He also served as treasurer to Church House.
Mr Henry Walter Coningsby Erskine (1872-1933) 1930 to 1933	Educated at the Charterhouse and Oxford University, he was a pianist. Further information in *SNCSN*.
Bernadette Mary Farrell (b 1957) 1994 to 1998	Music advisor to the Archdiocese of Westminster from 1988, member of Music in Worship Foundation council. Married to Owen Alstott.
Mr Christopher William Field JP, MA, ARAM, ARCM (b 1940) 1985 to 2005	A Choral Scholar at Trinity, Cambridge, he studied at RAM and taught at Dulwich College. Assistant choirmaster at Bromley Parish Church, he was conductor of the Bromley Male Voice Choir from 1969 to 1983.
Sir Henry Murray Fox MA FRICS FAI (1912-1999) 1979 to 1988	Member of the Worshipful Company of Chartered Surveyors and Lord Mayor of London 1974/75.
Ian Fraser 1996 to 2000	A Chartered Accountant.
Mr Spencer William Freeman MBE (b.1929) 1995-????	Formerly Head of Copyright at Novello with whom he had a 50 year career. He served on the Executive Committee of the Methodist Church Music Society and was DOM at Central Methodist Church in Eastbourne for over 40 years (from 1967). Awarded MBE in 2013.

Prof Richard John Barrett Frewer MA, RIBA (ret), Hon HKIA, ARB (b 1942) 1990 to 1997	Choral Scholar at Gonville & Caius, Cambridge, and sang tenor in the choir of St Margaret's, Westminster, for 10 years. Architect and member of Arup Associates 1966 to 1991, Professor of Architecture at University of Bath 1991 to 2000 and at the University of Hong Kong 2001 to 2005.
Ven Oswin Harvard Gibbs-Smith (1901-1969) 1948 to 1955	The Archdeacon of London and Canon Residentiary at St Paul's Cathedral 1947 to 1961, Dean of Winchester 1961 to 1969.
Mr John Robert Griffin CBE 1959 to 1964	General Secretary of the Royal British Legion until retirement in 1959.
Dr George Howell Guest CBE, MA, MusD, FRSCM, (1924-2002) 1983 to 1998	Born in Wales, after wartime service in the RAF, he became assistant organist at Chester Cathedral. He became organ scholar at St John's College in Cambridge, and on graduation took up the post of College Organist, retiring in 1991. He was an RSCM Special Commissioner.
Sir David Harrison CBE, FREng, FRSCM (b 1930) 1996 to 2005	Chairman of RSCM Council from 1996 to 2005, Vice Chancellor of the University of Keele 1979 to 1984, Vice Chancellor of the University of Exeter 1984 to 1994, Master of Selwyn College, Cambridge 1994 to 2000.
Mr Sidney Brayshaw Heys LL B 1957 to 1984	General Manager of the National Provincial Bank from 1958, he served on the GPC until 1984.
Lady Elizabeth Higgs (1924-2013) 1986 to 1987	Chairman of the Arkleton Trust from 1986 until 2004. The Trust was set up in the 1970's by her husband John, Secretary of the Duchy of Cornwall and Keeper of the Prince's Purse. They farmed in Enstone, Oxfordshire.
Revd Brian Hoare BD (b 1935) 1994 to 2000	Entered Methodist Ministry in 1968, Deputy General Secretary of Methodist Home Missions and member of Music in Worship Foundation council.
Michael Brett Hockney MBE, BA, FRSA 2002, FCIM, FRSCM (b 1949) 1986 to 2004	Vice-Chairman of Council from 2000. Organist of All Saints' Church, East Sheen, London 1976 to 1998.
Mr Roger D Houghton (1908-1988) 1962 to 1987	Solicitor, lifelong chorister of St John the Baptist, Broughton, Preston.
Sir Hugo Baldwin Huntington-Whiteley (1924-2014) 1969 to 1986	A chartered accountant, he succeeded to the Baronetcy on the death of his father in 1975.
John Maxwell Hutchinson (b 1948) 1996 to 2000	Architect and former President of the Royal Institute of British Architects. He founded the charity Architects For Aid (A4A) after being caught up in the 2004 Boxing Day tsunami.
Revd Canon Ronald Claud Dudley Jasper CBE (1917-1990) 1973 to 1979	Educated at Leeds University and ordained after study at the College of the Resurrection in 1940. Vicar of Stillington 1948 to 1955, Succentor of Exeter Cathedral until 1960, Lecturer in Liturgical Studies at King's College London and Canon of Westminster in 1968, Archdeacon of Westminster 1974, Dean of York 1975-1984.
Alderman Sir Brian Garton Jenkins GBE, MA, PCA (b 1935) 1987 to 1997	Chairman of the Woolwich Building Society and Lord Mayor of London 1991.

Revd Marian Jones 1987 to 1995	Methodist minister in Normanton, West Yorkshire.
Prof Sir Ivor Christopher Banfield Keys CBE (1919-1995) 1975 to 1989	A child prodigy pianist, he became the youngest ever [at that time] FRCO. After study at the RCM he was assistant organist at Christ Church, Oxford. He was professor of music at Belfast, Nottingham and Birmingham universities and was also music editor for the Addington Press.
Mrs Charles William (Grace Mary Thyrza) Kimmins DBE (1870-1954) 1947 to 1953	Wesleyan deaconess working mainly at the Methodist West London Mission. She was made CBE in 1927 promoted to DBE in 1950.
Rt Revd Eric Henry Knell (1903-1987) 1961 to 1966	Bishop of Reading 1954-1972, educated at Trinity College, Oxford, ordained in 1929. He was Archdeacon of Berkshire before elevation to the Episcopate. On the RSCM Council he was Representative of the Incorporated Guild of Church Musicians.
Ven Graeme Paul Knowles CVO (b 1951) 1996 to 2001	General Synod Appointee to the Council. Archdeacon of Portsmouth 1993-1999, Dean of Carlisle 1999-2003, Bishop of Sodor and Man from 2003 to 2007 and Dean of St Paul's Cathedral, from 2007 to 2011.
Rt Revd David Konstant (b. 1930) 1978 to 1986	The 8th Roman Catholic Bishop of Leeds from 1985.
Mr Charles Sidney Lake (1872-1942) 1932 to 1937	Council representative of affiliated choirs.
Admiral Sir Charles Edward Lambe GCB, CVO (1900-1960) 1957 to 1960	After an illustrious naval career, he retired as Admiral of the Fleet in 1960, but died a few months later. He was an able pianist.
Mr Clive Letchford MA ACA 1989 to 1994	Former choral scholar at New College, Oxford, teaches Classics and Ancient History at the University of Warwick and was interim DOM of Holy Trinity, Stratford-upon-Avon in 2012.
Revd John Reginald Bertrand Bradley Lumb (1890-1955) 1936 to 1945	Vicar of Bickley. For further information see *SNCSN*.
The Revd Nigel Simeon McCullock KCVO, MA (b 1942) 1982 to 2000	Chaplain to Christ's College, Cambridge, from 1970 to 1973, Diocesan Missioner in the Diocese of Norwich from 1973 to 1978, Archdeacon of Sarum and Rector of St Thomas's, Salisbury from 1978, Suffragan Bishop of Taunton from 1986. In 1992 he was translated to be the Bishop of Wakefield and then Bishop of Manchester 2002-2013.
Rt Revd Thomas McMahon (b. 1936) 1987 to 1990	Trained for the priesthood at St Sulpice in Paris. Chaplain to Essex University from 1972 to 1980 and R/C Bishop of Brentwood from 1980 to 2011.
Sir Stanley Robert Marchant CVO (1883-1949) 1932 to 1949	Assistant organist of St Paul's Cathedral from 1903 and full organist from 1927. Principal of the RAM from 1936, he was Chairman of Council from 1947 until his death.
Sir John William Denys Margetson KCMG FRSCM (b 1927) 1987 to 1994	Chairman of Council (see above).

Revd Francis John Marsh BA, DPhil, ARCO (b 1947) 1994 to 2000	Vicar of St Thomas's, Ossett. Former organ scholar of York Minster and research student at York University. Gained a doctorate with a study of Samuel Wesley. Now Priest-in-charge, Emley and Flockton.
Mr D R Martin-Smith 1962 to 1982	An architect.
Mr Frederick Alexander Martin-Smith (1886-1968) 1930 to 1962	Bank Manager, Hon Treasurer of RSCM from 1951 to 1962. For further information see SNCSN book. It was noted in the Finance Committee minutes in Oct 1960, that since his appointment as Hon. Treasurer in January 1951, he had only missed one Finance Committee meeting.
Roy Cyril Massey D Mus, FRSCM (b 1934) 1983 to 1998	See under Wardens.
Sir William Neil McKie MVO MA DMus Hon RAM FRCO (1901-1984) 1945 to 1952 and 1961 to 1966	Was Organist and Master of the Choristers at Westminster Abbey from 1941 until 1963, a Member of the Athenaeum.
Revd Thomas Caryl Micklem (1925-2003) 1975 to 1992	A Minister in the Congregational and United Reformed Churches, he was a hymn writer and religious broadcaster. He was Chairman of the Hymn Society of Great Britain and Ireland, and of the URC Musicians' Guild.
Mr George W A Miller FCIS 1956 to ????	Managing director of Eastwoods Ltd., brick, cement, tile and concrete products manufacturers.
Mr Lewis W Moody 1962 to 1970	Of Macclesfield. Lewis Walton Moody MBE the rugby player is his son.
Revd Canon Dr Peter C Moore OBE (1924-2000) 1965 to 1980	Educated at Cheltenham College and Christ Church, Oxford. Ordained in 1948, he served as a minor canon at Canterbury Cathedral, curate at Bladon, chaplain at New College, Oxford, Vicar of Alfrick, Canon Residentiary at Ely Cathedral and Dean of St Alban's from 1973 to 1993.
Lord Mottistone OBE, FSA, FRIBA (1899-1963) 1957 to 1959	Henry <u>John</u> Alexander Seely, 2nd Lord Mottistone, of the architect firm of Seely & Paget. Educated at Harrow and Cambridge. During WWII he served in the Auxiliary Air Force and at the Ministry of Works. In 1947 he succeeded to his father's title. He was Surveyor of the Fabric of St Paul's Cathedral, architect to St George's Chapel, Windsor and a Lay Canon and architect at Portsmouth Cathedral.
Mr Norman C R Nash 1985 to 1997	A partner in Nash, Broad & Co, London, Chartered Accountants. Chairman of Calibre (recorded books for the visually impaired), he sang in St Margaret's, Putney, choir and, after retirement at Holy Trinity in Sibford, Oxon.
Mr Michael Bernard Nicholas FRCO(CHM), Hon. FGCM,. Hon. DMus UEA (b 1938) 1978 to ????	Organist and choirmaster of St Matthew's Church, Northampton 1964 to 1971, organist of Norwich Cathedral 1971-1994, Chief Executive of the Royal College of Organists 1994-1997.
Mr Archibald Keightley Nicholson (1871-1937) 1934 to 1937	Sydney Nicholson's brother — a stained glass architect. For further information see *SNCSN*.

George M Nissen CBE, Hon FRAM (b 1930) 1992 to 1999	Member of the Stock Exchange from 1956 to 1991.
Ven Hugh Ross Norton OBE MA (1890-1969) 1958 to 1964	Precentor of Wakefield Cathedral from 1921 to 1924, Chaplain to the Forces from 1924 to 1945, Archdeacon of Sudbury from 1945 to 1962 and Canon Residentiary of St Edmundsbury Cathedral from 1958 until 1964.
Mr Richard Bruce Hamilton Ottley (1890-1947) 1937 to 1945	A City Banker and Hon Treasurer of the RSCM from 1937 to 1939. A supporter and connoisseur of music and the ballet. Also Chairman of the United Kingdom Gas Corporation.
Dr George D Parkes MA BSc, DPhil (d. 1967) 1960 to 1967	Of Keble College, Oxford, Senior Proctor in 1935, organist of Newington Parish Church. Curator of Oxford University Parks until retirement in 1967, his son David was an Addington Student.
Mr Archibald David Barclay Pearson (b 1900) 1936 to 1944	Member of the Stock Exchange. For further information see *SNCSN*.
Mr Frederick David Linley Penny CBE, Hon Life RSCM (1896-1978) 1930 to ????	Organist St Mary's, Prittlewell, RSCM Representative for Chelmsford. For further information see *SNCSN*.
Revd Ian Pitt-Watson (1921-1995) 1969 to 1971	Graduate of the University of Edinburgh and the RAM. He became a Presbyterian Minister in 1950, serving at the Cathedral Church of St Giles in Edinburgh. He taught at Aberdeen university until 1980 when he took up a professorship at a seminary in Pasadena, California. He resigned in 1971 to save the RSCM the cost of his visits to Council Meetings from Scotland.
Col The Hon Stuart Pleydell-Bouverie DSO OBE (1877-1947) 1933 to 1946	Director of Phoenix Assurance Company. For further information see *SNCSN*.
Mr Christopher Peter William Regan B Mus, FRAM, FRCO, HonRCM (b. 1929) 1975 to 1993	Educated at Christ Church Cathedral Choir School, taught at Sedbergh School, was a professor at the RAM and organist of Lincoln's Inn Chapel. He retired to Tewkesbury.
Andrew Milton Reid (b 1929) 1987 to 1990	Investment advisor of Pensford Bristol.
Mrs Mildred <u>Betty</u> Ridley DBE (1909-2005) 1953 to 1978	Dame Betty Ridley, who preferred to be known as Mrs Ridley, was Third Church Estates Commissioner at Church House from 1972 until retirement in 1981. Her *Guardian* obituary read 'It was on the playing fields of Cheltenham Ladies College that Betty Ridley, who has died aged 95, became convinced that women ought to be ordained priests. It was a cause to which, in her sensible way, she was to devote a large part of her life. She never wished to be ordained herself, but blazed a trail for other women until she became one of the most influential lay people in the Church of England, as well as one of the kindest.'
Rt Revd Edward James Keymer (k/a Ted) Roberts FRSCM (1908-2001) 1957 to 1977	See above — Chairmen.

Revd Dr Erik Reginald Routley BD, DPhil, FRSCM (1917-1982) 1968 to 1982	Educated at Lancing College and at Magdalen and Mansfield Colleges in Oxford, he was chaplain of Mansfield from 1948 to 1959. A noted hymnologist, he was a Congregational Minister in Edinburgh from 1959 and in Newcastle-upon-Tyne from 1967. Appointed a Professor at Westminster Choir College in Princeton, New Jersey, in 1975, his enthusiastic work for the RSCM continued with him setting up and serving as President of RSCM America.
John Milford Rutter CBE, MA, MusB, MusD (Lambeth), FRSCM, (b 1945) 1990 to 1993	Studied at Clare College in Cambridge and was director of music there from 1975 to 1979 after briefly teaching at Southampton University. A widely known composer, especially for his choral music and carol settings.
Major Richard Shuldham Schreiber JP (1907-1978) 1953 to 1968	Served in the Coldstream Guards from 1926 to 1951, ADC to the Governor General of South Africa from 1933 to 1955. A Commissioner of the St John's Ambulance Brigade. A street in Ipswich is named after him.
Sir Charles Hilary Scott (1906-1991) 1973 to 1985	A partner in the international London law firm of Slaughter & May from 1937. The Annual Report 1986 notes that 'Sir Hilary and Lady Scott had, for many years supported the work of the RSCM and continue to do so upon his leaving the Council.'
John Gavin Scott LVO, MA MusB, FRCO (1956-2015) 1994 to 2000	A former chorister at Wakefield Cathedral and organ scholar at St John's College in Cambridge. Sub-organist of St Paul's Cathedral, then full organist from 1990 to 2004 and at St Thomas on 5th Avenue in New York until his death.
Dr Martin Edward Fallas Shaw OBE FRCM (1875-1958) 1935 to 1936	Composer, conductor, theatre producer. Later in life he became involved with church music and he received a Lambeth Doctorate in 1932.
Mr Robin Treeby Sheldon MA, FRSCM (b 1932) 1990 to 1992	First Director of the Music in Worship Foundation 1984, organist All Souls', Langham Place 1958-1965, Director of Music at Lancing College, organist at Holy Trinity Church, Hounslow, until retirement. In 1992, on becoming special advisor to the RSCM (60 days a year), he had to relinquish his council seat.
Ven Canon Jane Elizabeth Margaret Sinclair (b 1956) 1994 to 1997	From 1993 to 2003 she was Canon Residentiary and Precentor at Sheffield Cathedral and from 2003 to 2007 she was also Honorary Canon at the Cathedral. From 2003 to 2007 she also served as Vicar of Rotherham Minster until appointment as Archdeacon of Stow and Lindsey in the Diocese of Lincoln. Since 2014 she has been Canon Steward at Westminster Abbey.
Mr Archibald Slater 1941 to 1944	Solicitor in Tenbury Wells.
Sir Arthur Somervell (1863-1937) 1930 to 1937	Studied at Cambridge University with Stanford, at the RCM with Parry and in Berlin. He was a professor at the RCM from 1894 and was Chairman of Council from 1930 until his death.
Revd Mgr George Stack BEd, (b 1946) 1996 to 2000	Ordained priest in 1972, he served in various parishes before appointment as Administrator of Westminster Cathedral in 1993. He became Archbishop of Cardiff in 2011.

Sir Angus Duncan Aeneas Stirling Hon FTCL (b 1933) 1996 to 1998	Was appointed to be Chairman of Council in 1996 on his retirement as Director-General of the National Trust, but withdrew after it became apparent that major fundraising was necessary and he felt that he could not give enough time to this. He did however serve on Council.
Mr Jerry Sterling Stover Jr. (b 1950) 1986 to 1993	Lawyer and Principal of Bruern Abbey School.
Lt Cdr Kenneth Raydon Swan Kt; OBE, QC, Hon Life RSCM, (1877-1973) 1937 to 1967	Barrister educated Rugby School and Balliol College, Oxford.
Mr Eric Gerard Lumley Temple (1911-1972) 1938 to 1969	Solicitor, educated at Eton, Cambridge and the RCM, he was a student at Chislehurst in 1932 and organist of St John's, Holland Road, London. He loaned his Blüthner grand piano for use in the Great Hall at Addington, and it subsequently moved with the RSCM to Cleveland Lodge.
Sir Reginald Sparshatt Thatcher OBE, MC FRCO, DMus, HonRAM (1888-1957) 1950 to 1955	Studied at the RCM and was organ scholar of Worcester College, Oxford. After distinguished service in WWI, he was DOM at the Royal Naval College, Osborne, at Charterhouse and Harrow Schools before appointment as deputy DOM at the BBC in 1937. He joined the RAM as Warden in 1944 and served as Principal from 1949 to 1955. He was knighted in 1952.
Howard J M Thomas 1995 to 1999	Chartered Surveyor.
Mr Ronald Tilbury 1973 to 1976	A solicitor in Thornton Heath and Mayor of Croydon 1969/70.
Rt Revd Mgr Canon George (k/a Tommy) Tomlinson (b 1985) 1968 to 1977	Educated at Keble College, Headmaster of the Oratory School in Woodcote from 1943 to 1953. Parish priest at St Patrick, Soho Square, and Chaplain to London University until 1964 when he became Administrator of Westminster Cathedral, serving until 1967.
Dennis Townhill OBE, DMus, FRSCM (1925-2008) 1990 to 1998	Studied with Gordon Slater at Lincoln Cathedral. Was organist of Louth and Grimsby Parish Churches before serving at St Mary's Cathedral in Edinburgh from 1961 to 1991. Over this same period he directed 21 RSCM courses, mostly in Scotland.
Mr Richard William Trumper CBE, FRICS (1900-1989) 1955 to 1980	Educated at Repton School, he was Senior Partner in the firm of Messrs Clutton, Agents for the Commissioners of Crown Lands. He served as President of the Institution of Chartered Surveyors.
Mrs Janet H Unwin MA, BPhil, ARCM 1990 to 1998	Served in HM Diplomatic Service, chiefly at the UK Mission to the UN in New York. She worked for the Carnegie Endowment for International Peace in New York, at the Royal Institute for International Affairs in London and she devised fundraising musical events for the National Arts Collection Fund.
Mr William Graham Wallace 1951 to 1952	Chartered Accountant.

Revd Prebendary Newell Eddius Wallbank MA PhD MusD (1914-1996) 1966 to 1978	Representative on Council of the Incorporated Guild of Church Musicians. Rector of St Bartholomew the Great in the City of London. Prebendary of St Paul's Cathedral.
Mr Theodore Hunter Hastings Walrond (1872-1935) 1932 to 1933	Sydney Nicholson's assistant at Carlisle Cathedral, succeeded him as Acting-Organist in 1908 until 1910. After leaving Carlisle he worked for the Board of Education and became one of H M's Inspectors of Schools.
Revd Norman Leonard Warren MA (b 1934) 1990 to 2000	Ordained in the Church of England in 1960; curate of Bedworth, Warwickshire, 1960-63; vicar of St Paul's Leamington Spa 1963-77; Rector of Morden 1977-89; Archdeacon and Canon of Rochester from 1989 to his retirement in 2000. A founder member of Jubilate Hymns.
Mr James Irvine Watson OBE, 1975 to 1989	Deputy Lieutenant of North Yorkshire resident of Fulford, York. A former Secretary of the British Council.
Revd Dr Francis Brotherton Westbrook FRSCM (1903-1975) 1971 to 1975	Ministerial Secretary of the Methodist Church Music Society, Director of the Williams School of Music.
Miss Seymour Whinyates OBE HonRAM FRCM (1892-1978) 1960 to 1961	Director of the Music Department of The British Council. A violinist and President of the Society of Women Musicians from 1961 to 1963.
Mr Sidney Wild 1977 to 1984	A former executive of the National Westminster Bank, he served on the GPC.
Sir David Valentine Willcocks CBE, MC, FRSCM (1919-2015) 1958 to 1989	A former chorister at Westminster Abbey from 1929 to 1934, he was a music scholar at Clifton College, Bristol, and then organ scholar at King's College, Cambridge. After serving at Salisbury and Worcester cathedrals, he was organist at King's College, Cambridge from 1957 until 1974 when he became Director of the RCM. According to Wikipedia, his honorary degrees number over fifty.
Rt Revd John Leonard Wilson KCMG (1897-1970) 1952 to 1957	Chairman of Council (see above).
Henry Woods Wollaston (1916-1989) 1970 to 1986	After graduating from Cambridge he went to the Home Office. His father, Sir Gerald Wollaston, was Garter Principal King of Arms and it was he who signed the Grant of Arms to the RSCM in 1945.

Appendix 3. Non-teaching staff at Addington Palace

Bursar

Jackson, Alec W. Hon RSCM[299]: d. 30th Sept 1974. He joined the staff at Chislehurst on 20th April 1931 and was appointed Bursar of SECM in 1943. His job was to keep accounts and be responsible for increasing sales of RSCM publications; the journal *PCM* was his brainchild. He and his wife managed Roper House in Canterbury when it was the students' hostel. He was described in *ECM* May 1956 as 'kindly and self-effacing.' He retired as Bursar at the end of 1966, and became Publications Manager until March 1968. He was succeeded by Mr Vincent Waterhouse. From 1954 he lived at a house purchased for £4250 in 1954 by the RSCM (Mactrevor, Coombe Lane, Addington). The initial rent was five guineas per month. Jackson lived there until 1968. The house was then to be converted into two flats, but the Planning authorities would not permit this.

Accountant

Kerrigan, Michael: He was appointed in June 1985 as Accountant, a new post (financed for the first five years by Hymns A&M). He became Finance Director in 1992 and resigned in May 1996 to become Chief Accountant to the Haberdasher's Company in the City of London. He was instrumental in the introduction and integration of computer technology into the RSCM offices.

Public Relations Officer (and Appeals Secretary)

Rivers, Capt William (Billy) Elphinstone, Hon RSCM: b. 1900: d. March 1993. He was a former officer in the 10th Ghurkha Rifles and 20th Burma Rifles. Known as 'Billy', he was Appeals Secretary, and (from 1965) also Public Relations Officer. A scheme inviting subscribers had been launched, and Captain Rivers was appointed after the move to Addington to 'find further means of achieving freedom from financial anxiety.'[300] He had been Bursar of St John's School in Leatherhead. He began by asking affiliated choirs to sing carols for RSCM funds over Christmas 1954, bringing in £275 from 75 participating choirs, and the following year £300 from 90 choirs. In 1959 the carol appeal produced £501 from over 500 choirs. Made Hon RSCM in 1969, he retired at the end of 1971 after 17 years of

---

[299] See *SNCSN*.
[300] *ECM* Jan 1955.

service. The Annual Report for 1972 notes that 'His greatest contribution was through the regular visits which he made to choristers' courses, to festivals and other events up and down the country. He endeared himself to a large number of people and many, including former students of the College of St Nicolas, have cause to remember him with gratitude and affection. He was much-loved by the staff at Addington and, after retirement, he was allowed to partake of a weekly free lunch at AP to 'keep in touch with the staff.' One student recalls that he 'always came through the Common Room and invariably took an interest in us all.'

Roger Allen (1970/71):

'He was referred to as 'everyone's mobile bank'. ' [He cashed cheques for the students].

Roy Massey:

'Billy Rivers was another great character. By designation he was the Appeals Secretary but spent a lot of time chatting to the students and staff, and was always ready to pop out to the White Bear for a quick one. He seemed to have an encyclopædic knowledge of organists and music staff at countless public and preparatory schools and he also had an eye for appropriate furniture for the Palace at knock-down prices. I'm sure he was a splendid ambassador for the RSCM as he travelled round courses and festivals, and I hope he made some money.'

Left: Captain Rivers, Middle: [unknown] Right: Leslie Green

Antonia Harman (1970-1974):

'Capt 'Billy' Rivers was a legend. He was always there, every day in a voluntary capacity, driving up from his home in Ashtead, Surrey. He was particularly helpful to overseas students who might have problems with their passport, visas, money exchange etc, and he was always there to help. I became particularly friendly with him when he discovered my father had been in the 6th Gurkha Rifles regiment during the war while he (Billy) had been in the 10th Gurkhas. He and his patient wife Judy (Billy was always on the go!) came and stayed with my parents in Fowey, Cornwall, and they even came out to Australia and stayed with Michael [Deasey] and me in Sydney. He was related to Napoleon (he owned one of Napoleon's relics) and was very interested in history, so to see where Captain Cook had landed in Botany Bay (the very rock!) was quite something for him.'

Ian Barber (1960-65):

'An eccentric man, a terrible driver but a driving force for the RSCM!'

Publications:

Fortune, Mrs Noreen: Appointed as Bursar's Secretary then, from 1968, in charge of the Publications Department under the Bursar and then, in 1973, became Publications Manager in succession to Mrs Amos. She retired in November 1982, after 18 years with the RSCM, being succeeded by John Sansom.

Jackson, Alec W: see Bursar.

Sansom, John: He succeeded Noreen Fortune as Publications Manager in January 1983. Previously he was in academic publishing since 1962. On his retirement, Vincent Waterhouse wrote, 'his experience [in educational publishing] became evident in the reorganisation and subsequent growth of sales... with beneficial results for the purchasers — and for the sales figures.' On retirement, he and his wife Doreen moved to Wales. He was succeeded by Peter Wright in 1992.

Wright, Peter: Joined as part-time Publications Marketing Consultant in Summer 1991, in part subsidised by a grant from the Rayne Foundation. He replaced John Sansom in 1992 in the new role of Publications Director. He studied at Christ's College, Cambridge, and previously worked with Penguin Books and the Open University Press. He was made redundant in October 1996.

Secretarial/ Administration Staff (in alphabetical order):

Ainger, Tom: External Courses Organiser 1988-1992.

Amos, Mrs: Formerly Mrs Clegg, widow of the late David W. Clegg (a tenor in Canterbury Cathedral Choir who also worked at AP until he died Nov 1963). She re-married in 1970 but still continued to be known as 'Cleggles'. She was assistant from 1956 and then manageress of the RSCM's publications department until retirement in April 1973. One student observes that 'Mrs Clegg WAS publications.'

Mrs Clegg at work in the Publications Dept

Roy Massey:

'Mrs Clegg, the widow of one of GHK's Canterbury tenors was in the publications department and was marvellous at finding music for me and also giving me brown paper with which to cover my organ music. She also had a wicked sense of humour.'

Amuaku, Patrick: Assistant in the Publishing Director's Office ca 1989-1992 and looked after the Courses Library.

Barrow, John James Benson GRSM FRCO, LRAM, ARSCM: b. 1926, Chelmsford; d. 28th May 1992. He was a student at the RSCM in Canterbury in 1948 and also studied at the RAM. After teaching at Malvern College and Twyford School, he was organist at St Peter's in Bexhill-on-Sea, before joining the AP staff in 1967. At this time he became organist of All Saints', Benhilton (Sutton), and later served as assistant at St Michael's in Croydon. He became Assistant to the Secretary, mainly dealing with Commissioners' visits, the CTS and the Guild Choirs. He was promoted to Assistant Secretary in August 1977 and then in August 1984 he became the RSCM's first Computer Manager. He was the main administrator for the Diamond Jubilee service at the Royal Albert Hall in 1987 and was made ARSCM that year. He retired in November 1991 after 24 years' service. On retirement, he worked two to three days a week for the RCO, at the request of Vincent Waterhouse, helping them to computerise their membership records, a job he had done for the RSCM ten years previously. Harry Bramma feels that he was rather undervalued and comments that he was able to work for the RSCM because he also had a private income. Harry recalls:

> 'There were many others working for the RSCM in the Addington years who had a real sense of vocation and who did not argue too much about the pay cheque! One such was John Barrow. He had been a student at the College of St Nicolas at Canterbury in the post-war years, contemporary with Michael Fleming, Arthur Wills and Timothy Lawford. His father Canon Barrow, had been a member of RSCM Council and it seemed natural that he should give his life to supporting the organisation. He was a man who really enjoyed 'backroom work.' This extended to all practical matters like hanging the huge portrait of Sir Frederik Ouseley which came to Addington on the closure of Ouseley's College of St Michael at Tenbury. No job was beneath him — even the unblocking of drains during the six-week Summer Courses where the influx of 40 people put very great pressure on the drainage system which had been designed for a small number of residents when people generally took baths less frequently. He was in fact, as Assistant Secretary, the Odd Job man as well.

> But his command of administrative detail was formidable, especially when organising the great RSCM Festivals at the Albert Hall, when up to a thousand singers had to be marshalled off the stage and had to do all manner of organisational things. I experienced this in 1991 when he organised 'The Glory of the Psalms'[301] — a joint venture between the RSCM and All Souls', Langham Place, with RSCM choristers from around Britain and the All Souls' Orchestra performing to a full house. This was the last of the great festivals which started with Sydney Nicholson at the Albert Hall and Crystal Palace. John Barrow relished the challenges of these great occasions. His dedicated contribution could so easily be forgotten.'

---

[301] See p.224.

Barrow, Sylvia: Clerk in the General Office. She left in the summer of 1991, to be replaced by Rose Pettet.

Bass, Mrs C: In the Duplicating Room at AP December 1980.

Bates, Jonathan: Membership Administrator from 1996 to 2001. For the RSCM's move from Dorking to Salisbury he was Relocation Project Manager.

Besant, Miss: Office staff 1954/55.

Brawn, Mrs J: Worked in the Publication Sales Dept December 1980.

Burrows, Helen: succeeded Stephen Liley in the 'other publishers' department from 1991 to August 1997.

Carnes, Peter: b. 11th Jan 1930. He had been a chorister under Sydney Nicholson at Chislehurst. An employee of the National Westminster Bank, he was seconded by them to the RSCM into a new post as Public Relations and Appeals Secretary, serving from March 1986 until March 1989. This was an initiative set up by the Nat West to provide staff to charities for projects that might not otherwise find funding.

Right: Peter Carnes at the launch of *SNCSN* in January 2012

Cast, Mr I: In Publication Sales Dept 1989.

Charman, Mrs Jean: Clerk in the General Office ca 1989-1992.

Child, Mrs Nell: Began as a junior in the General Office in October 1958 and was upgraded in 1960 as Cashier, retiring at the end of 1978 and replaced by Mrs Eve Passow.

Church, Lily: Worked in the post department at AP from 1981 until retirement on 1st August 1995. *CMQ* in October 1995 estimated that she had despatched some 3 million letters and parcels in her 14 years at AP.

Churchill, Jo: Appointed January 1994 to run the Development Appeal and by the end of the year was also Affiliates Co-ordinator.

Clark, Mrs Margaret: Resigned from the Accounts Dept in 1992.

Clegg, Mr & Mrs: See under Amos, Mrs.

Coleman, Miss Amanda: Secretary in the Chief Executive's Office from ca 1992, External Courses Organiser 1994.

Cookman, Bernard: He was a former employee at the Bank of England, associated with the RSCM for many years, organist and choirmaster of a Surrey church. After taking early retirement he joined the AP staff part-time as link-person for overseas members on 1st May 1979 (and was still there 1989).

Cookman, Mrs B: Assistant in the General Office at AP in December 1980.

Coppen, Mrs Claire: On the Switchboard in the General Office ca 1989-1992.

Coulter, Mrs Kay: A member of the administrative team (looking after the membership records) for nearly 25 years. She retired in December 1979 for health reasons and died in 1980. RSCM Council made her Hon. Life Member in 1973.

Dauris, Mrs M: replaced Mrs Palmer in the Bursar's office from August 1958 to February 1959.

Davies, Mrs Anne: Assistant in the Duplicating Room ca 1989-1992.

Davenport, Janet: PA to Lionel Dakers 1981-1985, succeeded by Marian Hughes.

Davis, Mrs J: In Publication Sales Dept in 1989.

De Boise, Mrs Vera: Secretary in the Finance Director's Office at least 1980-1992.

Dobson, Margaret: Personal Secretary to Vincent Waterhouse for 11 years. She retired in 1983, and was succeeded by Jill Scriminger. Her husband Philip was Father Christmas at the AP Fair for several years. Her two sons Henry and Andrew both served as Head Chorister in the AP Chapel Choir.

Doyle, Mrs Maureen: Succeeded Mrs Clark in the Accounts Dept 1992.

Dumbleton, Miss: Office staff 1954/55.

English, Jonathan: He replaced Gordon Larkman on his early retirement in 1988 to administer the external courses. When the first 'desktop publishing' equipment was purchased in 1990 JE was appointed and trained to operate it. In 1994 he became Assistant Accountant. He left in 1996 to pursue a professional singing career.

Fawcett, Mrs Hatty: Marketing Executive with the role for encouraging new affiliations from September 1994.

Fellowes, Eileen: Assistant Accountant from January 1992 to August 1993 replacing Ken Meekison.

Ferguson, Ida: Personal Secretary to Vincent Waterhouse until her retirement in 1971. She dealt with Cathedral Courses and the appointment of Representatives.

Ferguson-Smith, Mrs I: Member of the Accountant's staff 1971-1986.

Foat, Miss Lilian: b. 1907. Book-keeper in the Bursar's Department from 1955 until retirement in 1971.

Roy Massey:

> 'Old Miss Foat was another stalwart of the Publications Department. She sang at St John's, Upper Norwood, with a voice described by her choirmaster as 'like a fruitcake with a wobble', but she was a delightful person.'

Franks, Mrs I: Assistant to Frank Johnson in the Other Publishers Office at AP December 1980.

Fraser, Mrs E: Assistant in the General Office at AP December 1980 (still there 1989).

Froud, Derek: b. 1951. Graduate of Birmingham University, worked for 20 years in the financial world, latterly at Citibank. Organist (for 10 years) of St George's in Brighton at the time of his appointment to succeed Victoria Hook as Director of Communications in December 1993, he was also treasurer of the Brighton Festival Chorus. He became Head of Member Services from 1996 with oversight of Music Supplies until made redundant in October 1998. Organist of the Church of the Good Shepherd in Brighton.

Goodall, Richard: Assistant in the Sales Dept. ca 1992. Organist of St Margaret's Church in Oxford since 2003 and Senior Organ Consultant for Makin organs.

Gosling Miss A: Shorthand typist in the Bursar's office from 1955, to Publications Assistant in 1957.

Grainger, Mrs L: In the Accounts Office at AP ca 1980-1982.

Green, Mrs: part-time assistant in the General Secretary's office resigned Mar 1960 and was replaced by Mrs Kettle working full-time.

Green, Mrs M: Worked in Publication Sales Dept. Left 1989.

Gunstone, Mrs Jean: A secretary in the General Office, who was recorded as being in post in December 1980, retired in September 1994.

Haines, Mrs M E: Worked in the Publication Sales Dept December 1980.

Halsey, Diana: Secretary to the Warden then Director of Studies. She worked during school terms only, but this was not enough so she retired at Christmas 1994.

Hamilton, Mrs S: Assistant in the General Office at AP December 1980.

Harman, Mrs C: In the Cashier's Office at AP December 1980.

Harrison, Mrs B: In the Accounts Office at AP December 1980.

Hebblewhite, Mrs B K: Worked in the Post Room at AP December 1980.

Henderson, Ian: He worked in the general office from November 1961 until December 1965, organising one day events and Commissioners' visits.

Hepburn, Mrs M: Worked in the Publication Sales Dept. December 1980.

Hobbs, Mrs M: Worked in the Publication Sales Dept. December 1980.

Holmes, Mrs S W: part-time accounts clerk in the Bursar's office in 1957/58.

Hook, Mrs Victoria: Began work in September 1992 as Communications Director but left a year later to have a baby, returning part-time afterwards. In her first year she had travelled widely to see Area Committees who found her 'a breath of fresh air.'

Howard, Miss Betty: A Secretary at AP from 1954 (moved from Canterbury where she was secretary to Leslie Green) until at least 1961.

Hubble, Mrs M: On the Switchboard ca 1989.

Huggett, Miss M: Office staff replaced Miss Dumbleton.

Hughes, Marian: PA to Lionel Dakers from 1985 and then to Harry Bramma.

Inge, Miss: Secretary March 1955 to November 1966. Her successor was Mrs Patrick.

Irving, Mrs Q D: Assistant in the General Office at AP December 1980.

Jackson, Mrs E P (Pat): d. 31st Mar 1984. From 1972 until retirement in 1982, she was responsible for dealing with advertisers in the *PCM* and *CMQ* magazines. Latterly she was also secretary to R S McDowall (editor of *CMQ*).

Janes, Victor: d. 15th Mar 1984. Joined AP staff on 1st January 1981 to a new post as co-ordinator of work done by local committees: he had recently retired as Head of Statistics at Church House, Westminster.

Johnson, Frank W: b. ca 1923; d. 4th July 1987. He was in charge of the 'Other Publishers' section of the RSCM Publications Dept. from 1973 until his sudden death in July 1987, although he was off for almost a year (1978-79) because of a broken leg. He was, for 25 years, choirmaster at Kemsing Parish Church in Kent.

Julier, Mrs E: In the Cashier's Office at AP December 1980.

Kettle, Mrs: In the General Secretary's office from at least 1959 until at least 1971 recording orders, filing and duplicating documents.

Lance, Mrs Janet: Worked in Accounts. HB on retirement mentions that she was the only person on the staff with longer service than himself so she must have started before February 1989 and during 1989 she was responsible for the computers.

Larkman, Gordon W: He organised residential choristers' courses, and other external courses from 1972 until retirement in January 1988 on health grounds.

Lee, Mrs A L: Worked in the Publication Sales Dept in December 1980.

Liley, Stephen: Graduated from Liverpool University in 1988 and joined AP in August 1988, He worked with John Ottley in the 'other publishers' department left in the summer of 1991 to study at the RCM. He was replaced by Helen Burrows.

Lomasney, Mrs A: Worked in Publication Sales Dept. ca 1989-1992.

McBride, Andrea: Secretary to the Director of Studies Geoff Weaver from 1994.

Markley, Mrs S: Worked in the computer room in 1989 (had left by 1992).

Meekison, Kenneth: Appointed Bursar in 1968 until 1992, when he was given responsibility for maintaining contact with Area Committees at home and abroad. Ken was a member of the Iona Community and of St Columba's Church of Scotland. He was actively involved with running a residential home for the elderly in Putney owned by St Columbus's Church. His wife Christine, editor of the popular cookbook *The Palace Kitchen*, was a Deaconess in the Church of Scotland. He and his wife lived in Mactrevor House (later known as 120 Coombe Lane and previously occupied by Alec Jackson) owned by the RSCM and which was sold to the United Reform Church in 1994.

His successor Michael Kerrigan was retitled 'Accountant'.

Ken Meekison **in his office ca 1979**

Milnes, Michael: Appeal Secretary from 1968 to 1971. He was a professional fundraiser, from the Appeal Consultants Messrs Hooker, Craigmyle & Co Ltd of Dublin.

Molineux, Mrs E: Worked in the Publication Sales Dept December 1980.

Morgan, Clifford A: Retired from the Post Office in 1972 and acted as honorary courses librarian at AP from 1972 to December 1985. He was organist of East Sheen URC for over 50 years.

Morris, Mrs P: Worked in the Publication Sales Dept. ca 1980-1989.

Murray, Mrs: Part-time in the General Secretary's office in 1959 and in the Bursar's office in 1960.

Nash, Mrs B W: In the Accounts Office at AP in December 1980.

Nichols, Dorothy: Sales supervisor in Publications Dept at AP ca 1986.

Oliver, Mrs M: VEW's secretary in 1989.

Palmer, Mrs E M: full-time accounts clerk in the Bursar's office from April 1957 until July 1958, replacing Mrs Holmes.

Paschalides, Caroline: Appointed to the Publishing Dept in 1994.

Passow, Mrs Eve: Cashier from 1978.

Patterick, Mrs K: A secretary from November 1966.

Perrott, Mrs Kay: Worked in Publications from 1956 to April 1983, latterly as PA to the Publications Manager. Her successor was Mrs Dorothy Nicholls.

Pettet, Rose: Clerk in the General Office from 1991, succeeding Sylvia Barrow.

Pratley, Miss: Office staff from 1955 to 1958, replacing Miss Besant.

Probert, Miss: Member of AP office staff 1955, promoted to Typist and General Assistant in 1957.

Pryce-Davies, Miss S: Shorthand typist in the Bursar's office from 1954.

Radford, Adrian: Finance Manager from 1996 until 1998.

Rhodes, Mrs B: In the Cashier's Office at AP December 1980.

324

Roden, Mrs R: Assistant in the Bursar's office from 1954.

Rogers, Arthur J: Appointed to the Publications Department at AP in 1953. Left in 1955 to work for A R Mowbray & Co.

Sanders, Miss Marjorie: Secretarial assistant to Alec Gurd until his post ended in 1973 when she continued with the day-to-day running of the Appeal on a part-time basis. She took over running the Christmas Fayre from 1975 until she retired at the end of 1977.

Scoble, Mrs M: Worked in the Publication Sales Dept December 1980.

Scott, Mrs K: Started work March 1959 in succession to Miss Dauris.

Schirok, Beatrix (Trixi): Assistant to the Director of Studies from 1995.

Scriminger, Jill: Personal Secretary to Vincent Waterhouse from 1983, and after a short break away from the RSCM to Martin How from 1987 and then to John Wardle.

Seagrove, Miss: Started work in the General Office November 1958.

Silver, Mrs G: Secretary to Mrs Fortune at AP December 1980.

Simpson, Mrs D: Worked in Publication Sales Dept 1989.

Squibb, Mrs Shirley: Clerk in the General Office ca 1992.

Steel, Mrs J: Office staff started September 1959.

Stevens, Mrs A: Worked in the Publication Sales Dept in December 1980.

Swallow, Mrs: part-time assistant in Publications Dept from 1957.

Symonds, Mr D P: Worked in the office at AP in 1954/55.

Tadman, Mrs Elsie: Was responsible for the non-residential three-day courses for choristers from 1972 until retirement at the end of April 1987. On retirement, she flew to Mexico to assist in completing a translation of the New Testament into the native language of the Chontal Indians.

Tarlton, Miss: Office worker at AP from 1955, promoted to shorthand typist in 1958.

Taylor, Julie: Secretary to Chief Executive Charles King from 1994.

Tolley, Mrs Rosamund: Secretary in the Chief Executive's Office ca 1992.

Trailing, Mrs N: In the Bursar's Office at AP December 1980.

Trillo, Miss Kathleen: Succeeded Dorothy Yorke as secretary to the Director in 1973.

Wade, Mrs I: Worked in the Publication Sales Dept in December 1980.

Wheeler, Mrs Jenny: Worked in Publication Sales Deptartment ca 1989-1992.

Williams, June: P/A to Harry Bramma from ca 1994 and then John Harper. She retired in 2000.

Williamson, Mrs Mary: Started in February 1966 and was Martin How's secretary for 21 years and also Secretary to Colin Yorke. She retired in July 1987. Her successor was Jill Scriminger.

Willson, Howard: Was organist of St Augustine, Bermondsey, and sang at St Mark's, Purley. For ten years (from 1962) he organised the residential and three-day instructional courses promoted by HQ until his retirement in September 1972. His work was continued by Gordon Larkman.

Woodhead, Graham: Succeeded Eileen Fellowes as Accountant in September 1993 and was succeeded by Jonathan English in April 1994.

Yorke, Dorothy M (known as Dot): d. 3rd February 1989. She was GHK's secretary throughout his directorate (and also to successive Wardens). She started at Addington in January 1954 at a salary of £400 p.a., and retired in April 1973, having stayed to see LD safely settled in. When she first arrived at Addington the builders were still in situ and she recalled that her first piece of equipment was not a typewriter but a broom! She held sway in an office just off the main entrance and often was the first person visitors met. After her death in 1989, she left a five-figure legacy to the RSCM.

Martin How describes her as a 'smiley sort of person with a perky voice.'

Roy Massey:

> 'I shared a secretary with the Director, and Miss Dorothy Yorke was a great support and help to me. She was a good church lady from Sanderstead and she adored GHK who, of course, wrote letters in meticulous style which delighted her heart. At first I was less assured in this area as I'd never dictated a letter in my life, but she politely corrected my infelicities of language and kept a wary eye on my timetable. She was an absolute treasure.'

Domestic Staff:

Housekeepers

Gordon, Chloe (known as 'Ma'): d. 1994. She was housekeeper at Addington in succession to Mrs Audrey Taylor from the Summer Term of 1959. GHK wrote in *PCM* Oct 1971 'she has battled successfully with the formidable demands of a very large house and of its population, many of whom could be described as young, exuberant, untidy, enthusiastic or any one of a number of other adjectives' and 'She set a standard of what she called 'Palace manners' which is for ever imprinted on the consciousness of all who came into contact with her.' She moved out of the Palace on 21st Aug 1971, her departure remaining unknown to all but a few of the staff.

Adrian Adams (1967-70) wrote in *CMQ* April 1995.

> 'Mrs Gordon was a power and a personality that no-one could forget. If you wanted to find her, all you had to do was stand and listen, and it would not be long before her penetrating voice would locate her. If you were a student and wanted to stay in bed in the morning, you did not stay for long! Undaunted, Mrs G would invade your privacy with 'I shouldn't worry, my dear, I've seen it all before!' remove the bed covers and physically tip the mattress and its occupant on to the floor. Midnight

pranks were severely reprimanded, but usually with a twinkle in her eye, except if the bath overflowed into her flat! Chloe ruled over the 'domestics', the students and Gerald Knight with not quite a rod of iron, but certainly with a firm hand.'

Another student (1969-70) recalled his role as fortune teller at the Autumn Fayre, when he had been persuaded to 'read the hands of many who paid good money for me to do so[302]. Not having done it before, it was quite unnerving to 'guess' right. Mrs Gordon the Housekeeper had put me up to it, and with Mrs Gordon you didn't say 'no'. Two other students recall that she 'ruled with a huge amount of fairness mixed with firmness, and ran a tight ship' and 'she ran the residential side with a rod of iron and was a *grand dame* of the old style.' She was offered an RSCM Honorary award but declined!

Roger Allen (1970/71):

'A formidable but wonderfully kind-hearted housekeeper (and her daughter Anthea), she was a grand Victorian lady with an insatiable appetite for sherry, who had somehow strayed out of her era. I well remember how she used to hold court at dinner after she'd had perhaps one sherry too many — much to the consternation of Freddie [the Warden] and Beryl Waine. Mrs Gordon could wrap Gerald Knight around her little finger — and frequently did.'

Roy Massey:

'I rapidly discovered that the mainspring of life at the college was undoubtedly the Housekeeper, Mrs Gordon. She was a quite remarkable woman in her capacity to organise the workings of a great house, and though I never discovered her antecedents I'm quite sure she had been brought up in a large country house somewhere. She had high standards in everything she did as she organised the various routines necessary to make the place run smoothly. Mrs Gordon also made herself responsible for the flower gardens behind the Palace, and her green fingers regularly produced a splendid array of colour in the Summer, and there was little that went on in the college that she didn't know about. She was quite demanding in her relationship with the students and her admonition to an individual that such and such behaviour was not 'Palace manners' pulled up many a student who might have erred and strayed. On the other hand, she had a heart of gold, and any youngster with a problem would often seek her out for a bit of comfort and motherly advice.'

Michael Deasey (1969-1971) remembers:

'When someone dared put up a Labour poster during an election campaign she ordered it down saying 'This is a Conservative household'.'

Benson, Michael: Chef at AP from 1972, appointed Assistant Housekeeper in 1991 and then promoted to the position of House Manager in 1994. He was still at AP as Curator in 2013.

---

[302] Every year she would coerce some unsuspecting student into palm-reading. She gave some guidance to them on what to say and every year the booth produced a good sum of money.

Alan Snow (1972/73):

'The longest-serving member of the non-music staff, what a patient and enduring man he was. A cheerful smile greeted us each day at breakfast — and so did the quality of his cooking!'

Antonia Harman (1970-1974):

'... I had moved to the 'Women's Wing' for accommodation. These rooms were down behind the kitchen and Michael was always giving us special treats and left overs. We girls became very friendly with him and we had lots of laughs and jokes with him.'

Blacktin, Harry: d. 1972. Harry was Steward at AP from 1954 until his death in late 1972 from leukaemia. One of his many duties was the ringing of the rising bell. One student remembers that it was Harry who put the urn on and made tea, and quotes 'that urn would nearly take off.'[303]

[AH] recalls:

'He had a long drawl when he talked and was most famous for his boiled eggs (they were always hard!) and we just called them 'Harry's eggs!' whenever we had them for breakfast.'

Boniface, Colin and Daphne: Appointed 1989 as Steward (post vacant for 15 years) and Assistant Housekeeper. They lived in the Bungalow vacated by Martin How, who moved out of AP. Mrs Boniface was promoted to Housekeeper in August 1990.

Boon, Mrs Joyce: On the domestic staff at AP ca 1992.

Bowkley, Miss V: see under Students.

Chambers, Mrs Ethel F: She repaired choir cassocks and surplices from 1954 until retirement in 1972. She is especially remembered for her work at the St Nicolas Fayres and Summer Parties. She was made an Hon Life Member of the RSCM in 1964. She was also the mother of Christopher Chambers, a leading college chorister.

Chilvers, Mrs Jean: On the domestic staff at AP ca 1992.

Dakers, Mrs Elisabeth: Housekeeper 1974 to 1988 — see under 'Directors'.

Duffy, Mr and Mrs Angus: Mr Duffy was handyman/gardener and Mrs Duffy was assistant cook from September 1974. They lived in Stable Lodge at AP and resigned in July 1975. Stable Lodge was then leased to the Golf Club for one of their employees.

Ferns, Margaret: see under 'Wardens'.

Field, Mrs E: On the domestic staff in 1989.

Fogden, Mr G: Handyman from 1953 to the end of 1973. His wife Iris also worked as an assistant cook.

Frier, Miss A: AP Cook from November 1957.

---

[303] See also Roger Allen's recollections on p. 76.

Harwood, Mrs Janet: Assistant Housekeeper (resident) began in August 1987. She succeeded Elisabeth Dakers as Housekeeper from January 1988 and left in August 1990.

Heinemann, Therese [or Teresa]: She worked in the Palace kitchen in the late 1960's, and also 'guarded the entrance to the female quarters.' The female students lived in the former servants' quarters behind the kitchen, and were strictly segregated from the men. She was a German cook who 'produced cuisine of a very high standard'. It was Therese, a keen photographer, who took the photograph of Addington Palace in the snow on the weekend of the November Fayre in 1969. Following overnight snow, she got up early and 'trekked around the edge of the golf course so that she could have a perfect picture — without footsteps.' Two students mentioned this and Catherine McClurg (1969/70) went on to recall: 'that evening a lot of students, including me (a married woman of 28 years) 'borrowed' some steel trays from the kitchen and used them as sleighs. It was great fun.'

November 1969, Snow at Addington (without footprints) photographed by Teresa, the cook

Michael Deasey (1969-1971) writes:

'It was during one of Martin How's choir training lectures in November that suddenly the snow started to fall. It was my first experience of falling snow and it was a heavy storm. Martin likes to remind me, even five decades later (and tells anyone else) how he lost me that day. I just simply pushed my chair to the window and stared out for the remainder of the lecture.'

Elizabeth Salmon (1962/63):

'I think it was the night when the death of President Kennedy was announced [and] very few of us students were in for the evening meal. Therese prepared two main dishes. I don't remember the one we all chose, but the salmon in aspic which she had made with considerable care and creativity remained untouched by the end of the meal, at which point it was thrown with great vigour and chagrin against a wall.'

Roy Massey:

'Teresa, the German cook was a wonderful character with a slightly mercurial temperament, but the meals she produced were of a high standard, and in my three

329

years at Addington I put on weight. Teresa also had the endearing habit of putting out some food by the kitchen door for the foxes in the park.'

Hicks, Miss O M: Assistant Housekeeper, leaving in April 1987.

Hughes, Miss Bronwyn: On the domestic staff at AP ca 1992.

Hunt, Mrs G C (Trudy): b. 1908. A member of the domestic staff at AP for over 29 years. She was 77 in 1985 and attended a Buckingham Palace Garden Party along with Michael Benson and John and Sylvia Barrow. She was made Hon Life RSCM that same year and was still on the staff in 1992 (age 84).

Roy Massey:

'Little Mrs Hunt looked after my bungalow as if it were her own, and made a lovely job of treating my wooden block floor with non-slip. She also made my bed daily.'

Laird, Mr D: Handyman in 1989.

Mellor, Mrs Joanna: On the domestic staff at AP ca 1992.

Meyer, L: AP Cook succeeding Miss Pontefract from April to November 1957.

Milner, Sheila: Assistant chef to Michael Benson in 1984.

Moyse, Gladys: Retired as Assistant Chef in 1991.

Newcombe, Linda: Assistant Cook from 1991 to 1993.

Osborn, Jean: Assistant Housekeeper in 1991.

Pontefract, Miss: Cook in 1955/56.

Robertson, William (Bill): Appointed as Resident Cook in March 1992, but made redundant, along with all the other domestic staff in November 1993.

Selemann, Mrs M: On the domestic staff in 1989.

Sibley, Mrs K: On the domestic staff in 1989.

Smith, Mrs J: On the domestic staff in 1989.

Taylor, Mrs Audrey: See under 'Wardens'.

Taylor, Mrs M: On the domestic staff in 1989.

Weston, Elizabeth: On the domestic staff at AP from October 1967. In October 1992 a party was held at AP in honour of her 25 years of service.

Yeoman, Miss Frances SRN: Appointed in 1971 as successor to Chloe Gordon. She was a former Matron of Brentford Hospital, Organist and Choirmaster of St Michael's, Chiswick, and RSCM Secretary for the Archdeaconry of Middlesex. She left in the summer of 1973.

[AH] recalls:

'She had a King Charles Spaniel that was like a child to her (she was not married). We always had to leave a chair for it at the table and it would have its slobbery lips on the table! We students did not approve of that!'

Addington Palace Staff on 31st May 1996, one day before the move to Cleveland Lodge began

Appendix 4. Non-resident staff: field officers and others

Anderson, Bryan FRCO(CHM), LRAM, FRSCM: b. 1935. Bryan was a boy chorister at All Saints', Margaret Street in London. He was Choirmaster of St Mary Redcliffe in Bristol and Head of Music at St Mary Redcliffe and Temple School from 1968 before being appointed Commissioner for the Midlands and South West on September 1st 1980, a newly-created

post. In addition to his other Commissioner's responsibilities, he developed the Cathedral Singers Choir (now titled 'Midlands and South West') started by Martin How and he was the driving force behind the residential courses at Dillington House and Kingswood School in Bath. He was awarded the ARSCM in 1986. Bryan retired in August 1995 and wasmade FRSCM the following year. After retirement he returned to be active at St Mary Redcliffe as churchwarden and lay-reader. Harry Bramma writes:

> 'He was a relentless visitor and became a much loved advisor and teacher as he travelled vast distances through his area.'

Appleton, Gordon BEd, LRSM, Hon FGCM, FRSCM: b. 1947, Stockton-on-Tees. Gordon trained as a teacher of Divinity at Christ Church College in Canterbury and was organ scholar there. He was a teacher to Jamaica and directed the choir at Kingston College before moving to Guildford Grammar School in Western Australia. After serving as Master of the Music at Perth Cathedral in Australia from 1987, he was appointed as RSCM Regional Director for the North in September 1993, succeeding John Cooke. He became Warden in 2004 following Michael O'Connor and was made ARSCM that year. Although re-organisation of the RSCM later reduced his role, he continued to direct the Northern Cathedral Singers until retirement in 2014 when he was made an FRSCM.

Harry Bramma writes:

> 'When the Southern West and Midlands Regional Directors were made redundant, he stayed on as Co-ordinator of the Areas. The importance of his work in this role cannot be over-emphasised, he kept things going at the regional level; the very survival of the RSCM had a lot to do with him.'

Barber, Geoffrey FRMCM: d. 29th April 1974. On leaving military service after the war, he abandoned his pre-war career in business and became a student at the Manchester College of Music. He became DOM at Stockport School, organist of St Paul's, Heaton Moor, was on the RSCM's Musical Advisory Board from 1958 to 1962 and was a Special Commissioner from 1959. He maintained a very high standard of choral music at Heaton Moor and between 1960 and his death he directed 51 RSCM courses. He was appointed Commissioner for the North in 1971. He was elected FRMCM in 1973.

Roy Massey:

'Barber was an absolute wizard with boy choristers, extracting marvellous results in a short space of time, and I learned a great deal from him.'

Above: RSCM 3-day school at St Paul's Heaton Moor December 1967: Geoffrey Barber in action

Left: Martin How with Geoffrey Barber 1972

Cooke, John GRCM, ARCM, ARCO, FRSCM: b. 1930, Barnstaple; d. 1st July 1995. John was educated at Barnstaple Grammar School and the RCM. He was DOM at Cheshunt Grammar School and organist of Cheshunt PC prior to appointment as Northern Commissioner from 1st January 1975, after the death of Geoffrey Barber. His 'patch' was formidable, covering the North of England, Scotland, Ireland and North Wales. In 1986 he had a coronary thrombosis and was off work for three months. Colleagues mention that he was a particularly fine accompanist, a skill he passed on to many young organists on courses at Addington and to adults on courses in the North of England as well as at Cathedral

Courses. He retired as Regional Director for the North in September 1993, a post he had held for 18 years, but, sadly, had a rather short retirement before another and fatal heart attack. Harry Bramma writes:

'He inspired great affection and was a diligent visitor and excellent with the Northern Cathedral Singers. He became very well-known in his area and much valued.'

Ogden, David BA, FRSCM: b. 1966. A graduate of Bristol University, David was DOM at Clifton RC Cathedral from 1991. He was appointed as Regional Director of the Midlands and South West, to replace Bryan Anderson in 1995. He was a founder contributor to the *Sunday by Sunday* planner from 1997. He succeeded Gordon Stewart as Director of the RSCM Millennium Youth Choir in 2004, relinquishing this post in 2014. He now directs the RSCM Chamber Choir. David has composed and edited much music for RSCM Publishing. In addition to his RSCM work, David has been DOM at Westbury-on-Trym PC in Bristol and conductor of both the City of Bristol Choir and the chamber choir 'Exultate'. He was made ARSCM in 2004, upgraded to FRSCM in 2015.

Poole, Revd Canon Joseph Weston, FRSCM: b. 25th March 1909, Gravesend; d. 7th July 1989. Poole was educated at King's School in Canterbury and went on in 1929 to be organ scholar and classical exhibitioner at Jesus College, Cambridge. Whilst training for ordination at Westcott House in Cambridge in 1933, he became friends with fellow student Cuthbert Bardsley[304]. After the latter became Bishop of Coventry in 1956, he suggested that Poole be appointed Precentor of Coventry Cathedral[305]. Poole took up the post in 1958 at which time GHK wrote in *ECM*

> 'Mr Poole has given skilled and stimulating instruction in 'singing and saying the services' at all the courses which have been held at Addington for ordinands and clergy and he hopes (we are glad to say) to be able to continue this work from Coventry.'

It was whilst he served as Precentor of Canterbury Cathedral from 1938 until 1949 that he and GHK became close friends. During that time he was lecturer in liturgiology to the RSCM at Roper House in Canterbury, resigning when he became Rector of St Katharine's Church, Merstham, Surrey (from 1949 until 1958). His close association with the RSCM continued and his flair for creating acts of worship found an outlet in major RSCM festivals[306] and in the themed Festival Service books and devotional liturgies published by the RSCM[307]. In 1977 he was made FRSCM and retired from Coventry Cathedral. A fuller account of his life and work can be found in *In Tuneful Accord: The Church Musicians* by Canon Trevor Beeson, SCM Press, 2009.

---

[304] Bishop Bardsley was Bishop of Croydon in 1954 and so presided at the opening of AP. He was also on RSCM Council from 1952 to 1956.

[305] Poole was responsible for the magnificent opening service of the new Coventry Cathedral in 1962.

[306] Royal Albert Hall 1965, Rejoice 1977, Jubilate Deo 1979.

[307] FSBs Nos.6-10, *Our Heart's Joy* 1980, *The Birthday of Christ* 1980, *From Gallows to Glory* 1981, *The Christian Race* 1982, *The Mystery of Faith* 1984.

Sheldon, Robin: b. 1932. A graduate of Cambridge University, he was DOM at All Souls', Langham Place, London, and also taught at Eton and Lancing schools. Appointed as part-time Special Advisor from 1992 at which time he was at Holy Trinity, in Hounslow. He was Director of the Music in Worship Trust (now Foundation).

Wardle, John MA, FRCO(CHM), ARSCM: b. 1948. A graduate of Caius College, Cambridge, John was organist of All Saints', Crowborough, in Sussex and taught at Beacon College there. He replaced Martin How as Southern Commissioner in September 1992, his title being changed to Regional Director for the South. Amongst his many remits were those of Director of RSCM Southern Cathedral Singers and RSCM Awards co-ordinator. In 2003 he was awarded the ARSCM. He retired in 2013.

Harry Bramma writes:

'He brought many musical and organisational skills with him — he actually liked 'small print'!'

Hon Librarians:

Charles Edward Scott Littlejohn	1946-1958
Post vacant	1959-1986
John Parkinson	1986-1995
Dr John Henderson	1995-

Littlejohn, (David) Charles Edward Scott MusB (Oxon), FRCO: b. 10th June 1879, Broughty Ferry, Dundee, d. 3rd July 1959, Winchester. Littlejohn was a student contemporary with Sir Sydney Nicholson at the RCM. After serving as organist at Holy Trinity in Notting Hill and St Saviour's in Sunbury (1899 to 1901) whilst at the RCM, he taught at Repton School from 1901 to 1912. He then served at St John's Episcopal Church in Coatbridge (1912 to 1916), at St Barnabas in Paisley (1916), was acting organist at St Mary's Cathedral in Glasgow (1916/1917), and, following war service, was organist of Christ Church in Falkirk (1919-1931). He then served at St Paul's in Knightsbridge (1931-1934), at St George's in Beckenham (1931-1934), became a resident student at St Nicolas College in Chislehurst in 1935 and in the following year was appointed a tutor there. He moved to Great Warley in Essex ca 1938 and, after the war, to Hunstanton. He was employed by

RSCM Council in 1940 to catalogue a very large library bequest by William Arthur Ellington and the following year moved to Tenbury as assistant organist to SHN at St Michael's College. In May 1943 he briefly took over editorship of *English Church Music* relinquishing this later in the year to C H Phillips. From 1946 he was RSCM librarian at Canterbury and then Addington[308], despite being concurrently organist of the Parish Church in Hunstanton in Norfolk. He was also a musical advisor to The Faith Press and editor of *A Scottish Choir Book* 1931. After retirement he became a Brother of St Cross near Winchester and he died there.

Parkinson, John A: b. 1919; d. 18th Feb 1995. Hon Librarian at AP from 1986 until his death. He was DOM at Trinity School in Croydon and director of the Orlando Singers. He had also worked at the British Library. The author of several musicological books: *An index to the vocal works of Thomas Augustine Arne and Michael Arne* 1972, *18th Century Song Collections: A Classified Index* 1985, and *Victorian Music Publishers: An Annotated List* 1990, he also edited several pieces of choral music for publication and ran a small second-hand book business from his home in Selsdon.

Henderson, John Christopher MA, MBBChir, MRCP(UK), MRCGP, DRCOG, ARSCM: b. 1945, Derby. Educated at Magdalen College School, Oxford, St John's College in Cambridge and Osler House, Oxford, John retired from his medical career in 1992. He has been organist of Wroughton Parish Church near Swindon since 1996 having previously served at Fairford Parish Church in Gloucestershire from 1974. He became Hon Librarian of the RSCM in May 1995, served for ten years as Chairman of the Bristol & Swindon Area Committee, was a founder contributor to the RSCM's *Sunday by Sunday* planner and his book *A Directory of Composers for Organ* won the 2006 Oldman Prize from the International Association of Music Libraries. He was made ARSCM in 1996.

The original *Sunday by Sunday* team in 1997, L to R: Revd Ian Forrester, David Ogden, Geoff Weaver, Robin Sheldon and John Henderson

---

[308] He can be seen on the library photograph on p. 15.

Appendix 5. RSCM Facts, Figures, Finances and Appeals

In the pre-war years at Chislehurst the SECM, as it was then, barely managed to keep its head above water financially. Without Sir Sydney's personal generosity[309], the many donations from *Hymns Ancient & Modern*, of which he was a 'Proprietor' — a kind of share-holder, the SPCK, personal supporters (many of them clergy) and legacies, it would have foundered. The One Guinea[310] choir affiliation fee was never going to support the College and its outreach into the dioceses of the UK, let alone the whole world.

As Sir Sydney explained in his *Musings of a Musician*:

> 'The original body of Proprietors mutually agreed that any profits of the undertaking should be devoted to Church work, at the discretion of the individual members. In later years, under the Chairmanship of Bishop Frere, the proprietors agreed to enter into a voluntary Trust, by which the profits should be distributed by corporate grants to specified branches of Church work, including a percentage to the Central Board of Finance of the Church Assembly. So that the valuable property in the book is not and cannot be used for private enrichment, but after the deduction of ordinary expenses the income is all devoted to some form of Church work, such as missions, education, church music and similar objects. It was largely my election to a proprietorship that enabled the School of English Church Music to be founded and its College of St Nicolas to be maintained, and without this source of help it is very doubtful whether such an undertaking would have been practicable.'

So what was the situation after WWII? Well, to be truthful, it was exactly the same! The constant striving to get more affiliates on board continued, personal 'subscriptions' were encouraged with these donors later being formalised as 'Members', legacies were sought, but the affiliation fee remained remarkably low. Churches have never been known for their wealth, but it has always been the case, and still is today, that many, presumably non-musical, PCC Treasurers on seeking to balance the books have looked at the RSCM affiliation and thought that it might be something to cut. This became especially so during the last twenty years at Addington when many small churches began to see a decline in or the disappearance of their choirs. The RSCM has always taken the view that it is not only there for churches with choirs, but can provide musical advice to any church[311]. It was usually observed that, when an increase in affiliation fee was made, a significant number of churches ceased to be affiliated.

---

[309] Sir Sydney bought the College buildings at Chislehurst himself and eventually donated them to the RSCM. He also worked as Director without payment.

[310] Although the Guinea, originally a gold coin containing ¼ of an ounce of gold, technically disappeared in the 19C, the name continued until decimalisation of the UK currency in 1971. It meant 21 Shillings i.e. One pound and One Shilling (£1.05 in decimal currency). Fees were commonly charged and paid in guineas until decimalisation.

[311] 1995 was designated 'The Year of the Small Church' by the RSCM and both John Wardle and Gordon Appleton gave many workshops around the country in that and the following year. RSCM Publications also provided resource books for churches with limited musical resources.

Graph 1: RSCM Choir Affiliation Fee 1951-2003

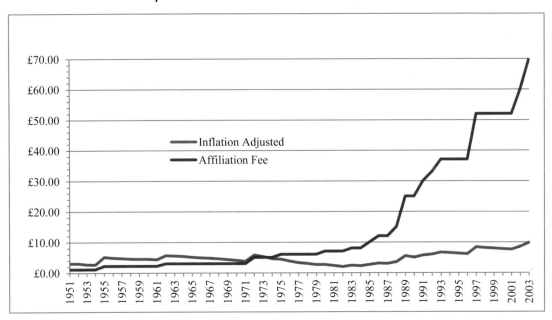

Amazingly the one guinea per annum affiliation fee continued until 1955, when it was increased to two guineas. There was always a reluctance to increase this fee lest there was a backlash of resignations but, taking into account UK Government inflation figures, the affiliation fee has always been good value for money as Graph 1 above shows.

UK inflation figures are adjusted to a notional baseline which was set at 100 in January 1974. This means that the affiliation fee of 1951 is adjusted upwards to £3.06 for 1951 and in 2003 adjusted downwards to £9.79. This means that, in real terms, the cost of church affiliation increased from 1951 to 2003 by slightly more than three times[312]. I think most of those reading this would feel that the great variety of services provided to members and affiliates by the RSCM today is well worth this relatively small increase. To put things in perspective and using the same inflation adjustments, the cost, in real terms, of The Daily Mail increased by a factor of four between 1974 and 2014 and a First Class Stamp has doubled in price over that same period.

The total number of affiliates from year to year has been surprisingly difficult to identify. Numbers reported in CMQ, in the Annual Reports, in publications and in Council Minutes varied depending on what time of year the figures were taken and they are rarely the same. There is no archival record book and so there are gaps for some years, but Graph 2 on the next page gives an overall impression. The apparent drop in numbers during 1970 was due to the removal from the register of churches that had not paid their subscription for several years. A large proportion of these were overseas churches.

---

[312] In recent years the adjusted figure has fluctuated between £8.80 and £10.00, also around three times that of 1951.

Graph 2: SECM/RSCM Affiliations 1931-2000

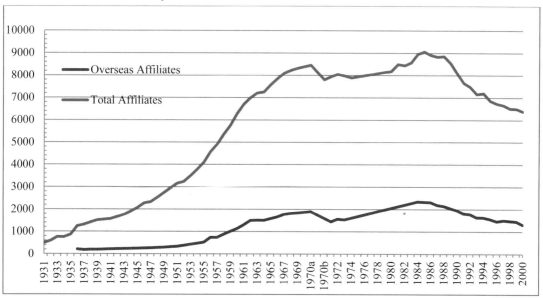

What cannot be shown on Graph 2, because data is unavailable except for five widely separated years, is the rapid growth in the number of Friends and Personal Members over recent decades, a considerable number that goes a long way to offset the loss of income from affiliation fees.

Graph 3: Affiliation Fees as a % of total RSCM Income

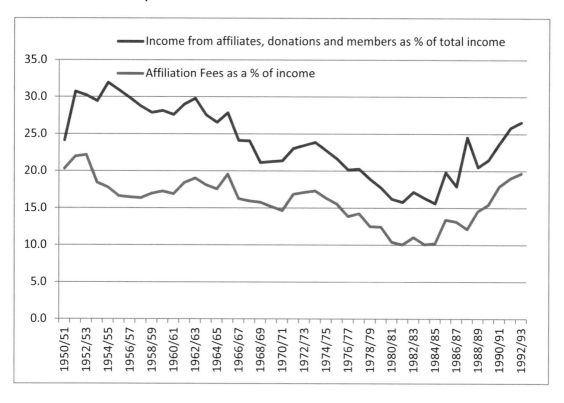

It is commonly thought that the affiliation fee paid by churches is a major part of RSCM income, but, during the 40 years at Addington, this was not quite the full picture. It can be seen in Graph 3 that, during the RSCM's Addington residency, affiliation fee income generally only provided slightly under 20% of total income. Taking into account the extra income from members and donations, the figure is just around 25%. During the period 1975 to 1985 it can be seen that there was a decline in the proportion of RSCM income derived from affiliation fees. This corresponds to the massive rises in interest rates experienced at that time which had the effect of greatly increasing investment income, a great bonus for charities such as the RSCM, but a double-edged sword for such a bonanza rarely continues.

Both Sir Sydney and Gerald Knight were aware that churches, church musicians, choirboys and their parents often had limited financial means and, ever since the Chislehurst days, they were keen to keep courses affordable. Many of the legacies received in the early years went to fund bursaries for students and choristers. The keeping of prices as low as possible whilst continuing to survive financially was a difficult juggling act, but the management was greatly helped by the RSCM Council members with financial skills.

Graph 4: Profit from the sale of publications

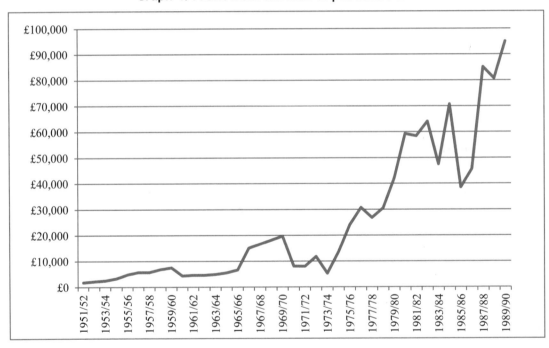

Nicholson and Knight were also keen to provide good music at a reasonable cost for choirs, and the publication of so many books of compilations was a testament to this, for they give greater value for money than single editions. The additional carrot of a 50% discount on RSCM publications sold directly to affiliated choirs kept many an affiliation fee safe. In January 1993 this discount was reduced to 25%, though, at that stage, postage and packing remained free. It was gradually recognised that publishing music also had another spin-off, namely that it was a good source of income. By the time the RSCM left Canterbury, profit

340

from publications was running at about £2000 pa, though this figure is deceptive because it does not include staff costs or postage. After 1990 the way the annual accounts were presented also makes it impossible to calculate a profit on publishing. Ignoring these final years, Graphs 4 and 5 show the actual profit from sales and the contribution made by publishing profit (not publishing income) to the total RSCM income.

Graph 5: Publications Sales as a % of Total RSCM Income

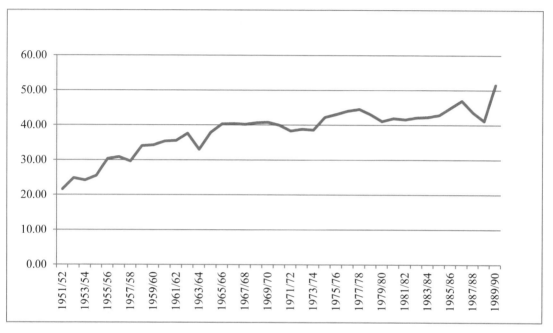

So, as a generalisation, around 25% of income is derived from affiliation fees, donations and subscriptions, with 40% from publications, this making up about two thirds of RSCM income. Where did the other 35% come from? Mostly from legacies, investments, course fees and royalties. During the high interest rate years of the 1970's and 1980's mentioned earlier, charitable organisations with healthy capital assets were exceptionally lucky and, helped by shrewd investment, the RSCM tripled its capital assets which stood at £300,000 in 1976 over the ten years to £964,000. Investment income rose substantially and in one particular year, 1982, the RSCM's investment income at £59,565 exceeded even the £58,397 total income from Affiliation Fees. 1990 was the first year when total income topped £1 million, though there was £23K deficit that year.

The very low interest rates prevailing in recent years have been a serious problem forcing charities to seek other income sources.

Appeals

1948: The Nicholson Memorial

Because Sir Sydney took no salary, there was an urgent need after his death to make provision for a paid successor and this was the main reason that a new Director for the RSCM was not appointed when the founder died. Before a job could be offered, there was the need to find sufficient funding and 'The Nicholson Memorial Appeal' was the outcome. This was first outlined by Hilary Chadwyck-Healey, Hon Treasurer of the RSCM, at the AGM in 1948. The Archbishop of Canterbury Geoffrey Fisher at a Council meeting (appropriately in the Jerusalem Chamber at Westminster Abbey where Sir Sydney's original vision was first unveiled) at St Nicolastide in 1948 said:

> 'The Appeal... ought to hold the attention of Churchmen in General, who should realise the essential work done for the Church by the RSCM.[313]'

The appeal was for £60,000. Although this does not superficially seem very much, the equivalent sum today (2015) would be over £2 million. Interestingly the comparative figures for the next two major RSCM appeals were £200,000 sought in 1970 (equivalent to £2.8 million today) and £1.5 million in 1994 (equivalent to £2.7 million today) – all significant sums.

As part of the appeal, the RSCM published *The Sydney Nicholson Commemoration Book*, a book devised by the Musical Advisory Board to be used as a Festival Evensong resource book with Nicholson in D-flat as the canticles and a selection of hymns and anthems, mostly by Nicholson. There was also a chanted version of the canticles for the use of smaller choirs. Priced at three shillings (£4.76 today) it sold fairly well, but even though various publishers waived their copyright (as did Ernest Bullock and William Harris who contributed anthems) the sum raised by this project was probably not large.

In *ECM* April 1950 the organising secretary of the appeal noted that only £1934 had been raised and bemoaned the fact that many affiliated choirs had 'done nothing' to contribute. Choirs and individual choirboys then seemed to make more effort and the figures increased to £2628 in July, £6500 in October. By July 1952 £20,000 had been raised but, with only £1.723 of that received between May 1951 and May 1952, it was decided that the appeal had run out of steam and was not worth continuing and so Council decided to close it.

1970: The Development Appeal

The next major appeal was the Development Appeal seeking £200,000 in 1970. Information about the aims and objectives of this appeal was sent out in leaflets with the RSCM magazine. The authors have not been able to find one of these, but it is thought that the principal aim was to make provision for extra full-time staff. Michael Milnes, a professional fundraiser, from the Appeal Consultants Messrs Hooker, Craigmyle & Co Ltd of Dublin was appointed Appeal Secretary from 1968 to 1971. The RSCM had been trying hard to get

---

[313] *ECM* Jan 1949

charity appeals on the radio and television and they eventually succeeded on 24th August 1969, when Professor Sir Bernard Lovell[314] broadcast on behalf of the RSCM in 'The Week's Good Cause' on BBC Radio 4 raising £678/5/0d. On 25th January 1970 ITA (Granada) broadcast a television appeal for the RSCM with actress Violet Carson from 'Coronation Street' as presenter. A rather disappointing £240 was the response.

The appeal proper began with a press conference on 7th April 1970 in the Jerusalem Chamber at Westminster Abbey. The Appeal Committee was under the Chairmanship of Lord Rupert Nevill. It was recognised that using a professional fund-raising firm would involve considerable expense, but this was regarded as essential as no one in-house or on RSCM Council had this kind of expertise. In September Alec Gurd[315] was appointed to replace Michael Milne as Appeal Secretary for a period of three years until 1973, by which time it was hoped the appeal would be complete. By the time of his appointment, the Development Appeal had raised £86,500 but Appeal fees and expenses came to £19,536. A large proportion of this money came from HM The Queen, Industry, Trusts, Banks and private donations with very little from the membership. Progress of the Appeal was slow but steady − £101,200 by May 1971 and £121,000 by January 1972. The Annual Report in July 1973 noted the end of the Development Appeal. With interest and some late pledges, by July 1973 a total of £136,000 had been raised after expenses, very valuable 'but somewhat short of the £200,000 target.' There was enough money however to appoint Martin How and Geoffrey Barber as Commissioners for the South and North respectively, but not enough to appoint a full-time Commissioner for Congregational Singing which had been first on the list of RSCM needs when the appeal was first launched. Second on that list was a new Clerical Commissioner, also not appointed; third on the last were the two Commissioners for North and South mentioned above; fourth was a full-time Commissioner to develop work overseas (not appointed) and lastly, a third of the amount was to be used to expand and modernise the School. In retrospect these were good but unrealistic goals.

Although technically over, appeal money continued to come in and, when the extra bonus of tax claimed back from covenants was added, Alec Gurd noted on his retirement as Appeal Secretary at the end of 1973 that the final total raised was £152,000 (£1.64 million today).

---

[314] Bernard Lovell OBE FRS (1913-2012) was himself an organist, serving at Swettenham church until well into his eighties. Whilst exploring the universe with the giant radio-telescope at Jodrell Bank, it was commonplace for him to disappear for a few hours to play for services. He also served as president of the Incorporated Guild of Church Musicians.

[315] Alec Gurd was also RSCM Secretary for the Diocese of London (for 14 years retiring at the end of 1983). He had served as an organist in Winchester, Guildford and London, latterly of St John-the-Baptist in Isleworth from 1977 until his final illness. He was responsible for organising the movement and seating of the 700 singers at the 50th Anniversary Festival in the RAH in 1977. He was made Hon Life RSCM 1977.

1994: Sing with the Spirit

The third major appeal was the 'Sing with the Spirit'[316] appeal of 1994, launched with a Service of Dedication in Westminster Abbey on 3rd June 1994 in the presence of HRH The Duchess of Gloucester, The Archbishop of Canterbury, The Dean and Chapter and with the heads of other denominations and the Lord Mayor and Lady Mayoress of Westminster.

Harry Bramma, who organised the service, writes:

'I had my worries that it would be a half-hearted occasion but in the end it turned out to be a very great event indeed. The Abbey Choir conducted by Martin Neary sang at the service which included a specially-composed anthem by John Rutter — a setting of the RSCM motto 'I will sing with the Spirit' and Walton's *Coronation Te Deum*. The sermon was preached by Timothy Bavin, Bishop of Portsmouth, and the Blessing was given by George Carey, Archbishop of Canterbury and President of the RSCM.

The Queen (Patron of the RSCM) was represented by HRH the Duchess of Gloucester. As I and Roger Butler (Acting Chairman) waited to welcome her near the west Door, we stood for half an hour greeting the congregation as they arrived. This was a very moving experience, people arrived from far and wide — and they kept on coming in an ever increasing stream so that, as six o'clock approached, the Eastern limb of the Abbey, the Choir, Crossing and Transepts were filled by a congregation of around 1,000 people. This included many distinguished supporters who had made the effort to be there.'

Harry continues:

'The success of the Abbey launch bode well for the Appeal. In the end, by 1996, something like £560,000 had been raised to fund the move to Cleveland Lodge and to provide extra services and resources to benefit the membership.

The Appeal had two prongs. The first was an appeal to Trusts, Charities and to business. We had the professional services of Tim McDonald with whom I worked closely for a year with some success. He was able to put us in touch with charities who gave considerable sums, but it was not easy convincing those bodies to give to a network rather than to a clearly-defined project. We had success both in terms of bricks and mortar and the funding of the educational programme. We wanted to start a Liturgy Planner (now transformed into *Sunday by Sunday*[317]). I wrote to the Abbot of Nashdom suggesting this might interest the 'Pershore, Elmore and Nashdom Trust.' He wrote back by return enclosing a cheque for £5,000. I quote this as an example of such approaches which yielded moderate amounts which added up to a sizeable sum. Sometimes the grants were bigger — the Livanos Charitable Trust gave

---

[316] John Rutter's anthem of the same name was composed for the appeal.
[317] This began in 1997 and is still published quarterly. It is arguably the most useful initiative from the RSCM in the last 20 years. A photograph of the original team of contributors is in Appendix 4.

£25,000 to fund the moving of the Harrison organ from Addington to Cleveland Lodge.

The second prong of the Appeal was to the membership. This was very ably organised by Jo Churchill who came to Addington (and then Cleveland Lodge) several times a week. She established good relations with the Area Committees, many of whom worked very hard to raise considerable sums. The financial benefit to the RSCM was clear; and the involvement of the members was an important morale boosting exercise which was a major factor in the Appeal's success. The pity was, that after the move to Cleveland Lodge in 1996, the momentum was not maintained.'

Humphrey Norrington was Chairman of the Appeal Committee and Jo Churchill, organiser of the appeal, wrote a regular column in *CMQ* offering various suggestions for fund-raising events. Of course there were the usual coffee mornings, sponsored sings and the like, but members came up with other ideas including Church-Crawls in the City of London, bell-ringing, choral vespers, the sale of Addington Bears (wearing chorister robes and ruff) and even RSCM 'luxury chocolate bars' bearing the appeal logo.

During December 1994 a joint venture with The Children's Society was initiated, whereby members and supporters of both organisations were encouraged to go carol-singing, especially in public places and pubs. The Children's Society provided boxes and badges and the two organisations would share the profits. During the same month, it was noted in *CMQ* that the first six months of the appeal had raised £200,000 with 648 members having donated and 304 having pledged to raise money. *CMQ* wryly noted that this was 'just 8% of Affiliates and Friends and our hope is that many more will be encouraged to contribute in 1995.'

The first year of the appeal raised £360,000 and was enough to launch the RSCM's regional education programmes at Portsmouth and Huddersfield Universities and at the Colchester Institute, where courses towards the RSCM Foundation Certificate in Church Music would be taught. The plan was to open further centres in Cardiff, Liverpool, Buckfast and Doncaster during 1996 with the added role of offering some of the traditional courses, such as the 'Reluctant Organist' courses, together with other not-so-traditional courses which were formerly held at Addington Palace. Some of the money was also used to start essential works at Cleveland Lodge prior to the move.

On Bank-Holiday Monday 6th May 1996 22 RSCM Areas arranged 100 events for a 'Sing with a Holiday Spirit' event raising around £5000. Later that month a Royal Reception was held at St James's Palace. A ticketed event, whole coach loads of members attended and musical activities were on offer in the many rooms opened for the reception. The day raised over £15,000 and by the summer of 1996 the appeal total reached £560,000. One further use of the money was to appoint seven Assistant Regional Directors.

In October 1996 it was announced that the RSCM had been successful in securing a Lottery award of £1,153,000. The first phase of building work at Cleveland Lodge was entirely funded by the RSCM's own resources, principally from appeal funds supplemented by legacies. One stipulation of the Lottery award is that funds could only be used for capital work and not for other RSCM work.

In February 1997 Martin Neary directed a 'come and sing' performance of the *Requiem* by Gabriel Fauré in Westminster Abbey. The 1000 singers' tickets rapidly sold out and many remember this day with pleasure, though who knows what Fauré would have made of such a massive performance! The appeal ended after three years in June 1997 having raised £620,000; however, following the success of the Westminster Fauré, 18 further 'come and sing' events were arranged — 8 more of Fauré's Requiem and 10 of Stainer's *Crucifixion*.

Course Statistics

Records of attendance at AP courses in the early years are not available, but a register exists for the period from 1987 to 1995. One notable observation is how few courses were cancelled through lack of interest.

Addington courses in the final years

Year	Term	Courses	Cancelled	Residential	Full	Attendance
1987	Michaelmas	24	0	9	6	823
1988	Spring	24	2	10	3	507
1988	Summer	21	0	8	6	587
1987/88	*Academic year total*	*69*	*2*	*27*	*15*	*1917*
1988	Michaelmas	23	0	11	3	768
1989	Spring	23	1	10	3	515
1989	Summer	23	0	9	3	604
1988/89	*Academic year total*	*69*	*1*	*30*	*9*	*1887*
1989	Michaelmas	21	1	10	7	665
1990	Spring	24	5	10	7	560
1990	Summer	19	0	7	1	400
1989/90	*Academic year total*	*64*	*6*	*27*	*15*	*1625*
1990	Michaelmas	18	1	8	5	382
1991	Spring	19	4	8	4	396
1991	Summer	23	4	8	5	811
1990/91	*Academic year total*	*60*	*9*	*24*	*14*	*1589*
1991	Michaelmas	25	1	6	11	648
1992	Spring	22	1	8	7	679
1992	Summer	18	4	7	5	527
1991/92	*Academic year total*	*65*	*6*	*21*	*23*	*1854*
1992	Michaelmas	24	4	8	7	473
1993	Spring	22	2	7	6	658
1993	Summer	24	3	8	4	579
1992/93	*Academic year total*	*70*	*9*	*23*	*17*	*1710*
1993	Michaelmas	20	0	6	10	688
1994	Spring	24	5	0	n/a	640
1994	Summer	17	1	3	1	545
1993/94	*Academic year total*	*61*	*6*	*9*	*11*	*1873*

1994	Michaelmas	24	4	0	n/a	605
1995	Spring	20	4	0	n/a	453
1995	Summer	16	4	3	n/a	214
1994/95	Academic year total	60	12	3	0	1272
	8-year Total	518	51	164	104	13727
	Annual Average	65	6	25*	16*	1716

* Because complete information is not available for 1994/95, these averages only relate to a 6-year period.

External RSCM Summer Courses 1990-93

Very few other course figures are extant. The tables on the right and below show the numbers attending some of the courses mentioned in Chapter 5. The numbers for 1967 to 1976 include both AP and external courses.

b = boys, g = girls, y = young men, a = adults, m = men

		1990	1991	1992	1993
Edinburgh	bgy	100	—	—	—
St Andrews	bgy	—	—	55	—
St Andrews	bgya	—	—	—	89
Abbots Bromley	bgy	110	138	83	92
Lincoln	gm	45	45	45	48
Chetham's	bgy	—	—	69	60
Chetham's	bgya	—	138	—	—
Bath	g	86	105	119	120
Bath	bya	104	85	103	79
Salisbury	a	40	44	42	41
Total		485	555	516	529

RSCM Course Statistics 1967-1976

Year	67/68	68/69	69/70	70/71	71/72	72/73	73/74	74/75	75/76	9 year Total	Annual Average
Res Juniors	1585	1860	1735	1878	2091	1681	1145	1602	1584	15161	1685
Res Adults	100	69	242	236	233	182	223	n/a	n/a	1285	184
Non-Res Juniors	1495	1359	2040	2026	1997	1784	3133	2094	2150	18078	2009
Non-Res Adults	50	96	104	80	76	64	150	n/a	n/a	620	89
Total Juniors	3080	3219	3775	3904	4088	3465	4278	3696	3734	33239	3693
Total Adults	150	165	346	316	309	246	373	n/a	n/a	1905	272

Appendix 6. Rediffusion Choristers' Award 1975-1992

In 1976 the television company Rediffusion wished to encourage the work of church choirs[318] and approached the RSCM for advice. The competition was initially called the 'Choristers' Award Scheme' though it was sometimes popularly referred to as 'Chorister of the Year' which later led to some confusion with the BBC2 awards of that name. The various names of the competition are listed below with the main prize-winners.

The RSCM organised the awards on behalf of the sponsor Rediffusion. In the first year the 28 finalists were chosen by the staff from boys on the Residential and Cathedral Courses that summer[319]. The adjudicators each year from 1975 to 1988 were Lionel Dakers and David Willcocks together with a guest celebrity, that being Sir Charles Groves for the first competition. The final always took place at St George's, Hanover Square, and Martin How was the accompanist until 1989, with John Cooke playing for the final three years.

Rediffusion Choristers' Award 1975-1984

1975		Age		Prize
1	Matthew Billsborough	13	All Saints', High Wycombe	£1000 to church + stereo equipment
2	Iain Simcock	11	St Alphege, Solihull	£250 to church + personal gift
3	Martin Ford	11	St James, New Malden	£100 to church + personal gift
4	Nicholas Sears		Christ Church, Beckenham	£50 to church + personal gift
5	Gavin Spears		St Michael, Maidstone	£50 to church + personal gift
6	Jonathan Kirk		St Mark, Woodthorpe, Notts	£50 to church + personal gift
The other 22 finalists also received personal gifts				
Guest Adjudicator: Sir Charles Groves				

1976		Age		Prize
1	Stephen Drummond	12	Holy Trinity, Cockeridge, Leeds	£1000 to church + colour TV
2	Angus Day	10	St John, Greenock	£250 to church + personal gift
3	Jonathan King	13	St Philip, Norbury	£100 to church + personal gift
The other 15 finalists received personal gifts + £50 for their church.				
Guest Adjudicator: The Lord Bishop of Ely				

---

[318] No particular reason was given for their interest in church music; this initiative was announced in the Annual Report of 1976. It was subsequently reported that Lord Buckhurst, Chairman of Rediffusion, had a personal enthusiasm for the project.

[319] Existing Cathedral Choristers were excluded from the competition.

1977		Age		Prize
1	Andrew March	12	Holy Trinity with Christ Church, Tunbridge Wells	£1000 to church + stereo equipment
2	Angus Day	11	St John, Greenock (then to Glasgow Cathedral)	£250 to church + stereo equipment
3	Philip Hollows	12	St Peter, Ruddington	£100 to church + stereo equipment
The other 13 finalists received a cassette recorder + £50 for their church.				
Guest Adjudicator: Ernest Lough				
A power cut in central London threatened this competition, but the candidates arrived and proceeded with candles. There was apparently enough light for the Adjudicators to see each boy and it was thought the standard of singing was the highest yet.				

1978		Age		Prize
1	Simon Carney	13	St Peter, Stockton-on-Tees	£1000 to church + colour TV
2	Stephen Cooper	15	St Mary-le-Tower, Ipswich	£250 to church + music centre
3	Paul Orchard	12	St Mary, Beddington	£100 to church + cassette recorder
The other finalists received a cassette recorder + £50 for their church.				
Guest Adjudicator: Joseph Cooper				

1979		Age		Prize
1	Simon Minns	13	Bath Abbey	£1000 to church + colour TV
2	David Hunt	13	St Paul, Crofton	£250 to church + stereo equipment
3	Richard Cooke	13	St George, Stockport	£100 to church + stereo equipment
The other finalists received a cassette recorder and a music stand + £50 for their church.				
Guest Adjudicator: Sir Peter Pears				

1980		Age		Prize
1	Timothy Attree	13	Christchurch, Bexleyheath	£1000 to church + colour TV
2	Steven Gunter	12	St Mary, Cheshunt	£250 to church + stereo equipment
3	Barry Bladon	10	St James, New Malden	£100 to church + stereo equipment
The other finalists received a cassette recorder and a music stand + £50 for their church.				
Guest Adjudicator: Richard Baker				

1981		Age		Prize
1	Andrew Hopkins	12	St Philip, Norbury	£1000 to church + gift
2	David Morris	11	Sacred Heart, Middlesborough	£250 to church + gift
3	Kevin Beck	12	St Woolos Cathedral, Newport	£100 to church + gift
The other finalists received a gift + £50 for their church.				
Guest Adjudicator: Steve Race				

1982		Age		Prize
1	Robert Saunders	12	St John, Ranmoor, Sheffield	£1000 to church + colour TV
2	Paul Clay	14	St Edward the Confessor, Romford	£250 to church + stereo equipment
3	Vincent Penfold	13	St Philip, Norbury	£100 to church + stereo equipment
The other finalists received a cassette recorder and a music stand + £50 for their church.				
Guest Adjudicator: Ian Wallace				

1983		Age		Prize
1	David Clegg	10	Romsey Abbey	£2000 to church
2	Laurence Pittenger	13	St David, Baltimore, USA	£500 to church
3	Oliver Dracup	12	St Mary and All Saints', Bexley	£250 to church
Guest Adjudicator: Donald Swann				

1984		Age		Prize
1	David Pickering	12	St Edmund, Roundhay, Leeds	£2000 to church + colour TV
2	Christopher Bruce	13	Newcastle Cathedral	£500 to church + stereo equipment
3	Keith Holah	12	Bridlington Priory	£250 to church + stereo equipment
Com-mended	Richard Riley	12	Our Lady of Lourdes, Lee, SE London	
The other 11 finalists all received £100 for their churches + a personal gift				
Guest Adjudicator: Dame Janet Baker				

It was announced in *CMQ* that Rediffusion no longer existed and that Anglian Windows would be the new sponsor in 1985.

Anglian Windows Choristers' Awards 1985

1985		Age		Prize
1	Jonathan Cunliffe	14	St Helen, Waddington, Yorks	£2000 to church + personal gift
2	Paul Stevens	12	St Edmund, Riddlesdown, Surrey	£500 to church + personal gift
3	Gareth Markes	13	Preston Parish Church	£250 to church + personal gift
Com-mended	Stuart Hetherington	12	St John, Knaresborough	
Guest Adjudicator: Sir Geraint Evans				

For 1986 Anglian Windows' parent company BET took over responsibility.

BET Choristers' Awards 1986-1988

1986		Age		Prize
1	Daniel Ludford-Thomas	13	St Matthew, Northampton	£2000 to church + personal gift
2	Anthony Liddell	14	Radley College Chapel Choir	£500 to church + personal gift
3	Robert Byatt	13	St Andrew, Coulsdon	£250 to church + personal gift
Com-mended	Mark Gonzales	13	St Michael and All Angels, South Beddington	
Guest Adjudicator: Lady Barbirolli				

From 1987 only half of the finalists were selected from RSCM courses. Individual entries were allowed and there were 16 finalists in all, 8 recommended from RSCM courses and eight from regional semi-finals arranged by BET.

1987		Age		Prize
1	Adrian Phillips	12	St Michael, Macclesfield	£2000 to church + personal gift of £250
2	Gareth Child		St Luke, Cardiff	£500 to church + personal gift
3	Mark Brignall		Emmanuel Church, Saltburn	£250 to church + personal gift
Com-mended	Sam Barrett		Bristol Cathedral School	
Guest Adjudicator: Lady Solti				

For the 1988 competition, John Rutter composed the original 2-part version of his *Angel's Carol*.

1988		Age		Prize
1	Andrew Quartermain		St Mary-le-Tower, Ipswich	£2000 to church + personal gift
2	?	?	?	?
3	Keith Lines	12	St Mary's, Wroxham	?
Guest Adjudicator: ??				

From 1989, Harry Bramma, as the new Director, took Lionel Dakers' place, David Willcocks retired from the panel and two guest adjudicators were invited each year. The competition also changed to having just two awards, one for boys and one for girls, and all entries were on a Free Entry system, no finalists being selected from RSCM courses. The name was also changed to 'Choirboy and Choirgirl of the Year'.

BET Choirboy and Choirgirl of the Year 1989-1991

1989		Age		Prize
Boys	Edward Snow		Hexham	£2000 to church + personal gift
Girls	Rhiannon Williams		Barry	£2000 to church + personal gift
Guest Adjudicators: Andrew Lloyd-Webber and Peter Skellern				

1990		Age		Prize
Boys	Duncan Watts		St Thomas on the Bourne	
Girls	Paula Bishop		St Matthew's, Darley Abbey	
Guest Adjudicators: ??				

1991		Age		Prize
Boys	Oliver Sammons	12	All Saints', Gresford, Clwyd	£2250 to church + personal gift
Girls	Joanne Lunn		Leicestershire	£2250 to church + personal gift
Guest Adjudicators: David Hill and Michael Ball				

Choirboy and Choirgirl of the Year was run in 1992 by Kestrel Communications (on behalf of BET) 'on a shoestring, with the RSCM providing help in kind', that is advertising it in *CMQ* and providing judges. If no further sponsors could be found by Kestrel/BET this would be the last competition, and this proved to be the case.

Kestrel Communications Choirboy and Choirgirl of the Year 1992

1992		Age		Prize
Boys	Gavin Moralee	12	St Barnabas, Dulwich	
Girls	Fiona Wright	14	Sutton Valence School Chapel Choir, Maidstone	
4000 entries were whittled down to 18 finalists				
Guest Adjudicators: ??				

There are numerous photographs of the winners. A selection can be found on the next two pages.

Above: 1978 winners (L to R) Stephen Cooper, Simon Carney, Paul Orchard
Left: 1976 winner Stephen Drummond 'Singing in the rain'

The 1984 winners with (L to R) Richard Baker, Donald Swann, Steve Race, Dame Janet Baker, David Willcocks, Lionel Dakers and Ernest Lough

Holy Trinity, Tunbridge Wells: Andrew March (Left), The Rediffusion £1000 Prize in 1977 purchased a piano for the church, Martin How seated

1986 winners: (L to R) Robert Byatt, Daniel Ludford-Thomas, Anthony Liddell

Appendix 7. An Addington and RSCM Diary

1952

June 20th	GHK appointed Director.
July	First public announcement of proposed move to Addington Palace made in this month's *ECM*.
July	The work of transforming AP began, but major building work did not start until July 1953.
July 16th	Announced that HM the Queen had consented to become a Patron of the RSCM, in addition to HM Queen Elizabeth, the Queen Mother.
July 18th	The Archbishop of Canterbury wrote to approve that the RSCM should offer help to choirs 'in the [other] recognised Christian Churches' but noted that 'I am quite clear that the Unitarians ought not to be admitted' (and goes on to explain why). RSCM Council subsequently decided to admit non-Anglican churches but call them 'Associated Choirs' rather than 'Affiliated Choirs'.
Sept 30th	Revd Cyril Taylor appointed Warden and Chaplain and Revd Horace Spence appointed Clerical Commissioner.
Oct 28th	Planning consent received from the Town Clerk of Croydon.
Dec 23rd	All furniture and equipment was now removed from No 17 The Precincts and stored in Roper House and the Deanery.
Dec 31st	GHK steps down as organist of Canterbury Cathedral. He was succeeded by Dr Douglas Hopkins.

1953

Jan 1st	GHK begins as Director of RSCM.
Feb	The RSCM was responsible for 'redecorating and dilapidations' on leaving 17 The Precincts. The cost was to be £602, but the Dean and Chapter were prepared to settle for just £400.
Mar 12th	With Roper House full of furniture and equipment, three further rooms were needed as office space and as overflow accommodation for the hostel. An agreement was reached with Edred Wright to rent three rooms in his own house.
Mar 12th	It was agreed to award a prize at each Instructional Course for Choirboys for the boy who had shown himself to be the best all-round chorister. It was suggested that Sir Sydney's *Peter the Chorister* would be an appropriate book.
Apr	*ECM* Apr announced that Mr Stephen Dykes Bower, surveyor of the fabric of Westminster Abbey, had given his services to draw up plans for the Chapel at AP.
Apr 11th	Clerical Commissioner, Revd Horace Spence, began his duties.
Apr 30th	The lease for AP was signed and sealed by the Executive Committee at 5 Amen Court in London. This was the regular meeting place for the committee, being

the residence of Dr John Dykes Bower, organist of St Paul's Cathedral and Chairman of the committee since it began in 1951.

The lease between RSCM Council and Croydon Corporation would run for 50 years from 25th March 1953, even if the RSCM did not pay rent from that date. Rent was fixed at £1000 per annum, but at this point the Golf Club were still in occupation of part of the Palace and a rent rebate and starting date for the rent had not been agreed.

May	The Home Guard vacated the rooms rented to them by Croydon Corporation.
May 8th	The RSCM Coronation choir of 20 boys were resident at Addington Palace until June 3rd.
June	Dr Sidney Campbell accepted the offer to be Director of Musical Studies at AP.
July	*ECM* announced that 'At the Annual General Meeting it was stated that the Council had decided on a change of emphasis in the School's objectives. Hitherto its efforts have tended to be concentrated mainly on church choirs and the technical improvement of their singing. Hereafter it will work on a broader basis by giving its attention to all musical aspects of public worship.'
	'In future encouragement and advice... will no longer be offered solely, or even mainly to organists and choirs but also to clergy and congregations.'
July 16th	It was decided that the Music Advisory Board would consist of five permanent members (GHK, Dr John Dykes Bower, the Chief Commissioner, the Warden, the Clerical Commissioner) and ten elected members with one third retiring annually.
July 27th	Building work begins at Palace with exterior painting. The major work involved a complete electrical wiring, the installation of 'new heating apparatus', the building of a new kitchen and the conversion of a conservatory and men's changing room into the Chapel of St Nicolas. Redecoration 'on a modest scale, of about 100 rooms, as well as the painting of three hundred windows, was also undertaken.' Messrs E H Burgess were the contractors. A major company, who worked in the London area and whose clients included London Underground, they are long since defunct. Work continued until lunch time on 10th July 1954, the day of the opening, but enough work was complete to allow term to start in January 1954.
Sept 1st	The Revd Cyril Taylor takes up duties as Warden. He was asked to take up residence and supervise work in progress, and with the help of Mrs Taylor, compile a list of furniture, fittings and equipment required. In fact they both did more than supervise, and engaged in real 'hands on' physical work.
Sept 17th	It was noted that there was a vacancy on RSCM Council and it was suggested that a woman be appointed. Mrs Fisher (wife of the Archbishop of Canterbury) was invited to suggest suitable persons, from business or industry.
Oct	Guy Stanford, son of Sir Charles Villiers Stanford, bequeathed the copyright in all Stanford's unpublished music, books, royalties and performing rights to his

sister and then on her death to the RSCM. This occurred in 1956. He also gave the bound manuscript of Stanford's complete Service in C to the Colles Library.

1954

Jan	The first van load of furniture arrives at AP from Canterbury in the second week of Jan.
Jan 22nd	Term starts; the first students arrive.
Feb	In the first week of Feb, the RSCM office moved from Roper House, Canterbury; in all there were 20 van loads transferred over four weeks. The cost of the move was subsidised by The Pilgrim Trust (£1000) and Hymns A&M (£850 towards establishing a Chapel).
Feb 2nd	Blessing of Palace by Bishop of Croydon, Rt Revd Cuthbert Bardsley.
Feb 4th	Opening of RSCM office at Addington for business.
Feb 11th	The Executive Committee approved the sale of the Lease of Roper House to the National Institute for the Deaf for £1000. In 2015 it is still a residential home for the RNID.
Mar 29th	First of four courses for theological students.
Apr 3rd	St Mary Cray was the first affiliated choir to begin the tradition of visiting AP to sing Saturday Evensong.
Apr 19th	First residential course for choirboys (Easter Monday).
May 6th	Recently-formed AP boys' choir (The Tallis Choir) sang service for first time.
May 7th	The Mayoress of Croydon and about 50 other ladies prominent in the life of the Borough, accepted an invitation to tea at the Palace, and to hear from the General Secretary and Warden about the history of the RSCM and the part it was hoped that Addington would play in its future.
July	GHK wrote in *ECM* 'My present aim is to see for myself the state of music in churches in as many dioceses as possible, so that future policy may be firmly based on first-hand knowledge and experience.' He travelled 20,000 miles in pursuit of this aim.
July 10th	Official opening of AP in the presence of HM Queen Elizabeth the Queen Mother and dedication of the chapel to St Nicolas by the Archbishop of Canterbury. The anthem *Behold the Tabernacle of God* was especially composed by Sir William Harris for the occasion. Two boys from each of the following cathedrals formed the choir: St Paul's, Westminster Abbey, Canterbury, Southwark, Rochester, Blackburn, with two boys from the Chapel Royal and included men who had sung at the first service at Chislehurst in 1929. The cost of tea for 2000 guests plus marquees was just around £500. Guests (except dignitaries) were asked to make a donation to expenses but the event made a disappointing deficit of £365.3.11d.

358

Sept	RSCM Hon Treasurer F A Martin-Smith purchased Sir Sydney's Myrtle Cottage from the RSCM.
Sept 13th	Edred Wright resigns as Choirmaster.
Sept 23rd	GHK reported in the 27th Annual Report 1954 that:

Sept 23rd   'The establishment of our new headquarters is most expensive and, I believe, one of the most far-seeing things which the RSCM has done. The purchase of additional equipment has naturally been essential, and the cost of this has partially been met by generous gifts from affiliated churches, choirs and private individuals for which the RSCM is very grateful.'

Sept 23rd	Captain Rivers appointed Appeals Secretary.
Oct	The Finance Committee noted that cost of providing four meals a day to resident staff was 5/9½d. The budget allowed for 5/6d. Mrs Audrey Taylor was asked to take steps to reduce the cost of meals to 5/6d a day, and to buy provisions wholesale, as far as possible.
Nov 11th	The Director recommended to the Executive committee that Hubert Crook be appointed Headquarters Choirmaster provided that a suitable person could be found to take his role as full-time Commissioner. Melville Cook of Leeds Parish Church was approached but declined the offer.
Dec 4th	The Warden and Fellows of the College of St Nicolas met at Addington for the first time (their 11th meeting).

1955

Jan	Martin How arrives as a student.
Jan	The second choir of boys at AP (The Nicholson Choir) is founded.
Feb	*Choral Service Book No. 1* published.
Apr	*ECM* mentions that organ recitals have been given by George Thalben-Ball, Alwyn Surplice, Dr Henry Ley and Conrad Eden.
Apr 26th	First of annual regional conferences for Representatives held at AP.
Apr 28th	Martin How appointed HQ Choirmaster [Charles Cleall had already been interviewed and rejected] for the academic year 1955/56.
June 16th	Mr Sidney Humphreys, leader of the Aeolian String Quartet, gave a violin recital.
July	It was noted with approval that Mrs Taylor's efforts to economise on food had been successful with the cost of meals in the last six months being now £1/10/9d compared to £2/0/6d in the previous six months.
July	The Finance Committee authorised the Director to commission original compositions up to a limit of £100 p.a. on the advice of the MAB (Musical Advisory Board).
July 9th	The first Summer Garden Party at which the College students gave a recital of secular music in the Great Hall.
Sept	Diocesan & Archdeaconry Representatives first appointed.

Sept	Martin How starts work with the Tallis and Nicholson Choirs.
Sept 23rd	Autumn Term starts with 17 full-time students.
Oct 19th/20th	GHK (who also held the post of Organist to the Archbishop of Canterbury) provided two choirs of twelve boys (two each from AP and from major churches and cathedrals around London) to sing at the re-dedication of Lambeth Palace Chapel in the presence of HM The Queen and members of the Royal Family.
Nov	Annual Report noted that we joined IAML[320] (and we are still corporate members).
Dec 10th	GHK leaves for first overseas visit paid for by a 1947 Hymns A&M donation in memory of SHN. Council appointed Dr John Dykes Bower as Deputy Director during GHK's absence. He received the gift of a clock in recognition of services rendered.

1956

Spring	Mr E H Warrell joined teaching staff as Plainsong tutor. David Gatward chosen (by fellow students) to be Head Student for the year. Dr Sidney Campbell steps down as resident Director of Musical Studies at AP.
Spring	Recitals by the Choir of the Russian Orthodox Church from Paris, by the Ripieno Choir and by Nigel Coxe (piano student at the RAM).
Mar 22nd	The recently published *Cross of Christ* was performed for the first time in the Great Hall directed by MJRH. The congregation was so large it spilled into adjacent rooms. It was the first time that all the boys, from both choirs and probationers, had sung together.
Apr 18th	The choristers directed by MJRH gave a 'show' at St John's, Selsdon, depicting the life of choristers through the ages — entitled 'Then and Now' — see p.146.
May	It was announced in *ECM* May 1956 that the journal would be published three times a year instead of quarterly due to increased costs. [It reverted to quarterly in 1963.]
May	*ECM* also reported that the 70-80 College choirboys were divided into two large choirs, Nicholson and Byrd, and two groups of probationers to fill vacancies.
May	'Recommended Lists' of anthems, upper-voice canticle settings first published.
June 11th	MJRH and the College choir with student Allen Sever at the organ, sang at Lambeth Palace Chapel at the request of the AOC for the consecration of the Bishop of Madagascar.
June 12th-13th	The 50th birthday celebrations of The English Hymnal were held at AP during the Hymn Society's Annual Conference, the many lecturers included RVW[321], Prof Arthur Hutchings Joseph Poole. Students and college choristers sang

---

[320] IAML — International Association of Music Libraries.
[321] See p. 69.

	hymns, directed by MJRH, with Derek Holman, organ, in West Croydon Methodist Church on 13th June.
July 2nd	Leslie Green noted in his Newsletter to Representatives that a 35mm filmstrip entitled 'A day at Addington Palace' was available to borrow to illustrate talks on the work of the RSCM at local or church events. The popularity of this and the large number of bookings required several copies of the film to be made. To the authors' knowledge, none have survived.
July 19th	GHK returns from overseas visit.
July 21st	Summer Party at AP; 500 guests attended and GHK gave talk on his recent overseas visit. The college Choristers acted as stewards and sang Evensong.
July 24th	End of term final 'full boys' service in St Mary's, Addington, and attended by many parents followed by tea. [Stanford in B-flat and Nicholson *Let us with a gladsome mind*.]
July	GHK notes in the Annual Report that choirs were weaker numerically than 40 years earlier except in the well-run choir and that 'almost everything depends on the personalities of the parson and choirmaster.' Sixty years on from this the same is true.
Winter Term	Concerts in the Great Hall by the Ionian Singers directed by Graham Stewart, the St George's Singers from Ashtead directed by Geoffrey Morgan.
	The BBC again invited the College Choir to pre-record a 15' programme of Christmas music for transmission overseas.
	Recently left student David Leigh recorded a programme of organ music on the Chapel organ for transmission in Hong Kong on Christmas Day.
Nov	It was decided to give all non-executive office staff a bonus equal to one week's gross pay. This became a regular and welcome boost to staff who were considerably under-paid by any standard.
Dec 8th	First St Nicolas Fair at AP.
Dec 22nd	Recital of Advent and Christmas music in the Great Hall.

1957

Jan	The Trustees of the Stanford estate advised that the Stanford royalties were steadily rising (£2794 during 1955/56) and that the RSCM would have to pay estate duty on these.
Jan 31st	Concert in the Great Hall by the Orlando Singers directed by John A Parkinson, later Hon Librarian at Addington.
Mar 19th	The first concert in the Great Hall given by the students themselves. The concert concluded with Stanford's *Songs of the Sea* for which Sir William Harris was the piano accompanist.
May 16th	Constitution for the management of Overseas Branches promulgated and branches were formed in each of the states of Australia and New Zealand.

June	The Finance Committee approved the sale of confectionary and tobacco to staff and students.
June 6th	Recital in the Great Hall by the Dingwall Ensemble, DOM Dennis J Grew.
June 27th	Recital in the Great Hall by students with friends from the RCM.
July	Insurance on Chislehurst discussed by council — still owned by RSCM and on lease to Kent Education Committee.
July 13th	Summer Party at AP. The Choir sang Evensong [Wise in E-flat; *O Lord God*, Brewer; *Praise to God*, Campbell].
July 14th	The students and boys were invited to Lambeth Palace for tea which was followed by Evensong [Wise in E-flat and Redford *Rejoice in the Lord*] and presentation of the ADCM awards to Dennis Townhill and Robert Joyce.
July 23rd	The choir recorded Psalms 23, 62 and 68 for an RSCM Record. GHK directed with MJRH at the organ.
July 24th	Last day of term concert of anthems by the Chapel Choir, featuring anthems learned for chapel services during the term.
Aug 1st	International Congress of Organists in London visited AP. The RSCM also arranged two choral workshops in St Sepulchre's, Holborn, on July 30th/31st. In the week following the Congress, AP arranged two three-day courses for overseas' visitors attending the Congress (at a cost of $20).
Oct 12th	First Festival Service sung by boys' voices in St Paul's Cathedral.
Oct 17th	Concert in Great Hall, at which the newly-restored (by Mr Applegate of Selsdon) chamber organ was heard for the first time in a concert with the Morley Chamber Orchestra conducted by David Gedge.
Nov	It was agreed to buy a Bevington organ from St Edmund's Church, New Addington, for installation in the Robing Room. The costs were £100 for the organ and £120 for removal, repair, installation and electrical work.
Dec	New vestments donated anonymously to the chapel.
Dec 7th	2nd St Nicolas Fair at AP.
Winter Term	Gift to the library by Mr J L Crawford of metrical psalters and hymn-books collected by his grandfather Major G A Crawford, a contributor to *Grove* and *Julian*.

1958

Jan	Piano recital in the Great Hall by Croydon pianist Miss Dorothy Grinstead [d. 1974, she taught at the Tobias Matthay Pianoforte School and frequently broadcast on the BBC].
Jan 23rd	GHK leaves on his second overseas visit, to Africa. Again John Dykes-Bower appointed temporary Deputy Director during his absence (to May 1958).
Jan 25th	Three choristers appear in a performance of Britten's *St Nicolas* at the RAM (trained by MJRH). Two further performances were given on 20th May 1959 and 3rd June 1959.

Feb	Several College choristers are auditioned by Benjamin Britten for a part in Britten's new opera *Noyes Fludde*. Brian Weller gets the part.
Mar 20th	Brian Fairfax gave an organ recital in the Chapel.
Mar 21st-23rd	College choristers have a choir weekend at the Palace.
Spring Term	Recitals in the Great Hall by Banstead Musical Society (conducted by Derek Holman), a song recital by Miss Mary Blake (soprano) and Miss Evelyn Dacker (piano), winners at the 1957 Croydon Music Festival, and the Croydon Music Circle.
Spring Term	A new Lenten altar fontal donated anonymously, designed by Mr Stephen Dykes Bower and executed by Mrs Ozanne of Sawbridgeworth.
Spring	Hubert Crook had a heart attack in Blackburn, but recovered in time for the Summer Courses.
May 9th	GHK returns.
May 15th	AP Chapel choir sing at Lambeth Palace, ADCM diplomas awarded.
May 17th	Choral Concert in the Great Hall arranged by students Phillip Cooper and Walter Sutcliffe. The students sang with an orchestra from the Guildhall conducted by Michael Hamm (a student and later professor of conducting at the Guildhall).
July 4th-6th	College choristers have a choir weekend at the Palace.
July 8th	AP Chapel choir sing Evensong at Lambeth Palace for Bishops attending the Lambeth Conference.
July 10th	The students sing a Eucharist at St Sepulchre's, Holborn.
July 10th	*Triennial Festival Service* in the Royal Albert Hall [a Thursday] in the presence of HM Queen Elizabeth The Queen Mother and nearly 200 of the Bishops and Archbishops attending the concurrent Lambeth Conference. The Triennial should really have been in 1957, but was delayed a year to coincide with the Lambeth Conference.
July 16th	The students and boys gave a recital in St Mildred's, Addiscombe.
July 17th	Council appoints a Commission to look at the work and organisation of the RSCM.
July 18th	Evensong and Admission of Choristers as full members. Parents invited.
July 21st	The students and boys repeated their Addiscombe recital in the Great Hall as an end of term concert with MJRH directing and GHK as accompanist. *ECM* notes that MJRH encountered considerable difficulties in the recent musical events caused by London students being able to practise and sing on one day but not on the next. All this extra work was, of course, in addition to the regular Chapel services.
July 22nd	AP Chapel choir sing Evensong at Lambeth Palace for Bishops attending the Lambeth Conference.
Aug 31st	Retirement of Revd Cyril Taylor as Warden.

Sept	Leonard Blake resigned as editor of *ECM* after 10 years in the post. CVT invited to take over but declined. So GHK and HLAG edited the next issue.
Sept 19th	The New Warden Revd George Sage installed in AP chapel by the Bishop of Malmesbury.
Oct	*ECM* notes that there are now over 5000 affiliated choirs and over 2000 personal members.
Oct	*ECM* notes that recitals had been held in the Great Hall by The Goldsmiths Madrigal Choir (conductor Brian Brockless), The Dolmetsch Consort, The St Michael's Singers (conducted by Dr Harold Darke), The Croydon Music and Recording Society, The Chapel Choir of The Bishop Strachan School for Girls, Toronto (conductor John M Hodgins).
Oct	Annual Report for 1958 notes that during this year recommended lists of carols for Christmas, Epiphany and Easter and a list of graded organ voluntaries were published.
Dec 5th-7th	College choristers have a choir weekend at the Palace.
Dec 12th	End of term concert.
Dec 17th	Croydon Youth Choir Concert directed by MJRH in the Great Hall.
Dec	This year there were two carol evenings directed by MJRH, both of which featured instrumental music. A recording of carols was also made for the BBC Overseas Service.
Winter	The college choir sang at Lambeth Palace for the meeting of the British Council of Churches.

1959

Jan	Gramophone records of a recording of the 1958 RAH Festival were being held up by a copyright problem over the organ voluntaries. 270 orders had been received of the 300 requested. By April they had all been delivered and 50 more were ordered.
Feb 1st	Nicholas Andrew Holman, the 2nd child of Mr & Mrs Derek Holman was baptised in the Chapel.
Mar 6th-8th	College choristers have a choir weekend at the Palace.
Apr 30th	GHK reported to Council that the reduction of *ECM* to three times a year had been a great mistake. Since Leonard Blake had resigned as editor they had not been able to find someone suitable, and GHK and HLAG had been sharing the work. He also said that 'The Chorister's Leaflet' is 'a very slight and shoddy publication. We are glad to know that it gives great pleasure to the boys who are lucky enough to get copies, but it compares very unfavourably with 'The Chorister' which we published in pre-war days and which ceased publication in 1939.'
May 7th	Lambeth Palace garden party and ADCM presentations. The College Choristers sing Evensong.

May 18th	The College Choristers sing Evensong in Chichester Cathedral.
June	*ECM* June 1959 notes that, for this academic year 58/59, AP has had full capacity — 17 full-time students and 12 'London' students, with the majority from abroad.
	ECM also notes that the boys' choir has made two BBC TV appearances with MJRH.
	ECM notes concerts in the Great Hall at AP by Valerie Tryon (piano); The Holiday Singers (directed by Miss Vally Lasker), Herr Rudolf Strahlendorf (piano); singers and players from the Guildhall (with AP students) performed under Michael Ham and Walter Sutcliffe (including the Fauré *Requiem*); Mary Illing (Sop) and David Winnard (bass) with Winifred Boston (piano).
June 19th-21st	College choristers have a choir weekend at the Palace.
June 27th	College Choir participated in the Chelmsford Diocesan Pilgrimage at Bradwell-on-Sea.
July 11th	Summer garden party, 400 members attended. Evensong was sung by the College Choir (Walmisley in D-minor and Batten *Sing we merrily*).
July 16th	End of term recital by boys' choirs with instrumental items.
July 16th	GHK reported to Council that Morley College Chamber Choir directed by Denys Darlow and the Purley Circle Singers directed by John Odom had given recitals in the Great Hall.
July 22nd	Ten choristers sing for a wedding at Lambeth Palace.
July 24th	It was reported in June that nine students had defaulted in paying their fees. By July five had now paid, three had promised to pay and one was being followed up with legal action.
July 24th	The idea of selling the Chislehurst property arose again. Cecil Clutton[322] reported that the situation had not changed since his report of 1954 i.e. the freehold of the property is not worth much more than a mere capitalisation of the rent received. Kent County Council had the property valued (£86,750) for insurance purposes.
Aug 18th-25th	Demand for places at the annual Summer School is so great that a second one (at Darley Dale) was arranged for 120 boys and 14 choirmasters.
Sept	Term started with 26 students (15 AP and 11 'London').
Sept 1st	From this date a free lunch was provided at AP for administrative staff. 3 reasons were given '1) Our isolated position with only one small café available in the village where there is not a very good service; 2. Practically every business firm in London provides its staff with luncheon vouchers every week; 3. Several members of our staff are married women who have domestic duties to complete before starting work with us at 9.00am. They have little opportunity of preparing sandwiches for themselves.' This privilege continued until the closure of AP.

---

[322] This is the same Cecil Clutton who was an author of books about organs and clocks.

Sept 22nd   The College Choir sings Evensong in Lambeth Palace.

Oct 20th   The first RSCM course devoted to Plainsong begins at All Saints', Margaret Street, with six one-hour weekly sessions directed by Arthur W Clarke, director of the Gregorian Association.

Nov 28th   St Nicolas Fayre opened by popular singer Michael Holliday, at which sit-down lunches were provided for the first time. Over £500 raised.

Dec 5th   Students and boys sang a St Nicolastide Eucharist at St Sepulchre's, Holborn. (Darke in F) conducted by MJRH with GHK at the organ. The RSCM AGM was then held in Cutler's Hall and the choir sang again for Evensong at St Sepulchre (Sumsion in A and Handel *Let their celestial concerts all unite*) with GHK directing and MJRH at the organ.

Dec 4th-6th College choristers have a choir weekend at the Palace.

Dec 17th   GHK leaves on third overseas visit (South Africa, South America, Caribbean and North America, accompanied by student Lindsay Colquhoun). He directs the first Summer School at Cape Town. In *ECM* Oct 1959 GHK says 'Lest it should be supposed that these travels cost the RSCM a lot of money, I should like to make it clear that this tour, like the two previous ones, has been made possible by the generous contributions of the Proprietors of *Hymns A&M* to the RSCM Overseas Development Fund.' Again John Dykes-Bower appointed temporary Deputy Director during his absence.

Dec 19th   The choir sing carols at the Golf Club.

Dec 21st/22nd Carols in the Great Hall.

1960

Jan-Feb   The Plainsong course of last October was so successful (40 attendees each week) that a further course was arranged at All Saints', Margaret Street, directed by Alfred Batts, organist of Banbury PC and DOM at St Stephen's House, Oxford. In fact these courses continued to be popular for several years.

Spring   Martindale Sitwell joins the staff as organ tutor and Michael Fleming as tutor in plainsong.

March   *God so loved the world* published.

April   Council member Eric Temple loaned his Blüthner grand piano for use in the Great Hall.

May   A confidential report of the Commission appointed by RSCM Council was received (see Appendix 11).

May 19th   Concert in the Great Hall by the Elizabethan Singers conducted by Louis Halsey.

July 5th   A short two-piano recital for students and staff by Sir William Harris and Dr John Dykes Bower.

July 14th   Nigel Coxe gives his third piano recital. The same evening Senior Choristers with MJRH gave a recital of arias and songs.

July 16th	Summer Garden Party at which GHK was welcomed back from his third overseas visit.
Sept term	Michael Brimer is appointed temporary HQ Choirmaster whilst MJRH attends Cambridge University to finish his degree.
	Term started with a full house of students (18 AP and 12 'London').
Sept 13th	Hubert Crook, Chief Commissioner since 1944 died — Memorial Appeal launched.
	GHK was ill around this time, and MJH stood in for him on several occasions. GHK was back to direct a boys' Festival of 250 voices in St Paul's Cathedral on 15th Oct.

1961

Feb	*ECM* Feb 1961 reports that the Goldsmiths Company had pledged £3300 for three years for scholarships to British students to study at AP. The Gilchrist Trust pledged another donation to enable Commonwealth students to travel around England hearing the best choirs.
Mar 24th	The Archbishop of Canterbury (Dr Fisher) conferred a Lambeth DMus on GHK at Lambeth Palace. Addington boys and students sang at the service, which included Stanford in A and *In exitu Israel* by Samuel Wesley.
Mar 27th	At a performance of *Elijah* in the Royal Festival Hall, AP chorister (Graham Madeley) took the role of the 'youth'.
May	The books in the Colles Library on loan from The Hymn Society were made a permanent gift.
June 29th	The Chapel Choir gave a recital in St Michael's, Croydon, with some of the organ students contributing solos.
July 8th	Summer Garden Party: Evensong in the Chapel included S S Wesley's *The Wilderness*.
Summer	The 'Thirty-two Choir' of Bristol University gave a recital in the Great Hall directed by Dr Willis Grant.
Sept 27th	GHK leaves on fourth overseas visit for Japan and Korea, a trip suggested by the former AOC Dr Geoffrey Fisher, who has visited this area and thought that a visit by the Director of the RSCM would be useful. John Dykes Bower again in charge with *ECM* listing him as 'Deputy Director'.
Dec	Piano recital in the Great Hall by Miss Barbara Hill (Mrs Martindale Sidwell).
Dec 19th/20th	Two evenings of Carols Services.
Dec 21st	Departure of Michael Brimer to be Lecturer at the University of Western Australia.

1962

Jan	The affiliation fee rose to £3 UK and £2 Overseas. The previous year's accounts showed a positive bank balance of only £23 at July 31st 1961. RSCM Council

decided that in order to expand the work of the RSCM and replace the late Hubert Crook, an increase was necessary.

Jan 29th   The Archbishop of Canterbury and Mrs Ramsey visited AP.

Feb   *ECM* Feb 1962 reports the gift of books to the library from the late Maurice Frost (1899-1961), hymnologist and Vicar of Deddington. This, now known as the Frost Collection, was collected personally by Leslie Green from Deddington Vicarage.

               Also a gift of paintings of AP by Archbishop Sumner were presented by the Master of the Temple.

Feb   *ECM* Feb 1962 announces a series of lectures to help organists and choirmasters who are preparing for the new Archbishop's Certificate in Church Music inaugurated by the Incorporated Guild of Church Musicians and for which the first examination was in Dec 1961. It was GHK's hope that many RSCM members would enter for this. This Archbishop's Certificate is open to any member of the Anglican Church unlike the Archbishop's Diploma which may only be taken by those who hold the FRCO(CHM).

Mar 1st   Peter White starts as Headquarters Choirmaster.

Mar 8th   Recital by Maurice Bevan (baritone) and Anne Alderson (piano) [also his wife!].

May   An invitation is received from the organisers of the 1963 Anglican Congress to be held in Toronto, to run a UK-style Cathedral Course in Toronto. *ECM* Oct 1962 revealed details of the plans.

May 17th   Concert in the Great Hall by the Elizabethan Singers. Also piano solos that evening by student Michael Beynon.

June 18th   Retirement of Revd Horace Spence, Clerical Commissioner since 1953.

June 21st   Piano recital in the Great Hall by Dr Roy Jesson (RAM).

June 23rd   The College Choir sang Evensong in Westminster Abbey.

June 29th   GHK returns from fourth overseas visit.

July 7th   Summer Party.

Autumn   Prof Arthur Hutchings of Durham University spent three days at AP teaching in the Michaelmas Term.

Sept 13th-16th The Prayer Book Psalter Commission were in residence.

Dec 6th   St Nicolastide Celebrations: Eucharist at AP, Lecture by John Joubert at Cutlers' Hall about 'Church Music Today', Lecture–Demonstration at St Sepulchre's in the evening with illustration sung by Croydon PC Choir and Addington students directed by Peter White.

1963

Jan 1st   *RSCM News* first appeared together with *Promoting Church Music* (both quarterly). The increase in sales of 'other publishers' music now necessitated a leaflet to advertise and review these offerings.

Easter	Three-day residential course for the 60 singers chosen for the 'Cathedral Course' to be held at St James' Cathedral in Toronto, which replaced the usual annual Cathedral Course.
May 15th	*English Church Music* first appeared as an annual 'learned' journal.
May 20th	HM Queen paid official visit to AP. See Chapter 4(I).

1964

	ECM 1964 has a report of the 'Enquiry into the appointment of organists'.
Jan 4th	A reunion was held for those who had visited Canada in 1963 (49 attended).
Feb	*RSCM News-Notes* No. 208 Feb 1964 lists 'What we did in 1963':
	401 visits by Special Commissioners to affiliated choirs.
	17,522 singers, representing 922 choirs, attended 71 festivals organised by the RSCM.
	516 adults attended 27 RSCM short courses at Addington and elsewhere.
	34 One-Day Schools for junior choristers were held.
	822 boys and girls attended 16 local Three-Day Courses.
	441 more choirs became affiliated.
	242 new Personal Members joined.
	25 Half-Day Courses were held.
	16 Representative Conferences and meetings took place.
	7,792 orders for publications or badges were received from affiliated choirs alone.
	635 Written requests for advice were received.
June 14th	Death of Warden Revd George Sage — succeeded by Derek Holman, previously Sub-Warden and Tutor.
July 11th	Summer Party.
July 31st	H Leslie A Green retires as Secretary after 36 years.
Aug 1st	Martin How starts as HQ Commissioner, he lived in the top floor of Golf Cottage.
Aug	LD was examining for ABRSM in Rhodesia and South Africa. On the same trip he visited and held a festival at Port St Louis in Mauritius.
Oct 17th	Choirboys' Festival Evensong in St Paul's directed by Martin How. He travelled 1000 miles to the eleven rehearsals for this.
Dec 6th	Eucharist at St Sepulchre, two talks, the first in Cutlers' Hall Bernard Rose on 'The Interpretation of 16C Church Music' and then, after tea, in St Sepulchre by John Whitworth on 'The Counter-Tenor Voice'.

1965

Jan 1st	Commander A H W Byng appointed Secretary.
Jan 7th	A conference was held at Church House to discuss MJRH's proposed CTS.
Mar 31st	Derek Holman resigns as Warden.

Apr 1st	Roy Massey appointed Warden and Revd Anthony Caesar appointed Chaplain.
July 7th	Choral Festival Service at Royal Albert Hall, attended by HM Queen Elizabeth the Queen Mother and The Archbishop of Canterbury.
July	*PCM* notes that Peter Burton's setting of the Communion Service had been translated into Braille and deposited in the RNIB Library along with other RSCM publications.
Nov 18th	The Cathedral Organists' Association annual conference was held at AP [only 18 were present].
Dec 4th	RSCM Chorister Training Scheme launched along with the Junior St Nicolas/St Cecilia Awards at a public demonstration at the RCM. It was supposed to be held at the RCO in Kensington Gore, but the large numbers who wished to attend forced a change of venue.
Dec 11th	AP was visited by The Organ Club. 47 members signed the visitors' book.

1966

Feb	The CTS caused so many enquiries (900 in 2 months) that MJRH was given a part time Secretary, Mrs M Williamson.
June	Work began on the project to expand AP, twelve new practice rooms and the conversion of the existing practice rooms into rooms for the Publications Department.
July 9th	Summer Party with distribution of honours attended by CMS as part of their 60th birthday celebrations.
Aug 10th-17th	First residential course for (101) girls at St Elphin's School, Darley Dale.

1967

Jan 1st	Mr A W Jackson retired as Bursar after 36 years, and was appointed Publications Manager — Vincent Waterhouse appointed Bursar.
Jan-Feb	GHK leaves on fifth overseas visit.
July 1st	New practice rooms at AP opened by Bishop of Ely (Chairman of Council) at Summer Party.
Aug 13-20	First Summer School on Eastern side of USA.
Nov 15th	New gas boilers were installed costing £2440.
Dec 15th	An Extraordinary General Meeting was held to alter the Memorandum of Association so as to extend full membership of the RSCM to all churches having membership in the World Council of Churches and to the Roman Catholic Church. Before this time any non-Anglican members of the RSCM were known as 'Associated Choirs' rather than 'Affiliated'.

1968

Jan 15th	Martin How appointed Headquarters Choirmaster, Vincent Waterhouse appointed Secretary and Chief Administration Officer.

370

Mar 4th	Kenneth Meekison starts work as Bursar.
Mar 15th	Alec Jackson retires as Publications Manager after 36 years of service.
Mar 16th	One Day Conference between RSCM and 23 Theological College Representatives at AP.
Apr	Vincent Waterhouse becomes Secretary on the retirement of Commander West Byng.
Sept	The smaller of the two big Cedar trees (actually a Deodar) in AP gardens was washed away in a storm.
Oct	Young Membership (under 18) introduced.

1969

Apr 25th	The Mayor of Croydon plants a new 15ft high Cedar (Cedrus Deodara, Himalayan Cedar) tree.
July 5th	Summer Party held at Chislehurst instead of Addington to mark 40th anniversary of the setting up of the College of St Nicolas. The Chairman of Council presented the diplomas and awards, and Evensong was sung on the terrace by the College Choir directed by Martin How. Among the attendees were: Sir Ernest Bullock, Mr H P Chadwyck-Healey, Leslie Green and Mr A W Jackson.
Sept	When the new boilers were installed, the estimate of annual running costs by the South Eastern Gas Board proved to be wildly incorrect by a factor of 100%. A lengthy negotiation failed to get the Gas Board to put the RSCM on a business tariff, but in the end Vincent Waterhouse managed to agree a revised tariff and an £800 refund in respect of the first 18 months of use. VEW wrote in a report to the GPC on 25/9/69: 'A great deal of time has been spent on these negotiations — the inefficiency of the Board is indescribable. After meeting staff at various levels, I feel a certain amount of sympathy with an individual who has to work for an organisation of this type which is bedevilled by frequent changes of policy and even more frequent changes of senior staff.' [Nothing changes!]

1970

| Apr 7th | In the Jerusalem Chamber at Westminster Abbey a press conference launches a £200,000 RSCM Development Appeal. The Appeal Committee was under the Chairmanship of Lord Rupert Nevill. |
| May 21st | Inspection of AP by H M Inspectors from the Department of Education and Science following an application to have the College of St Nicolas recognised as an 'efficient independent establishment of further education.' The Secretary of State for Education subsequently wrote in January 1972 to say the application was approved and was back-dated to 1st Sept 1970. |

June 25th	Festival Service *Jubilate Deo* held in the Albert Hall attended by HM the Queen.
July 23rd	Following a significant bad debt of an Australian student, it was noted in the GPC Minutes 23rd July 1970 that the committee 'viewed the financial position of foreign students with some concern and approved the suggestion that the amount of the deposit paid by overseas students, at the time when their applications are accepted, be increased from £10 to £50.'
Summer	The Chapel was redecorated and the 'necessary wiring for stereo recording apparatus' was installed.
Sept	*PCM* January 1971 reports that the academic year started with 33 students, 10 from the previous year and 23 new students including 4 from USA, two from Australia and two from Canada.
Sept	Senior St Nicolas/St Cecilia Awards are launched.
Sept	Alec Gurd appointed as Appeal Secretary for three years.
Sept 1st	Colin Yorke appointed Resident Choirmaster.
Oct	*PCM* Oct 1970 reports the appointment of Revd Leslie Katin as Chaplain of Addington and Revd Mark Tweedy as Lecturer in Liturgical Studies.
Oct 29th	In a report, GHK noted that during the past year the Addington boys' and students' choirs had sung in St John's, Smith Square; Southwark Cathedral; Chichester Cathedral and regularly in St Michael's, Croydon. The male students had also sung Evensong in St Mary Aldermary; Southwark Cathedral and Salisbury Cathedral.
Autumn	A pedal piano was donated by Mrs Parkes in memory of her late husband Dr George Parkes, RSCM Council Member.
Dec 3rd	A further inspection of AP by HMI.

1971

Jan 1st	GHK awarded CBE in the New Year's Honours list.
Mar/Apr	*CMQ* reports that boys from the AP Choir had taken part in six performances of Covent Garden's production Wagner's *Parsifal*.
May 3rd	The inaugural meeting of The Society of St Nicolas, formed to bring together all past and present members of the College of St Nicolas. There had been a previous St Nicolas Society, started and based in Canterbury but this was wound up in 1957 and the funds transferred to start a new St Nicolas Bursary.
May 22nd	Addington Palace Singers conducted by Colin Yorke perform Fauré's *Requiem*, RVW *Mass in G-minor* and two Holst *Psalms* in Addiscombe Parish Church with the Erato Chamber Orchestra, one of the 'May Concerts'[323].
Aug 21st	Chloe Gordon retired.
Sept 1st	Geoffrey Barber begins as Commissioner for the North (Province of York, Scotland, and the Welsh Dioceses of Bangor and St Asaph). This appointment

---

[323] See p. 56.

was actually made by RSCM Council on 15th Oct 1970. Martin How returns to his old post as Headquarters Commissioner with responsibility for the South (the Province of Canterbury and the southern Welsh dioceses). Both of these posts made possible by the raising of more than half of the £200,000 appeal.

Oct 5th   GHK reports that, although he had been appointed to hold the office of Director until 1978, it had been suggested that the vacant post of Warden might be combined with that of Director and he would be prepared to step down sooner and adopt a role of Commissioner for Overseas. A committee of five members was established to consider the RSCM's future.

Dec 31st   Frederic Waine (Warden) retires [on health grounds].
            Captain Rivers also retires after 17 years of service.

1972

Jan   The Department of Education and Science recognised the College of St Nicolas as an 'efficient independent establishment of further education.'

Jan 27th   The committee considering the future of the RSCM reported to RSCM Council. The contents of the report and the extensive discussion were not minuted.

Feb 25th   An advertisement for the post of Director of the RSCM and Principal of the College of St Nicolas was placed in *The Times* and the *Times Educational Supplement*. There were five applicants of which John Bertalot and Lionel Dakers were interviewed.

Mar 23rd   Piano Recital given by (7) students.

Apr 14th   LD offered the appointment as Director (subject to medical review) with a review of the appointment every third year.

April   *PCM* Apr 1972 GHK announces his intention to retire. He also mentions that he will be in hospital for three weeks in April 'for a final clearing up after my illness.' He would continue to live at AP and RSCM Council asked him to be the first Overseas Commissioner.

Apr   *PCM* Apr 1972 announces the new joint course (actually started Sept 1971) approved by the Department of Education linked to the RAM/RCM/TCL.

June 3rd   AP Summer Party with presentation to Capt Rivers and presentation of RSCM Honorary awards.

June 17th   AP Singers, Boy choristers and Erato Chamber Orchestra conducted by Colin Yorke perform *Messiah* in St Mildred's, Addiscombe. [Another 'May Concert'.]

June 22nd   Following a satisfactory medical report, Council noted that LD had accepted the appointment of Director. At the same meeting GHK's resignation was accepted and he was duly appointed Commissioner for Overseas.

Sept 30th   Croydon and District Choristers' Association held an 'Open Evening' at AP.

Dec 31st   Gerald Knight retires as Director.

1973

Jan	Lionel Dakers starts as new Director of RSCM.
Mar 23rd	Council approves the Director to order a two manual and pedal organ from Peter Collins at a cost of £2478.
April	In *PCM* Apr 1973 LD notes that of 34 students in residence for the 72/73 academic year, they include a Cambridge don on sabbatical and a R/C priest from Leeds.
Apr	AP choristers and students record Series 3 Communion music by John Rutter and Richard Shephard onto a 7-inch LP.
May 24th	First meeting of the Musical Advisory Board at Church House, Westminster. The board was reconvened by LD to 'assist me shape certain aspects of RSCM activity, especially publications.'
May 26th	AP Singers, Boy choristers and Erato Chamber Orchestra conducted by Colin Yorke perform Handel, Elgar and Haydn in St Mildred's, Addiscombe. [Another 'May Concert'.]
May/June	LD began the now established tradition of regional meetings between the Area Representatives and RSCM Senior officers.
June 30th	AP Summer Party with presentation of RSCM Honorary awards.
July 14th-15th	Croydon Flower Society held a Flower Festival in aid of the development appeal. 2600 people attended, recitals were given by Addington students and by the Morley College Chamber Orchestra. Just over £500 was raised.
Oct	*PCM* Oct 1973 p.1 The Bishop of Ely, Chairman of Council, announces that the one year course for intending professional musicians was to be replaced with a comprehensive programme of short courses from the autumn of 1974. From the end of the academic year in July 1974 the title 'College of St Nicolas' would lapse.

1974

Jan	Mrs Dakers appointed Housekeeper of Addington.
Jan	The choristers of Salisbury Cathedral stayed for two days whilst making a recording in London for Decca.
Mar	LD arranges with Dr Watkins Shaw at the RCM for the 'Frost Collection of Hymnody' (over 550 books) to be housed at the RCM on permanent loan, the arrangement to be terminated by either side on giving six months' notice.
Apr	*PCM* Apr 1974 outlines the new role of AP as an education centre.
Apr	Following the Easter residential course for boys, it was announced that next year's course would be, for the first time, for girls. However there is no evidence that a course was held in the following year or in any subsequent years.
May 16th	The Archbishop of Canterbury and Mrs Ramsay came to dinner as guests of the staff and students.

374

June 8th	AP Singers, Boy choristers and Erato Chamber Orchestra conducted by Colin Yorke perform Elgar, Warlock, Leigh and Mozart's *Requiem* in St Mildred's, Addiscombe. [Another 'May Concert'.]
June 22nd	AP Garden Party included a recital by former students. Instead of the usual Evensong there was a Service of Thanksgiving with music from recent RSCM publications. There was also an exhibition of books from the Colles Library.
June 29th	Members of the IAO were entertained by Lionel and Elisabeth Dakers. [LD had just concluded his term as President of the IAO.] Westminster Choir College of Princeton University held a summer course at AP.
July 10th	20th Anniversary of the Dedication of the Chapel, the service attended by serving and former RSCM staff.
July 18th	GHK gives an address in Chapel marking the closure of the College of St Nicolas.
Oct 10th	The retiring RSCM President, the Archbishop of Canterbury and Mrs Ramsey arrived at the Jerusalem Chamber in Westminster Abbey at the end of a Council Meeting. They were thanked for their interest in the work of the RSCM and entertained for luncheon. The next AOC, Dr Coggan, had agreed to be the next President.
Dec 26th	LD visits Rhodesia, Mauritius, Hong Kong and Australia (a 3 week trip).

1975

Jan 1st	John Cooke begins work as Northern Commissioner.
Feb 8th	Service of thanksgiving for life of Sir Sydney Nicholson held at Westminster Abbey, and a wreath laid on his grave in the cloisters. Singers from RSCM affiliated choirs conducted by MJRH. MF played the organ for the service, Stephen Cleobury played before and after. Addresses by both GHK and LD and both the Archbishop of Canterbury (RSCM President) and Bishop of Ely (Chairman of Council) were present together with a congregation of over 2000.
June 18th	Concert by the Addington Palace Singers and Croydon PCC directed by John Ottley and Julian Drewett.
June 28th	AP Summer party and presentation of Diplomas. Also a preview informal recital on the Peter Collins organ by Michael Fleming.
July 2nd	Official Inaugural recital on the new Peter Collins organ by Gillian Weir.
July 18th	Recital on the Peter Collins organ by Francis Jackson.
Sept 20th	MJRH auditions singers at AP for Cathedral Singers and for the 1976 summer courses.
Oct	More than 100 Methodist Church musicians visited AP.
Oct 30th	The finals of the first Rediffusion Choristers Awards in St George's, Hanover Square. Boys who attended RSCM Instructional courses between April and Oct would be 'in the running' and selected by course staff. 28 boys were selected

	for the finals, with three prizes and three runners-up being awarded. See Appendix 6.
Oct 9th	Recital on the Peter Collins organ by Margaret Phillips including a *Toccata* by Alan Ridout specially composed for her and the organ. This remains unpublished.
Nov 6th-8th	Conference of RSCM Area representatives (12 attended).

1976

Apr	*PCM* April 1976 announced a new service — 'Train by Tape' whereby choirs send a cassette tape of themselves recorded singing or rehearsing on one side. The two commissioners, John Cooke and Martin How, would then return the tape with informal comments on the other side.
Apr 10th	The Marriage of LD's daughter, Rachel, took place in Addington Chapel.
May/June	*PCM* July 1976 notes that during these two months, in addition to all the usual courses, there were 25 occasions when the house was used by outside organisations ranging from Young Wives' Groups and Townswomen's Guilds to a meeting of the Royal Institute of British Architects, a concert by the Croydon Youth Orchestra and an evening for The National Trust.
June 26th	Summer Garden Party.
July	*PCM* mentions a new initiative 'Organ Lessons at Addington Palace' under the direction of Allen Ferns. To commence Monday evenings in October.
July 7th	Recital on the Peter Collins organ by Martin Neary.
July 16th	Recital on the Peter Collins organ by Arthur Wills.
July 31st	Council Report notes that over the previous year the external courses had been subsidised to the tune of £9517 in order to keep the fees down, especially for boys and girls. Council was anxious to ensure that such courses are available for all who wish to attend.
Summer	Restoration of the chandelier in the Great Hall, made possible through the generosity of Mrs Marjorie Battis in memory of her son, Raymond Wyckoff, a student at Addington in 1974 who died soon after leaving. She sent $2000. There was also a grant of £500 from Croydon Borough Council and £300 from the GLC. Between them, these covered the total cost of around £2000.
Aug	Redecoration of the dining room made possible by the sales of *The Palace Kitchen* (220 recipes, published at the end of 1974), compiled by Christine Meekison, wife of the Bursar. (By 1980 this had sold 5000 copies.)
Sept 18th	MJRH auditions singers at AP for Cathedral Singers and for the 1977 summer courses.
Oct	LD begins a two-year term as President of the RCO.
Oct 19th	The URC Guild of Church Musicians held their second AGM at Addington.
Nov 18th-20th	Conference of RSCM Area representatives (5 attended).

Late Dec	Some scenes for Michael Caine's film *The Silver Bears* (released Apr 1978) were filmed in the Great Hall.

1977

	Wrought-iron gate to the garden and five water colours in the music room given in memory of Sir William Harris's gifted son-in-law Michael Brockway.
	The Revised CTS with provision for 'ex-trebles' was launched during 1977.
Apr 1st-4th	The choir of St John & St Philip from The Hague in The Netherlands were resident for a choir course, the first of at least four biennial weekends. In the intervening years LD went to tutor them in The Hague.
Apr 21st	The GPC Minutes record that, after agreeing to buy a new Opel Kadett estate car for £2414 for the Southern Commissioner, the chairman should 'write to Mr How stressing that, in view of the heavy increase in the cost of providing and maintaining a car, he must take greater care of the new vehicle than he had of his previous two cars.'
Apr 21st	Another GPC Minute noted that LD had been elected to the Athenaeum Club in London (SHN and GHK were also members). The RSCM paid his joining fee and first year's membership. The Inspector of Taxes had been consulted and 'it appeared likely that he would be allowed the subscription, as use of the club premises could be regarded as essential to the promotion of Mr Dakers' work as Director of the RSCM.'
Apr 26th	Jubilee Dinner held at the Assembly Rooms in York with address by the Archbishop of York.
May 6th-8th	(Jubilee) Flower Festival at AP.
May 18th	The Taskin Harpsichord Trio gave an evening concert.
June 30th	Golden Jubilee Festival of Thanksgiving and Dedication in Albert Hall, attended by HM The Queen Mother and the Archbishop of Canterbury.
July 2nd	50th Anniversary Garden Party at AP, 14 recipients of Jubilee Honours presented by Bishop of Ely, Chairman of Council (who actually retired on June 30th, having served from 1957). The AP Madrigal Group sang under MJRH.
July 7/8th	Flower Festival at AP arranged by the Surrey Flower Arrangers' Association, included displays sent by affiliates in Australia, Canada, Holland, Kenya, Mauritius, Rhodesia, Singapore, South Africa, Norway and USA. 3500 visitors attended.
July	LD disbands boys' choir at Addington.
July	During the annual Summer 'Overseas Course', visitors include the Archbishop of Canterbury and Herbert Howells. Indeed, every Summer, eminent guests came to meet the students, and AOC Coggan and Herbert Howells visited again in Summer of 1980.
Summer	HM The Queen donates a Wedgwood coffee set.

Summer	During re-decoration of the small dining room, once a chapel in Archbishop Benson's time, murals depicting biblical scenes were found. Believed to have been painted by one of the Archbishop's daughters, they were covered up with new wallpaper.
Oct	*PCM* Oct reports that the IAO had presented a table lamp for the dining room as a 50th anniversary gift to the RSCM.
Oct 6th	GPC minutes mention an approach by A R Mowbray to set up a joint publishing company with the RSCM [this would become the Addington Press].
Oct 20th	Jubilee Dinner (the 2nd) held at The Connaught Rooms in London with address by the Archbishop of Canterbury.
Oct 25th	Jane Parker-Smith gives a recital in the Great Hall on the Peter Collins organ.
Nov 9th	(Jubilee) Hymn Singing Festival at St Columba's Church of Scotland in London directed by LD with MJRH at the organ.
Dec 4th	A new ciborium was dedicated by Revd Paul Rose at the St Nicolastide Eucharist in AP Chapel in memory of Canon Horace Spence, Clerical Commissioner from 1953 to 1962.
Dec 10th	Launch (at the RCM) of the Adults Training Scheme 'the brain child of Martin How.' Also a revamp of the original CTS with a new module to help ex-trebles with changing voices devised by Michael Rhodes organist of Stoke-on-Trent PC.

1978

Jan	Martin How visits Australia and NZ where he directs Summer School in Sydney and Nelson.
Jan	John Barrow appointed Assistant Secretary, a new post, though he had been functioning as such for several years.
Jan	Two pieces of furniture were stolen from the Palace and a successful insurance claim was made.
Feb	New arrangements for adjudication of St Nicolas Guild applications came into force.
May	John Cooke made a tour of Ireland and plans were made for an increase in RSCM activity there.
24th May	AP closed and all staff had a coach outing to Wells. The Bishop (Chairman of RSCM Council) and Mrs Bickersteth invited them all to tea at the Bishop's Palace.
June	The GPC minutes reported that the formal publishing agreement between the RSCM and A R Mowbray to bring the Addington Press into being had been signed.
June 24th	AP Summer Party.
June 26th	GHK moved out to a flat in London. The GPC agreed to continue GHK's membership of the Athenaeum as long as he wished to retain his membership.
July 31st	GHK retires as Overseas Commissioner.

Nov 2nd	Launch date of Addington Press.
Nov 25th	Addington Palace Fayre renamed 'St Nicolas Fair'.
Dec 9th	St Nicolastide Eucharist 11.15, sung by the Southern Cathedral Singers directed by MJRH.
Autumn	LD visited Canada, South Africa, Rhodesia and Kenya.

1979

Jan	LD in USA.
Jan 1st	Michael Fleming, Warden, relinquishes this post to Allen Ferns (and his wife) and becomes full time Staff Tutor.
Jan 30th	Presentation ceremony by Mr and Mrs Roland Michener of a bronze bust of Healey Willan, the work of Canadian Sculptor John McCombe Reynolds. This was commissioned through the generosity of Mrs Michener, the wife of the former Governor-General of Canada, who was a pupil of Willan before her marriage.
Mar	An agreement with American publisher Hinshaw Music Inc. was signed permitting Hinshaw to print items from the RSCM catalogue for sale in the USA with 10% commission on sale price going to the RSCM who shared it 50/50 with composers.
May 1st	Bernard Cookman joins the staff part-time as link-man for overseas members.
Jun 23rd	First AP Open Day — Flower arrangements, Ecclesiastical Embroidery, Choir-training demo by MJRH and RSCM publications.
July 10th	Silver Jubilee service in Addington Chapel: CVT returned to celebrate the Eucharist with music sung by the summer overseas course members under Roy Massey. The new RSCM flag flew for the first time that day, six feet square and made by Miss Dorothy Wigg and Mrs Dakers.
Summer	The Faith Press had ceased its printing and publishing activities. The new Addington Press took over and purchased the stock of *The Parish Psalter*.
Sept 16th	Death of GHK, a simple private funeral in AP Chapel. His ashes were buried at St Michael's College, Tenbury, on 29th September at his request[324].
Autumn	*CMQ* January 1980 notes that the first R/C church choir to sing Evensong in the Addington Chapel was that of St Chad, South Norwood.
Oct	*CMQ* Oct mentions the appointment of J Wippell & Co Ltd as 'Robe Makers to the RSCM.'
Oct 11th	Service of thanksgiving in Holy Sepulchre, Holborn, for the life of GHK.
Nov	LD awarded Lambeth DMus.
Dec 8th	St Nicolastide Service (Evensong) sung by Northern Cathedral Singers under John Cooke.

---

[324] His ashes were transported to Tenbury by Lionel Dakers. By chance LD was staying at the Athenaeum Club on the night before his journey to Tenbury, and thought that GHK would be pleased to know that his last night above ground was spent in the club which was a large part of his social life.

1980

Announced in Jan *CMQ* that the Society of St Nicolas (for past students) cannot continue, due to lack of support. It was finally wound up at a meeting in July when it was decided that money remaining in the bank account should be invested with income generated to be used for a Gerald Knight Memorial Prize for organ service music accompaniment.

Jan 1st   New Syllabus for St Nicolas and St Cecilia Awards comes into force.

Jan   *CMQ* announced a Gerald Knight Memorial Fund to improve the Colles Library.

Mar 13th   Council noted that there had been 40 applications for the new post of a third Commissioner. Five candidates were to be interviewed.

Apr   *CMQ* April p.4 notes that the 'Meet, Eat and Sing' events have become very popular in RSCM areas. Martin How has directed 98 of them and sold RSCM publications to the value of £2000 at them.

May   GPC Minutes note that £861 had been donated to the fund set up in memory of GHK. This would be spent on improvements and additions to the Colles Library.

July   *CMQ* announces that the AP Madrigal Society founded by MJRH will be reformed as the Nicholson Singers to sing Evensong in Home Counties Cathedrals about four times a year, under the direction of Michael Fleming. In their first year they sang at Canterbury, Rochester and St Albans cathedrals.

Aug   GPC minutes report that, because of unsatisfactory service to affiliated choirs, the RSCM could no longer recommend Thomas Pratt & Sons with whom there had been business links for over 50 years. A new arrangement had come into force with J Wippell & Co.

Summer   Michael Fleming tours the USA.

Sept   Robert Kennedy was appointed to set up an American office to promote the RSCM. The RSCM in the USA introduced a new membership level *The Friends of the RSCM* at $15 pa.

Sept 1st   Bryan Anderson starts in a new post as Commissioner for the Midlands and South-West. His post was financed for three years by the All Saints Trust. [The All Saints Educational Trust is one of a small group of unique church-based charitable trusts, each established with the proceeds of the sale of teacher training and higher education colleges, in the case of the All Saints Educational Trust, the College of All Saints at Tottenham. The College was closed upon merger with Middlesex Polytechnic (now University) in 1978.]

Oct   The Annual Report announces that the organisation at the areas level is to be improved. Until now it has been according to Diocesan boundaries. This is not always ideal and Council approved a scheme by LD to regroup areas with a greater consideration for access and population.

Nov 27th   LD receives honorary FRCM from the Queen Mother at the RCM. Fellow recipients were Sir George Solti, Robert Tear and Gerald Moore.

Dec 13th/20th Carols in the Great Hall.

1981

Jan 1st	LD in Canada.
Jan 3rd	Evensong in Canterbury Cathedral was the first performance by the Nicholson Singers directed by Michael Fleming. In their first year they sang at Canterbury, Rochester and St Albans cathedrals.
Jan 17th	Piano Trio Concert.
Feb 20th	Concert by the Newstead Singers and other artists.
Mar	The RSCM took delivery of its first computer. The first task was to transfer membership records to this.
Apr	*CMQ* notes that the Gerald Knight Memorial Fund to improve the Colles Library has exceeded £1000 and that Dr Watkins Shaw will be making recommendations to improve and extend the range of material available.
May	The RSCM in America was incorporated as a Not-for-Profit organisation in May 1981 under the laws of New York State with Erik Routley as President (Routley had moved to Princeton University in 1975).
July 18th	The Chairman of RSCM Council, the Bishop of Bath and Wells, held a garden party at the Bishop's Palace attended by 180 RSCM supporters. The event, which featured madrigals, a wind ensemble and cream teas, heralded the formation of a new RSCM Area Committee.
July 21st	A private visit by the Queen Mother was cancelled at the last minute due to her indisposition. She was due to meet the overseas (Commonwealth) students on the summer residential course.
Summer	LD visited South Africa.
Nov	A burglary took place in which five chairs from a set of six were removed from the room called Wellington.
Dec	The Great Cedar sustained grievous damage.

1982

Spring	A GPC Minute in April notes that the cataloguing of the Colles Library was well advanced.
Apr 19th-23rd	Course by the Panel of Monastic Musicians.
May 1st-3rd	Arts and Crafts at Addington, 7000 people attended, 11 craft groups provided displays including wood carving, silverware, glass engraving and early musical instruments. The chef baked 1500 scones and could have done more. After expenses £4500 was raised towards re-decoration of the Great Hall.
July	The Annual Report begins: 'The state of music in churches affiliated to the RSCM is a matter of the greatest interest to the Council and to the Headquarters staff, and a good deal of information comes through the reports made by the three Commissioners following tours of their respective areas, but so far as is known, no-one has attempted a comprehensive survey designed to provide a detailed picture of music in affiliated churches. With the assistance

of Dr Berkeley Hill of Wye College in the University of London, a questionnaire was prepared and distributed to all affiliated churches in April [1980]. Replies are being analysed and a detailed report will be published early in 1983. One of the objects of the survey will be to provide information which will allow the RSCM to plan for the needs of members in the coming years. The Council acknowledges with gratitude the grant from the Ecclesiastical Insurance Office to cover the cost of this survey.'

Aug   Allen and Margaret Ferns retired (earlier than expected but necessitated by her ill health).

Sept 1st   Janette Cooper, formerly DOM at Roedean School in Brighton, takes over from Allen Ferns as Warden. She was already well-known at AP through her popular 'Reluctant Organist' courses which began in 1974.

Sept 1st   A new assistant housekeeper appointed to occupy the flat formerly occupied by Mrs Gordon and Miss Yeoman. This was currently occupied by Michael Fleming, but he agreed to move out of the AP.

Autumn   LD in Canada, New Zealand (1 week) and Australia (7 weeks).

Oct 8th   Death of Erik Routley. He was succeeded as President of RSCM America by Revd John Andrew, Rector of St Thomas' Church in New York.

Nov 20th   At St Michael's, Cornhill, the first Gerald H Knight Memorial Prize was awarded to Adrian Lenthall aged 16, organist of St Mary's in Manuden, Essex.

Dec 18th   Annual Carols in the Great Hall sung directed by MJRH.

1983

Feb 7th-22nd   MJRH visits USA.

Jan-Mar   LD visited seven Theological Colleges to speak to ordinands.

May 1st   LD received the CBE from HM The Queen Mother conferred in the New Year Honours list.

May 13th/14th   Overnight a burglary took place in which a set of chairs from the Great Hall and silver were removed from the Chapel Vestry.

June 28th   The Bishop of Bath and Wells presents the RSCM Honours at a ceremony in AP.

June 29th-July 13th MJRH visits USA.

Summer   LD visits Luxembourg, Belgium, Holland, Gibraltar and the Pacific coast of North America from San Diego to Vancouver.

Aug/Sept   Following the Summer Course for overseas students, the Great Hall and Chapel underwent major renovation over an 8-week period. The Chapel Central windows were removed for restoration and replaced temporarily by a timbered wall. The work was in part funded by a grant from the London Borough of Croydon [the RSCM's Landlord].

Oct 10th-14th   A 'Reluctants' Reunion' course was held for some of the many organists who had passed through Janette Cooper's hands over the years [since her courses began in 1974].

382

Nov 26th	Annual Fair Raffle included a gift from HM The Queen Mother.
Summer	Canon Gwilym Morgan of Manchester Cathedral donated to AP six framed prints including signed work by John Piper and Molewyn Merchant.
No date	The silver chalice, paten and wafer box were stolen from AP Chapel. St Sepulchre loaned replacements.

1984

Jan-Feb	RSCM Membership records were transferred to a computer system provided by Minerva Computer Systems with hardware by Data General. Transfer of accounting records and stock control were added over the next six months. John Barrow took a key role in this IT project and was promoted to Computer Manager from 1st Aug. Roger Butler was a key member of the GPC in ordering and overseeing installation of this system.
Feb 14th	Burglary in Vincent Waterhouse's flat.
Apr 13th	There was another burglary at AP, but on this occasion the van containing the stolen furniture was stopped by police and the thief taken into custody.
Summer	LD visits East and South Africa on a six-week tour.
Oct	A two-day Anglican/Roman Catholic conference was held at AP arranged by RSCM Council.
Oct	A re-organisation of Australian committees was to be undertaken because of the vast distances between centres of population.
	For the first time since 1972, the financial year ended with a deficit (£23,000).

1985

Jan	*CMQ* lists LD's overseas visits for the year — 3 to the USA, 2 to Canada and one each to East Germany and Scandinavia.
Apr 20th	AP hosted the reception for the marriage of Michael Fleming to Anne Abbott which took place in Croydon Parish Church.
Summer	Two altar frontals donated to AP Chapel.
	AP boilers needed replacement. Over half the cost of this was met through a legacy from Miss G R Russell.
July 25th	Organ Recital by Peter Hurford on the Peter Collins Organ as part of the summer Overseas Course.
Autumn	Mr Frederick Shorrocks, a local historian, published a book *Addington Palace: History and Description* (ISBN 854021477) jointly with Vincent Waterhouse who contributed a short chapter about the work of the RSCM.
Oct	The RSCM bought houses for Mr & Mrs Kerrigan and for Mr & Mrs Meekison being partly funded by the sale of 120 Coombe Lane. The Meekisons moved in on 8th November but unfortunately Mr Meekison suffered a coronary thrombosis on 28th Oct and was admitted to Croydon Hospital. He returned to

work in January 1985. The Kerrigans moved into their house in Selsdon on 3rd Dec and subsequently bought it from the RSCM.

1986

Jan 25th	Publications 'Open Day'.
Mar 18th	Peter Carnes, a former SECM chorister at Chislehurst now working for the National Westminster Bank, was seconded to AP for Fundraising and public relations work under a NatWest scheme to assist charities.
July 23rd	Organ Recital by Peter Hurford on the Peter Collins Organ as part of the summer Overseas Course.
Oct 11th	Following the success of the Publications 'Open Day' held in January, this was repeated.

1987 (Diamond Jubilee)

Jan 20-Feb 4th	MJRH in USA.
Apr 28th	Diamond Jubilee Festival Dinner at the Civic Centre, Leeds. Lord Coggan guest speaker.
May 2nd-4th	Open weekend with Arts and Crafts Exhibition.
May 4th	The first outing of the Nicholson Girls' Choir (aged 14-21) singing Evensong in Southwark Cathedral under their founder and director Michael Fleming.
May 6th	Diamond Jubilee Festival Dinner in the Middle Temple Hall, London, with Rt Hon Edward Heath as guest speaker.
May 27th	Celebrity Recital in the Great Hall by John Shirley-Quirk.
June 20th	Garden Party at AP at which the Bishop of Bath and Wells presented the RSCM Hon Awards including a much deserved FRSCM for Leslie Green.
June 26th	'At Home' with the Director and RSCM Staff.
July 2nd	Goodbye lunch-time party for Mary Williamson.
Sept 14th	Celebrity Recital in the Great Hall by the King's Singers.
Sept 27th	A major exterior repair and redecoration of the Palace commenced. Estimate £33,445 but this became £43,000 + VAT by October 1988.
Oct 15th	The gales brought down many trees.
Oct 24th	Publications 'Open Day'.
Oct 31st	The Art of Accompaniment, a practical demonstration by Martin How.
Nov 10th	RSCM staff party (old and present) 100+ people present.
Dec 2nd	Westminster Abbey Evensong sung by the Nicholson Singers under Michael Fleming with MJRH at the organ.
Dec 24th to Jan 4th	AP closed for Christmas and the New Year possibly for the first time. Until this time there were post-Christmas courses.

1988

Mar 17th	At the AGM, the Rt Revd John Bickersteth, Bishop of Bath and Wells, stepped down as Chairman of RSCM Council. He was succeeded by Sir John Margetson KCMG, former British Ambassador in The Hague, and also a former choral scholar at St John's College, Cambridge.
Apr	*CMQ* revamped with Richard Morrison as the new Editor.
July 1st	Party for Billy Rivers.
July 27th	Peter Hurford gave a recital on Collins organ in the Great Hall.

Oct 11th-17th MJRH in USA.

Oct	*CMQ* reviews the changes in Canon B20 mentioned above (Oct 1985) and announces that a 'model contract' for the employment of organists has been jointly devised by the IAO, ISM, RCO, RSCM and the Legal Advisor to General Synod.
Dec	At the end of the month LD retired as Director and the following month he and ED moved to Salisbury.

1989

Feb	With several substantial legacies being invested over recent years, it was noted in the GPC minutes that the net assets of the RSCM had exceeded £1 million for the first time.
Feb 1st	The Summer six-week residential courses for overseas students that began in 1975 was not well attended in 1988, and by the beginning of 1989 it was clear that there was not enough support to run a 1989 course which was duly cancelled.
Mar 1st	Harry Bramma commissioned as Director at a Eucharist in AP Chapel celebrated by the Rt Revd Ronald Bowlby (Bishop of Southwark). Chairman of Council, Sir John Margetson gave an address and the Rt Revd Nigel McCullough (Bishop of Wakefield and RSCM Council Member) performed the commissioning. The organ was played by MJRH who directed a small professional choir.
Apr	'Sing Aloud' scheme launched in *CMQ*, superseding the original Chorister Training Scheme.
June 1st	The Auriol String Quartet give a concert in the Great Hall.
June 22nd	Nigel Clayton gives a piano recital in the Great Hall.
July	The Annual Accounts show a deficit (£11,345) for the sixth year running, on the other hand the balance sheet has grown to pass the £1 million mark for the first time, mostly due to £205,000 of legacy gifts.
July	Negotiations with the Borough of Croydon began to consider a new lease for AP, although this was not due to run out until 2003. The RSCM was seeking to rent out AP to commercial concerns, an enterprise not permitted by the current lease.
July 28th	Peter Hurford gives a recital.

Summer	The winners of the first Annual Harold Smart Competition are announced and published.
October	Richard Morrison relinquishes editorship of *CMQ* to move to *The Times*. Karin Brookes, editor of *Music Teacher* magazine, steps in as editor in the interregnum.
Dec 27th	MJRH leaves for Australia (Summer School in Adelaide) and NZ Summer School returning 23rd Jan.

1990

Jan	Gales uprooted two cedar trees at AP, but the great cedar tree suffered only minor damage. Part of the Director's house was damaged.
April	*CMQ* Editorship taken over by Trevor Ford.
June 13th	Reception at AP to mark the retirement of Vincent Waterhouse.
July 25th	Organ Recital by Peter Hurford in the Great Hall.

1991

Feb 2nd	The first Addington examinations for the new RSCM Young Organist's Certificate.
July 13th	The first RSCM Annual Day of Celebration held at Southwark Cathedral.
June 26th	Organ Recital by Peter Hurford in the Great Hall.
Sept	The first auditions were held for girl choristers to join the RSCM's three Cathedral Singers choirs.
Nov 25th	The first mention of negotiations which had been going on confidentially with Lady Susi Jeans regarding the bequest of her home in Dorking to the RSCM.
Dec 27th	MJRH to South Africa to direct summer schools, returning Jan 13th.

1992

Jan 5th/6th	Burglary and theft of computer equipment. [Security remained a constant problem.]
Jan 25th	Michael Fleming held auditions for a Southern Cathedral Singers Girls' Choir in St Alban's, Holborn.
Mar 28th	Northern Cathedral Singers new Girls Singers sing their first service in St Wilfred's, Harrogate, under their founder John Cooke. Their first cathedral day was 20th July in Wakefield.
June 28th	This date was selected for Britain's first 'National Music Day'. This idea was also taken up internationally as World Music Day on 21st June every year and in later years by the RSCM to promote a 'Music Sunday'.
July	*CMQ* notes that the RSCM runs (or is planning) Organists Training Schemes in Cornwall; Devon; Somerset and South Avon; Bristol and Swindon and Birmingham and is setting up schemes in Wessex and Gloucestershire.

July 8th	Peter Hurford gave an all Bach recital on the Peter Collins organ in the Great Hall. 134 attended.
Nov 10th	A fund-raising Gala Dinner and Concert at the Guildhall, to be attended by the Duchess of Kent. £15,750 raised.
Nov 17th	Two framed panels listing RSCM Directors and Secretaries were unveiled by 89 year old Leslie Green. They were the gift of LG's brother Mr F E W Green. Also present were Messrs. Harry Abbott, Edred Wright, Monty Durston and Vincent Waterhouse – i.e. the surviving three of the RSCM's four Secretaries were present.
Nov 23rd	The GPC recommends to RSCM Council that the RSCM should now give Croydon notice to quit AP.

1993

Jan 1st	From this date all affiliation renewals would be on Jan 1st.
Apr 8th	Michael Fleming retires.
Apr	*CMQ* notes that it is the 10th anniversary of the RSCM Local Training Centre in Egham, Surrey. During this time over 2000 organists, choirmasters and singers have availed themselves of the courses on offer. Run by the RSCM Guildford Diocesan Committee, it is just one example of how RSCM training was gradually and successfully decentralised from Addington.
Apr	*CMQ* prints in full a letter sent by Sir John Margetson, Chairman of Council, to the Archbishops of Canterbury and York, this being a considered response by RSCM Council to the Archbishops' 'In Tune with Heaven' report.
May 19th	Harry Bramma, Sir John Margetson, Chairman of Council, and Peter Wright, publications director, attended a forum held by the Archbishop of Canterbury at Lambeth Palace to discuss important issues affecting Church Music.
May 20th	A Grandfather clock valued at £600-800 was stolen from the staircase.
May 25th	HB reported to council that approximately 1750 persons attended a course at Addington per annum and that he had appointed Gordon Appleton as Regional Director for the North.
July	Confirmation in *CMQ* of the move to Cleveland Lodge. Redundancy notices were issued to all domestic staff except the Housekeeper and Steward.
July 7th	Peter Hurford gave a recital on the Peter Collins organ in the Great Hall. 107 attended.
Sept 1st	Gordon Appleton succeeds John Cooke as Regional Director for the North.
Sept 30th	Llywela Harris retires as Warden.
Oct 18th-22nd	The last Adult residential course at AP. On the penultimate day there was a celebration of the organs of AP. The readings, organ music and plainsong sung in procession from room to room were recorded and issued as an audiotape by PH Music.

Oct	The RSCM launches its now familiar series of publications known as *RSCM Classics*.
Oct 29th-31st	The final junior residential course at AP (a weekend for young organists, directed by Gordon Stewart).

1994

Apr	In *CMQ* HB lists the organs at Addington and invites bids for the four instruments for sale.
Mar 17th	Bryan Anderson reported to Council that during 1993 he had driven around 31,000 miles in his work as Regional Director and had also used public transport.
June 3rd	Launch of 'Sing with the Spirit' appeal to raise £1.5 million with a service at Westminster Abbey.
	Launch of RSCM Foundation Certificate in Church Music Studies.
June 22nd	Peter Hurford gave a recital on the Peter Collins organ in the Great Hall.
July 11th	The bedrooms and kitchen were re-opened and staffed for a trio of Summer courses ending 13th Aug. This was a great success.
Oct 12th	Retirement Dinner for Sir John Margetson, Chairman of Council.

1995

Feb 25th	A repertoire day was held by the RSCM Publishing staff. There were workshops by Martin How and by various publishers. Over 500 people attended and many further applicants were unable to register due to the large numbers.
Mar 31st	On this day the lease with Croydon for AP expired but the Borough of Croydon was happy for the RSCM to remain at AP after this date.
July 10th	The bedrooms and kitchen were re-opened and staffed for two Summer courses.
July	*CMQ* announces that, after a one year pilot at Huddersfield University, further courses have been arranged for the 'Foundation Certificate in Church Music Studies'.
July	HB receives an Honorary Doctorate at Bradford University.
Oct	HB reports in *CMQ* that three of the four organs for disposal have now been sold.
Nov 28th	On this day the General Synod of the Church of England voted by a substantial majority that the RSCM be appointed the official agency for music in the Church of England from April 1st 1996. This was a proposal that came out of *In Tune with Heaven: Report of the Archbishops' Commission on Church Music 1992*.

1996

Jan 6th/7th The successful repertoire day held in Feb 1995 was repeated as a whole weekend.

Jan 20th Tea, a tour of the Palace, Candlelit Dinner with entertainment by the Southern Cathedral Singers.

Feb 17th Reunion of past students at AP, with a tour of the Palace, exhibition of memorabilia of SHN and the College of St Nicolas, Dinner and an impromptu concert.

Mar 2nd Making Music at the Palace — Come and Sing Handel's Four Coronation Anthems with John Wardle, with an intermission for 'Pizzas at the Palace'.

Mar 16th Grand Auction of all goods not going to CL (this was the last advertised 'course'!) with supper included. Charles King was the auctioneer.

Mar 23rd Farewell dinner, with talk by Harry Bramma.

Mar 24th Farewell service at AP, with Nicholson Singers, conductor Michael Fleming and Martin How, organ. All the music before, during and after this service was composed by past and present members of RSCM staff (except for RVW *Te Deum* and the hymn tune 'Nun Danket').

May 29th Royal Event at St James's Palace. Raised over £15,000.

June RSCM moves out of AP to Cleveland Lodge. 36 Pantechnicons, 2000 Pickford crates were used and there were 16 tons of music. It was noted that, due to moving the whole of the reference library, removal costs were now £2000 over budget.

After moving out there were still many leftover items. Of these, twelve beds, blankets, bed linen and towels were sent to Bosnia, a local Croydon charity helping refugees had further items, some furniture was sold at Sotheby's, with the final item being removed on June 25th.

In October 1996 a Heritage Lottery award of £1,153,000 was announced.

Sing with the Spirit

APPEAL NEWS [5]

Goodbye and Hello

Goodbye to Addington Palace

It's going to be a long goodbye because after 40 years at Addington Palace, we know that many members of the **RSCM** would like to have the opportunity of visiting once more. Therefore the **Goodbye to Addington Palace** will take place from January to March 1996. Inside this issue are details of special events being held at the Palace to which all members are invited. In addition members are being given the opportunity to say farewell to the Palace in their own way.

Hello to Cleveland Lodge

Work has now started on the repair and refurbishment of Cleveland Lodge. The picture shows Charles King, our Chief Executive, and Michael Benson helping to carry in the first piece of furniture from Addington Palace although we hope the bulk of the removals will be done through a door rather than a window!

Cleveland Lodge will become the administrative and publishing headquarters of the RSCM with all the office equipment needed to take us into the 21st century. It will also provide us with a permanent home in perpetuity, one that will be easy to maintain at low cost.

Appendix 8. Honorary Awards

Prior to 1963 there were three categories of 'Fellows of the Royal School of Church Music'[325]. These were not honorary awards but a 'working' post, akin to that of School Governor. They met three or four times a year.

(i)   Honorary Fellows (appointed for life)

(ii)   Ordinary Fellows (elected for 7-year terms)

(iii)   Ex officio Fellows:

      The President of the RCO

      The Principal of the RAM

      The Principal of the RCM

      The Organist of Westminster Abbey

      The Organist of St Paul's Cathedral

      The Organist of St George's, Windsor

      The Organist of Canterbury Cathedral

      The Organist of York Minster

It was a condition of Fellowship that the holder be a communicant member of the Church of England, a condition which had, in the pre-Addington years, caused several eminent musicians to decline the invitation to be a Fellow. Between 1936 and 1954 Fellows occasionally moved from one category to another. The appointment of Fellows to the various categories was made at meetings of the Fellows of the College of St Nicolas.

In 1963 RSCM Council took the decision to issue its own diplomas 'because it wishes to show its gratitude to those who have worked untiringly for the cause of good church music and for the RSCM.'[326] This did not contravene the Founder's desire that he did not wish students of the College to receive diplomas at the end of their training, for these new diplomas were to be honorary in recognition of work done in the field of church music rather than earned by passing an examination[327].

Initially there were three diplomas:

FRSCM[328] The initial awarding of a Fellowship was to the 17 existing Fellows in the categories above, together with six others deemed to have made a substantial contribution to church music. These were Dr Herbert Sumsion, Prof Arthur Hutchings, Dr Greenhouse Allt, Mr George Maybee (of Canada), Dr Leo Sowerby (of the USA) and Mr David Willcocks.

Hon RSCM The Honorary Members of the RSCM were 'practising musicians who have contributed to the improvement of music in the Church and have given of their time, energy, knowledge and experience to serving the RSCM in many ways.'[329] The first batch of recipients were Mr Cecil Adams (organist of Dursley Parish Church), Mr C A Bryars (organist

---

[325] From 1936 to 1953 they were titled 'Fellows of the College of St Nicolas'.

[326] *RSCM News* No 2 April 1963.

[327] See Appendix 11, Recommendation 12.

[328] The first non-Anglican FRSCM was awarded to Revd Dr Erik Routley in 1965.

[329] *RSCM News* No 2 April 1963.

of Chesterfield Parish Church and Special Commissioner), Mr Mervyn Byers (organist of St Andrew's Cathedral in Sydney and Special Commissioner), Mr Charles Hutchings (organist of St Peter's Collegiate Church in Wolverhampton and Special Commissioner) and Dr Arthur Pritchard (organist of St John's Wood Church and Special Commissioner).

ARSCM Associate Membership of the RSCM was 'reserved for those who had been students with the RSCM and have begun to make their mark in the world.'[330] Three awards were made in this category in 1963 — to Mr Martin How, Mr Malcolm Cousins (organist of Mansfield Parish Church and Special Commissioner) and Mr Michael Fleming.

The requirement to be a former student of the college had to be dropped when the college closed in 1974.

Honorary Life Member of the RSCM Council also decided to thank a group of people 'Without [whom] the RSCM could not render so effectively the services that it provides for its members'.[331] This was not a diploma and carried no right to use the letters after the recipient's name. The first six elected were all Area Representatives and Secretaries who had given service for more than 20 years. Altogether, between 1963 and 1986, 62 people were so honoured. No more awards were then made and the award was discontinued in 1991.

Except in 1981, 1983 and 1986, no diplomas of any kind were awarded during the period 1978 to 1990 apart from an 'Hon Life' to 77 year old Trudy Hunt of the AP domestic staff in 1985. In 1991, at Southwark Cathedral, Harry Bramma instituted the first of what is now an annual event, that is 'RSCM Celebration Day'. As part of this great occasion, 20 new diplomas were awarded and presented in a separate ceremony[332]. *CMQ* July 1991 announced that:

> 'we are therefore delighted to recognise the work of the following men and women who have made notable contributions to the life of the Church through music. They come from many countries and traditions.'

Whereas in the early years most of the awards were made to musicians with very close RSCM connections, in the later years awards have been to a broader cross section of people and organisations concerned with church music including liturgists, hymn and song writers, organ builders, directors of notable non church choirs, composers and the Taizé community. It has also been a common practice to 'promote' some award holders from ARSCM to FRSCM.

---

[330] *ibid.*
[331] *ibid.*
[332] They are now presented during the service, see p. 236.

The current criteria for making awards, with the total number of recipients since the awards began and correct to 2015 is:

FRSCM (191)

For achievements in church music and/or liturgy of international significance, or for exceptional musical and/or liturgical work within the RSCM.

ARSCM (169)

For achievements in church music and/or liturgy of national significance, or for important musical and/or liturgical work within the RSCM.

Hon RSCM (99)

For exceptional or very significant work that has contributed to the cause of church music and/or liturgy at international or national levels, or within the RSCM, but which is not primarily musical or liturgical.

Certificate of Special Service (136)

First awarded in 2000, this rewards significant administrative work as a voluntary officer or member of staff within the RSCM, or an award for a significant contribution to church music and/or liturgy at a local level.

A full list of the 642[333] holders of these awards from 1946 to 2015 can be found on the RSCM web page www.rscm.com [follow links — 'about us' — 'honorary awards'].

---

[333] The numbers do not appear to add up due to the 'promotion' of some award holders from one category to another.

Appendix 9. ADCM/ACDCM

In the very first SECM *Quarterly News Sheet* in April 1928, Sydney Nicholson noted that 'No 'Degrees' or 'Diplomas' will be issued by the School. Students will be encouraged to present themselves for the choir-training examinations of the Royal College of Organists.' This subject was however re-visited at the 62nd meeting of the Council of the SECM in February 1936 when there was discussion about a diploma or certificate to be awarded 'after a test of musical efficiency and liturgical knowledge' to those who completed courses at the College of St Nicolas. It was decided to consult the President (the Archbishop of Canterbury, Cosmo Lang). Archbishop Lang, after consultation with the Royal College of Organists and his own advisors, reported that he would like to make it the *Archbishop of Canterbury's Diploma in Church Music*. By the summer of 1936 the RCO and SECM had approved the musical syllabus and testing arrangements, and Lambeth Palace had finalised the liturgical syllabus and assessment procedure. The Archbishop issued a press-release on 4th June 1936:

The Archbishop's Diploma in Church Music

In order to emphasise the importance of music in the life and worship of the Church, the Archbishop of Canterbury has decided to institute a diploma in Church Music. Candidates will be required to show a knowledge of all branches of church music and of liturgical subjects, and a necessary preliminary is that they should be Fellows of the Royal College of Organists and have taken the RCO diploma in choir training. The examination will be conducted by the School of English Church Music. Particulars may be obtained from the Secretary, College of St Nicolas, Chislehurst, Kent.

The requirements to enter the examination were stringent, for the candidate had to be an FRCO holding the CHM (Choirmaster) diploma. The following September (1937) it was reported that seven candidates had entered for the examination.

At this first examination in October 1937 the examiners were Dr William Harris for the SECM, Sir Ivor Atkins for the RCO and the Revd Canon J H Crawley for Lambeth Palace[334]. One candidate failed and one did not attend, this being Sydney Campbell, whose subsequent career did not appear to have been held back by not achieving this diploma! The five who passed[335] were Gerald Hocken Knight, Leslie Alfred Lickfold, Charles Henry Phillips, Richard Francis Cutbush and Arthur Morgan Stacey. They received their diplomas from the Archbishop at a special service in Lambeth Palace Chapel on St Nicolas Day, 6th December 1937.

The following year a formal constitution for the diploma was agreed by all three parties and it was requested of the Archbishop that the ACDCM be permanently established. In

---

[334] The three examiners for the ADCM were elected at meetings of the Fellows of the College of St Nicolas.
[335] Biographical information about these musicians can be found in SNCSN.

1938 there were three entrants all of whom passed — John Eric Hunt (blind), Frederick Vernon Curtis and Philip Benjamin Tomblings.

Examinations were suspended during WWII but further examinations were then held in 1947[336], 1949, 1951-1953, 1956-1976 and 1978-1990. The post-war regulations were amended to specify that candidates would be accepted from 'any church which is a member of the World Council of Churches and to members of the Roman Catholic Church.'

At their meeting in June 1957 the Fellows of the College of St Nicolas decided to revise the syllabus. The 'special subject' choice which had previously only contained music up to the end of the 18C was now extended to 1950. The Viva voce examination was replaced by a general paper covering the whole field of church music. Abolition of the 'Viva' enabled overseas candidates to be accepted, and on 28th January 1963 John Boe of St Luke, Evanston, Illinois, a former student at Canterbury, was the first successful ADCM candidate to be examined outside England. There was no practical element to the examination — it was assumed that possession of the FRCO(CHM) had tested these abilities. The examination consists of three written papers:

Part I   Requires an exact knowledge of the substance, history and use of the Book of Common Prayer.

Part II   Is a general paper on Church Music requiring a wide general knowledge of music in worship, church music 1550-1950, plainsong, Anglican chant, Canticles, hymns, anthems and voluntaries.

Part III Special Subject, in which a precise and detailed knowledge is required. The candidate chooses one of six categories. This paper requires musical quotations and the writing of accompaniments and arrangements.

The diploma was formally presented by the AOC at Lambeth Palace when a service was sung by the Addington Chapel Choir. If the presentations were in the summer, then there was usually also a garden party.

Around 1971, when the RSCM policy was to become actively ecumenical, the ADCM changed its title (but kept the initials ADCM) to the 'Archbishops' Diploma in Church Music', dropping 'Canterbury' and moving the apostrophe to imply inclusion of the Roman Catholic Archbishop of Westminster who was made a Vice-President of the RSCM in 1971. The liturgical examiner for the diploma was however still chosen by Lambeth Palace.

The initial high pass rate was not maintained and, in 1967, only one candidate out of eight passed. It was possible to pass the three sections of the exam on separate occasions and so there were many 'resits'. Annual courses were held in Addington to assist candidates in preparation for the exam, with special emphasis on paper-work, church music history and liturgy. In total, 158 individual examinations were held between 1936 and 1990. 72 passed, 76 failed and there were 52 'resits' — indeed one candidate sat on 10 separate occasions without success. There have been no further candidates since 1990 when the successful

---

[336] From this time 'ACDCM' was shortened to 'ADCM'.

candidate was Gordon Busbridge FRCO(CHM), BA, LRAM, ARCM, now DOM at Cheltenham College.

With a minimum requirement of FRCO(CHM), this diploma was really too specialised to ever expect a wide uptake, but this was an era where diplomas were thought to be highly prestigious. Candidates for cathedral organist posts today are generally not judged on the letters after their names, but by their practical work and proven experience.

ADCM Awards 1963, GHK with Michael Smith (L) and Roy Massey (R)

Lambeth Degrees

By virtue of the Ecclesiastical Licences Act 1533, the Archbishop of Canterbury has the power to award degrees. Although these are commonly termed 'Lambeth Degrees', the Archbishop is not a university and the degrees he awards are full degrees of the Realm.

The degrees may be obtained either following an examination or thesis and under the direction of the Archbishop's Examination in Theology, or by the awarding of upper degrees (often, though not always, doctorates) in a range of disciplines to those who have served the Church in a particularly distinguished way and for whom an academic award would be particularly appropriate. It should also be noted that Lambeth Degrees can only be awarded to those who are capable and willing to take the Oath of Allegiance to the Queen[337].

When GHK received his Lambeth D Mus, the *Choristers Leaflet* of June 1961 commented that:

> 'An interesting feature of the ceremony [of presentation] is the way in which the Archbishop 'knocks' the degree into the recipient. The recipient kneels in front of the Archbishop while the Archbishop says 'I hereby make you a Doctor of Music' — or whatever kind of doctorate he is conferring; but on the three words 'Doctor of Music' he gives the person receiving the degree three hearty whacks on the head with a mortar-board which he is holding upside down in his right hand, as if to accent those words. The noise made by the whacks on the afternoon we were there was considerable, but all agreed that the noise made by Dr Knight's head was far more resonant and musical than either of the others we heard!'

Michael Fleming about to receive his Lambeth MA from Archbishop George Carey in 1999

---

[337] Information from the Lambeth Palace Website.

Appendix 10. Principles and Recommendations of the RSCM

'The RSCM does not seek to impose uniformity on its affiliated choirs in matters of detail, but it sets before them certain broad Principles as a guide for their work and offers certain Recommendations for their consideration.'

Principles:

1. A technical standard is requisite for church choirs at least as high as that expected from secular choirs, in:

   (a) Correctness of notes.

   (b) Singing in tune.

   (c) Quality of tone.

   (d) Attack and unanimity.

   (e) Blend and balance of voices.

2. In church choirs, even more than in secular, there is a need for:

   (a) Absolute clearness of words.

   (b) The utterance of the words in responses, psalms and canticles with proper emphasis and without distortion.

3. In the work of a church choir the proper rendering of the simpler parts of the service is of first importance.

4. Those responsible for the choice of the music to be used in church should take every care that it be worthy of its purpose.

5. The choir are responsible leaders of the congregation, whether in 'singing' or 'saying'.

Recommendations

These are not printed here as they were mainly concerned with intoning at Matins, Evensong and Communion, which, for the most part, has little contemporary relevance. What is worth quoting is a statement from the Appendix of the 1957 edition of 'Principles':

PURPOSE AND AIM

Statement of policy by the Council of the Royal School of Church Music, dated 27th Jan 1953.

I   THE ROYAL SCHOOL OF CHURCH MUSIC is established to promote the study, practice and improvement of music and singing in connection with the services of the Church of England and of Churches in communion with the Church of England.

Note: These activities are not confined to the work of choirs but embrace the use of music in worship generally.

It is not required of members that they conform to one pattern of music in their worship. The criterion must be whether the offering is of the highest standard possible in the given circumstances.

II   IT IS THE AIM OF THE RSCM:

(a) to arouse in the Church the desire to achieve the best of which it is capable;

(b) to show how this may be achieved.

In order to succeed in this aim, the RSCM needs:

(1) to secure for its work the support of Bishops and the rest of the Clergy as well as of church musicians, members of choirs and congregations;

(2) to provide advice and practical help for all who are responsible for the music of the services;

(3) to take steps to raise the general level of musical taste and attainment through education of all faithful church people; and

(4) to maintain at headquarters a constant standard of well-ordered worship, to serve as an object-lesson and inspiration to those anxious to learn.

Appendix 11. The 1960 Confidential Report

In July 1958 the RSCM commissioned a confidential report with four major terms of reference:

1) To examine the RSCM, its work, activities and organisation, in relation to Purpose and Aim.

2) To consider in what ways if any the RSCM can be of increased usefulness to the Church.

3) To consider staffing in relation to 1) and 2) above.

4) To report and make recommendations where desirable or necessary on all the above matters upon completion of the enquiry, or at the end of twelve months which ever is the earlier.

The Commission consisted of the Rt Revd E J K Roberts, Bishop of Malmesbury, Dr Dykes Bower, Mr E W Bishop and Mrs Ridley.

They met for 16 whole-day sessions with Mr Bishop as Secretary at Dr Dykes Bower's home at Amen Court. All of the current RSCM officers were interviewed to elucidate their thoughts on the work and organisation of the RSCM.

This report, although its existence is virtually unknown to all but a few, proved to have far reaching consequences for the RSCM. During the early 1960's major changes were made in response to its recommendations — a new structure at area level and at Headquarters, a new aggressive publication strategy, honorary diplomas and a major change in RSCM magazines.

Amongst the many recommendations of the report, a few stand out:

2a   'That in spite of the present shortage of full-course students, care be taken to select only those who are of such a standard as to be capable of benefitting from the training provided at Addington.'[338]

2e   'That the special courses for clergy, ordinands, organists, choirmasters, teachers, readers and choristers, etc. at Addington be steadily developed since there is scope for continual expansion both at Addington and elsewhere to meet the growing and varied musical needs of the Church.'

5   '… give urgent consideration to the development of the RSCM's services to the whole church and in particular -

      (i) to new housing area churches;

      (ii) to country churches where the music is solely or mainly congregational and where congregations are small.

---

[338] This was a splendid ideal but, especially in the later years of full-time students at Addington, it became necessary to fill student places in order to survive financially. A number of students of low ability were admitted whose parents could afford the fees. Ironically the less-able students took longer to achieve or attempt their ARCO and so were in residence for some time.

In the Commission's opinion, the development of the RSCM's work along these lines is most likely to succeed if undertaken through diocesan initiative.

7a   'That the administrative staff at headquarters be:

(i) The Director,

(ii) The Chief Administrative Officer and Secretary,

(iii) The Chief Accountant and Publications Manager.'

7b   'That in addition to these three executive officers there should be:

(iv) the Warden of Addington,

(v) The Clerical Commissioner,

(vi) The Chief Commissioner.'

[At the time of this report these last two posts were vacant.]

7c   This recommendation laid out proposed salaries for the main officers. Allowing for inflation since 1960 these roundly equate to:

Director:	£30,000 including £10,000 for board/residence.
Secretary:	£25,400
Accountant/Publications Manager:	£23,400
Warden:	£20,400 including £10,000 for board/residence.
	Plus an entertainment allowance of £2000
Chief Commissioner:	£26,400 (for a future appointment)

Regarding Choir Correspondents and Representatives the Commission:

'considers that the vital link between the affiliated choir and the RSCM should be the Choir Correspondent since it believes that both in fostering the purpose and aim of the RSCM and in raising funds for its work, the parish is the best unit.

The Commission also considers that the policy of appointing Representatives for each rural deanery, archdeaconry and diocese is likely to result in an increase **nominal** rather than **active** representation. (If all these possible appointments were made, there would be approaching 2000 Representatives in England alone.)'

It was therefore recommended that no more Local Representatives be appointed and that 'as a matter of first importance great care be taken to secure suitable Choir Correspondents.' The Diocesan Representatives were recognised as 'key men in organising the work of the RSCM in the diocese, and for convening meetings of Choir Reps.' They were also encouraged to work closely with the Diocesan Choral Associations and Church Music Committees.

The appointment of further Deanery Clerical Representatives was encouraged in place of Local Clerical Representatives.

10a 'That the production and sale of music, books and other articles be steadily increased. But that care be taken not to lose the goodwill of the music publishers by developing a competitive business, since the RSCM is dependent on them for permission to use copyright material.'

10b 'The Commission further recommends that consideration be given to the free distribution of a popularly edited periodical with the objective of interesting choir members in the many activities of the RSCM and its affiliated choirs, etc.; and as a means of strengthening the link between the affiliated choirs, annual subscribers and the RSCM. And that ENGLISH CHURCH MUSIC either be discontinued or published annually as a learned review...'

Honorary Diplomas

12 After consultation with the Incorporated Society of Musicians, it is recommended:

'That the Constitution of Director and Honorary Fellows adopted by the Council on 21 July 1955, be annulled, and that, in its place, honorary diplomas be granted to Church musicians of distinction, and to others who have rendered outstanding service to the cause of Church music in general or to the RSCM in particular, subject to the right of existing Honorary Fellows to retain their honorary fellowship should they not wish to receive an honorary diploma.

The Commission stresses that the greatest discretion would have to be exercised at all times in awarding such honorary diplomas and particularly when awarding them to persons not already holding some recognised musical qualification.'

Appendix 12. Further Student and Staff memories

Whilst many anecdotes and comments have been incorporated in the chapters above, some more general reminiscences are printed here, including several lengthy offerings.

Paul Spicer (1970/71)

'I went to live at Addington Palace as what we referred to as a 'Londoner'. In other words I was a student at the RCM who just lived at the Palace. In return for this privilege those of us on this ticket would take part in everything we could, singing in choirs, playing for services when required and generally helping out when we were around. We could practise on the various organs, use the practice rooms (some of which had pedal pianos) and of course eat with everyone and use the gracious rooms of the building. The ethos of college life was very much modelled on an Oxbridge college: candlelight for evening meals, staff wearing gowns and so on.

It was a beautiful place to live and in many ways it was an unreal existence. The library was often used for after dinner socialising and I remember smoking cigars and drinking some probably very cheap alcohol and thinking I was very grand with my friends. The gardens were lovely too. The amazing cedar tree at the back of the palace with its ancient branches propped up to prevent their collapse was a memorable feature. The golf course at the front (probably very expensive for members) was the scene of much late-night revelry and on more than one occasion a car being driven over it.

I shared a room called Manners Sutton (named after the Archbishop of Canterbury 1825-1828) with Robert Gower, James Lancelot and Julian Drewett. Robert and James have remained lifelong friends along with Roger Allen who was at Addington with us. James was the genius of the student body whose prodigious keyboard skills we often called upon him to exercise. I remember asking him to transpose Bach's Prelude in A minor up or down a tone (I can't remember which) and he did it at sight, flawlessly. We all learned hugely from two of the Addington staff in particular, Martin How and the late lamented Michael Fleming. What different people, but what remarkable skills they effortlessly demonstrated. Both had (Martin, of course, is happily very much still with us) the kind of organ management skills which made the instrument simply come alive in a way which simply defeated those would say it was an unmusical instrument. Their last verse re-harmonisations of hymns and psalm accompaniments were the stuff of legend and fed our hungry, impressionable minds. How hard we tried to imitate the essence of these skills!

Gerald Knight was the Director of the RSCM to begin with when I arrived. He was a slightly odd character who I found difficult to connect with. I think he bonded better with the students who were full time at the RSCM. Lionel Dakers, when he came, was more approachable but I instinctively felt that he was not such a good musician. We all had much exposure to the young South African Colin Yorke who took many rehearsals and services in which we played or sang. He was enthusiastic, although his constant smoking had a feeling of slight desperation about it. The weekly Evensong at Croydon Parish Church[339] (now Minster) was always a highlight and we enjoyed the cathedral-sized four manual Hill organ which had recently been restored by Harrisons.

I was essentially very happy during my three years there. Student life seemed very staid and respectable compared with the freedom which current university students enjoy. We were a fairly conservative lot even though those who know me now would be amazed by my flared trousers, wide lapels, thick-rimmed Buddy Holly glasses and masses of thick curly hair (almost Afro-like) which I despaired of, but did little in reality to tame. In my final year I became the proud owner of a terribly unreliable VW 'Beetle' and I spent an inordinate amount of time putting floor repairing material in it to stop it leaking. I vividly remember driving back from Durham, near where my parents lived, in a rainstorm and my feet sloshing about in inches of water!

The other students at Addington were a mixed bunch but there were notable exceptions including the urbane Christopher Moore, the extraordinary improviser Nigel Allcoat, Peter Philips who later founded the Tallis Scholars, Duncan Faulkner and Richard Dacey.

One or two things remain vividly in the memory: Robert Gower's sandals. He wore them all day every day (and, some believed, at night as well!). The ritual burning of said sandals was an historic occasion and the cause of no small upset which we fear may have caused permanent psychological damage! The other, rather more seriously, was Michael Fleming asking me to buy the new record (LP) of Howells' *Hymnus Paradisi* which had just been issued (Willcocks with the Bach Choir). I duly went to HMV in Oxford Street and purchased the disc not having any idea what riches were contained therein. I was studying composition with Howells and had been a devotee of his music for years but at that stage knew nothing of this extraordinary choral work. In my corner of Manners Sutton by the windows I had a record player on which I endlessly played English music (Vaughan Williams' *5th Symphony* and *Oxford Elegy* were favourites), but I rapidly added Howells' work to my own collection and so took a further step along the path which led me to writing his biography and much besides about him. I remember Howells ringing me one day on the college public phone which the students used. He simply wanted to change a lesson time. The student who answered it heard a voice say 'It's Dr Howells here, may I speak to Paul Spicer?' in his attractive Gloucestershire burr. The student was speechless in awe of hearing the voice of a musical god in that place (it was, after all, the <u>Royal</u> School of

---

[339] [AH] also remembers the weekly Evensongs: 'Local boys came on certain days for choir training, culminating in weekly Evensongs at Croydon Parish Church [with Colin Yorke]. They formed the treble line for the male RSCM students. Us girls, whether 'Addington' or 'London' students used to attend weekly — another way I learnt so much repertoire just from listening.'

Church Music) and I have never forgotten the beatific look on his face as he came to fetch me to the phone. Little things sometimes create big impressions!'

James Lancelot (1970/71)

'Addington proved the perfect antidote to the city life of London. I shared Manners Sutton with Paul Spicer, Robert Gower and Julian Drewett; three of us have stayed in touch, and the four of us made a happy team with our own particular brand of humour and insanity, even if my copy of Vierne 2 still bears the scars of a water-fight one evening.

London students were expected to join in much of the life of the community, with regular worship in Chapel, choir training lectures from Martin How and Colin Yorke, and (towards the end of the year, for he had been in poor health) tuition from Gerald Knight. I particularly remember a morning in the Empire Room where he and I took opposite grand pianos and played through some of the works of John Stainer for the benefit of the assembled company; music which Gerald then proceeded to trash comprehensively. Jeremy Dibble would not have been impressed! Martin How in particular was generous with his time and gave me much-needed help with choir training. I was always in London at the time of Michael Fleming's plainsong tutorials — very much my loss — but he did give me valuable experience in accompanying at Croydon Parish Church; it was here that I first locked horns with *Stanford in A*.

Addington boasted a weird and wonderful collection of organs, varying from the rather successful multum-in-parvo in the Chapel (I remember Gerald Knight making it sound like a cathedral organ) and the relatively large Harrison in the Robing Room to the noisy 'Classic' organ in the basement and the unspeakable Bevington in the conservatory. My uncle Wyndham Tye had built the organ in the Lecture Room, a Cousans (the family firm)[340]. That room also contained a good grand piano which took many of my hours — I took ARCM in piano performance during the year, and sadly have never had so much time for piano practice since.

Since so many students held church posts which took them away from Addington on Sundays, and since London students were out on weekdays, the liturgical highlight of the week was the 7.30 Communion on Friday mornings. This was made possible only by the rich, sweet tea prepared for us beforehand by the housekeeper, the formidable Mrs Gordon. Even then wakefulness came only gradually during the course of the service. Loyalty forbids me to name the organist who dropped the copy of Jackson in G on to the pedalboard while I was trying to conduct it.

Mention of Mrs Gordon reminds me of other staff; Leslie Katin, the Chaplain; Captain Billy Rivers, with whom to be a passenger in his Rover was, it seemed, to dice with death; Vincent Waterhouse, whom I came to know much better in his later days at the RCO; Harry Blacktin, odd-job man, always ready with a cheery word; and Freddie

---

[340] See 'The Cleverley Organ' Chapter IX.

Waine, the Warden, loveable if not always effectual. 'Isn't this fun, James?', he said to me during a Guy Fawkes party, walking up to me with a lighted firework in each hand. Hesitant though I was in my youth, my advice to him was curt and prompt.

We had our share of jollifications, the ultimate being a ball held during February[341]. Preparations involved not only the laying in of much alcohol but also the inflation of five boxes each containing 144 balloons. Not everyone found my jumping up and down on them outside bedroom doors the following morning as amusing as I did. Among other delights — and many of them had better go with us to our graves — were moped races up and down the drive; two students owned these machines, but since one had a higher top speed than the other there was a certain predictability about the outcome. It seemed amusing to climb on to the Palace roof and play with the fire hose, sometimes to the disadvantage of golfers on the adjacent course; and one day, having discovered a flag bearing the Welsh Dragon, we hoisted it on the flag pole — to my delight it was still flying bravely when I returned from London the following day. I draw a veil over my first visit to the Cricketers, when I was persuaded to down three gin and oranges. The ladies amongst us were all too easily persuaded that the Palace was haunted; a game of 'murder in the dark' came near to producing heart attacks, encompassing as it did the entire building including the basement (what happened to the nameplate from the steam engine Saint Nicholas which lived on the wall down there?)[342].

For all the study and all the fun, there was still time for other pursuits. Afternoons at the RCM were often followed by a stroll across Hyde Park to see what was going on at Paddington station (afternoon tea in the Great Western Hotel was a bargain at five shillings — decimal currency was introduced during the course of the year). Despite copious organ and piano practice I found time to read voraciously — indeed, at no time since have I had the amount of free time that the year yielded. It was possible to enjoy concerts in the RFH; determined to witness Otto Klemperer conducting before it was too late, I splashed out on the one remaining ticket for one of his last concerts — a seat in a box at £2, a huge sum for a student in those days, but never regretted (no cashpoints then; I had an 'arrangement' with a bank in Kensington, where I cashed a cheque for £5 each week). Above all, I made lifelong friendships, and that, along with the preparation I was given for the demands of Cambridge and what lay beyond, is my greatest debt to Addington.'

---

[341] [AH] recalls: 'The students ran a ball at least two years running. These were very successful and Addington Palace was a great place to have such a function.'

[342] When GWR Locomotive 2926 'St Nicholas', built 1907 in Swindon, was scrapped in September 1951, one of the nameplates was acquired by the choir of St Augustine's Church in Swindon who made a gift of it to the RSCM. We have newspaper cuttings of the presentation, but the quality of the photograph does not bear reproduction here. The nameplate was sold off during the RSCM's Dorking years along with Sir Sydney's desk and other items of furniture.

Lionel Sawkins (1958/59)

'During my time at Addington, there were some very memorable musical experiences. One evening, we sang through the choruses of Bach's B-minor Mass, accompanied on 2 pianos by Dr John Dykes Bower and Sir William Harris. On Christmas Day, my fiancée, Maureen and I were the guests of Sir William on the organ screen at St George's, Windsor. In those days there were twin consoles, and Sir William shared the accompaniment to the Christmas Oratorio (Part 1) with his assistant, while Maureen and I turned pages for them! Unforgettable!

At Easter, we were (with some other Australians at Addington, including Ian McKinley and Jim Britton) guests of David Willcocks at Cambridge. Thanks to the Hymns A&M trust, we were lodged in the Blue Boar while spending each day at King's choir practice, then to Evensong. On Easter Day, we attended all services, followed by tea in David Willcocks's apartments and then a private recital by him on the Chapel organ (he must have been exhausted but his hospitality never wavered). The next day, we were at Ely, attending Arthur Wills' boys' practice, and then Evensong. I think that we probably owed all these extraordinary experiences to the initiative of Gerald Knight.

The proximity to London was a great boon to us overseas people. I went to a performance of *Turandot* at the Royal Opera House, to hear Mahler 8 under Jascha Horenstein at the Albert Hall (a work rarely played in those days), and Anna Russell at the Festival Hall when I feared Norman Hurrle was going to suffer a heart attack as he laughed so much. Numerous other concerts at the RFH followed, including organ recitals by GTB, the blind André Marchal (whom I had previously heard in Sydney), and on Sundays, I inevitably went to the Temple Church where the virtuoso organ playing was matched by the extraordinary unanimity and sheer beauty of the choir (it's still like that today). At Croydon Parish Church, we also heard Derek Holman's wonderful choir — the hair stood up on one's neck when his boys sang those stratospheric trios in the Kodály *Missa Brevis*; in the Christmas Oratorio, he paced the work so wonderfully — 'if angels thus did sing' coming hard on the heels of the previous chorus, never to be forgotten.'

Roy Massey writes:

'After graduating[343], I did a Dip Ed in the University's Education Department and during this year decided to attempt the CHM diploma and took advantage of the revision course offered by the RSCM. This was my first acquaintance with Addington Palace and I was bowled over by the building and the wonderfully friendly atmosphere and tone of the place. I also thoroughly enjoyed the course which was taken by a very young Martin How who, I think, had recently been appointed College choirmaster. The Revd Cyril Taylor was the gracious Warden and there was a small choir present, the St Martin's Singers, presided over by a Revd Kennedy-Bell[344] — and George Thalben-Ball listened in an avuncular manner

---

[343] From Birmingham in 1956 with a BMus.
[344] Prebendary W D (k/a K-B or 'Jim') Kennedy-Bell (1915-2001), was also a musician and broadcaster. Despite a long attachment to St Martin-in-the-Fields where he was first a tenor in and then director

to our efforts with the choir. I remember becoming very friendly with a young Michael Fleming, Brian Runnett and Jack Longstaff, a slightly older man, who were also on the course. On the Sunday night, Fleming, Runnett and myself belted down to St Michael's, Croydon, to have a look at their Father Willis organ recently rebuilt by the new firm of N P Mander. Leslie Betteridge[345], the organist who later went on to Bermuda Cathedral, gave us a warm welcome and we all had a play. All four of us were successful in the exam and Michael Fleming was awarded the John Brook Memorial Prize for the highest marks. He attributed this to the fact that the choir had rarely sung any plainsong so he had to do some really basic work with them. This was typical of Michael's modesty which I got to know well my later years, as he was a truly magnificent choirtrainer even in those early days and thoroughly deserved the award.'

Robert Gower (1971)

'I well remember my first evening at Addington, sitting down in the elegance of the candlelit dining room and wondering if all student life could be like this. The College of St Nicolas was surreal indeed — a small number of students, perhaps thirty, from around the world, some there for full time study, others using the place as a base for their courses at one of the London conservatoires. There was a vast range of experience and ability, with those competing for Oxbridge organ scholarships on the one hand and those struggling to acquire basic keyboard skills on the other, representing a need for differentiated learning and teaching with a vengeance.

The community or 'court' — for it had that sort of feeling — was presided over by Dr Gerald Hocken Knight who seemed rather impervious to the liberalising climate of the early seventies. His travels on behalf of the RSCM made him a somewhat irregular presence for his students. If they joked about his perceived propensity for musical austerity (rehearsing ferial responses was a house speciality), then equally, his weekly 10 am Tuesday morning seminars on Church Music History, held in the capacious sitting room of his flat, were a mine of information for his charges who, like Manuel, knew nothing. Using his *Treasury of English Church Music* volumes, GHK shared enthusiasm and precious insight, building foundations for knowledge of the repertoire which we were able to consolidate by browsing and purchasing sheet anthems from the RSCM shop in the basement. The flat was also the venue for those privileged to be invited to play Scrabble. That chance was only afforded to me on a single occasion, when I made the ill-advised error of winning.

The two greatest staff influences on me were Michael Fleming and Martin How. Michael's musicianship oozed consistently. With his genial smile, his flapping of his tie and murmuring (followed by laughter), Michael was adored for his modesty, talent and for his empathy with the young. I learnt so much about accompaniment and organ management

---

(from 1947 to 1995) of the St Martin's Singers, he was also appointed in 1955 to the Temple Church with George Thalben-Ball, serving as Reader there and singing the services for forty years.

[345] Formerly a pupil of Herbert Brewer in Gloucester and after retiring from his day job at Lloyds Bank, Leslie Betteridge (1903-1998) served at Bermuda Cathedral from 1964 to 1979, before a final retirement back to England.

from him, as well as fundamental instrumental technique and repertoire in our lessons. His plainsong lectures and accompaniments were wonderfully crafted, plainsong evensong on a Wednesday afternoon at 3.15 being a highlight of his week. Fr Mark Tweedy came from the Community of the Resurrection in Stepney to take this office. Clothed in his grey habit, with his prominent nose and teeth (would they shatter when he closed his mouth?) and a strained tenor voice produced from the back of the throat, Mark cut a distinctive figure. But his sincerity won over the student body, who were full of admiration for his way of life and humility. Mark loved Bach (pronounced *Baaark*) and would extol his works with a knowledge born of study. He loved his connection with the RSCM and many of us continued to see him after we had left the College (in my case, he was visiting Radley where I worked 15 years on).

Plainsong evensong would be followed by tea in the common room, with Choral Evensong on the radio (a double dose for us students, therefore). At around 5.15 pm, GHK (if he was in residence) would walk through to catch the 5.30 post from the private collection provided for the RSCM offices with a hand-written card for the cathedral organist concerned. I often wondered what was said if the music was not well received.

On a Wednesday evening, Michael Fleming took a car of students to supplement the singers of Croydon's Bach Society. Rehearsals were held in the hall of the Parish Church (where he was organist). I recall the excitement and dynamism of his preparation of Handel's *Dixit Dominus*. These were different times and so, without seatbelts, we would visit a hostelry, where Michael provided drinks before driving us home. On arrival at the Palace entrance, it was not uncommon for the car to leave the drive and take a detour around a few bunkers of the golf course, to the merriment of all.

Martin How resided in the small bungalow to the north east of the Palace. As commissioner, he was often on the road, work-shopping for the RSCM. His home was a mass of music and books and his work was his life. His commitment and energy were (and still are) impressive. A fastidious choir trainer, his logistical organisation of the local children who rehearsed at Addington was as meticulous as his preparation of the music sung and his use of the RSCM chorister training scheme, with all its coloured stickers, gradings and awards. Underpinning this was a wonderful musician, an organist with a rare gift for extemporisation and harmonic invention, whose thrilling last verse accompaniments made such a lasting impression.

The Chaplain in my time (1970-72) was Leslie Katin, brother of concert pianist Peter, who also lived in Croydon. A devoted Anglican priest of a Catholic persuasion, Leslie presided at the weekly 7.30 am Friday Eucharist, at which it was a student tradition to provide a cold bath afterwards to those who failed to rouse themselves to sing. I fear the choral efforts at that time of day lacked certain finesse.

Having Roger Allen (passionate and authoritative as ever on Wagner), Christopher Moore (refined, cultured and knowledgeable in so many areas) and the consummate musician — organist, choral trainer, composer and luxuriant counter-tenor — Paul Spicer (devoted to

Howells, with whom he was then studying composition and to whose work he listened on headphones pretty well each evening) amongst the student body brought lasting personal friendships. James Lancelot, then en-route from Ardingly College to King's College, shared my (non-partitioned) room in my first year, together with Paul and Julian Drewett. James's self-discipline marked him out even then, for he would keep a strict routine whilst we led each other astray. On too many occasions, I fear I tripped over his bed on returning home after late night revelries. We were (I was?) youthfully irresponsible in the 'jolly jape' of re-siting exactly the contents of a room overlooking the golf course on the flat roof over the front porch. From that same roof, we also disgorged the contents of the fire hose onto the unfortunate Colin Yorke, a rather detached young South African choirmaster, whose continual nervousness was not assuaged by chain smoking.

Serious musical intellects at Addington included Peter Phillips (of the Tallis Scholars) and Daniel Leech-Wilkinson (now Professor at King's College, London) who were students in my time, as was the brilliant improviser Nigel Allcoat. The visiting staff too had real strength — academic tuition from the late lamented musicologist Anthony Greening, singing lessons from Norman Platt (artistic director of Kent Opera) and piano lessons from the adorable Noretta Conci, through whom I got to know her foremost pupil Leslie Howard.

For me, these years were absolutely life-changing; inspired by talents greater than mine, I practised and worked as never before, so completing the majority of my diploma work before entering university. I was able to gain experience as organist of St Matthew's, East Croydon, being in post in both the old church opposite East Croydon station and in the replacement building in a nearby residential area, with its brand new two manual Mander classical organ opened by Peter Hurford — as much a musical deity to students then as now. External outings by the student choir — singing Sydney Nicholson's elegant Propers in St Sepulchre's Holborn for the annual feast day service for St Nicolas at the start of December or providing an anthem in Lambeth Palace chapel for the Archbishop's conferment of diplomas — live vividly in the memory.

In recalling my two years at Addington, I have an immense amount for which to be grateful: these were carefree, happy times before facing the realities of a rather crueller world.'

Anita Banbury (1963-66)

'I was a 'London' student, i.e. I lodged at Addington, travelled up to town for classes, and loved coming back to fresh air. The air got fresher at each stage — Bakerloo (no Victoria Line in those days) the deepest part of the journey; Circle or District line (nearer the surface) delivered me to Victoria where we could see daylight once more! Train to East Croydon, then the 130 (I think it was) to the bottom of the drive.

Being able to practise on the organs; use the library; sing services (the women were all sopranos); mix with Church Musicians from all over the world and live in great comfort was a wonderful experience. The proportion of men / women [30/5] was also a particular learning curve.

410

I had my 21st in the Colles Library... party involving many residents.

Giving my residential address to (for example) the local music shop in Marylebone was fun. 'Addington Palace' I would say (so obviously a student and wearing my RAM scarf). 'Addington Palace' was written down. Things usually arrived!

The surroundings were gracious... how many students sat doing harmony with a view of the golf course and fountain out the window? The people were so friendly and the company always congenial. I consider I was extremely fortunate to have had the 'Addington experience.' I may say that writing these reminiscences has inevitably brought a smile to my face.'

James Burchill (1960-62)

'I remember one Monday morning after playing for Morning Prayer I was waiting with the rest of the students in the rehearsal room for our first class when Gerald Knight came in and, without mentioning any names, made it quite clear that I had played 'St Stephen' much too fast. While I am certainly not trying to claim any credit for this I have observed that English organists now play hymns much faster than they did fifty years ago; I remember last hearing a gathering note some years ago at a conference in England attended mainly by North Americans: many of the verses of the hymns began as a two-part round with the visitors starting with the organ and the locals coming in a beat later.'

'Toward the end of my time at Addington I had the honour of being asked to play a service at Westminster Abbey which was sung by the College choir. In preparation for this, Sir William McKie allowed me to join him in the organ loft for a service. One of the points that he made was that in Westminster Abbey the organist had to play ahead of the choir in order that it would sound together; I realised that this must have been second nature for Sir William when I heard him accompany a choir in a much smaller church — I felt sorry for the choir director who clearly couldn't bring himself to say 'Um, Sir William, um, we seem to have a problem ...''

Ian McKinley (1958/59)

'My singing teacher, Robert Poole, 'discovered' that I had a good voice. As a result, I had a lot of solo baritone work, especially enjoyable in excursions to such places as Chichester Cathedral and Lambeth Palace. I became keen to hear professionally-performed music in London, and every weekend saw me at the Festival Hall or elsewhere, where I heard magnificent performances by the likes of Fischer-Dieskau. A masterclass by Lottie Lehmann was an unforgettable experience.

In a wonderful experience to remember, an American lady visitor was so impressed that she paid the expenses for the overseas students to spend Easter weekend with the choir of King's College, Cambridge, and to stay at the 'Blue Boar.' How marvellous was all that!'

John Morehen (1960/61)

'On reflection, the year was slightly incestuous, and one needed to get out of the place from time to time to maintain one's sense of reality. But it was a year on which I look back with much pleasure. Most of my fellow students were from abroad, and some of them — such as Barry Smith, Foster Diehl and David Marsden — had fine careers in South Africa, the USA and Canada. Many of the friendships I made there have endured to this day.'

Peter Phillips (1972)

'I was only there for two terms — the spring and summer of 1972 — before going up to Oxford as Organ Scholar of St John's... The general memory I have now was that the atmosphere was rather claustrophobic, I was there because I couldn't really play the organ despite my scholarship and, despite John's [Morehen] best efforts, never did learn to. I easily failed the ARCO.'

However he goes on to say:

'John Morehen and Martin changed my life for the better; the other teachers made little impression... 1However the in-house choir provided an opportunity which I grasped eagerly, on one occasion making the entire college get up ten minutes earlier than the already very early start to sing Eucharist before breakfast. I thought the music I had chosen would need extra time (Victoria's *Missa O quam gloriosum* was the ordinary, I forget what the anthem was). I even begged Martin to sing tenor, which he did, though he asked to be relieved of it! He said quite rightly that we didn't need the extra time, and I had lots of tenors already. I was not so popular at the breakfast which followed. The first Tallis Scholars concert followed in Oxford only sixteen months after I left Addington Palace, so the education I got there clearly forwarded my ambitions, even though choir conducting was not the primary purpose of my being there.'

Father Anthony Cridland (1969-1971)

'I was the second Roman Catholic Priest to be sent there [AP]. In 1968 Fr Michael Hennesy, a Redemptorist Priest had been sent there. He was in his second year when I joined him in 1969. We had both been sent because we Catholics were adjusting to celebrating the Mass in English.

I was a student at Addington Palace for two years. It was well run. I enjoyed my time there. My most amusing memory concerns the Grand Piano in the main hall. It belonged to Dr Gerald Knight. Whenever he left to pay visits as Head of The RSCM, especially if he was going overseas, an impromptu concert would take place in the main hall using his piano. It seemed this always happened almost as soon as his plane took off.

My two years at Addington Palace gave me an opportunity to improve my musical skills and to get to know a lot about the Anglican Musical Tradition and major repertoire. At the start of my second year I became the choir master at our seminary near Guildford where I had a chance to develop my conducting skills. The knowledge acquired at that time has stood me in good stead ever since.

As I sit here recalling my life at Addington Palace, there are one or two of its strengths I would like to mention. The tradition of singing Evensong every day gave us students the opportunity to gain experience that was second to none. On a completely different plain, the food and all the domestic arrangements were excellent. The candle light dinners every evening created an atmosphere that did everyone good.

I remember that I found Martin How's boys' choir excellent. I remember Michael Fleming, my organ tutor with affection because I realised he accepted where each one of us was musically and built on our skills. Two of the visiting professors come to mind as well, Norman Platt, who taught me things about the human voice that still stand me in good stead 40 years later and my piano teacher, whose name I have forgotten. I simply remember her as a very nice Italian Lady, who had won Moscow's prize for the best pianist several years before and who taught me valuable lessons about performance.

I remember really enjoying our visit to sing in Salisbury Cathedral, the Festival in the Albert Hall, which the Queen came to, the concert we gave in The Anglican Parish Church in Addiscombe and the annual Ball in my first year in the main hall at Addington.

During my years of priestly ministry I have done many things. All through these 45 years the knowledge I gained at the RSCM of music, musicians and their ways has been invaluable. Over the years I have run choirs myself but for most of the time I have recruited others, sometimes musical virgins, to do so. My ability to understand musicians has served me well. Over the first six months of my fourteen years of ministry in Peckham we only had one Mass with hymns. By the time I left we had a Traditional Choir, an absolutely excellent Folk Choir and an African Choir of Ghanaians. All three choirs sang every week. They helped our weekly congregation to grow from 300 to 800 and were a great joy.'

Robert Smith (1961-63) recounts the following anecdote concerning a wedding at Lambeth Palace, at which the College Choir had been asked to perform.

'...[Our] choirmaster, Michael Brimer, after checking we were all brushed up and resplendent, gave the order to proceed from our west end robing vestry, at exactly the same moment the archbishop's procession started out from the east end vestry. Two processions approached each other from opposite ends meeting in the very middle of Lambeth Palace Chapel. Fortunately our leading choirboys had the grace and presence of mind to withdraw deferentially to the north followed by the rest of us, as archbishop and regalia glided by. We were then able to close ranks and proceed in as dignified a manner as previously. Chaos reigned at the psalm, though, when it was discovered the pointing in the beautifully-printed order of service was markedly different from that in our Parish Psalters.

John Morehen struck up Mendelssohn's Wedding March with his customary panache as the wedding party moved gracefully to the archbishop's vestry for the register signing, then realising his error performed a masterly improvised seamless parade of composers' styles from Mendelssohn via Spohr to S S Wesley, to introduce the motet.'

He goes on to recall the following: 'There was a famous electricity sub-station debacle which blacked out a huge area of south east England in 1961 or 62, during one of our late Evensongs. We had reached the Gloria of Howells' *Collegium Regale* Magnificat, when all lights were suddenly extinguished. The organ died a few seconds later, and as the choir gradually did likewise, the lone brave voice of choirmaster Michael Brimer continued from memory to the Amen. Warden Revd George Sage then announced solemnly 'We will say the rest of the office.' Candles were hurriedly put into alternative use, including one from the altar conveyed heroically by Revd Horace Spence who kindly offered it to some Cantoris sopranos. Barry Smith claims to have heard his wife Margery's indignant Irish Whispered riposte (lower pitched than Horace's) 'Not them you fool! ... US!'

For my first English Christmas, Peter Partridge and I were two indescribably lucky 'Commonwealth' students nominated by Revd George Sage to be guests at Allan Wicks' home at Canterbury. Allan had us in cassock and surplice and injected into the choir before we could breathe in! This was my first visit to Canterbury and I was — and remain — lost for words to describe the Cathedral's overwhelming effect on us both. We were equally guests of the choir, joining in wonderful walks in the glorious Kentish countryside. Allan graciously had me back for the following two Easters and Christmas. At this second Christmas, when it came to the Feast of St Thomas of Canterbury four days after Christmas, it had been and probably remains the custom for the final voluntary at Evensong to be the Bach 'Great' G minor Fantasia and Fugue. Of course I had heard it the previous Christmas, but now, out of the blue, Allan invited me to play it! I was astounded but of course accepted this considerable challenge. The famous Willis stretches away along four bays of the South Quire Triforium, each division with its individual time delay. I struggled grimly to a triumphant ending, exhausted after this huge test of nerve! Allan also rang me one day at Addington, inviting me over to join the expanded choir for a Vaughan Williams G minor Mass performance, again a most memorable event.

We all loved the fine little Chapel Harrison. A former bass at Sydney Cathedral used to enthuse over this 'little cathedral organ.' None of us was used to a Contra Fagotto and I always felt poor Horace and Margery Spence earned the George Cross for their daily endurance of endless hours of Full Swell floating in from the adjacent chapel! I am still proud of two musical uses I found for the unusual Great to Swell coupler. In the Stanford in G Magnificat I began with Swell 8' and 4', with Great Clarabella uncoupled for the spinning wheel obligato. At 'He hath shewed strength' the left hand is required to jump from Swell onto the prepared coupled Great — at Addington already in use for the uncoupled obligato! This was the point for drawing Great to Swell, with both hands remaining where they were! In preludes and fugues for example it is common to alternate between Great and Positiv, and on the Addington Harrison one might begin and end on the Swell with flues, Octave, Unison Off and Great to Swell with Great 8' and 4', then jump down to the uncoupled Great for episodes. For extra strength at the end cancel Unison off!

Canadian John Goss was a direct descendant of his illustrious namesake. One weekend he felt obliged to visit some relatives deeper into the Surrey countryside who seem to have been members of an extreme evangelical sect and were out to 'save' him. He arrived back at Addington mentally and nervously totally exhausted!

I gained ARCO, FRCO and (CHM) in 1962, my second year, finally managing the Durham BMus in 1967, four years after leaving Addington where Derek Holman had given me expert tuition. In September '62 I became Head Student by default — I had already done three years' school teaching so I was the eldest left. Chris Phelps described me as the vaguest HS ever — never knew what was happening!

I had become Sub-organist at St Bride's, Fleet Street for my last 18 months at Addington, then accepted the post of organist/choirmaster at Halifax Parish Church Yorks. In my two years I had built the choir from 6 trebles to 23 when St Bride's invited me back to be Director of Music where I remained for 6 1/2 years. I followed this with seven years at the fine 1902 Ninian Comper church of St Cyprian, Clarence Gate, in Sir John Betjeman's favourite church, described by Jonathan Clancey in his excellent, much treasured little book *John Betjeman on Trains* as 'a few piston strokes from Marylebone Station'! In the same period I taught organ and general musicianship at London's Guildhall. I played recitals at Coventry Cathedral, New College Oxford, Jesus College Cambridge, Pershore Abbey, All Saints' Margaret Street, St Michael's Cornhill etc. I married a former organ student Susan Styles who is now married to Nicolas Kynaston.

In September 1967 I was appointed to a class music teaching position at Chiswick Grammar School, W4. I [then] discontinued class teaching, and from 1973 taught individual organ and piano lessons first at The Mall (independent boys') Prep School, Twickenham. In 1981 I returned to Australia to St Thomas', North Sydney, am now remarried and back at my previous job at famous Australian Victorian-Gothic-Revival architect Edmund Blackett's magnum opus: Goulburn (NSW) Anglican Cathedral with a glorious 1884 Forster and Andrews organ to match! [I taught] at a number of independent girls' schools, mainly in Sydney, from which I have now retired.'

Revd Michael Smith (1955/56)

'My connections with RSCM began in around 1954 when I was living and at school in Berkhamsted — where Horace Spence was the Rector. Horace of course became Clerical Commissioner of the RSCM and was well connected to its leading lights and introduced me and Peter White (Organ Scholar of St John's, Cambridge and Organist of Leicester Cathedral) to RSCM by enrolling us in the 1954 Summer School.

When in 1955 I had a year to work out before going up to Cambridge (I was organ scholar of Queens', Cambridge, from 1956-59) I had the benefit of the Hymns Ancient & Modern Organ Scholarship at Addington.

So in September 1955 I left home to spend a year with the RSCM. I remember the surprise with which I discovered Addington — bigger than anything I had known before — and grander too.

Cyril Taylor was the Warden — aided on the domestic front by his wife Audrey — and they kept a very tight but friendly ship — I suspect that by today's standards we were all of us really spoilt.

The house was not of course designed for teenage students. I slept in a grand room called Manners-Sutton (the rooms were named after former archbishops) and I remember particularly the en-suite bathroom where plumbing and drainage was managed by heavy and elaborate brass fittings that would not have been out of place in the Ritz.

The residents were headed of course by Gerald Knight who resided when not on overseas tours and Hubert Crook too from time to time. Captain Rivers and Leslie Green kept the office alive with a wonderful secretary [Dorothy Yorke]. Teaching was facilitated by Martin How, Derek Holman, E H Warrell (wonderful plainsong sessions), Sidney Campbell, William Harris — and of course the Warden. We were very fortunate to be close to London and were given opportunities to experience much of the scene there — and to be involved with Sidney in Southwark Cathedral. It was when Sidney moved from Southwark to Canterbury that William Harris took over some of his teaching. Organ practice was challenging — so many students and just two organs — supplemented by the pedal pianos in the basement!

Students of my day were led by David Gatward — senior student. Others I remember include Michael Holman — with whom I later worked at Uppingham, Peter White, Derek Ferris — a brilliant organist who moved I think to the USA, Allan Sever — an American with a splendid keyboard technique and Morgan Simmons — another American whose feet never became at home on the pedalboard! Then there was Bek Lim from Singapore and David Leigh from Hong Kong where his father was an Archdeacon, whose family had built a well-known Chinese church in Kowloon City. I visited David on a number of occasions in Hong Kong: he was an ordained priest, in charge of the church that his father had built, much respected among the Chinese speakers and working well over the age of 80 because they needed him: he had produced a new Hymn Book for the Chinese Church. Michael King came from Grahamstown [South Africa] and provided a link to yet another part of the Anglican Communion — with Michael Brimer from Cape Town. Bill Pierce was from Sydney and a very down-to-earth Australian. From England we had a splendid Devonian Stuart Smith and of course David Parkes who later was ordained — and died far too young and Vivienne Bowkley — a splendid lady from Malvern.

I remember Saturday afternoons — spending many an afternoon playing the Chapel organ for a visiting choir — lots of *Wood in D* and *Wood in E-flat*!

I remember evenings of entertainment and education after Dinner: Gerald and Hubert playing *Marigold*! William Harris and Gerald playing duets too... these 'oldie' musicians were immensely gifted and such an inspiration to us.

Addington was a great place. It sounds frightfully precious in modern thinking — but it wasn't. It was a good, down-to-earth, foundation in the A to Z of church music that was ideal for the day. We probably weren't too adventurous — but this was the 1950's and the greatest excitement was to look for the girls who were alleged to exist in the aptly-named Feather Bed Lane. I never found them!'

Michael Bailey (1960-63) recalls some moments of humour:

'All students sang Services in the beautiful Chapel of St Nicolas. For many of us it was often challenging to sustain an appropriate respectful and reverent disposition.

1. During one Service in the Autumn Term, we sang *I saw the Lord* (Stainer). A short while prior to this, Mrs Gordon, the housekeeper and a keen gardener, had lit a large bonfire of Autumnal and combustible leaves. Unfortunately a window had been left open, and a lively breeze was blowing towards the Chapel. You can imagine the ensuing and serious problem when attempting to sing the repeated imitation: 'The house was fill-ed with smoke ... The house was fill-ed with smoke ... The house ... ' A Divine intervention?

2. Hooi Hin Kiong (Richard Hooi), a newsreader from Kuala Lumpur with a fine natural baritone voice, came to the RSCM as a mature student to study singing with Mr Poole. Richard had great difficulty with English when he first arrived and on one occasion, the choir had equally great difficulty in retaining solemn composure when he attempted to read the first lesson. He started well enough. 'Here beginneth the first lesson'. Then, after many pauses and futile attempts at pronouncing 'Ecclesiasticus — Chapter3', he followed up with 'werses eleven to one.' We always looked forward to Richard singing the Nunc Dimittis in *Stanford in G*, when he would embellish it with wondrous and patently self-indulgent glissandos. Couldn't stop him! Stanford would have done!

3. We always took it in turns to read the lessons, accompany and conduct the choirs. On one occasion John Gadsden, another mature student, was playing the voluntary on the lovely Harrison organ. In those days, organs were by no means as well equipped to deal with registration changes as their more modern counterparts. To compensate for this, John had become adept at adding or reducing stops with whichever part of his body was available at the time — usually his feet or teeth. Unfortunately, on this occasion as the choir recessed, his dentures failed him in spectacular fashion and he loudly uttered his usual one syllable expletive which cannot be printed here. Suffice to say, it rhymed with 'affidavit.' We had great difficulty pretending to be deaf!

4. One or two were able to afford old bangers (of the motor car variety; we were then innocent of other varieties), and it was fun to race from the corner chalet (the abode of Derek Holman) to the end of the drive. The drive was wide enough to race at the start but, soon after the Chapel it narrowed dangerously between the two tall trees and uncomfortably near to the first green of Addington Palace Golf Course. Much screeching of ancient brakes would therefore generally ensue, resulting in complaints from enraged golfers on the green. Most of them would have missed anyway; but it is indeed said by some that the enragement of golfers was one of the main reasons as to why the RSCM had to leave Addington Palace[346].

5. Language could sometimes be a problem, even at the RSCM. Jim Briton, a mature student from Australia, was rather concerned and perplexed when a young lady assistant in

---

[346] Not, of course, true!

the offices down below seemed startled when he called in the college shop and asked for some durex. Durex was then Sellotape in Oz, where he came from.

6. A young American, Craig Smith, bought a very old Jaguar to remind him of his very old Cadillac back home. It smoked enormously (as he did), and would often break down. It spent most of its life on tow.

7. Mrs Gordon the greatly admired housekeeper, and 'bonfiring pioneer', was certainly a force to be reckoned with; from the lowliest student to the most elevated and exalted of the staff. She took no prisoners from either. They don't make them like her anymore.

8. Whenever there was a fall of snow, we would be amused to see Campbell Hughes, a keen fan of Gillian Weir, carrying that very lady down the drive to catch the 130 bus, to keep her dry for her journey to London. No mean feat. Would and could he still do that today? ... and would she let him?

9. We all looked forward to the new weekly music list posted in the Common Room by the formidable and proud Dorothy Yorke, the Warden's secretary. On one occasion, 'Panis Angelicus' was incorrectly spelt [as 'Pan is Angelicus.' We were all most intrigued. Could such an item possibly exist? What did Cesar Franck know that we didn't? It only happened once.

10. The Reverend and Mrs Horace Spence were a lovely couple who lived on the other side of the Chapel. They were extremely generous and kind to all the students and staff. They would occasionally offer a lift in their car. There are many stories about their driving skills, which were variable. They were known and feared by most local drivers in the South East. Horace was inclined to drive slowly, whilst Marjory favoured much higher speeds and would therefore be constantly urging him to overtake. Horace did this once, under the usual duress, not realising that the vehicle in front was under tow. 'Get back, Horace, you fool!' yelled Mrs Spence. Poor Horace, it was always his fault.

11. The extravert Nicholas Zelle (a young student) bought an old Austin Seven (yellow with a black top). To celebrate the end of one particular term, it was pushed late at night through the main doors of the palace (the perpetrators respected the building far too much to drive it in), and parked in front of the huge fireplace in the Great Hall[347]. I was accused of being the ringleader of this prank, but it wasn't me! Had I been the ringleader, I would have made a proper job of it and got the car up on the roof somehow.'

Michael Bailey also recalled that 'Many fine people worked in the offices. All shared lunch in the main dining room during weekdays. A real family atmosphere prevailed – almost ALL the time!' and he remembered Scrabble sessions with Dr Knight and jogging with Martin How and others around the golf course estate.

---

[347] Other students mention the car ending up in the Great Hall, but the photographs on pp. 72/73 confirm that the car only reached the Common Room.

418

Tim Schofield (1972/73)

'It was a very intense, inward-looking place in some ways for an 18 year old, but in my time there, at least, this was more than compensated for by the friendships made and the quality of the teaching staff. I was taught harmony and counterpoint by Anthony Greening who was inspiring, rigorous and quite mad (on the way back from the pub one night in his old Morris Minor he drove down the wrong side of the dual carriageway quite deliberately. I wasn't in the car but Richard Dacey was and it scared the life out of someone who wasn't scared by much). John Morehen taught me the organ and again brought great intellectual rigour and humour to all we did. Noretta Conci-Leech taught me the piano and was wonderful as a person and a teacher (she herself had studied with Arturo Benedetti Michelangeli).

For me the daily round of worship in the beautiful chapel made a lasting impact and was probably life-changing, although I didn't know it at the time. It almost certainly prepared the way for my call to ordination.

One of the other lasting things Addington left me with was the quest for excellence in all things. Working with people like Simon Lindley and those mentioned earlier meant that there was a culture that frowned on second-best. We learnt a huge amount from Simon Lindley about choir training, often delivered with un-PC comments such as 'given your lack of rhythm I pity your future wives.''

One practical advantage of AP for the 'London' students is remembered by **Antonia Harman** (1970-74):

'I lived at Addington with its wonderful wing of practice rooms. While all my friends had limits to practising in their 'digs', I never did; we could practise any hour of the day or night without disturbing anyone.'

She also comments:

'The ratio between girls and boys was about 1:6 so us girls had a wonderful time and were mostly spoilt, especially Monday evenings after the formal dinner, when we usually went out to the pub. There was one famous pub that had about forty varieties of homemade wine. The damson was the most well liked and I still like damsons to this day! One student who loved **all** the girls was Jeryl Taylor, a blind student from Canada. We would all scatter when we heard the tap, tap, tap of his stick and he particularly liked Christine Asher, and, in his Canadian drawl, he would bellow out 'Christine (Asher) the smasher'. Everyone knew when Jeryl was around. He returned to Canada and we heard that he did eventually get married so we were all very happy for him! Most of us girls ended up having a boyfriend(s) and several, like myself, resulted in marriage.'

Attacks of mirth in Chapel have been mentioned above by [MB] and are also remembered by [AA]:

'The chapel as well as being the centre of activity was, because of the intimate nature of the space, the place where any mishaps would result in uncontrollable giggles. Many the times when Michael Fleming would disappear behind a *Manual of Plainsong* which did little to provide cover. Afterwards Michael would, of course, come out with something like 'too much, too much!' with hand on tie and heart.'

He goes on:

'Another strong recollection was the evenings when one returned from 'The White Bear' or the 'Sandrock' and someone, often Roy Massey, Michael, Martin or Gerald, would be playing the piano in the Great Hall lit only by those dim standard lamps with their treacherous wires strung across the deeply polished floor. You became conscious of a small audience of students draped on a sofa or chair soaking up the atmosphere. And, of course, that was the great charisma about the place, atmosphere, music exuding from all quarters at all times of day and night. Wonderful!'

Appendix 13. The AP Choristers' Reunion 2013

On 25th September 2013 a group of former boy choristers and students met together at Addington Palace, for a memorable reunion. Peter Hood, one of the organisers for this reunion, commented; 'It all started over lunch on Martin How's 80th birthday on 3rd April 2012. Three of his 'Grandads', as he calls us (Colin Creed, Tony Clarke and I), took him out to lunch at 'The White Bear', a much-favoured hostelry not too far from Addington Palace. We drew up the initial list of former choristers and the idea of the reunion was born.' Others then came on board, including Peter Grover to assist in what was a considerable 'tracking-down' enterprise.

The fine autumn day saw Addington Palace at its best, and brought back many memories for the 70 people, which included some 50 old choristers, travelling from all over the UK, France, Holland and even one who had travelled from California, to attend this reunion. There was a display of RSCM archive material in the old Robing Room, and a selection of artefacts, including a scout uniform worn by the chorister-scouts, in the former Music Room. Lunch was served in the Great Hall, and guest speakers included RSCM Director Andrew Reid, who presented a stirring vision for the RSCM of the future, the Vicar of Croydon, Canon Boswell, former chorister Brian Weller, Harvey Cousins who presented Martin with a hand-made box and pen and a record, and of course the guest of honour, Martin How — who, after praising the efforts of the organisers — said: 'It was delightful —

as if we had never had the 55 year break, as if we had carried on from where we left off.'[348]

Peter Hood then presented Martin How with a commemorative book containing memories from the following former choristers: Ray Ghent (1954-1958), Harry King (1954-1958), Robin Jenkin (1954-1957), Bill Jennings (1954-1956), Ian Clifton-Everest (1954-1957), Peter Grover (1954-1958), David Ursell (1954-1958), Colin Creed (1955-1959), Paul Rangecroft (1955-1960), John Ellis (1955-1959), Brian Weller (1955-1961), Tony Clark (1955-1957), Colin Sell (1956-1959), John Woodland (1956-1958), Dick Gilbert (1956-1958), Roger Durston (1956-1958), Pete Crofts (1956-1962), Chris Chambers (1956-1961), Chris Rutter (1957-1961), Geoff Thomas (1957-1963), Martin Skeet (1958-1963), Geoffrey King (1959-1964), Bob Atkinson (1960-1964) and of course Peter Hood (1957-1963). Also the following students made a contribution to the book of

Address by Martin How

memories: Jonathan and Moira Gatward (1955-1957), Michael Bailey (1960-1963), Adrian Adams (1967-1970), Christopher Tinker (1968-1970), Colin Atree (a member of the Southern Cathedral Singers) and Bruce Ruddock, Canon Precentor of Peterborough Cathedral, who had attended RSCM courses as a treble.

Amongst the memories included in the above list, some delightful anecdotes have emerged, as well as an insight into the routine at AP from a boy's point of view.

> 'On arrival for choir practice we would be given a sandwich and a glass of orange. There was then some free time when some of us would play table tennis. In the same room [the Robing Room] was a large organ complete with its pipes. One evening a number of table tennis balls somehow found their way into the organ pipes. It would have been marvellous to see the look on the organist's face when he began to play, and the balls came flying out of the pipes, however that was not to be — and surprise, surprise no-one ever mentioned it.' (Ray Ghent, who goes on to admit that he was the culprit!)

Another chorister (Robin Jenkin) remembers '....jam, margarine and white bread for tea, doing my homework before choir practice ....playing table tennis ....cricket matches on the park below the Palace gardens, having my cassock, surplice and ruff sorted out by 'Ma' Gordon ....[and] the fun and games with the other boys of the choir.' Another chorister recalls 'they never seemed to run short of jam sandwiches!' (John Ellis)

---

[348] *The Croydon Advertiser* 5th October 2013.

Before singing a service attended by the Queen and Prince Philip at Lambeth Palace, Bill Jennings recalls: 'On the way to the Palace from Addington, four of us in the back of the coach decided to try smoking. Martin was not amused.'

'Those cross country runs around the golf course, I think Martin ran for Cambridge ....anyhow we could never keep up with him.' (David Ursell)

A common theme of memories runs through most of the entries which, apart from the sheer joy engendered by Martin How of singing and being part of a team, may be summarised as follows (in no particular order): jam sandwiches, cross country runs, football, snooker, table tennis, choristers' week-ends, scout camps, away singing fixtures and comic-reading. Former chorister Paul Rangecroft in his own tribute, sums up Martin's contribution to the choirs at AP: ' What followed [his being admitted to the choir] will be echoed by generations of RSCM-ites, within and without the nurturing and astonishingly grand, historic 'arenas' provided by Addington Palace — you took charge of a significant element of our growth and development.... choirs, church music, scouts, sports, visits/trips — which were underpinned by your unrelenting pursuit of excellence, discipline, fun, team-working, recreation [and] social interaction.'

After lunch there was the opportunity to wander round the various rooms in the Palace, and then reassemble in the Chapel for a final act of worship, before dispersing. Afterwards, Colin Creed commented, 'It was like being reunited with a family member. We had a wonderful day.'[349]

Photo display in Robing Room

[349] *ibid.*

Appendix 14. The RSCM Coat of Arms, The Chorister's Prayer, The CD

On being granted a Royal Title in 1945, the *RSCM* applied to the Heralds' College for a coat of arms and these were granted in December 1950 being:

Argent five Barrulets Azure over all a lyre between six Nightingales three and three respectant in pale Or on a Chief of the second an Open Book proper between two Stars of eight points of the third and for the Crest On a Wreath of the Colours A Semi figure of St Nicolas vested in Pontificals proper Mitred and holding in his dexter Hand a Pastoral Staff and in his sinister Hand three Purses Or.

The five blue barrulets on silver ground represent the music stave; the lyre is one of the most ancient instruments; the nightingales are singers. In the chief the two stars are taken from Sir Sydney's coat of arms and the book represents learning (rather than the Bible). The crest is St Nicolas the patron saint of the school, the pastoral staff indicating his episcopal authority and the three purses one of his legendary good deeds in Myra.

Sir Gerald Woods Wollaston (1874-1957) was Garter Principal King of Arms and it was he who signed the Grant of Arms to the RSCM. His son, Henry Woods Wollaston, a senior civil servant at the Home Office, was a RSCM Council Member from 1970 to 1976.

The Chorister's Prayer

> Bless, O Lord, us Thy servants, who minister in Thy temple.
> Grant that what we sing with our lips, we may believe in our hearts,
> and what we believe in our hearts, we may show forth in our lives.
> Through Jesus Christ our Lord. Amen.

The Chorister's Prayer in its most common form was first published by the School of English Church Music in 1934 in the *Choristers' Pocket Book*. No indication of its origin was given there and it had been assumed by many that this may have been the work of Sir Sydney Nicholson and/or Cosmo Lang, Archbishop of Canterbury and a keen supporter of Sir Sydney and of the School of English Church Music.

The prayer does however have origins which extend back at least to the 4C, for the tenth canon of the fourth council of Carthage (c.398 AD) decrees that cantors should be blessed with the words 'Vide, ut quod ore cantas, corde credas, et quod corde credis, operibus comprobes' ('See that what thou singest with thy lips thou dost believe in thine heart, and

424

that what thou believest in thine heart thou dost show forth in thy works'[350]). The same Latin text is also used in the *Pontificale Romanum* of 1595/6 in both the form for admitting a psalmista or cantor and also at the ordination of priests. The earliest English versions seem to date from the 1840's with two, one for use before with a second version for use after Divine Service, published in a booklet entitled *Historical Notices of the Office of Choristers* 1848 by the Revd James Millard. Within a few months the 'after service' version of that prayer also appeared in the journal *The Parish Choir*[351] — 'Grant, O Lord, that what I have said and sung with my mouth, I may believe in my heart; and what I may believe in my heart, I may steadfastly fulfil, though Jesus Christ our Lord' and this identical prayer was published again in *The Choir and Musical Record Almanack*[352] in 1866. It may be that Sir Sydney modernised the language of The Chorister's Prayer[353], but we who pray these words weekly carry on a tradition of many centuries and hopefully we both 'steadfastly fulfil' and also 'show forth' the tenets of our faith in our lives and music.

The CD   Time

1. Sir Sydney Nicholson: An extract from his speech rhythm lecture with vocal extracts sung by Harry Barnes. Recorded in 1931   3.08

2. Address by GHK at a BBC broadcast of Choral Matins on 24th November 1957 live from AP Chapel, followed by the singing of the hymn *Let all the world in every corner sing*. The St Nicolas College Choir is directed by Martin How with Derek Holman at the organ.   12.51

3. Stanford B-flat *Magnificat* from the RSCM 21st Birthday Recording made on Dec 6th 1948 in St Sepulchre's Church, Holborn. 220 voices from 12 affiliated choirs directed by Hubert Crook. GHK and Sidney Campbell accompanied the choir in this recording but it is not known who played for this particular track. The whole service was issued on five 78rpm records.   4.02

4. Plainsong hymn *Most holy God and Lord of heaven* from Choral Evensong broadcast live from the Ely Cathedral Course on 11th August 1971. Conductor Martin How, organist John Jordan.   2.05

5. Parry *Blest Pair of Sirens* from a BBC Choral Evensong broadcast live from Westminster Abbey on 28th Aug 1987 conducted by Martin How with David Briggs at the organ.   10.27

6. Tomkins *5th Evening Service* from a BBC Choral Evensong broadcast live from the Wells Cathedral Course in 1980. Conductor Martin How, organist Adrian Lucas.   9.07

---

[350] Translation from the preface of *A Handbook of Church Music* by F Clement Egerton, London, R & T Washbourne Ltd., 1909.
[351] *The Parish Choir* May 1849 p.172.
[352] *The Choir and Musical Record Almanack* in 1866 p.11.
[353] Though 'show forth' seems to have already replaced 'steadfastly fulfil' by the 1909 translation quoted above.

7. Anthem *And I saw a new heaven* by Edgar Bainton from a Choral Evensong broadcast live from St Paul's Cathedral Course on 28th Aug 1957. Conducted by GHK with Derek Holman at the organ. 5.49

8. Anthem *Bless, O Lord, us thy servants* by Martin How and directed by him at a Canterbury Cathedral Course. The year is unknown. 3.14

9. Psalm 143 sung to plainsong by students of the College of St Nicolas directed and accompanied by Michael Fleming. Recorded 1969 in All Saints', Margaret Street, London. The Cantor was the Revd Anthony Caesar. 3.28

10. Psalms 59 and 60, as set in *The Parish Psalter*, recorded at the Canterbury Cathedral Course in 1986. Conductor Martin How, organist Timothy Lawford. 7.57

11. An improvisation in 1996 by Martin How on the Harrison organ in Addington Chapel after it had been cleared of furniture. Note the extra resonance of the empty chapel and marvel at how this small 10-rank instrument sounds almost like a cathedral organ and wonder at how many different timbres could be produced upon it. 15.20

With the exception of Michael Fleming's plainsong in track 9, which was recorded for an RSCM LP record, and Martin How's setting of the Chorister's Prayer, recorded at a Canterbury Course concert, all of these recordings were made live during church services. Some taken from radio broadcasts and others tape-recorded by the late Mr John Huntley at Martin How's Cathedral Courses[354].

The RSCM owes a tremendous debt of gratitude to Mr Colin Brownlee who has transferred many of the RSCM collection of 78s, LPs and tapes to a digital format. No noise reduction techniques have been used and so these recordings are offered 'warts and all.' Several of the major Albert Hall Festivals were recorded and issued in LP or CD format, but copyright issues prevent us from reproducing extracts from these.

We hope that this CD, in addition to allowing listeners to hear the voices of both Sydney Nicholson and Gerald Knight, will demonstrate the high standard of singing and chanting by ordinary boys and men from parish churches around the country who attended these courses.

---

[354] John also sang alto on the courses.

Epilogue

There is a perception in some quarters that the Addington years of the RSCM were the 'golden years' of the organisation. Whilst researching our first book, *Sydney Nicholson and The College of St Nicolas: The Chislehurst Years*, we came across a similar perception that, after its closure, the Chislehurst years were thought by some to be the 'golden age.' Neither statement carries much weight when viewed in any detail. Firstly, the RSCM is not in the business of looking back but, as our Founder always upheld, looking forward. Vision rather than nostalgia has been the guiding precept of the RSCM from its very conception, and this remains true to this day. The Chislehurst years were beset with teething troubles, ranging from a slow uptake of church affiliations, attracting enough students to make the College viable, domestic staffing problems and a hazy idea what the RSCM (then SECM) had to offer, not helped by confusion over what the College and the School represented: A view which persisted, despite attempts at clarification. Likewise the Addington years, throughout the RSCM's tenure, were plagued with similar financial problems to the Chislehurst years.

A popular view that Addington was a gentlemen's club, with its preponderance of male staff and students, together with its candle-lit dinners and gown-wearing collegiate regime giving more than a whiff of 'Oxbridge', would seem to give emphasis to this perception. To a certain extent, this was the way things were in the fifties. True, there was a certain elegance of style surrounding activities in the Palace, reinforced in no small measure by Gerald Knight's insistence that all things should be done properly. Many of our contributors noted, and were impressed by, the atmosphere thus engendered when they were students there. However, towards the end of the Addington era, it was increasingly being viewed, again reinforced by some of our contributors, as something of an expensive anachronism — with some justification perhaps. This was a problem which Lionel Dakers, the succeeding Director, sought to rectify by the closure of the residential college and the introduction of a wider variety of short courses.

Barry Sampson in his Sheffield MA Thesis suggested that:

> 'Thus it can be said that 1963 was a peak in the history of the School. In that year public recognition of the RSCM's work was given by the Queen's visit, the Council began to use its powers to confer diplomas; two new magazines and a publications pamphlet appeared, reflecting the changing climate in Church Music; and the annual Cathedral Course — the climax and 'showpiece' of the RSCM's work with choirs — took place on an international plane; during the Congress of Anglican Bishops in Toronto.'

Viewed from the perspective of 1971 (the publication date of Sampson's thesis) this may have seemed the case, but we hope that we have shown that further significant peaks in activity were still to come, especially in the 1970's and 1980's — and all that despite the closure of the College to residential students in 1974.

Conscious that there was no full account of the Addington era, and prompted by requests from a number of former staff and students, we have set out to provide a record of those years, before such memories fade into obscurity. We have been delighted by the response and enthusiasm for this project, and hope that we have managed to cover most of the significant landmarks.

We have considered in some detail what the RSCM and its principal officers have done through these Addington years, but we have not really fully considered the RSCM at work in churches and schools at the 'coal face.' The paid Headquarters staff and roving commissioners, most of whom we hope have been acknowledged in these pages, are but the tip of an iceberg. There was, and still is, a vast network of committed church musicians, organised into areas with committees, who arrange activities at a local level. Most of these people are unpaid volunteers, many are just as dedicated to the cause of the RSCM as the leading musicians on the staff at Addington had been, many have given a lifetime of service and loyalty to the objectives of the RSCM, many — from the most eminent cathedral organists to the most humble beginning organists and singers — acknowledge a debt of gratitude to the courses made available, and the tuition and practical help that Addington offered, either at Headquarters or out in the field. Few of these faithful church musicians are mentioned by name in these pages but we would like to dedicate this book to them, for without church and school affiliations, friends and individual members, there would be no RSCM.

By the end of the Addington era, church music and liturgy had already entered a period of change. In the Church of England especially, there was an air of uncertainty, as an alternative to the perceived inflexibility of the *Book of Common Prayer* was being actively sought. This led to a period of flux which, even after the publication of *Common Worship*, continues in the 21C, with no clear endpoint. The shrinking number of choirs, and especially boy choristers, together with those changing styles in church worship has led to a decline in RSCM membership and influence. Whilst the 1960's to 80's may represent the peak of the RSCM's activity, if not necessarily its 'golden age', and will always be looked back upon with considerable pleasure and nostalgia by those who remember it, this is not to say that the RSCM has little role in the future of church music and the education of church musicians. Far from it — the RSCM has always, and will always, adapt to the circumstances facing it. That basic responsibility to provide training and resources for contemporary church musicians, together with the principles stated on every affiliation certificate, has not changed from Sir Sydney Nicholson's day; and the desire to raise standards in a world where so many everyday values sink to the lowest common denominator, is as vital today as it ever was.

John Henderson and Trevor Jarvis
Salisbury, 2015

Afterword by RSCM Chairman of Council, Brian Gill

John Henderson and Trevor Jarvis are to be congratulated on having recorded the history of RSCM from sources of evidence that have not been available until now.

In their account of the Chislehurst years, they gave us a valuable history of the beginnings of RSCM and captured the ambition and the energy with which Sir Sidney Nicholson created it and developed it. In this volume they have chronicled the work of those directors who have inherited Nicholson's vision and carried it forward into a society and a musical world more diverse than Nicholson could ever have foreseen.

This volume confirms that the mission of RSCM is as worthwhile today as it was in Nicholson's time. It is a testament to the work of those who have preserved Nicholson's legacy and handed it on to us as a living tradition.

In these uncertain times, this history gives us cause for optimism for the future of church music. It will inspire all who express their faith through this most sublime form of Christian worship.

Brian Gill

The Rt Hon Lord Gill, also an organist and singer, became Chairman of RSCM Council in 2010 after serving as Chairman of the Royal Scottish Academy of Music from 1999 to 2006. He has had a distinguished legal career in Scotland. A Senator of the College of Justice from 1994, he was Chairman of the Scottish Law Commission from 1996 until 2001, Lord Justice Clerk until 2012 and Lord President of the Court of Session until retirement in 2015.

Index

432